DESTROYER ACTIONS

SEPTEMBER 1939 TO JUNE 1940

by

Harry Plevy

The History Press

British Library Cataloguing in Publication Data:
A catalogue record for this book is available
from the British Library

Copyright © Harry Plevy 2006

ISBN 978-1-86227-483-9

First published in the UK in 2006
This paperback edition published in 2008 by
The History Press Ltd
The Mill, Brimscombe Port
Stroud, Gloucestershire. GL5 2QG
www.thehistorypress.co.uk

1 3 5 7 9 8 6 4 2

Printed in Great Britain

Contents

Acknowledgements

I am indebted to very many organisations and people, some of whom are sadly no longer with us, for their help in the research for, and preparation of, this book. In preparing my acknowledgements I have made every effort to trace and contact copyright holders or their next of kin. However, given the passage of time since the events described in the book took place, with changes among publishing houses and organisations over the years resulting in transfers of copyright ownership, I have – despite extensive enquiries – been unable to trace a few of the copyright holders. I will make every effort to remedy the mistake or omission in any subsequent reprint or edition of the book.

The following persons have shared with me their memories of service on wartime destroyers or, as copyright owners, have allowed me to quote from the documents of relatives who did. Wherever known I have given the last title or rank of the person quoted; otherwise, I have given the title or rank at the time of the event described or of writing the memoir. I have chosen not to include honours and decorations in my acknowledgements, simply because I have been unable to guarantee the accuracy or comprehensiveness of such a listing. I hope that my contributors will understand and forgive this decision. For their permissions I am indebted to:

Mr H. Barwick
Mr M. Bell Macdonald for Captain A.M. Bell Macdonald, BEF
Mr J. Cannon
Mrs J.F. Childs for Second Engineer H. Saville
Mr D. Courage
Mr P. Court-Hampton for Lieutenant E.A. Court-Hampton
Captain R.D. Franks
Mr J.G. Gemmell
Mrs B. Grandage for Lieutenant G. Grandage
Lieutenant Commander J.F. King, for Captain H.A. King
Commander P.N.T. Lesisz

Mrs D. Lumsden, for Captain G.J.A. Lumsden
Mr R. Lush
Commander P.J. and M. Mosse for Commander J.P. Mosse
Mrs D. Neale for Lieutenant Commander J. Neale
Mrs O. Nettle for Commander S.A. Nettle
Lieutenant Commander F.C. Rice
Mr G. Sear
Mrs Y. Shelley for Mr A.H. Turner
Mrs M. Slater for Mr R. Hooke
Mr T. Slessor
Mrs W.M. Snelling, for Chief Petty Officer F. Parker
Lieutenant J.P. Tumaniszwili
Lieutenant J. Wankowski
Mr D.C. Wilkin, for Vice Admiral Sir Alistair Ewing
Mrs S. de Winton, for Captain F.S.W. de Winton
Petty Officer B. Witkowski
Mr P. Yates

I wish to acknowledge and thank the following persons, publishers, authorities and agencies for kindly giving permission to reproduce extracts from books, newspapers and journals:

M. Brown for *Scapa Flow* by M. Brown and P. Meehan
Commonwealth War Graves Commission
M Connell for *Jack's War* by G. G. Connell
The Controller of Her Majesty's Stationery Office for *Naval Operations of the Campaign in Norway: April–June 1940* ed. D. Brown; *The Evacuation from Dunkirk: Operation Dynamo, 26 May–4 June 1949* ed. W.J.R. Gardner; *The Royal Navy Medical Service, Vol VII* by Surgeon Captain J.L.S. Coulter; and *The War at Sea 1939–1945* by Captain S.W. Roskill.
David Higham Associates for *Field Marshal Lord Allanbrooke: War Diaries 1939–45* by A. Danchev.
P. Finnigan of the HMS *Warspite* Association
Greenhill Books Ltd for *Memoirs: Ten Years and Twenty Days* by Grand Admiral K. Doenitz
Harper Collins for *Churchill and the Admirals* by Captain S.W. Roskill; and *The Navy at War* by Captain S.W. Roskill
Lieutenant (Rtd) E.P. Harrison of the HMS *Cossack* Association
Macmillan Publishers Ltd for *The Portsmouth Letters* by Admiral Sir William James
News International Newspapers
Orion Publishing Group for *The U-Boat Peril* by Captain R.F. Whinney; and *The Second World War, Vol 1: The Gathering Storm* and *The Second World War, Vol 2: Their Finest Hour* by W.S. Churchill

The Master and Fellows of Pembroke College, Cambridge for *Meredith Dewey; Diaries, Letters and Writings* eds A.V. Grimstone, M.C. Lyons and V. Lyons

Pen and Sword Books Ltd for *Dunkirk 1940: From Disaster to Deliverance* by P. Wilson

Periscope Publishing Ltd for *Destroyer Captain: Memoirs of the War 1942–1945* by Captain R. Hill Rogers

Coleridge and White Ltd, on behalf of Sir Ludovic Kennedy, for *On My Way to The Club* by L. Kennedy

Sheil Land Associates for *An Adventurous Life* by Admiral Lord Mountevans

A Suchcitz, Keeper of Archives, The Polish Institute and Sikorski Museum, London

The Telegraph Group Ltd

Mrs S Winton for *Carrier Glorious* by J. Winton

P. Ziegler and the Trustees of the Broadlands Archives for *Mountbatten: The Official Biography* by P. Ziegler

Information and quoted extracts from a number of other books and papers have also been incorporated into my writing and I wish to acknowledge their contribution. In my copyright search I have been greatly assisted by and thank: Mrs M. Ferre of the Office of Public Sector Information; Mr I. Hopkins of the Churchill Archives Centre, Churchill College, Cambridge; Mrs A. Littleboy of the Association of Royal Navy Officers; and Mr R.W.A. Suddaby, Keeper, Department of Documents, Imperial War Museum, London.

I would also like to acknowledge the authors of the following books, with thanks:

Lost Voices of the Royal Navy by M. Arthur
The Man who hit the Scharnhorst by J. Austin and N. Carter
Hitler's Naval War by C. Bekker
The Mountains Wait by T. Broch
Prologue to War: The Navy's part in the Norwegian Campaign by E. Brookes
Happy Odyssey by Lieutenant General Sir Adrian Carton de Wiart
Max Horton and the Western Approaches by Rear Admiral W.S. Chalmers
The Biography of Admiral Sir Bertram Home Ramsay by Rear Admiral W.S. Chalmers
The Fringes of Power: Downing Street Diaries 1939–1945 by J. Colville
Navies in Exile by A.D. Divine
The Merchant Navy Goes to War by B. Edwards
The Churchill War Papers: At the Admiralty. Vol 1 Sept 1939 to May 1940 by M. Gilbert
Everyman's History of the Sea War by A.C. Hardy

Battleship Barham by G.P. Jones
War Diaries and Letters: Life on the Battlefield in the Words of the Ordinary Soldier ed. J.E. Lewis
Narvik by Captain D. Macintyre
Assault from the Sea by Rear Admiral L.E.H Maund
Mountbatten: Eighty Years in Pictures by Lord Louis Mountbatten
The Kelly by K. Poolman
The Battle of the River Plate by D. Pope
Action This Day by Admiral of the Fleet Sir Philip Vian
Auchinleck: The Lonely Soldier by P. Warner

Extracts from documents and papers that I wish to acknowledge, but where I am again unable to trace copyright holders, include those of:

Captain P.J. Carsdale
Stoker F.W. Earridge
Admiral Sir Ralph Edwards
Petty Officer W. Elliott
First Circle Films
Admiral J.H. Godfrey
Able Seaman D.T.W. Harris
Vice Admiral Sir Charles Hughes-Hallett
Signalman J. Knight
Lieutenant Commander R. Leggott
Report M014793/40 re HMS *Whitshed*
Vice Admiral Sir William Robson
Rear Admiral M.W. Searle
Captain R.S. Sherbrooke
Captain Walsham, Royal Artillery
Admiral W. Whitworth
Captain V.A. Wight-Boycott
Commander G.H.D. Williams
Translated extracts from the logs of the German battlecruisers *Gneisenau* and *Scharnhorst*

The photographs in the book are by kind permission of the Trustees of the Imperial War Museum, London; Commander J. Lubkowski of ORP *Blyskawica*; Polish Naval Museum, Gdynia, Poland; and Mrs M. Slater.

My thanks go also to the staff of the Department of Documents and the Photographic Archive of the Imperial War Museum, of the Churchill Archives Centre, Churchill College, Cambridge, and of Codsall and South Staffordshire Public Libraries, for their help in dealing with my many enquiries, to Mr J.E.G. White for help with translations, and to Mrs W. Troman and Dr J. Wankowski for their help in tracing Polish persons and authorities.

Finally, grateful thanks go to my long-suffering family for their patience and understanding. To my wife Pauline, who has been a tremendous supporter of my writing, been a patient listener, and given unstinting help with word processing the various drafts and final copy of the book, as well as patiently dealing with the mass of correspondence arising from my researches; to my son Neil for facilitating much of my researches, proofreading and many helpful discussions and suggestions on content and direction; and to our daughter Julia for her encouragement and patient tolerance of my naval history obsessions.

Harry Plevy
Codsall, South Staffordshire

List of Maps

Introduction

The first nine months of the Second World War, the so called 'Phoney War' period prior to Dunkirk and the fall of France, were real enough to the destroyer crews of the Royal Navy. It was the Royal Navy that carried virtually the whole burden of the fight against the enemy, and it was the destroyers and their crews of that service that did the brunt of the fighting. The ill-prepared and poorly equipped small regular British Army took time to expand and equip, and was found wanting when it faced the vastly superior German Wehrmacht, firstly in Norway and then in France and the Low Countries, in the spring and early summer of 1940. From both Scandinavia and the Continent the beaten British Expeditionary Forces had to be evacuated back to Britain by ships of the Allied navies and merchant fleets, with destroyers of the Royal Navy playing a vital self-sacrificing role on each occasion. The Royal Air Force also took time to organise, only operating to a limited extent during the early months and was not called upon to play any prominent role in the early conduct of the war. Its time would come, gloriously, in the late summer of 1940 following Dunkirk and the fall of France in the Battle of Britain, when it took on and defeated the might of the German Luftwaffe.

The Royal Navy's time came immediately with the declaration of war. Straight away, and indeed for the whole six years of the conflict, the Navy was called upon to keep open the vital shipping lanes, and it fell largely to the destroyers and their crews to escort the convoys bringing the food, raw materials and war equipment to Britain, protecting the merchant ships from German sea and air attack.

The Royal Navy began the war in September 1939 with 184 destroyers, some new, but mostly old and of World War I vintage. Nine months later, by the end of the Phoney War in June 1940 following Dunkirk, it had lost 23 of them. Very many more had been badly damaged. The ships would be repaired and replaced, but not the very many experienced officers and men who were lost with them. Among those lost were destroyers and men whose gallantry and self sacrifice shone like a beacon in the dark days when

Britain was yet to come to terms with the later horrors of all-out war. Crews followed to the death the leadership and example of their captains: commanding officers like Captain Warburton-Lee and the crew of the *Hardy*, and Lieutenant Commander Roope and the crew of the *Glowworm*. Both captains were posthumously awarded the Victoria Cross in recognition of their, and their crews', gallantry and devotion to duty. Shamefully, the same recognition was not given to the captains of two other destroyers, lost together with all their crews except for one seaman from each ship, when they tried to save the aircraft carrier *Glorious* from the guns of the German battle-cruisers *Scharnhorst* and *Gneisenau*. Commander Glasford and the crew of the *Acasta* and Lieutenant Commander Barker and the crew of the *Ardent* never received the recognition and honours which were their due.

Destroyer actions during the early months of the war also brought to the fore other captains whose exploits caught the public's imagination and who would go on to high rank and commands in the Royal Navy and in State affairs. Men like Captains Vian of the *Cossack* and Mountbatten of the *Kelly*.

However, it was not all rearguard action against the overwhelming might of the German war machine in its first full flush of total supremacy in those early months of the war. While the German Wehrmacht and Luftwaffe might have swept all before them on land and in the air, at sea the German Kriegsmarine found the Royal Navy a much tougher proposition. The sea battles and encounters were much more evenly contested, especially in actions involving the destroyers of both sides. Thus while the Allied navies may have suffered heavy destroyer losses, in comparison the German Navy, with its numerically smaller destroyer force, suffered catastrophic destroyer losses. So much so that after the first and second battles of Narvik in April 1940, fought for the most part between destroyers, the German destroyer fleet was virtually eliminated. Only four serviceable destroyers remained. The German Kriegsmarine was thus in no position to escort troop transports for a sea-borne invasion of Britain two months later, following Dunkirk and the collapse of France, a factor which is frequently overlooked when evaluating why the Germans did not immediately follow up their success and invade Britain in the summer of 1940.

The men serving on destroyers, on both sides, had a hard war. Not only had they to contend with the various threats posed by the enemy, but there was always their common enemy, the sea, which posed its own trials and tribulations to the small, fragile destroyers and the men who sailed in them. This book seeks to pay tribute to those destroyers and their crews, friend and foe, who fought and died in the so-called Phoney War of 1939–1940.

I

The Navy Prepares for War

On 3 September 1939 the British and French Governments, quickly joined by Britain's self-governing dominions Australia, Canada, South Africa and New Zealand, declared war upon Germany in support of Poland, following the invasion of that country by Germany on 1 September.

Contrary to widely held expectation, the British populace was not immediately subjected to the privations of war; there were no massive air attacks upon her cities, nor were her people faced with immediate starvation. These tribulations were yet to come. Indeed, initially there could be said to be some welcome benefits. Unemployment, for example, fell from its high pre-war levels, as the country swung onto a wartime footing and expanded its manufacturing base for the production of armaments and munitions, and as civilians of military age in non-reserved occupations were called to service in the growing armed forces. There followed some months of what American journalists termed the Phoney War; Neville Chamberlain, the then British Prime Minister, called the Twilight War; and the pugnacious Sir Adrian Carton de Wiart,* a Boer War veteran, recalled as the Bore War.[1]

For the British Army and the Royal Air Force there were to be six months of gentle initiation into the war. Both services needed time to equip and train their new, largely conscript, servicemen and women. Within the first few days of war being declared the Royal Air Force sent squadrons and support units to France; and the British Expeditionary Force, made up of five divisions of regular home-based Army divisions, was assembled and dispatched to augment the large French Army facing the Germans behind their respective Maginot and Siegfried Lines (the *Westwall*). Months of stalemate then ensued on the continent. However, there was to be no gentle introduction for the Royal Navy. It alone carried the fight against-

---

* Lieutenant-General Sir Adrian Carton de Wiart fought in five campaigns spanning the period from the Boer War in 1901 to the Narvik Campaign in 1940. Severely wounded eleven times, losing both a hand and an eye, he was much decorated, including a Victoria Cross awarded in 1916.

the Germans in the first year of the war. Unable militarily, and unwilling politically, to raise the stakes by a direct attack on Germany in order to assist Poland, the Allies initially placed great faith upon world opinion and diplomacy to bring about a peaceful solution to the crisis. There was a widely held view that the war could be over by Christmas. Others thought that there was no immediate danger or cause for concern. In the meantime indirect pressure, short of all-out war, would be put upon Germany by imposing an economic blockade, a policy which, it was believed, given the perceived control of the seas by the Royal Navy, would rapidly bring Germany to the conference table.

> The war looks like being an immobile affair on the Western Front, with neither side bombing the other's civilian populations for some time to come, and the real tests being whether Germany's economic resources and the morale of her people can defeat the Navy's block- ade and the morale of the Allies. This will be dangerous because it will be boring; and in wartime boredom is certain to bring discontent at home. However I do not think the Germans will begin their pro- verbial "frightfulness" until they feel they are losing or winning so that London can probably sleep in peace for a good many weeks or even months to come.[2]

It was fortunate for Britain, and ultimately for the free world, that the Royal Navy was one allied service that was ready for war on the com- mencement of hostilities. It had been brought to a semi-war footing, and an awareness of modern wartime requirements, by the Abyssinian crisis following Italy's invasion of that country in 1935, and then, almost imme- diately afterwards, by the Spanish Civil War. Both of these conflicts had given the Royal Navy experience of the evacuation of refugees and British nationals and of blockade duties against contraband and gun runners.

In 1937, with the benefit of these experiences and with Hitler and Mussolini becoming increasingly belligerent and war increasingly likely, the Royal Navy started to overhaul its organisation and resources. In the mid-summer of 1937 Vice Admiral Sir Max Horton was given command of the Reserve Fleet, charged with the task of bringing this heterogeneous collection of elderly ships, large and small, onto a wartime footing. In naval circles the Reserve Fleet was considered, both literally and metaphorically, to be in the backwater of the Navy: at that time it was made up of some 140 ships of all classes, laid up in ports and inlets around the British Isles. They were manned, at varying degrees of readiness, by skeleton crews on a 'care and maintenance' basis. The Navy was fortunate in its choice of Admiral Horton, a distinguished submarine commander in the First World War and later to become equally distinguished as Commander-in-Chief, Western Approaches. He was a man of great drive and organising ability. His Fleet Secretary wrote of him:

Sir Max certainly put a new spirit into the Reserve Fleet by making people feel that they were doing a worthwhile job which was likely to come to fruition very soon. He insisted that everything should be looked at from the point of view of "What would happen to this on mobilisation?" One of his earlier measures was to carry out a mobilisation exercise on paper, but the facilities for victualling, kitting up and drafting the men, and the transport and labour for delivering the stores had to be actually there. This exercise proved to be most useful in showing up deficiencies in organisation, many of which were corrected before the Munich mobilisation in 1938. In addition to the measures taken within the Reserve Fleet, Sir Max kept up a constant pressure on the Admiralty to try to get made in advance those arrangements which he foresaw would be required.[3]

Following the Munich crisis of 1938, which spurred on the naval preparations, virtually the whole Reserve Fleet was ready by mid-summer 1939 to sail as soon as the ships' companies could be assembled.

Of the three British armed forces the Royal Navy was undoubtedly the best organised and most experienced. It was made up of dedicated, totally professional officers and men, steeped in naval tradition and highly disciplined. In the main, they were arguably more well trained than well educated, as a result of their recruitment into the service at an early age. The officers, traditionally from the middle and upper classes, joined the Navy at the age of thirteen, with a view to a lifetime career and a steady rise through the officer ranks. The apprenticeship was hard and long, the training unremitting, and the discipline harsh. Captain R. Whinney, later to become a distinguished destroyer captain and one of the Second World War's most successful hunters of U-boats, recalled his time as a cadet in the early twenties:

In the days before World War Two, The Royal Naval College, Dartmouth, produced nearly all those officers who would later be qualified to command HM ships at sea. They joined as small boys of thirteen and a half years of age, in uniform, as young officers and gentlemen. They had naval pensioner servants, who called them 'Sir', who made their beds, cleaned their shoes, and sent their laundry to the wash. Conversely, they were in for four years' sojourn of being chased around in an atmosphere of rigid (and in my day, uninspired) discipline which towards the latter months left many of them bloody minded.

They came, these young men, from fee-paying schools and were the sons of gentry, of professional men and, in some cases, of the aristocracy...the competition, the passing of the entrance exam, an interview and, of course, a medical were severe: forty-three were taken out of some two hundred applicants in my case. I passed in about twelfth but had the advantage of prep school where the alternative to working hard was a rare, effective, never resented walloping on the backside.

Dartmouth was in effect a public school run by a Captain, Royal Navy, with a naval staff and a headmaster with a civilian teaching staff...The Naval College was a vast, shiny, spotless place with highly polished floors throughout and the front of the buildings, seen from the outside, was impressive and elegant, built in red brick with white stone facings – again spotless with no sign of weathering permitted.[4]

Punishment for even minor transgressions was harsh:

A shirt folded with a button undone or a sock facing the wrong way, and the Cadet Captain made a tick in his notebook. Three ticks against anyone's name meant three cuts with the cane. Every night, after lights out, the defaulters were called from their beds in alphabetical order and, one by one, to the noisy swish of the cane dealt with...Serious offences, such as being found in possession of cigarettes or photographs of ladies without all their clothes on were awarded 'official cuts'. The offender was then held down over a horse-box in the gym while a Petty Officer performed the execution of six cuts.[4]

Other cadets were less concerned by the discipline but found other features of college life equally idiosyncratic:

Discipline at the College was obviously strict, but I do not consider that it was harsh. It was a full life but not unduly hard...Sports and exercise were taken very seriously at the College. Each cadet had to do an exercise log on every weekday. Participation in an organised game such as rugger or hockey constituted a whole log, while running to Black Cottage or a game of squash was only half a log. For some inexplicable reason having one's hair cut counted as a quarter log![5]*

The men, predominantly from the working classes or the ranks of the unemployed, usually joined at the age of sixteen and had their own shore-based training establishment, HMS *Ganges* at Shotley. Training and discipline were equally as severe as for the prospective officers. Signalman J. Knight, later to serve on the destroyer *Kelly*, retained his memories of his first days as a sixteen-year-old in the Royal Navy:

---

* Peter Cardale, later to become a Captain in the Royal Navy, entered Dartmouth as a thirteen-year-old in January 1933.

It must have been about five in the evening of 2nd November, 1936 when the train from Liverpool Street stopped at Harwich and the dozen or so of us got out to be met by a Petty Officer who said "This is it. If you've changed your minds you can go back now, but once across the water – tough." I wasn't going to change my mind, not after waiting six months since first going to the Recruiting Office in Whitehall. I was going to be a sailor, wear a blue collar and round hat, see the world, get all the girls, etc, etc.[6]

His introduction to naval life the next morning was quite literally a rude awakening:

…I must have slept in the end because the next thing I knew was a tremendous bang. There was a sort of oil-cloth table covering which was rolled up between meals, and one of the marine sentries who kept watch throughout the night had picked it up and banged it down on the table. "Come along" he yelled, "Stop sleeping, sun's burning your eyes out." Sun? In November? It was the start of a giddy round.[6]

After two years of training, ashore and afloat, the men signed on at the age of eighteen for an initial twelve years of service. After this they could leave the service for civilian life or transfer to the mercantile marine. They were retained by the Navy on reserve status for a set number of years, to be recalled to the service at times of national emergency. Some reservists had been called at the time of the Abyssinian crisis with Italy in 1935, and others at the time of the Munich crisis in 1938, when Germany had annexed Czechoslovakia and brought Britain to the brink of war.

The men who stayed on in the Royal Navy signed for a further ten years, leading to a full pension after twenty-two years of service. Such men, who in their second term of service had usually risen to Petty Officer or Leading Hand rank, formed the experienced and disciplined backbone of the Navy at the start of the war.

On 1 January 1939 the Royal Navy was made up of some 10,000 officers and 109,000 men. They were supported by a further 12,400 officers and men of the Royal Marines, who, in those days, manned a quarter of the armament of battleships, battlecruisers and heavy cruisers, carried out ceremonial duties, and provided, if required, landing parties for action or peace-keeping duties ashore. All the aforementioned officers, men and Royal Marines manned the ships in commission, staffed the bases and training establishments ashore, and provided 'care and maintenance' crews for the Reserve Fleet.

In addition, the Navy could call upon 73,000 officers and men reservists in the Royal Navy Reserve, which also included some men from the

Merchant Navy and fishing fleets who, while not having served in the Royal Navy, had joined the Reserve and received some naval training and recompense for their time and commitment. There were also some 6,000 Royal Naval Volunteer Reservists, amateur 'weekend' sailors who, somewhat analogous to the Army's Territorials, had undergone training and duties in their spare time. Thus the total strength of the Royal Navy at the outbreak of the war was some 200,000 men.

The next few years saw a massive expansion of these numbers. At its peak in mid-1944 the personnel of the Royal Navy totalled some 843,000 officers and sailors, including 73,500 of the Women's Royal Naval Service (WRENS). Although the vast bulk of this increase in numbers was made up of 'Hostilities Only' (HO) personnel called up for National Service, it was the comparatively small body of regulars, reservists and volunteer reservists serving at the outbreak of the war in 1939 who held the Navy together, trained the recruits for the Navy's expansion, and fought and died in the sea battles of the first year of the war.

As in 1914, so in 1939 precautions had been taken by the Navy in advance of the declaration of hostilities. On 15 June 1939 large numbers of officers and men reservists had been recalled. The Reserve Fleet, fully manned for exercises, had been inspected by the King on 9 August; and on 22 August further reservists had been recalled. On 24 August an Emergency Powers Defence Bill had been passed by Parliament and the Fleet ordered onto a war footing. The main Home Fleet had in fact been assembling for some weeks at its main base of Scapa Flow in the Orkneys.

The ships that the sailors were to man in that first year of the war comprised a mixed collection of various classes and sizes of vessel. In all, the Royal Navy had in commission, though not necessarily immediately available for service, some twelve battleships, three battle-cruisers, six aircraft carriers, fifty-two cruisers, six converted anti-aircraft cruisers, one hundred and eighty-four destroyers (see Appendix 1), fifty-five escort vessels of various kinds, and sixty-nine submarines. Most of them, especially the larger ships, were over twenty years old and were of First World War vintage; few of them had been modernised.

This was particularly so with the destroyers brought out of reserve. To their called-up crews, torn from their settled civilian life and home comforts, the prospects of life and conditions on these old ships must have been daunting. Captain P. Vian, recently appointed to take command of a flotilla of destroyers brought out of reserve, remembers of the crews:

> These, when they arrived, proved to be mainly veterans of the First War; their lives had been disrupted by mobilisation, which had come upon them so quickly that those who had grown moustaches had lacked time to remove them. Few had uniforms which fitted.

As veterans, they had clear memories of life in destroyers in Atlantic winters, and here they were, facing another dose of the same medicine, in the very same ships they had left in 1918, still without baths and drying rooms, or, in fact, any amenities whatever…In the event, the fortitude with which these Reserve destroyer crews faced their new circumstances was remarkable.[7]

The veterans' numbers were made up with young and inexperienced men. Eighteen year-old J. Knight, fresh out of Shotley, was one of their number. He joined the brand-new destroyer and flotilla leader *Kelly*, under the command of Captain Lord Louis Mountbatten, in August 1939.

I was in the draft which left Chatham Dockyard by special train for Hebburn-on-Tyne to commission HMS *Kelly*…The lower deck was cleared and Louis told us that our original store ship programme was meant to take three weeks but in view of the worsening international situation it had to be done quicker. Then came the shock! We had to do it in three days. No-one was going to sleep until it was done and then we would sail for working-up exercises at Portland. During those three days I was walking along the upper deck where I saw a pile of old-time cannonballs. 'What on earth do we want those for?' I wondered. Nine months later I was to find out.[6]

The nineteen-year-old, newly appointed Acting Sub-Lieutenant found his posting to a reserve fleet E class destroyer, *Escort*, being prepared at Chatham dockyard, equally daunting:

In most cases, two Acting Sub-Lieutenants were sent to each reserve fleet destroyer and my term mate Peter Eason joined Escort with me. I was allocated the job of navigating officer, torpedo officer and anti-submarine officer. I knew very little indeed about Asdics* and anti-submarine work, as I had not done a course on this. Most of the ship's company were reservists, either Royal Naval Reserve or RNVR. The RNR reservists were most experienced and mature. Some had been 'on the beach' for quite a while and so were pretty rusty. The Captain, Lieutenant-Commander John Bostock, was a very experienced, able and much respected destroyer captain. Besides the Captain, the First Lieutenant, we two Sub-Lieutenants, a Gunner (who happened to be an elderly Lieutenant) and a commissioned Engineer completed the officer complement.[5]

---

* Anti-submarine detection equipment named after Anti-submarine Defence Investigation Committee.

As some recompense for the harsh wartime living conditions in destroyers and other small escort craft the Admiralty paid a small 'hard lying' allowance to their crews. According to Captain Lionel Dawson, 'hard lying' was no misnomer. The term had originated from the living conditions on the first torpedo boats, forerunner of the destroyer, where:

> ...wooden planks were considered an admirable foundation on which to sleep at night and sit upon by day...life on the early destroyers was little better.[8]

As well as bringing into commission its reserve fleet of destroyers, the Admiralty also recalled ships from foreign stations in order to supplement the number of ships available and to concentrate them nearer home. Thus on the outbreak of war a flotilla of eight D class destroyers, built in 1932, was recalled to the Mediterranean from their China Station base at Wei Hai Wei, both to be on call nearer home, and to help counter the threat posed by Italy, should that country decide to enter the war on the side of its Axis ally Germany. The ships returned in something of a hurry. V.A. Wight-Boycott, then First Lieutenant on *Delight*, wrote to his mother on 4 September 1939:

> ...we have been steaming almost continuously at 20 knots. The ship is caked with salt from stem to stern. You can chip the salt off the funnels with a knife – (and we have) – a continued shower of spray over the whole length of the ship almost since we left.[9]

The hurried return brought other problems. *Diamond*, in 'peacetime condition', arrived in Malta complete with Chinese mess boys, twenty-two canaries, six pairs of lovebirds and two Siamese cats. As recalled by Seaman P. Yates, then serving on *Diamond*:

> However things were very soon to change. The Italians were rattling sabres and showing signs of joining the Axis, so the birds had to go. This presented no problem at all, they were simply given to numerous 'bar people' in Malta. The Chinese mess boys were a very different matter. They wanted to stay with the ship and the crew. This was not possible of course, so they were ordered to pack their belongings prior to being shipped back home. This created quite a rebellion among them, so much so that one went quite berserk with a meat cleaver on the torpedomen's messdeck. He was eventually subdued and locked in the switchboard compartment until he calmed down![10]

The overall position with regard to destroyer availability was complicated. Despite tight Treasury purse-strings the Admiralty had managed to secure, in each of the ten years preceding the outbreak of war, sufficient funding to be able to build a complete flotilla of destroyers, usually made up of eight or nine ships, one of which was a slightly larger flotilla leader. Thus of the one hundred and sixty-four destroyers actually available for service on 3 September 1939, approximately two thirds were of relatively modern construction (see Appendix 1).

Most of the remaining third were of First World War design or vintage. One of them was *Keppel*, a Thorneycraft class destroyer built in 1925 and destined to become the leader of the 17th Destroyer Flotilla, made up of old V and W class destroyers. In the early summer of 1939 Captain F.S.W. de Winton was appointed Captain (D) in command of the 17th Flotilla, and of *Keppel*:

> The flotilla consisted of the following 'V's and 'W's commissioned from the Reserve Fleet complement – *Versatile, Vimy, Warwick, Whirlwind, Watchman, Vidette, Velox* and *Vortigern*...These ships were about 1,750 tons and had complements of about 190...The flotilla was largely manned by reservists, men who had completed their twelve years in the R.N., and a certain number of pensioners. Three of the ships were commanded by retired officers and, with a few exceptions, active service officers comprised the officer complement of all ships...We were based in Portland and he [Vice Admiral Sir Max Horton, in command of the Reserve Fleet] gave me a very free hand with the ground plan and working-up to full seagoing and weapon efficiency covering a period of about three–four months.[11]

However, this apparently ample supply of destroyers was nowhere near enough to fulfil all the wartime duties required of them. Their duties had moved a long way from those originally envisaged at the time of their conception at the turn of the century. Destroyers did not have the long pedigree of battleships which went back to the days of 'ships-of–the-line', or of cruisers which had their origins in the frigates of Nelson's day. Destroyers were the consequence of two technologies introduced towards the end of the nineteenth century. These were the self-propelled torpedo and the marine turbine engine. Harnessed together in the form of small, very fast, torpedo boats, capable of hitherto unheard-of speed in excess of 30 knots, and able to discharge at long range lethal self-propelled torpedoes, these boats posed a considerable threat to the larger, cumbersome ironclads of the main fleets. As a countermeasure, equally fast Torpedo Boat Catchers were developed. These quickly became known as Torpedo Boat Destroyers and then simply as Destroyers. The first flotilla of twelve boats in this class was introduced between 1905 and 1908. They were known as the Tribal class – *Nubian, Maori, Zulu, Viking, Saracen, Amazon, Cossack, Mohawk, Tartar, Afridi, Gurka* and *Crusader*. As an evolving class they were all slightly different – *Tartar* was a shade faster than her sister ships, *Viking* had six funnels and *Crusader* had a powerful stern winch.[12] What they had in common was a speed of the order of 34 knots, two or three 18-inch torpedo tubes, a miscellany of deck guns, usually 18-pounder (3-inch) or 4-inch, and a displacement of 865–1,000 tons. They all served with distinction in the First World War, and had an eventful war* which, as will be seen, was to be repeated by their replacement class of Tribals in the Second World War.

By the outbreak of the First World War the destroyers' roles had been extended. Their duties were seen as, *inter alia*, screening and protecting the main fleets against attack by enemy torpedo boats; scouting and searching ahead of the fleets; harassing enemy torpedo boats, especially as they left or returned to their bases; and delivering torpedo attacks against the enemy fleets.

By the outbreak of the Second World War evolving technology, modern weapons and new strategies had made additional demands on destroyers. Their roles were now perceived as providing anti-submarine and anti-torpedo boat protection for larger ships of the Royal Navy; engaging in anti-aircraft and anti-submarine convoy escort work; carrying out limited offensive operations in narrow waters and against enemy-held coasts; engaging in mine-laying duties; and supporting other, larger, ships, and acting as fleet picket boats.

Winston Churchill, restored to his First World War post of First Lord of the Admiralty on 3 September 1939, was quickly on to the question of destroyer numbers. In a memorandum of 9 September to the Third Sea Lord, Rear Admiral R.A. Frazer,[13] he complained that only nine new destroyers were scheduled for delivery in the following sixteen months. This he thought was unacceptable.

The First Lord of the Admiralty was also concerned at the increasing complexity, and hence cost and construction time, of the destroyer class of ships. On 11 September he sent a memorandum[13] to the First Sea Lord, Admiral of the Fleet Sir Dudley Pound, welcoming the decision to take over six 'Brazilians'** which would become available for 1940, but deploring the fact that this modern breed of increasingly complex 'Fleet' destroyers, intended for work in conjunction with the larger ships of the Royal Navy, was not designed or suited for the more routine convoy escort duties. By 1939 the modern British 'Fleet' destroyer was approaching 2,000 tons displacement with a crew of more than 200, armed with 4.7-inch guns and up to ten torpedo tubes, and capable of speeds in excess of 35 knots (see Appendix 1).

---

* *Maori* and *Viking* were mined and sunk and *Mohawk* and *Viking* were damaged by mines. *Zulu*'s stern was blown off by a mine and *Nubian*'s bow by a torpedo. The two good halves were salvaged and joined to form a hermaphrodite ship, HMS *Zubian*.[12]
** Six destroyers being built in British shipyards on the outbreak of war for the Brazilian Navy.

The newly commissioned Alfridi (or Tribal) J and K classes of British destroyers were formidable ships whose all-round performance matched that of any destroyers of other navies. The 'Tribals' in particular, heavily armed with eight 4.7-inch guns, were graceful as well as powerful. A young Sub-Lieutenant Ludovic Kennedy remembers the impression created by his first sighting of *Tartar*:

> ...a little way downstream I glimpsed her for the first time – as sleek and elegant and powerful-looking ship as I have yet seen. From the bow there rose in successively higher tiers A gun, B gun, the convex armoured wheelhouse and – the high point of the ship – the open bridge, some forty feet above the waterline. At the back of the bridge was the foremast with its aerials, aft of that the raked funnel, and then in the waist of the ship the torpedo-tubes. Up again to the pom-pom and X gun and then down to Y gun, the quarterdeck and the stack of depth charges. The whole effect was one of symmetry and grace.[14]

If British destroyers of the era had one major weakness it was their wholly inadequate anti-aircraft armament. Their 4.7-inch guns could not be elevated above 40 degrees, and the secondary 0.5-inch machine guns and 2-pounder 'pom-poms' would prove no deterrent to a determined dive bomber or massed air attack. Some attempts had been made to improve the anti-aircraft armament of British ships, but the procurement of suitable weapons was proving difficult as all branches of Britain's armed forces strove to re-arm in the final years of peace. The then Lieutenant-Commander C. Hughes-Hallett, Captain of the destroyer *Valorous* of the 2nd Destroyer Flotilla between January 1934 and February 1936, had first-hand experience of the Admiralty's attempts to procure heavier anti-aircraft guns for the Navy's ships. Promoted Commander and appointed to a new staff position with the Director of Naval Operations in February 1936, he recalled:

> I was brought into the DNO's department to occupy a desk just established, responsible for all new guns being put into production, one of which in due course was the Oerlikon. I went to sea again in 1938 so that the following events occurred between 1936 and 1938. Before the Oerlikon...the Controller had endeavoured to place an order for Bofors (40mm) guns and mountings with the Swedish firm but was unable to do so because the firm's production capacity was fully committed for months, possibly years, ahead, largely owing to a big contract they had accepted from the War Office, and they were not prepared to increase their production unless we footed the bill for a new factory.[15]

The older destroyers of First World War vintage or design were even less well protected against anti-aircraft attack. The Captain of *Keppel*, lead ship of the 17th Flotilla, wrote:

> Although adequately armed against surface craft and U-boats, the flotilla was lamentably deficient in anti-aircraft armament. In *Keppel* I managed to get a couple of Lewis guns and a Maxim machine gun* fitted on the fore bridge. *Keppel*'s 3-inch AA gun was quite useless, which by the drill book required nine men to man it![11]

The relatively few modern fleet destroyers available to the Royal Navy in relation to the demands for their services, plus their increasing sophistication – and hence value – as warships, meant that when used in a convoy escort role they had become a more worthwhile strategic target for the U-boat than many of the smaller ships they were escorting. The hunter was increasingly becoming the hunted. This dichotomy between the role of the destroyer acting alone (or in concert with other destroyers or larger ships in naval actions), and that of destroyers acting as an escort for merchant ships in convoy, was becoming increasingly apparent following the Admiralty's reintroduction, on the outbreak of war, of its First World War convoy system, in order to give collective protection to merchant ships.

In contrast to the large but varied destroyer fleet of the Royal Navy, the German Navy, with a different remit and responsibilities, had only twenty fleet destroyers at the outbreak of war (see Appendix 2). However, these were all new, with the first one *Z1 Leberecht Maas* being built at Kiel in 1934-35. As a class, they were larger, at 2,100 to 2,400 tons, than their British counterparts, with a complement of 315 men. They were much more heavily armed, with five 12.7mm (5.1-inch) guns and a mine-laying capability for sixty mines, a factor which was later to cause great embarrassment to the Royal Navy. It was envisaged that one of their roles would be to escort the fast new German battleships under construction, and the battle-cruisers *Scharnhorst* and *Gneisenau*, so the destroyers had a designed top speed of some 38 knots.

However, this high-speed capability was only achieved at an operational cost. For propulsion, the ships used a high-pressure steam turbine system which proved unreliable in service, with frequent boiler tube problems – euphemistically termed 'growing pains' by the German naval authorities. A boiler tube had only to fail, filling the engine room with scalding steam, for a ship to lose speed or even to be forced to stop for emergency repairs. The German stokers and engine room artificers learned to deal stoically with the problem of a burst water pipe:

---

* Obsolescent light machine gun firing 0.303 small-arms ammunition.

We simply turned it off and ventilated it with cold air for twenty minutes. Though the fire-proof clay was still red-hot, one of us in heavy leather togs would then creep inside, detach the burst pipe, and put a patch over the hole. After two or three hours we might with luck get the boiler going again.[16]

The sea-going capabilities and effective range of the German destroyers were inferior to those of their British counterparts. Their forecastles were found to be too short resulting, even in medium seas, in the forward gun becoming unusable as both it and the bridge were engulfed with seas breaking over the bows. Their heavier armament also contributed to the ships becoming somewhat top-heavy and less stable in heavy seas, which necessitated the retention of a high, some 30% minimum, fuel reserve in the ships' tanks to ensure adequate stability. This in turn reduced operational range and endurance. These design and technical problems were to bedevil the activities of the German destroyers in the first year of the war.

However, the German Navy had one important strategic advantage. As a continental country, with the bulk of its food and raw materials obtainable from neighbouring countries and without the need to bring many of these essentials from overseas, the German Navy did not have the major problem of protecting its supplies with convoy escort ships. The problem facing the Royal Navy in giving collective convoy protection to the merchant ships bringing food and supplies to the British Isles, on the other hand, was a formidable one. The British merchant fleet at that time consisted of some 2,000 vessels, with between 100 and 150 ships – British, allied and foreign – arriving from or departing to destinations all over the world every day. The ships were of different nationalities, varying sizes and types, and travelled at varying speeds of between eight and fifteen knots. To organise these diverse ships and cargoes into groups and move them in convoy, under the protection of destroyers and other escort ships, with perhaps some overhead aircraft surveillance from Coastal Command or the RAF when in coastal waters, was a colossal undertaking. The threat of attack by aircraft, surface ships or U-boats was constant.

The threat from U-boats was one that would grow as the war progressed. At the outbreak of war Germany had fifty-seven operational U-boats of modern design. By 1942 Germany had built 304 U-boats, thirty -three of which were built in the yards of occupied France or Holland. At the end of 1942 Germany and Italy together had 485 submarines in service, of which sixty-eight were Italian.[17] By the end of the war, Axis submarines, Italian and Japanese as well as German, had sunk 2,828 Allied and neutral merchant ships totalling 14,687,231 tons, of which nearly 11,500,000 tons were from the British Merchant Naval Fleet. The Merchant Navy also lost 23,000 Merchant seamen, killed as a result of U-boat sinkings. In addition,

German U-boats had sunk 175 Allied warships, of which the majority were British.

It was not an entirely one-sided battle, however. Germany built a total of 1,162 U-boats between 1939 and 1945, of which 785, or two thirds, were lost. 632 of these were sunk at sea, of which 503 were accounted for by British ships and aircraft.[18]

The types and operational specification of the 57 U-boats with which Germany began the war are set out in Appendix 3. In essence these 57 submarines were developed from those in service in the German Navy at the end of the First World War. They were designed to patrol submerged at periscope depth, powered by electric motors, by day, and to patrol on the surface at night, using their diesel engines for both propulsion and to recharge their electric batteries. Later in the war larger, more advanced U-boats were introduced, capable of remaining submerged for longer periods.

Equally threatening in the early months of the war was the danger posed by powerful German surface raiders. Although the British and French navies were numerically greatly superior, in both capital ships and other surface vessels, to the German Navy in 1939, the German ships were generally speaking faster and more modern. Thus the threat from the fast 32,000-ton battle-cruisers *Scharnhorst* and *Gneisenau*, each armed with nine 11-inch, twelve 5.9-inch and fourteen 4.1-inch guns and capable of over 30 knots, plus that of the three 12,000-ton pocket battleships *Deutschland* (later renamed *Lutzow*), *Admiral Scheer* and *Admiral Graf Spee*, each armed with six 11-inch, eight 5.9-inch and six 4.1-inch guns and capable of 26 knots, was serious. Great Britain had only the three elderly battle-cruisers *Hood*, *Renown* and *Repulse*, and the French the new battleships *Dunkerque* and *Strasbourg* individually capable of catching and dealing with them in any running battle. In order to contain the threat of these surface raiders, the Allies had to provide shadowing task forces made up of battleships, battle-cruisers, and heavy 8-inch cruisers to protect the larger and more important convoys. This was in addition to the protection provided by the convoy's own 'close escort' of destroyers and other small escort ships. These shadowing heavy escort groups, in turn, also needed their escorting anti-submarine screen of destroyers.

There was one further consideration which prevented the Allied navies from bringing their numerical superiority fully to bear. Both the French and British were concerned about the intentions of the Italians in the Mediterranean and the Japanese in the Far East. For these reasons many allied warships, including destroyers, had to be kept dispersed throughout the world in order to protect overseas positions and lines of communication and commerce. As a consequence of all these considerations, the demand for destroyers was unremitting and could not be satisfied.

Since the first call on the modern destroyers being built in the 1930s would be to work with the main fleets, an acute shortage of vessels to

14

meet the very large demands for anti-aircraft and anti-submarine convoy escort duties was foreseen. From 1937 onwards the Admiralty took steps to combat this envisaged shortage in a number of ways. As an immediate step, six old 4,250 ton C class cruisers, launched in the First World War, and fifteen old destroyers of a similar vintage, were converted to an anti-aircraft escort role by re-arming them with 4-inch anti-aircraft guns. Even this step was to produce shortages of another kind in a Britain ill-prepared for war. The First Lord of the Admiralty's memorandum of 8 September 1939 to the Director of Naval Operations[13] reveals that the Royal Navy had only 520 rounds of ammunition for each of its main high angle 4-inch quick-firing guns.

The Admiralty also started to introduce new classes of vessel to take over the convoy escort roles of destroyers. They ordered specialist escort vessels of the generic type to become known as sloops. Displacing 1,000–1,250 tons, and armed with 4-inch guns, these vessels were slow but had a comparatively long sea-keeping endurance. By the outbreak of war some fifty of these sloops were in service. More analogous to the traditional destroyer was the small Hunt class destroyer; the individual ships were named after fox-hunts. These were of an entirely new design, a small and fast destroyer of some 1,000 tons displacement and capable of 32 knots. They were armed with a dual-purpose main armament of six 4-inch guns but carried no torpedo tubes. Twenty of these Hunt class ships were building at the outbreak of war, and a further sixty-six were included in the next two years of naval construction. Although of short sea endurance, they performed invaluable service throughout the War, in narrow seas and along the coastal shipping routes. Lastly, the corvette, another completely new type of small long-endurance escort vessel, designed on the lines of a whale-catcher displacing some 1,000 tons, armed with one 4-inch gun, was introduced. Although their small size and lively performance in rough seas made life very uncomfortable for their crews, they went on to perform yeoman service throughout the war. Their drawback was their top speed of fifteen knots, which was too slow to enable them to overtake a surfaced U-boat of the later types.

Few of these various convoy escort vessels were available when the Royal Navy went to war on 3 September 1939 with its miscellany of modern and obsolescent destroyers (see Appendix 1). By June 1940, nine months into the war, very many of these ships would have been sunk or badly damaged.

NOTES TO SOURCES

1.   Carton de Wiart, Lieutenant General Sir Adrian. *Happy Odyssey* (Jonathan Cape: London, 1950).
2.   Colville, J. *The Fringes of Power: Downing Street Diaries 1939–1945* (Hodder and Stoughton: London, 1985).
3.   Chalmers, Rear Admiral W.S. *Max Horton and the Western Approaches* (Hodder and Stoughton: London, 1954).
4.   Whinney, Captain R. *The U-Boat Peril* (Blandford Press: London, 1986).
5.   Cardale, Captain P.J. Papers 90/23/1. Imperial War Museum, London.
6.   Knight, Signalman J. 'Memories of a Miscreant'. Papers 87/15/1. Imperial War Museum, London.
7.   Vian, Admiral of the Fleet Sir Philip. *Action This Day* (Frederick Muller: London, 1960).
8.   Dawson, Captain L. *Flotillas: A Hard Lying Story* (Rich and Cowan: London, 1933).
9.   Wight-Boycott, Captain V.A. Papers 96/59/3. Imperial War Museum, London.
10.   Yates, Seaman P. Papers 92/27. Imperial War Museum, London.
11.   de Winton, Captain F.S.W. Papers 85/44/1 Imperial War Museum, London.
12.   Mountevans, Admiral Lord. *Adventurous Life* (Hutchinson and Co: London, 1946).
13.   Gilbert, M. *The Churchill War Papers, Vol 1: At the Admiralty Sept 1939– May 1940* (Heinemann: London, 1993).
14.   Kennedy, Sir Ludovic, *On My Way to the Club* (Collins: London, 1989).
15.   Hughes-Hallett, Vice Admiral Sir Charles. Ref H.U.H.T., Churchill Archives Centre, Churchill College, Cambridge.
16.   Bekker, C. *Hitler's Naval War* Trans Ziegler, F. (Macdonald: London, 1974).
17.   'The Battle of the Atlantic: The Official Account of the Fight against the U-boats, 1939-1945'. (HMSO: London, 1946).
18.   Roskill, Captain S.W. *The Navy at War, 1939-1945* (Collins: London, 1960).

II

The Opening Days

For the Polish and German navies, the war began in earnest on 1 September
1939. Poland's navy was both new and small, reflecting her recent emer-
gence as an independent country after centuries of partition and oppres-
sion by her immediate neighbours. It was formed from a small and miscellaneous collection of river gunboats, coastal patrol vessels, minesweepers
and torpedo boats; but it was not until the completion of the destroyer
ORP* *Wicher* (Wind) in 1929 that a sea-going Polish Navy emerged. Over
the next ten years, up to the outbreak of war, the Polish Navy grew in
strength as the almost-landlocked country sought to assert her independ-
ence and to demonstrate to her powerful neighbours Germany and Russia
her determination to defend her small coastline.

A further three modern and formidable destroyers were added to the
Polish Fleet between 1932 and 1938: *Burza* (Squall), *Blyskawica* (Lightning),
and *Grom* (Thunderbolt). In addition to these four destroyers, the Polish
Navy consisted of the small torpedo boat *Mazur*; the minelayer *Gryf*; five
submarines, *Wilk, Zbik, Rys, Orzel* and *Sep*; eight trawler-sized minesweepers; plus a dozen or so gunboats and coastal vessels. It was a very small
force to be matched against the might of the German Navy and from the
outset there could only be one outcome in any confrontation.

The *Mazur* was sunk by German bombers at the Gdynia-Oksywic naval
base at about mid-day on 1 September 1939. The *Wicher, Gryf* and some
minesweepers put to sea later that day on a mine-laying and sweeping
operation across the sea route between Pilan and Gdansk, where they were
attacked by formations of German Ju 87 Stuka dive-bombers. Although
damaged by near misses and bomb splinters, and suffering casualties,
they fought off the attackers and made their way to the naval base at Hel.
There the ships were bombed again; and on Sunday 3 September, the day
when Britain and France declared war on Germany in Poland's cause, the

---

* ORP is the abbreviation for Okret Rzeczypospolitej Polskiej, or warship of the Polish
Republic, being analogous to HMS.

ships were attacked in harbour by the two German destroyers *Leberecht Maas* and *Wolfgang Zenker*. *Maas* fired on *Wicher* and *Zenker* engaged *Gryf* at a range of some 14,000 yards. Already damaged, the immobile Polish ships, aided by a shore battery of four 6-inch guns, put up a doughty fight against the fast-moving German ships. Shortly before 0700 hours the leading German destroyer was hit and severely damaged by a salvo of return fire from the shore battery. A 6-inch shell struck the starboard fore-corner of the *Leberecht Maas*; splinters from the exploding shell scything down the gun crew behind B gun, killing four and wounding four.[1] Although not a mortal blow, the ship's firing and fighting power was diminished; and at 0735 the German destroyers broke off the action and withdrew under cover of a smoke-screen, leaving the *Wicher* and *Gryf* further damaged by the bombardment. The *Maas* alone had fired seventy-seven rounds of 5.1-inch (12.7mm) shells at the hapless *Wicher*. Two hours later the Luftwaffe took up the attack. *Wicher* was sunk at her moorings, and *Gryf* had every gun put out of action before finally succumbing to the air onslaught.*

Despite these Polish losses and setbacks, the German invaders did not succeed in eliminating the Polish Navy. In the days leading up to the conflict the British Admiralty had suggested that in the event of a German invasion some of the better Polish ships might try to escape to Britain to continue the fight rather than risk immediate destruction or capture. The proposal was accepted and the plan given the code name *Operation Pekin*. On 30 August, just before the German invasion, the Commander-in-Chief of the Polish Navy, Rear Admiral J. Unvug, received the order from the Polish Naval Headquarters in Warsaw to proceed with Operation Pekin, and the order 'Execute Pekin' was passed by semaphore from the Polish Fleet command to *Blyskawica*, the destroyer divisional leader.[2] The sealed orders of Operation Pekin contained the primary instruction:

> Destroyer division, consisting of *Blyskawica, Grom* and *Burza* to sail for Britain, reaching position between Borholm and Christians by sunset, passing Malmo at midnight. Departure immediate and arrival Britain during daylight.[2]

The Divisional Commander, Commander R. Stankiewicz, held a short meeting with his destroyer captains, Commanders W. Kodrebski (*Blyskawica*), A. Hulewicz (*Grom*) and S. Nahorski (*Burza*). At 1415 hours the three Polish warships weighed anchor and departed for an unknown destination and

---

* The naval base at Hel continued to defy the German invaders, aided by naval guns salvaged from the warships, despite Poland's increasingly hopeless position. At 0500 on 17 September Russia invaded Poland from the east, as part of the Russian-German Non-Aggression Pact signed on 23/24 August by Molotov and Ribbentrop, the respective Foreign Ministers. One of the clauses was an agreement to divide Poland between them. The naval base of Hel finally surrendered on 1 October.

an uncertain future. Increasing speed to twenty-five knots, Borholm was passed at 2140 and the Sund entered at 0010 on 31 August. Danish radio enquiries demanded identification and were ignored as the ships forged ahead. At sunrise the ships were in the Kattegat. At 1530, while on course for Scotland, a German plane was identified tracking the Polish warships. Course was changed to due West, 315 degrees, to outwit any U-boats being vectored into their path, and at sunset the course was reset. At 0925 on 1 September a radio message was received reporting the German attack upon Poland, and the warships were put on full alert. The crews knew that they had embarked upon a journey of no return, and that no quarter was to be asked or given in the future battles for their homeland. If necessary the ultimate sacrifice was expected of all of them, as expressed by an officer on the *Burza*:

> When we opened our sealed orders we learned that in the event of an attack by a strong force of German ships we in *Burza* were to fall behind and fight it out while the others went on. You see, they were much faster than us and much more valuable.[3]

At around mid-day the three Polish ships were met by the two W class British destroyers *Wanderer* and *Wallace* and escorted to Leith in Scotland. There they were welcomed as most valuable allies. The *Blyskawica* and *Grom* were new, and arguably the most powerful destroyers in the world at that time, with a displacement of 2,100 tons. Built at White's shipyard in Cowes, Isle of Wight in 1936, they each had a top speed of 39 knots and carried a formidable armament of seven 120mm (4.7-inch) guns, four 40mm and eight 0.5-inch machine guns for anti-aircraft protection. They also had six 21-inch torpedo tubes and a mine-laying capability of 44 mines. The *Burza* was older, slower and smaller. French-built in 1932, she displaced 1,540 tons and had a top speed of 33 knots. She was armed with four 130mm (5.1-inch) guns, two 40mm and four 0.5-inch machine guns. The *Burza* carried six 21-inch torpedo tubes and had a mine laying capacity of 60 mines. They were three very powerful destroyers that were to become an asset to the Allies and formidable foes to the Germans in the forthcoming months.

The flotilla's arrival in Scotland was to prove a lasting memory for two crew members. Commander T. Lesisz remembers:

> I was a young Sub-lieutenant on board ORP *Burza* when our squadron of three Polish destroyers...arrived on 1 September 1939 in Scotland, three days before England declared war. On Sunday, 3 September, shortly after 11.30 in the morning, a British admiral came on board our flagship *Blyskawica* to say to the officer greeting him at the gangplank 'Gentlemen, I am pleased to announce that we are at war with Germany.' [4]

Signal Petty Officer B. Witkowski has more personal memories of the time:

> ...met by British destroyers and escorted to outside of the Firth of Forth Bridge where we anchored and waited for permission to enter the harbour. There we were given provisions of white bread, butter and jam; what a treat. After some days we were given permission for some shore leave. Everyone received £1 to spend. I went by bus to Dunfermline to a dance hall where I had a little taste of Scottish dancing. After the night out I purchased a few trinkets and went back on board with five shillings left.[5].

The next few days were hectic ones for the Polish crews as they again prepared for sea. On 4 September the Commanding Officer of the Polish Flotilla, Commander R Stankiewicz, was called to London to see the First Sea Lord, Admiral of the Fleet Sir Dudley Pound. It was agreed that the Polish ships would sail under Royal Navy orders but be commanded by Polish officers and crewed by Polish seamen. Polish-speaking British liaison officers and signal coder specialists would serve on the ships to help overcome communication and operational problems. The first task allotted to the Polish destroyers was convoy escort duties in the Western Approaches.

> Soon after our destroyers were refuelled and three days later we were sailing around the north of Scotland to our new base at Devonport, Plymouth.[4]

Within a few days the three ships had been inspected by their new Commander-in-Chief, Western Approaches. He was obviously pleased by what he saw, as evidenced by the signal that he sent to the Commander of the Polish Forces on 12 September:

> I should like to express my admiration for the splendid spirit of your officers and ships' companies and their evident efficiency. I was much impressed with everything seen during my walk round your ships yesterday and am very proud to have them in my command. Although far away from Poland, the service you are performing is of the greatest importance to our common cause.[6]

Blyskawica and *Grom* were primarily built for service in the Baltic. Unfortunately, under wartime operational conditions in the autumnal Western Approaches, they were found to be top-heavy and hence unstable in the more turbulent seas of the North Atlantic and the increasingly wintry waters surrounding the British Isles. Under the direction of the ships' builders, J. Samuel White of Cowes, some interim structural modifications to reduce top weight were made in October to improve the ships' sea-going performance. On 29 October 1939 the three Polish destroyers were reassigned to Harwich and integrated into the 1st Destroyer Flotilla based there under Captain (D) G.E. Creasy, its commander.

An indication of the conditions under which the ships operated, and indeed of the operational conditions common to all destroyers and light escort vessels throughout the war, can be found in the report of an accident on board *Grom* sent to the Commander-in-Chief, Western Approaches, by the Senior Officer of the Polish destroyers, dated 30 September 1939:

Sir,

I regret to have to report the loss overboard at 10.00 on 29 September 1939 of Warrant Electrician Wladyslaw Kalinowski 2028/A.

The accident occurred in position 50degrees 09'N; 04degrees OOW course 300 degrees, speed 20 knots, sea 5 starboard quarter, wind force 7. The circumstances were as follows:

The ship rolled about 50 degrees to port under the action of an extra large sea and remained for some time in this position during which the port side of the deck was submerged from the break of the f'ocsle to the stern. A subsequent order of 'hard-a-port' brought the ship again upright.

Kalinowski at this time was standing by the after torpedo tubes and as these were almost completely submerged it is presumed that he was washed overboard.

There was some delay in the report of this reaching the bridge as the men in the immediate vicinity of Kalinowski did not observe the accident.

His companion however, with whom he was standing before the accident and who was completely submerged, observed the absence of Kalinowski when the ship righted herself and reported to the OOW Sub-Lieutenant Grochowicz, who immediately instituted a search for the missing man.

Meanwhile, shortly after 10.00 a report of 'man overboard' was received on the bridge via the Transmitting Station from the after superstructure. At the same moment however, a lookout on the bridge also reported 'man overboard' on observing that a seaman who was working at the time in the port sea-boat was completely submerged and lost to view.

Subsequently this report was disproved as the seaman referred to was found to be safe on deck, but the coincidence of the two reports was unfortunate since it led to the ship not being put about until 10.15.

The Captain altered course at this time, when the search for Kalinowski had failed, and returned to the position where the accident was presumed to have happened, but no trace of the man could be found.

The normal precautionary measures prescribed by our regulations for the safety of the crew at sea were being at the time correctly carried out.[7]

The three destroyers were not Poland's only naval contribution to the Allied cause. Immediately prior to the war there were two Polish Navy training ships at sea – *Iskra* and *Wilia*. Both had midshipmen and other trainees aboard, plus full complements of naval officers and instructors. Eventually these officers, instructors, trainees and crew made their way to Britain to provide the nucleus of the expanding Polish Navy.

Thus the outbreak of war found twenty year-old Midshipman Janek Wankowski,[8] one of sixty midshipmen, on board the Polish training ship *Iskra* (Spark), anchored at the French naval base at Casablanca, North Africa, undergoing their period of sea training. The *Iskra* was anchored near to the French fast mine-laying cruiser *La Tour d'Auvergue*, ex *Pluton*, 4,770 tons, the cruiser's decks loaded with some 125 mines.

Suddenly at 1040 on 13 September 1939 there was a massive upwards explosion on board the French cruiser as mines on her deck blew up. The explosion destroyed the French ship and the surrounding dockside, causing many casualties. Fortunately, the small *Iskra* was somewhat sheltered by the hull of the larger cruiser from the effects of the largely upwards explosion and escaped lightly, though one Polish officer had his knee-cap blown off and the decks of the training ship were littered with debris and human remains.

Midshipman Wankowski was working on one of *Iskra*'s six-oar rowing boats:

> Suddenly a roar of an explosion and a blast of air hit our ears and bodies, and a high fountain of water, smoke and huge slabs of metal rose up. The boat, shaken up, creaked ominously…The explosions repeated themselves, one after another, and our deck was being hit with great force by a variety of metal bits and splinters of steel, a rain of falling bits of wood and burning bundles of cleaning cotton…After perhaps one minute, or perhaps even less, the explosions ceased and the whole upper deck became alive, all having left the lower decks. Someone sounded the fire alarm. Everyone suddenly became fully conscious and found themselves right in their proper fire stations. Our motorboat was pushed away…and proceeded to pick up drowning survivors.[8]

After the trauma of that narrow escape the *Iskra* sailed to Marseilles, where the midshipmen were moved by rail to Brest, and then onward by sea to Plymouth. Here they were housed in a Polish liner converted into a make-shift training ship. After further training, those of the senior midshipmen able to pass with only a fortnight's notice the Oxford University English Language Examination were posted to Polish warships to gain sea-going experience. Thus Midshipman Wankowski found himself on November 1939, posted to *Burza* based at Harwich. He remained on the *Burza*, mainly engaged on convoy escort work along the East Coast of England and to and from Norway, until April 1940, before being promoted and posted to serve on motor torpedo boats.

As the last days of peace drained away the Royal Navy finalised its own preparations for war. At 1540 hours on Thursday 31 August a signal from the Commander-in-Chief was sent to all ships of the Home Fleet: "Complete fusing of all shells. Ship all warheads. PREPARE FOR WAR."[9] Then, at 1143 hours on Sunday 3 September, only a few minutes after Britain's official declaration of war, came the 'most immediate' signal from the Admiralty to all ships of the Royal Navy: "COMMENCE HOSTILITIES AT ONCE WITH GERMANY."[9]

The Royal Navy responded at once to its wartime footing with its usual mixture of hard work and humour:

> As the *Kelly* was intended for the Mediterranean Fleet she was painted light grey, but when the war began it seemed more likely that she would stay in home waters so on the Sunday afternoon everyone was over the side painting the ship dark grey. Some say the light grey was enamel paid for by Louis himself [Lord Louis Mountbatten, then Captain of HMS *Kelly*], but it was all covered by the dark grey. Even Louis was over the side in a white Daz-washed overall and the men on the next stage flicked paint from their brushes at him.[10]

For the British Navy there was to be no Phoney War, no phasing in. On the elderly destroyer *Walpole*,* engaged in convoy duties off Milford Haven, the Captain, Lieutenant-Commander Burnell-Nugent, received the Admiralty signal and within ten minutes had attacked a possible submarine contact with a pattern of depth charges: "The sudden realisation that there was a war on came as something of a shock to all on board."[11]

---

* The keel of HMS *Walpole*, a W class destroyer, was laid down in 1917. During the Second World War she served in the Western Approaches, in the Straits of Dover, off the East Coast and in the Channel. She also took part in convoys to Russia. She was mined in the North Sea off Schelde Estuary on 6 January 1945 and the extensive damage sustained led to her being finally broken up in 1946. The *Walpole* was adopted by Ely Urban and Rural Districts and the City of Ely in 1942, and her ensign was laid up in Ely Cathedral by the surviving members of the ship's company on 4 June 1980.

Late on 3 September, the Tribal class destroyer *Somali*, commanded by Captain G. Nicholson, captured the German merchant ship *Hanna Boge* in the North Atlantic, some 350 miles south of Iceland. The new 2,377-ton merchant ship, only completed in 1938, was carrying a £1million cargo of wood pulp, considered to be a strategic war material, from Nova Scotia back to Germany. The *Somali* captain put a ten-man boarding crew onto the *Hanna Boge* under the command of Lieutenant-Commander S. Tuke, the *Somali*'s First Lieutenant, and the ship and her German crew members were escorted to Kirkwall in the Orkneys. Her crew were interned and the ship taken over by the Merchant Navy.* It was the first of many blockade-runners to be seized by the Royal Navy in pursuit of the Allies' economic strategy.

That first day was also marked by controversy. On the evening of 3 September the liner *Athenia*, sailing from Liverpool to America and carrying women and children being evacuated to safety together with some 300 American civilians, was torpedoed and sunk by *U-30* commanded by Oberleutnant Lemp** with the loss of 112 lives, including 28 American citizens. Initially the German Government claimed that Winston Churchill had personally ordered a bomb to be placed on board the *Athenia* so that its subsequent sinking could be blamed on a German U-boat in order to bring America into the war on the Allied Side.[12] The attack, which alienated world opinion, was later defended by the Germans on the grounds that the U-boat commander had thought that the 13,000-ton *Athenia* was either a troopship or an auxiliary cruiser. It was a sinking that was to herald all-out, no-holds-barred, warfare between the U-boats and the Royal Navy.

Fortunately two patrolling Royal Navy destroyers, *Escort* and *Electra*, were able to rescue some survivors from the sinking of the *Athenia*, otherwise the loss of life would undoubtedly have been heavier. Captain P.J. Carsdale, then a Sub-Lieutenant navigator on *Escort*, recalled:

> *Escort* and *Electra* were barely a hundred miles away from *Athenia*'s reported position and we immediately proceeded to that position at high speed, and picked up survivors, most of whom were in boats, but some in the water on rafts. We then proceeded at 18 knots to Greenock. I managed to get a sun sight en route, which was just as well as when we were approaching the North Channel it came down foggy. We just managed to sight Altacary lighthouse on Rathlin Island and then the fog really came down. However, because of the injured on board, we did not reduce speed and the next thing we saw was the entrance to the Clyde off the Little Cumbraes. The Captain,

---

* The *Hanna Boge*, renamed the *Crown Arun* and used as a merchant ship by the British, was eventually torpedoed by a U-boat off Iceland a year later.
** Oberleaunant Lemp perished when his *U-110* was sunk in May 1941.

John Bostock, remained cool and calm throughout, but I remember the Chief Officer of the *Athenia*, who we had picked up, was somewhat alarmed. Remember that in those days there was no radar or radio aids and we did not have an echo sounder. Nevertheless all was well.[13]

The Admiralty's decision to re-introduce the First World War convoy system from the outset of Second World War was to prove a wise one. Although the Germans gained some initial successes from having placed the U-boats at sea before the war started, these early U-boat gains against the allied merchant fleets were not maintained. In the first fortnight of the war, before the convoy system was fully implemented, U-boats sank twenty-eight merchant ships totalling 147,000 tons. Over the next six and a half months, up to the end of March 1940, they sank a total of 229 ships, totalling some 764,766 tons. In the process they lost eighteen U-boats: more that one-third of their operational U-boat fleet at the outbreak of the war. Later in the war the pendulum of success was to swing markedly in favour of the U-boats, particularly during the battle of the Atlantic in the 1941–1943 period, before airpower and technological advances in underwater detection finally stilled the U-boat menace.

Nevertheless, in the first few weeks of the war German U-boats did secure some spectacular successes, against ships of the Royal Navy engaged on measures both defensive (as on convoy escort duties) and offensive (as in proactively seeking out the enemy submarines). One such offensive measure was the use of aircraft from fleet aircraft carriers, escorted by a screen of destroyers, on anti-submarine sweeps in the Western Approaches. It was to prove a costly and largely ineffective measure and the Royal Navy had an early escape from its consequences. On 14 September the aircraft carrier *Ark Royal* was looking for U-boats and German destroyers thought to be operating in the area. Sweeping down the north-west coast of Ireland to the west of the Hebrides in the direction of Rockall, she was unsuccessfully attacked by *U-39*. The aircraft carrier was escorted by five F class destroyers of the 8th Flotilla – *Faulknor, Firedrake, Foxhound, Fame* and *Forester*. As aircraft from *Ark Royal* searched ahead of the sweep, a distress signal was received from a merchant ship under attack. *Fame* and *Forester* were detached to go to her assistance and the remaining destroyer screen – *Faulknor, Firedrake* and *Foxhound* – closed on *Ark Royal*. In mid-afternoon, as *Ark Royal* was preparing to fly off a fresh air patrol, *U-39* chose that vulnerable moment to attack. Fortunately a look-out spotted the tracks of the two torpedoes speeding towards the carrier and as she turned away the torpedoes exploded harmlessly in her wake. Instantly alerted to the danger, the three escorting destroyers raced in to converge on the direction from which the torpedoes had come. It was to be a classic destroyer 'combing down the torpedo tracks' counter-attack against a submarine.

Almost immediately *Foxhound* made an Asdic contact and released a pattern of depth charges set to explode at shallow depth. *Faulknor* dropped another pattern. *Firedrake* followed up with a pattern set to explode at a greater depth. Deluged by depth charges from this concerted attack, *U-39*, a Type IX A boat, was forced to the surface only to find herself under attack and being hit by shellfire from *Faulknor* and *Firedrake*. Without any respite, the stricken surfaced U-boat was rammed by *Foxhound* racing in at full speed. It was too much, and the crew quickly abandoned ship before their U-boat sank with them on board, to be picked up by whalers from the destroyers. From Stoker Vernon Coles, on *Faulknor*:

> We sailed straight down the torpedo tracks, dropped a full pattern of depth-charges and up she came. It was *U-39*. We took them all prisoner; we rescued the men in the whalers and then brought them on board. They were badly shaken, as anybody would have been on the receiving end of couple of depth charges.
>
> Captain Daniels had the German U-boat captain interrogated. I talked to some of the German prisoners. They thought they were going to be shot and they were actually surprised at the way they were treated. We had to communicate with them in sign language, but we gave them cigarettes and things. They were rather wet when they came aboard, so they were supplied with blankets while their clothes and underwear were taken down to the boiler room to dry off. Their vests all had the German swastika on, so off they came during the night – they were taken as souvenirs. The Germans were most upset about that.[14]

Ark Royal's good fortune, and *U-39*'s misfortune, can almost certainly be attributed to faulty magnetic pistols fitted to the U-boat's torpedoes – a fault which was to dog the German U-boat fleet for many months to come and which certainly saved many allied ships from destruction. According to 'Axis Submarine Manual ONI 220-M', a wartime unclassified document from the US Division of Naval Intelligence:

> The explosive in the head of the torpedo is detonated by a 'pistol' which may fire on contact with the target or on reaching her magnetic field. Most (if not all) torpedoes carried by U-boats have combination pistols which will fire by contact or magnetically. A torpedo with a magnetic pistol may detonate without hitting the target, when making a faulty run or when completing a normal run – particularly in a rough sea.

Despite this lucky escape the Admiralty persisted for a time with the policy, as indicated by an entry in a naval officer's diary for Friday 15 September:

The Commander-in-Chief, Western Approaches, ordered the A/C HMS *Hermes* and the destroyers *Echo, Wakeful, Vesper, Venitia* and *Vanessa* to operate an anti-submarine patrol south of a line 250 degrees from Land's End. At the same time the A/C HMS *Courageous* and the destroyers *Inglefield, Ivanhoe, Impulsive* and *Intrepid* were ordered to patrol north of the line.[15]

Two days later, the Royal Navy was to be not so lucky. At 20.00 hours on Sunday 17 September, the aircraft carrier *Courageous* (Captain Makeig-Jones), a 22,500 ton ship with a complement of over 1,200 men and capable of carrying 48 aircraft, was torpedoed and sunk by *U-29* (Lieutenant Schuhart) off the south-west coast of Ireland, 330 miles west of Land's End, with the loss of 518 lives. Like *Ark Royal,* she had been engaged on an anti-submarine sweep, and in a similar fashion had been attacked at a vulnerable time as she turned into the wind to receive aircraft back on board. *Courageous* had been supported by the screening force of four destroyers, but two of these had been ordered away at the time of the attack to assist a merchant ship that had herself been attacked shortly before *U-29*'s attack on *Courageous.*

> From various positions which we plotted out it seemed that *Courageous* can only have had *Ivanhoe* and *Impulsive* on screen while *Inglefield* and *Intrepid* were hunting a submarine. [14]

It was almost a re-run on the attack on *Ark Royal,* but this time with tragic consequences. Over sixty years later John Cannon, then a sixteen-year-old on *Courageous,* recalled her final moments and his own survival:

> I was Captain Makeig-Jones's messenger on board, and Fred Ball was the Commander's messenger. Sadly, Captain Makeig-Jones refused to leave the bridge and went down with the ship. My lasting recollection of the sinking was the two hour swim without a lifebelt in a cold, rough sea – although the experience did prepare us for our next sinking by the Japanese when we were mature nineteen-year-olds.[16]*

Lieutenant E.A. Court-Hampton was resting in his bunk when the torpedoes struck. All the lights went out. By the time the order to abandon ship was given, the *Courageous* had a 45-degree list to port, and the assembled crew found it almost impossible to stand on deck without holding on to some part of the ship's structure.

---

* Three sixteen-year-old seamen who survived the sinking of HMS *Courageous,* Gordon Smerdon, John Cannon and Fred Ball, all later lived in the West Country and were still meeting up regularly sixty years after the sinking.

We all took off our shoes and clothes, and as I went to pull off my shirt, must have leant forward a bit too much and slid down the deck into a gun sponson [a small balcony] dislocating my right thumb and bruising badly the left elbow. Quickly pulling my thumb and clicking it back, I found myself afloat in a lovely lot of fuel oil and got smothered all over. This was a good point as I did not feel the cold during the three-quarters of an hour I was swimming for it, but a bad point from swallowing a few mouthfuls, point of view.[17]

After collecting three other swimming seamen onto a nearby floating plank of timber, they made their way, swimming and paddling, to the side of the rescuing destroyer *Impulsive*:

> ...doing a powerful breaststroke and pushed the plank...and then went alongside in fine style, saw all the men up, and then climbed up myself which was like pulling a ton of lead out of the water. I couldn't climb over the guardrails and had to ask the sailors to help me over, as a reaction was setting in when I realised I was safe. They took me aft and put me in a hot bath, wiped off most of the fuel oil, then wrapped me in a blanket and poured four neat whiskies down my neck. I slept for an hour and felt not too bad. About 10pm our destroyer had 300 men and 45 officers in addition to her crew on board and she set off at full speed for Plymouth.[17]

The loss of such an important capital ship so early in the war brought strong criticism from some of the press and some members of the House of the government's conduct of the war, particularly of the First Lord of the Admiralty, Winston Churchill. Even at that early stage of the conflict Churchill's forceful personality, his strong – not to say overbearing – influence in the government, and his frequent interference in the detail of Admiralty affairs were eliciting suspicion and even hostility in some quarters of the Commons and country. He was then a controversial political figure. He had been in the political wilderness for a decade, largely because of his powerful and influential criticism of his own Conservative party and of government policies, particularly its lack of response to Germany's increasing militarism through the Thirties. Winston Churchill was considered by many to be impetuous, unreliable, and too old; at the outbreak of the war he was by no means the much-admired and universally accepted great war leader that he was to become. John Colville, later to serve as Private Secretary to Churchill as Prime Minister, but at the outbreak of war a young diplomat seconded from the Foreign Office to serve under Prime Minister Neville Chamberlain at No. 10, reflects in his diary entry for Monday 18 September the uncertainty and division then afflicting the country:

I lunched at the Travellers, which had fortunately reopened, and learned that the *Courageous* (large aircraft carrier) had been sunk – our first naval disaster.[18]

Later that day, meeting with family and friends, he records:

We discussed the situation heatedly, and condemned the Government's inactivity severely (though one can but hope they are in reality doing more than they seem. But if they are, the Ministry of Information should give some indication of the fact, or the public will begin to lose confidence).[18]

Although the public at large did not then appreciate it, the basic cause of the sinking of the *Courageous* was the chronic shortage of sufficient destroyers to provide adequate screening of Royal Navy capital ships as well as meeting all the other demands being made of them. The minutes of the War Cabinet meeting[19] on the day after the sinking record Winston Churchill's observation that the loss of the *Courageous* had once again revealed the country's shortage of destroyers. He thought that once the United States Neutrality Act had been repealed the Royal Navy should try to purchase destroyers from the large stocks that the United States held, and that the purchase of even twenty of their older vessels would be of great assistance.*

The acute shortage was well understood in government and in naval circles. Vice Admiral Sir Max Horton, fresh from his highly successful term as Commander-in-Chief of the Reserve Fleet, was appointed on 18 September to take charge of the Northern Patrol. He was entrusted with the task of intercepting and searching, as part of the policy for the economic blockage of Germany, all merchant ships attempting to sail through the gap between Iceland and Scotland. He wrote to the Admiralty on taking up his appointment, taking the opportunity of reminding their Lordships of his own contribution to relieving the destroyer shortage:

I shall do whatever is possible to make things better in the way of assistance, but everybody is yelling for something, especially destroyers of course, despite the forty the Reserve Fleet produced ready before 'the day'."[20]

The chronic shortage was neither known to nor appreciated by the general public. This led to some ill-informed, perhaps naïve and unhelpful criti-

---

* A year later, in September 1940, America agreed to supply fifty First World War vintage 'four stacker' destroyers in exchange for the use of British bases in Bermuda and the West Indies.

cism from the press, the public and even from Members of Parliament not yet attuned to wartime conditions and the need to keep weaknesses hidden from the enemy. They were shocked by the early loss of the *Courageous*; and Churchill found he had critics even from within his own party:

Conservative MP: Can the First Lord of the Admiralty explain how it came about that a submarine was able to get within striking distance of the Courageous in view of the fact that the Admiralty have frequently assured the House that they can deal with the menace and that it is impossible for a submarine to get within striking distance?

Mr Churchill: The question is not one which can be dealt with in a supplementary answer, but I see no reason to doubt the soundness of the broad view, which the Admiralty expressed before the war, as to our means of coping with this particular form of menace.[18]

Winston Churchill's critics at this time were not solely confined to members of the press, public and Parliament. At times he could be his own worst enemy. His relentless energy, often conflicting orders and objectives, and a desire to be involved in even the minutiae of naval affairs, was upsetting the Admiralty; but if he had his critics he also had his friends, keen to protect him from his excesses. In his diary entry of 14 September, Henry "Chips" Channon, Conservative MP noted that he had seen Duff Cooper – another Conservative MP – in the House of Commons having a long heart to heart with Winston Churchill and that he had heard that Churchill was already driving the Admiralty to distraction with his interference.[19]

Captain S.W. Roskill is of the view that:

There can be no question that Churchill's return to the Admiralty in September 1939 was warmly welcomed throughout the Navy, though doubts soon began to arise regarding the soundness of some of his strategic and technical ideas. That he invigorated the whole administrative machinery of the department and made his personality felt far and wide is beyond doubt, but he also diverted to fruitless schemes manpower and materials which were sorely needed for more conventional purposes.[21]

At this time there were a number of problems between Churchill and the senior Admiralty staff. Perhaps the one causing most difficulty was:

Churchill's interpretation of the Orders of Council establishing that the First Lord was solely responsible to the Government and Parliament for all the Admiralty business. Some First Lords never found it difficult to reconcile that responsibility with leaving professional matters in the hands of the Sea Lords; but to Churchill such a delegation of his power and his rights was unthinkable, and his streams of proposals, suggestions and criticisms understandably irritated... [21]

A problem of a more practical nature was caused by differences in working hours and habits. Churchill spent his mornings in bed working on papers and correspondence, took a bed rest in the afternoon and reached a climax of activity in the evening stretching into the small hours of the next day. The staff at the Admiralty tended to work more conventional morning, afternoon and early evening hours. The working regime of the First Lord, and his lack of consideration of its effects upon others, was to be a source of strain and irritation to his advisers and staff, not only those in the Admiralty, in both world wars.

Whatever his perceived shortcomings however, the First Lord of the Admiralty was a brilliant orator and politician, and largely won over his Parliamentary critics in a debate on the U-boat war in the House of Commons in the week following the loss of the *Courageous*. It was apparently a barnstorming performance. He frankly answered further criticisms about why only two destroyers were attending *Courageous* when she was sunk, explained the range of problems being created by the U-boats and the meagre resources, particularly of destroyers, and that the country had to meet the threat. [19]

Churchill's speech turned away the criticisms of both his leadership of the Navy and of the conduct of the naval war, and established him as a strong future leader of the country's war effort. It was a speech that was praised from both sides of the House.

On 20 September, the day of the First Lord's initial dogged defence of his policies in the House of Commons, the Navy had provided its own riposte to his critics. A mixed force of ten destroyers from the 6th and 8th Flotillas, under Captain Daniel in the flotilla leader *Faulknor*, was searching for U-boats reported to be harassing and sinking fishing trawlers off the Butt of Lewis. At about 2300 hours, as night fell and under the lights of the *Aurora Borealis*, torpedo tracks were seen approaching one of the searching destroyers. The attack was avoided and the destroyer *Fortune*, nearest the line of attack, dropped a fending-off pattern of depth charges, followed by a further pattern set to explode at a greater depth. *Forester* regained Asdic contact and dropped a further pattern followed by one from *Fortune*. These attacks forced the type VIIA boat *U-27* to the surface astern of *Fortune*, who turned in a tight circle, opened fire and prepared to ram. The crew of the U-boat, now moving slowly ahead, rapidly abandoned ship. The destroyer broke off her attack, slowed, and sent over a boarding party to try to salvage documents and equipment from the U-boat before it sank. Meanwhile, whalers from *Fortune* and *Faulknor* picked up survivors as *U-27* slowly sank under the full glare of searchlights and of the Aurora Borealis. The survivors were patently grateful for their rescue and treatment on board, as witnessed by the translation of an entry made in an officer of the *Faulknor*'s autograph album by the commanding officer of the U-boat:

> May our seamen and officers of our valiant submarine U-27 sunk by British destroyer *"Faulknor"* never in word or deed denounce the Captain Commander, as my friend, who treated us with all respect and courtesy in our hour of distress. May I, on behalf of myself and crew, thank them and the Lord.
> Signed Johannes Franz
> Kapitan-Leutnant
> Commander, U-27 20 September 1939.[9]

In the early weeks of the war such successes against U-boats were hard won, and there were to be many setbacks. The U-boats were to gain a further major success on Saturday 14 October when the 29,000-ton R class battleship *Royal Oak* was sunk while at anchor in Scapa Flow by *U-47*, commanded by Kapitan-Leutnant Gunter Prien. 833 men lost their lives. It was a brilliant U-boat operation by Prien, who went on to become a leading German U-boat commander, striking at the heart of a major British naval base. Coming so soon after the loss of the *Courageous*, it placed further demands upon the already over-stretched destroyers, charged with screening Royal Navy capital ships whenever they left harbour and with the need to provide escorts for the merchant convoys.

NOTES TO SOURCES

1.   Whitley, M.J. *German Destroyers of World War Two* (Arms and Armour Press: London, 1991).
2.   Peszke, M.A. *Poland's Navy 1918–1945* (Hippocrene Books: New York, 1999).
3.   Divine, A.D. *Navies in Exile* (John Murray: London, 1944).
4.   Lesisz, Commander P.N.T. Letter to author, May 2001.
5.   Witkowski, Petty Officer, B. Letter to author, April 2001.
6.   Re. ORP Blyskawica. Ref MAR.A.V. 16/1. The Polish Institute and Sikorski Museum, London.
7.   Re ORP Grom. Ref MAR.A.V. 15/1 – 4. . The Polish Institute and Sikorski Museum, London.
8.   Wankowski, Lieutenant, J. P.N. Conversations and correspondence with the author, 2002/2003.
9.   Williams, Commander, G.H.D. Papers 90/24/1 Imperial War Museum, London.
10. Knight, Signalman, J. 'Memories of a Miscreant'. Papers 87/15/1. Imperial War Museum, London.
11. Wells, Captain J. *The Royal Navy: An Illustrated Social History 1870–1982* (Alan Sutton Publishing: Stroud, 1994).
12. Churchill, W.S. *The Second World War, Vol. 1: The Gathering Storm*   (Cassell: London, 1948).
13. Cardale, Captain, P.J. Papers 90/23/1. Imperial War Museum, London.
14. Arthur, M. *Lost Voices of the Royal Navy.* (Hodder and Stoughton: London, 2005.
15. Ewing, Vice-Admiral Sir Alistair. Papers 65/19/1-3. Imperial War Museum, London.
16. Cannon, J. Letter, *Daily Mail*, 4 September 2001.
17. Court-Hampton, Lieutenant E.A. Papers 99/75/1. Imperial War Museum, London.
18. Colville, J. *The Fringes of Power: Downing Street Diaries 1939–1945* (Hodder and Stoughton: London, 1985).
19. Gilbert, M. *The Churchill War Papers, Vol 1: At the Admiralty, Sept 1939– May 1940* (Heinemann: London, 1993).
20. Chalmers, Rear-Admiral W.S. *Max Horton and the Western Approaches* (Hodder and Stoughton: London, 1954).
21. Roskill, Captain S.W. *Churchill and the Admirals* (Collins: London, 1977).

III

Fleet and Convoy Actions: Duties and Distractions

Throughout the war convoy duty for the escorting destroyers and other light vessels was an exacting task that was, for most of the time, monotonous yet always dangerous, and at times extremely so. The early months of conflict were particularly trying for the over-stretched crews, as they tried to come to terms with wartime sailoring. The convoy ships and their escorts were threatened by enemy mines, torpedo attack from U-boats, torpedo boats and aircraft, bomb attacks by aircraft of the Luftwaffe, and shellfire from surface raiders. For the convoy sailors, naval and merchant, death was an ever-present companion; his scythe the swish of a torpedo or the crash of a bomb, mine or explosive shell; his lantern the flash of gunfire or the roaring flames of a burning sinking ship.

In those early autumn and winter months of the war, almost all U-boat activity was confined to the Western Approaches, the North Sea and coastal waters of the United Kingdom – especially the Eastern Coast. It was only later, with the coming of increasing numbers of more advanced submarines, that the U-boat war would spread out into the North Atlantic and to the eastern seaboard of America, the Caribbean, Mediterranean, South Atlantic and even the southern end of the Indian Ocean. In the later months of 1939, and the early days of convoy escort work, there was much to learn and much improvisation. Captain P. Vian recalls the communication difficulties encountered at this time on the convoys running to and from Scandinavia:

> There were no U-boats working on the run, escort being provided as a deterrent against surface and air attack. All would have been straightforward except for a curious but important oversight. There had been no signal book prepared with which to manoeuvre convoys. Since the Scandinavian convoys were large, and were formed mainly of ships of foreign nationality, alterations of course and formation on passage through the swept channels [cleared of mines] of the north-east coast of Scotland were no light matter.

34

Before dark each night it was necessary to send destroyers of the escort alongside every ship of the convoy, usually in bad weather, displaying on a blackboard the intended times for alteration of course. These times were, in fact, not accurately predictable, since they would depend on wind and sea, current and tide.[1]

About this time, *Kelly* was one of the destroyers engaged on convoy escort duties to and fro in the Western Approaches. Signalman J. Knight, one of her crew, wrote:

...for several weeks we were escorting convoys, three days into the Atlantic, pick up another convoy and three days back. Six days was about the limit of the ship's endurance at the slow speed of a convoy. For the whole of the six days the ..scuttles [portholes] and the dead lights were bolted down tightly. Unfortunately when the ship was painted dark grey the metal rims, which bedded onto the rubber in channels on the other part, had been painted as well. After six days being clamped down tightly the rims had stuck to the rubber and when the deadlights and scuttles were opened on returning to harbour for the first time the rubbers were pulled out. On the next trips in winter gales and heavy seas the scuttles were not watertight and each time a wave splashed against the side some of it came in and there was always an inch or so of water swilling around the mess.[2]

This was to bring additional problems:

In those days small ships were on what was known as 'canteen messing'. There was a weekly issue of tea, milk and sugar, a daily issue of meat, potatoes and also bread when in harbour and it could be obtained from a depot ship, or at sea whenever the cooks were able to do some baking. Anything else had to be got from the canteen and paid for at the end of the month, and food was prepared in the mess and taken to the galley to be cooked. All the tins of vegetables, fruit, etc., were kept in a locker fastened to the bulkhead between the messes and which opened at the bottom. Unfortunately the motion of the ship caused the locker lid to open allowing all the tins to fall out into the water swilling about. It didn't take long before all the labels came off the tins and it became the usual thing to open what it was hoped would be a tin of carrots to put in a stew only to find it was marmalade. This probably happened in other ships and word must have filtered back to the Admiralty because after a few months tins were issued without paper labels and what they contained was not painted on the outside, but seemed to be burned or branded on.[2]

For the crew members of *Kelly* there was yet another mealtime hazard – their captain Lord Louis Mountbatten's obsession with sailing at high speeds and executing sharp turns:

> I make no apology for referring to him as Louis, for that was how we spoke of him on the messdeck. Whenever the ship heeled in a flat calm someone was sure to say "Hello, what's Louis up to now?" It always seemed to happen at mealtimes. As soon as the plates were on the table, over went the wheel, over went the ship and there we were trying to keep three plates from falling with only two hands. We were convinced he did it deliberately.
> "What was that pipe Number One?" we imagined he said.
> "Hands to dinner, Sir."
> "Good, hard-a-starboard."[2]

Due to some extent to Captain Mountbatten's extravagant handling of the ship, *Kelly* was soon to be in difficulties, with a tragic consequence. Sent across the North Sea to try to intercept the *City of Flint*, an American merchant ship captured by the German pocket battleship *Deutschland* and now, with a German prize crew on board, making her way back to Germany through Norwegian coastal waters, *Kelly* was returning home on 3 November 1939 in high seas at some 28 knots when she turned abruptly as she was hit by a great wave and heeled over 50 degrees to starboard. All the boats, davits and guard rails on the starboard side were washed away, and a stoker was swept overboard and drowned. The ship's designer, Mr A.P. Cole, wrote to Captain Mountbatten congratulating him on his ship's lucky escape, with perhaps an hint of reproval of the Captain's handling of the ship and a note of self-satisfaction on his own design of *Kelly's* hull. The *Kelly* was among the destroyer classes built in the late 1930s with a 'longitudinal system' of construction intended to give greater strength to the ship's hull.

> The general opinion here is that the combination of sea and speed could quite conceivably have caused your terrific roll, which I believe is almost a record, and that very few ships could have survived it.[3]

The Captain of the *Kelly* was not alone at this time in facing criticism over his handling of his ship. Only a month earlier the C-in-C Western Approaches had found it necessary to caution his destroyer captains against travelling at too great a speed in heavy seas. From the diary of the then Lieutenant A. Ewing on the destroyer *Imogen*:

> ...From the movements signal it seems that the following ships are in the Western Approaches – *Eclipse, Wessex, Escapade, Encounter,*

Vanessa, Wakeful, Vansittart, Venomous, Vivacious, Venetia and *Viscount*. Some are with convoys and some patrolling. Entered Cardigan Bay at 5.30am. Fine and cold. Swept to the north around the Bay. Intercepted a signal from Impulsive that she had sustained structural damage caused by heavy seas…[later that day]…C-in-C Western Approaches has made a general signal to all destroyers in his command to the effect that the damage sustained by Impulsive would take three weeks to repair and warning commanding officers not to drive their ships at too high a speed into a head sea. Wars in the past have been won by seamanship etc. Poor old *Impulsive* is in the doghouse. It is a most difficult thing to judge, the time to slow down. You probably have been told to get to a certain position by a certain time and feel that you must get there if possible. And it is always the odd outsized wave that gets you. Then it is too late.[4]

Living and working conditions on board the destroyers and other small escort vessels must have been unbelievably hard as autumn turned into winter, and the sea turned ever more violent. G.G. Connell, who served on a fleet destroyer on the East Coast, recalls:

No special foul or cold weather clothing had been issued to the majority of the fleet so men wore a strange and mostly unsuitable mixture of clothing, private gear to supplement the inadequate issue gear and worn under issue oilskins in a vain attempt to keep out raw and freezing easterly winds.[5]

The provision of suitable clothing for the duty crews of the destroyers was an issue that Winston Churchill quickly took up and pursued with his usual persistence. He sent a note of the matter to the Admiralty staff on 6 December 1939[6] asking for precise information, to be obtained directly from Flotilla Captains, on the number of duffle coats available to destroyer crews working at sea, as against the authorised issue. He was evidently not satisfied by the response to his missive and followed up with a typically Churchillian broadside two days later to Rear-Admiral R.S. Arbuthnot, Fourth Sea Lord responsible for supplies and transport. Churchill expressed his concern on what he considered to be a lamentable situation and demanded an update every three days on the number of duffle coats being sent to which ships.It is little wonder that the First Lord's persistence over what they would no doubt consider to be undue interference with the minutiae of naval administration "was driving the Admiralty to distraction."[6]

Bad as the conditions must have been above deck on the destroyers, they were not much better below decks:

Battened down messdecks, dimly lit, overcrowded and damp with constant running condensation from steaming clothing, made living spaces cold, clammy and comfortless. Once hammocks were slung it became impossible to move around between decks unless bent double; there were few places that a man could stand upright. The constant bad weather of the winter of 1939 turned the messdecks of the East Coast convoy escorts into dreadful spaces of swirling water, spilt gash buckets and vomit; for men whose sleeping billet was on the deck below the mess tables shipboard life acquired an added torment.[5]

Many of the sailors, officers and men alike, and especially the recently-enlisted 'Hostilities Only' crew members must have suffered dreadfully from seasickness as the small escorts were tossed about in mountainous seas as they strove to hold their position in the escorting screen, all the time searching and keeping watch for enemy submarines and aircraft.

Petty Officer 'Bob' Burns recalls how appalling the conditions were:

Without doubt, throughout my experience, conditions in the old V and Ws were almost intolerable. Invariably fresh provisions were exhausted after three days at sea, the interminable diet of tinned food, no fresh bread, no vegetables caused more distress to the troops than any U-boat or aircraft attack. In addition the living conditions for the complement were primitive beyond measure, never enough billets for hammocks to be slung for more than half the troops, a place on deck sufficed for most. In the cold inhospitable Atlantic with salt water often awash in living places, no facilities to dry wet clothes resulted in complete misery. For H.O.s pitched after minimal shore training into these conditions it must have been heartbreaking. Many suffered permanent sea-sickness and their vomiting did not always take place on the upper deck. Vile smells from inadequate lavatory facilities permeated everywhere. [5]

Despite all this, watch-keeping, engine room and other duties and tasks could not be foregone or forgotten, however foul the weather and how-ever vile the vomiting. Some forty years later, CPO Easen of the destroyer *Kashmir*, writing to Captain H.A. King, his one-time Commanding Officer, asked:

Do you remember the torpedo man, while checking them in heavy seas up in the North Sea, was washed overboard and almost at once washed back again? His head was split open from back to front on the torpedo primer blades and you had to ask permission to alter course into the sea, so Doc could stitch him up. We held the Doc and his sick bucket while he did it.[7]

Even when not at sea the ships' crews found little comfort in Britain's wintry, blacked-out ports. For the warships stationed in northern waters, their base at Scapa Flow could not have been more inhospitable. A bleak stretch of water some ten miles by eight to the south of the mainland of Orkney, surrounded by islands bare of all trees and covered in grass, sheep and seabirds, its long winter nights were only lightened by a few hours of daylight and the winds seemed constantly to blow. Admiral Beatty in the First World War had called it 'the most damnable place on earth'. Now, nearly a quarter of a century later, little had changed:

> There were no women, shops, restaurants, just a couple of canteens that dispensed warm beer, a hall for film shows and the occasional concert party and football fields that too often displayed the sign "All grounds unfit for play". This was depressing for many, particularly the lower deck...[8]

In the winter months ships' crews had to find their own entertainment: card playing, "uckers" or ludo, reading. The officers too had to make their own entertainment. Ludovic Kennedy on the tribal class destroyer *Tartar* found:

> ...On the few days that we were in harbour each month we had enough to occupy us on board. We fed well, cigarettes and spirits were duty free; and sometimes in the evenings there would be darts competitions in the wardroom flat, 'tribal' parties where we and flotilla friends dressed up as Tartars, Eskimos, Bedouins, cinema evenings often improved by the last reel appearing first and upside down.[8]

However, other officers on *Tartar*'s sister-ships found Scapa Flow to be less appealing. Lieutenant-Commander R. Whinney, on *Cossack* in the summer of 1940, felt that:

> ...the ship, when not undergoing refit or repairs, was based at Scapa Flow, a bleak, dismal, God-forsaken place. It was made the worse because one could so easily see the sad battleship *Royal Oak*, only masts, a funnel and superstructure showing above the water, lying sunk on even keel, a reminder of the power of the U-boat. Scapa had its appeal only for the walks ashore across the heather and because there were to all intents and purposes no air raids to keep one awake at night in harbour.[9]

The First Lord of the Admiralty, Winston Churchill, recognised early in the war that the hard-pressed destroyer crews deserved better treatment in their all-too-brief spells in port. In September 1939 he wrote[6] to the Second Sea Lord and the Chief of Naval Personnel on the question of providing better facilities at Scapa Flow for the crews of the Home Fleet and the Northern Patrol. He envisaged a ship-based facility along the lines of that provided there by the SS *Gurka* during the First World War, and recommended that the provision should include a NAFFI* shop as well as a cinema and theatrical facilities. He asked for plans for implementation.

In the immediate press of war there was obviously little improvement at Scapa, and in December, Winston Churchill tried again to bring about change with a minute, dated 12 December 1939, to this time the First Sea Lord and to the Director, Naval Staff. He instructed:

> Every effort should be made to ease the strain upon the destroyer crews. At Devonport I am told admirable arrangements are made to relieve the flotilla complements as they come in from patrols, and that two or three days' rest in port brings them round in a wonderful manner. Similar arrangements are in force at Rosyth and Scapa, but I am told that the amenities at Scapa are so much below those of naval ports that the men are deeply disappointed when their brief spell of rest takes place there. No doubt in some cases this is inevitable, but I trust the whole question will be reviewed with the intention of comforting these crews to the utmost extent that operations will permit.[10]

Despite Churchill's efforts while he was at the Admiralty things had not greatly improved five years later when, in 1944, in preparation for the Normandy landings, ships were stationed there for bombarding practice at the many surrounding uninhabited islands. The destroyer *Jervis* was one such ship. Her captain, Lieutenant-Commander R. Hill, was to recall:

> One thing, incredibly, had not changed at Scapa and that was its lack of any kind of amenities. This was the fifth year of the war. The battlefleet of battleships, carriers and cruisers with their array of screening destroyers had been stationed there all the war. All the time there was a mass of other ships working up. The fleet went off for long sea periods covering the grim Russian convoys, or away in the Mediterranean for an assault landing, but back they all came to the dreary, treeless, austerity of Scapa Flow. There remained only a sordid, wet canteen for the sailors, and nothing for the officers.[11]

---

* Navy, Army and Air Force Institutes Founded in 1921, it was the official trading organisation catering for the needs of service personnel.

Yet these northern waters had a unique quality and appeal for the twenty- year-old Ludovic Kennedy, watchkeeping for the first time in the early months of the war on the bridge of *Tartar*. The destroyer was on passage from Greenock to Scapa Flow:

> The sun came up over Jura and the wardroom steward arrived on the bridge with a plate of hot buttered toast and a jug of tea. I leaned on the bridge counter, looked at the bows slicing cleanly through the calm sea, the ship lifting a little to the swell. I munched my toast and sipped my tea and thought that I had never been happier.[8]

Such moments of peace and contentment were rare; precious memories to offset the tedium and tiredness – and the times of terror – that pervaded the merchant and escort ships of a wartime convoy. Thus on Tuesday 10 October 1939 *Imogen*, *Ilex*, *Acasta* and *Ardent* were ordered to meet up with an outboard convoy of eight merchant ships, ranging in size from 3,900 to 8,000 tons, leaving from docks in South Wales. It was a typically mixed assortment of ships, cargoes and destinations making up a wartime convoy of the time.

Two of the ships, the *Heronspool* and the *Stonepool*, each some ten to twelve years old and owned by the Sir Robert Ropner & Co shipping company of Darlington, had embarked upon what was to be a traumatic voyage. The two ships had been hastily provided with a rudimentary defensive weapons system as part of Britain's emergency response to the expected U-boat onslaught upon her merchant fleet. Each had a First World War vintage 4-inch gun mounted on her stern, plus a light machine gun for use against aircraft attack. In charge of these guns were Royal Navy regular or reserve gunlayers from the recently formed Defensively Equipped Merchant Fleets force. Both the *Heronspool* and the *Stonepool* each had one such DEMS gunlayer. Their task was to form, train and lead a volunteer gun crew – "Pound and Pint Sailors" – from among the merchant seamen of the ship to which they were attached. The mettle of both gun crews was to be tested within a very short time.

The South Wales convoy was later joined by a group of merchant ships from Liverpool and they sailed together to their dispersal point. The *Heronspool* and *Stonepool* were soon struggling to keep to the convoy's mean speed of 9 knots, and were perhaps glad to be able to proceed at a more comfortable rate when the convoy dispersed at 1900 on Thursday 12 October.

> We reached the point of dispersal, 49°30′ N, 15°W, where we left and the [merchant] ships proceeded independently to their destinations. We turned to the N.E. for our rendezvous with a homeward bound convoy tomorrow morning. At 7.15pm we received from Ilex an SOS

41

from SS *Senneville* 'Submarine in position 50°10'N. 14°27'W attacking *Emile Miguet'*...we altered course and increased to 28 knots, going on to 30 as soon as the third boiler was connected. The position was some 50 miles away.[4]

Faced with this emergency, the C-in-C, Western Approaches, decided to split his force of four destroyers. *Imogen* and *Ilex* were ordered to proceed to hunt the U-boat attacking the *Emile Miguet*, while *Acasta* and *Ardent* went onto the appointed rendezvous with the in-bound convoy.

Meanwhile the gun crew of the *Heronspool* were being put to the test. After the convoy had dispersed, and the collier was proceeding on her way to the mouth of the St Lawrence, a lookout reported a ship on the port bow which turned out to be a tanker, apparently stopped, with a surfaced U-boat nearby. Flashes of gunfire revealed that the tanker, the unarmed *Emile Miguet*, was being shelled to destruction by *U-48* commanded by Kapitan-Leutnant H. Schultze. The 14,000 ton French tanker was already burning fiercely and her crew had taken to their lifeboats. Captain Sydney Batson, skipper of the *Heronspool*, wisely decided that his inexperienced gun-crew who had not yet fired their obsolescent 4-inch guns, was likely to be no match for the highly trained and practised gun-crew and the modern 88mm (3.5-inch) gun of the U-boat. The *Heronspool* tried to make her escape.

Having dealt with the larger tanker, the *U-48* turned her attention to the retiring collier. The U-boat had ample time to catch up with the *Heronspool*. Provided that she did not lose contact in the gathering darkness the Type VII submarine was capable of a surface speed of 16 knots, as against the *Heronspool*'s 9 knots. At 2000 the U-boat opened fire on the collier. Captain Batson now had the choice of abandoning ship or trying to fight it out, knowing that the U-boat could always submerge and sink them by torpedo if the gunfight got too competitive. The Captain decided to fight it out, and after a few rounds of return fire from the collier the U-boat submerged. Some two hours later the submarine was again spotted astern, creeping up on the collier. The *Heronspool* fired two shots and the U-boat again dived. This cat and mouse game continued until, shortly after 0100 on Friday 13 October, the U-boat gave up trying to sink the *Heronspool* by gunfire and fired a torpedo into her amidships. *Heronspool* was doomed and slowly sinking. Her crew took to the lifeboats after sending out distress signals and reporting both her position and that of the U-boat.*

At 2150 *Ilex* had taken on an emergency message to the effect that the SS *Heronspool*, one of the ships from the convoy that they had been escorting just a few hours before, was being chased by a U-boat. *Ilex* and *Imogen* raced

---

* Captain Sydney Batson was awarded the OBE, and Gunlayer John Pearson the BEM, on 15 December 1939, "for engaging the enemy before being torpedoed and sunk".

at 30 knots to this reported position about 25 miles away. Within a few minutes the ships' lookouts sighted flashes in the sky at an estimated distance of some fifteen miles. Both destroyer crews had high hopes of catching the attacking U-boat and saving the *Heronspool*, but it was not to be:

> We never saw a sign of *Heronspool* (or the U-boat attacking her). She must have sunk very quickly as it seems almost certain that we swept over her position having seen the flashes. But one never knows. We continued to search all night.[4]

However, the gallant crew of the *Heronspool* was safe. They were picked up shortly before dawn by the neutral American passenger liner *President Harding* which had heard their distress signals.

At daylight on 13 October the searching *Imogen* and *Ilex* sighted the *Emile Muguet* broken in two with her bows and stern, still afloat, alongside each other. After trying, with limited success due to the heavy swell, to sink the two halves with shells fired at their waterline, they only succeeded in sinking the stern portion. Not wanting to waste a valuable torpedo – British destroyers only carried one full charge of torpedoes in their tubes – they continued firing rounds at the slowly sinking, but still afloat, bow portion. They ceased when called away by a distress signal from the *Stonepool*, giving her position some one hundred miles to the south-south-west. In company with *Ilex*, *Imogen* set off at full speed for this new emergency. It was the start of an eventful two days for the two destroyers.

> We therefore set course for this position which according to our reckoning is some 100 miles S.S.W. By this time the original smoke that we had sighted turned out to be the SS *President Harding* steaming at high speed towards us. As she seemed to want to communicate with us we turned towards her and received the following "Have crew of *Heronspool* aboard" to which we replied "Thank you", made a complete circle round the ship at 28 knots while we read this semaphore message and then went off after *Ilex* who had continued her course. I dare say that a good many cameras clicked as it was a lovely sunny morning and her sides were lined with people.[4]

While these events were taking place the *Stonepool* was steaming some ninety miles away to the south at a steady eight knots. As the morning haze dispersed the *Stonepool* sighted a surfaced U-boat a few miles off to port. The U-boat had already seen them and almost immediately commenced firing. The first shell fell well ahead of the collier. Turning stern on to the U-boat and ordering full steam ahead, Captain Albert White the collier's skipper decided not to capitulate but to fight it out like his friend Captain Batson of the *Heronspool* had done. Their opponent was *U-42*, commanded by Kapitan-Leutnant Rolf Dau. The coming gunfight was the first blooding of both U-boat and collier.

Within two minutes of *U-42*'s first shot, the 4-inch gun on *Stonepool*'s stern had fired back. For the next two hours fire was exchanged shot for shot, with the collier at full speed constantly altering course to put off the U-boat gunners and with the wireless operator sending out distress calls and reports of her position:

> Five minutes after her first SOS message *Stonepool* sent out another message adding that she was being gunned. At 8.09am she sent a further amended position "*Stonepool* gunned by submarine". This we received at 9.10am. At 10.05am *Stonepool* gave her position as 48°36'N, 16°05'W. "*Stonepool* engaging submarine". She is doing well.[4]

After a time, accurate firing by the more experienced U-boat crew against the larger target of the merchantman resulted in *Stonepool* starting to take hits, destroying her two lifeboats and holing her near the waterline. It was not all one-sided however. *Stonepool*'s gunners were also landing shells close to the U-boat, forcing her commander to try an unsuccessful torpedo attack on the collier. Finally a shell from the *Stonepool* hit the U-boat near her 88mm gun position, forcing the submarine to crash-dive. *U-42* surfaced some distance away a few minutes later and made off on the surface, presumably damaged or holed and unable to proceed submerged. The *Stonepool*, her crew relieved to be still afloat, also steamed off but in the opposite direction. It was honours even.*

The two destroyers, *Imogen* and *Ilex*, were by now trying to reach the stricken collier, but their mission was interrupted by an unsuccessful hunt for a submarine and by the picking up of shipwrecked seamen from yet another sunken merchant ship.

> We now picked up two boat loads, leaving the third for *Ilex*. Our two boats contained nine officers including the Master and ten crew of the French ship *Louisiane* of 6,900 tons outward bound in ballast. The submarine stopped them at daylight, the first shot killing the First Officer on the bridge and wounding one man…They took to the boats at 8.30am and the ship was finally sunk by gunfire after thirty two shots had been fired. The U-boat remained with them and offered them food which they did not accept. She dived as soon as she sighted *Ilex*, one of whose shells they say fell very close as she went down. The Officers went into the Ward Room and the crewmen I put in the torpedo-men's mess. As soon as *Ilex* had picked up her

---

* Captain Albert White was awarded the OBE, and Gunlayer Frederick Hayter the BEM, on 1 December 1939, "for services in fighting off a U-boat".

boatload we set course for *Stonepool* again as meantime we had had the following signals: "From C-in-C. W.A. to *Imogen* and *Ilex*. Attack *Stonepool's* U-boat", and from *Stonepool* at 12.14pm giving another position and adding "S/M still in sight".[4]

Stonepool was now some sixty five miles away, and *Ilex* and *Imogen* set off at 30 knots, five miles apart, looking for both the collier and the submarine. When the two destroyers met up with the *Stonepool*, her captain reported that her attacker lad last been seen at 1300, on the surface, making off southwards. *Stonepool* was badly damaged from her gunfight, and although her skipper initially wished to continue his voyage, his ship's damaged condition made this an unrealistic proposition:

> *Stonepool* has one shell hole just above the waterline in No 1 hold which now has ten foot of water and No 2 hold has two foot of water. He first of all said that he was going to continue his voyage to St Vincent and was about to turn but as after twenty minutes he did not alter course we closed him again and spoke once more through the megaphone. This time he is quite certain he is returning to Barry Docks. I imagine that finding two perfectly good destroyers to escort him he thinks it is stupid to miss a chance like this. We congratulate him on his good effort in keeping the U-boat off and are amused to see that the crew who had their life-belts on when we arrived have now taken them off. Such is faith in the Royal Navy's protective powers.[4]

The *Ilex* took up on *Stonepool's* port bow with *Imogen* on the starboard bow and the trio set off at nine knots for South Wales. At 6.50pm *Ilex* suddenly altered course sharply to port and increased speed, signalling to her sister ship "Submarine this way". The U-boat had been sighted, surfaced, by the masthead lookout of the *Stonepool*.

> ...we followed at once and almost immediately *Ilex* hoisted the "Submarine in Sight" flag and opened fire. The U-boat was slow in diving but could be seen venting her tanks. Before she disappeared we got a range of 11,000 yards. At 6.57pm we told *Ilex* to reduce speed and start operating [her Asdic equipment] so that she did not overrun the position... At 7.02 *Ilex* had reduced speed and we did so five minutes later. *Ilex* was then 20° before our beam and about two miles off. At 7.17pm *Ilex* made that she was two miles past the diving position and she altered course 180° to port. Almost simultaneously we got contact and began passing ranges and bearings of the U-boat to *Ilex* at the same time taking over [as] Directing Vessel. *Ilex* closed and by 7.22pm also got contact. She attacked almost immediately dropping the usual pattern of five depth charges. Three minutes

later the U-boat suddenly came to the surface with a tremendous surge at about 20° to the horizontal and about 800 yards away. It was a most exciting moment and a loud cheer went up from the sailors and the Frenchmen who were watching. She righted herself at once and seemed to be in perfect trim. Both ships opened fire with our 4.7 inch guns. The result of this I think [was] *Imogen* – one hit, *Ilex* – two hits, one of which knocked their gun over the side. *Ilex* who was bows on went full steam ahead to ram, aiming to hit the motor room which is the largest compartment in the boat and is just abaft the conning tower. Just before she got there she stopped both engines and went full astern to reduce the impact and so the damage which she herself would sustain. She eventually hit with about six knots way on, or so the captain estimated. As she passed over their Torpedo Gunners' Mate fired the starboard depth charge thrower. Almost as soon as *Ilex*'s stern had drawn clear, the conning tower opened and an officer appeared waving a piece of white paper, then some sailors with their hands up. They were very nearly blown out of the water as, apart from *Ilex*'s after-guns which were trained on them at about thirty yards range, we were just about to open fire again in case they meant business. But it soon became quite apparent that they were leaving the U-boat so we closed and lowered the whaler.[4]

Imogen's boat picked up fifteen survivors, including the captain, navigating officer, engineer officer, three chief petty officers and nine ratings. *Ilex* picked up two ratings. The U-boat, *U-42*, sank within a minute of being rammed, taking twenty-six of her forty-three crewmen with her. It was the first voyage of the brand new U-boat, which had only been launched three months before on 14 July 1939. When the survivors went safely on board the two destroyers, they could not understand what had happened to them, why they had not succeeded in sinking the *Stonepool*, and how they had subsequently been found and sunk.

The Captain of the U-boat was most impressed by the tactics and gunnery of the *Stonepool* and asked if she was a special ship…The sailors [of Imogen] of course went to the extreme of kindness, treating them as long lost friends and all falling over themselves to give them cigarettes or have the distinction of lending them dry clothes. There was no feeling of animosity rather more that of two football teams meeting in the changing room after a hard fought game. The wet clothing was put down in the boiler room to dry. As far as the accommodation went I put the nine ratings in the stewards mess aft with a sentry on the hatch. The three chief petty officers in the petty officers mess and the officers in the captain's day and sleeping cabin also with a sentry outside.[4]

The two destroyers then set off to catch up with the *Stonepool*, plodding her way back to Barry Docks. *Ilex* and *Imogen* did not know it, but the next day was going to be even busier, and their ships become even more crowded.

By now the C-in-C Western Approaches, aware that these U-boat attacks on merchant ships were threatening to get out of hand, had ordered the *Inglefield, Ivanhoe, Intrepid* and *Icarus* to the area, with *Imperial* to join later. *Imogen* and *Ilex* continued to look for the *Stonepool** but shortly before dawn received an SOS from SS *Lochavon*, some thirty miles away, which had been torpedoed. Sighted at 0730, the *Lochavon* was still afloat but down by the bows and her crew had taken to the lifeboats. However, before a rescue could be effected yet another SOS was received, this time from SS *Bretagne*. This 10,000 ton French passenger liner was some fifteen miles away to the south east. At 0800 lookouts on the two destroyers found the *Bretagne*. She had been torpedoed and it later turned out, had a thirty-foot long hole on her waterline. She was already listing some 25° to starboard. There were eight corwded lifeboats nearby.

The two rescuers nearly brought tragedy rather than immediate succour to the shipwrecked survivors of the *Bretagne*. In the heavy swell, both destroyers had mistakenly taken two of the lifeboats for a surfaced submarine and opened fire at a range of some six miles. Fortunately no hits were made on the lifeboats. It was the beginning of a catalogue of confusion and poor communication which was to bedevil the actions of the two destroyers over the next few hours:

> We discovered afterwards that there never was a U-boat on the surface when we thought we had it in sight. All of us, the Captain and two Officers, The Yeoman of Signals and the Director Layer and Trainer all thought that what we were looking at was a U-boat which shows how easy it is to make a mistake. What we were looking at of course was two ships in line which from *Ilex* they could identify as boats as they were at a different angle. The reason that she did not tell us that we were firing at the boats was that she could not see our fall of shot and thought that possibly we could see something which she could not. By the grace of God we did not hit what we were firing at, but we never expected to we only wanted to make her dive. What the people on the boats thought we never heard, or at least not at that distance. It was a most unfortunate mistake as apart from the danger to the boats it affected the whole of our future

---

* The *Stonepool* had to make her own way home. She reached Barry Docks on 16 October, was repaired and sailed again. Her end came nearly two years later on 11 September 1941 when she was sunk off Greenland when part of Convoy SC42, which was massacred over a period of three days by a pack of ten U-boats, including *U-432* now commanded by Herbert Schultze, whose earlier U-boat, *U-48*, had sunk the *Heronspool*. Sixteen merchant ships were sunk in the action for the loss of one U-boat.

movements and decisions. We were convinced that we had seen a U-boat and that she had dived. So that when two minutes later we received an SOS from *Karamea* only 11 miles to the Eastward that she was being chased by a U-boat we knew or thought that we knew that it was another U-boat, different from the one which we were now hunting. In fact it was the same one that had attacked *Bretagne*.

Ilex slowed down and found out from people in one of the boats that the U-boat had made off over an hour ago. But owing to another mistake in signals we never got this information.[4]

Signals continued to pour in from the threatened *Karenea* asking for assistance, but since the destroyers *Intrepid* and *Ivanhoe* were within thirty miles of her reported position, and *Karenea* was steaming towards them and away from *Ilex* and *Imogen*, the decision was taken to concentrate on the survivors of the *Bretagne* and *Stoneavon* and leave the other two destroyers to assist the *Karenea*. At 1150 *Ilex* reported: "Lifeboat I passed this morning had injured men"[4] and so at 1200 *Imogen* began picking up the passengers and crew from the lifeboats while *Ilex* screened and guarded the operation against further attack. *Imogen* took on board four boatloads, totalling 156 passengers, 16 officers and 48 crew from the *Bretagne*.

It was a difficult job getting some of the injured out of the boats…We had about eight bad cases. The worst case, a leg injury we left in the after lobby, two went into my cabin, one in the chief's cabin. This left fourteen women to go down into the Wardroom. One very old Arab came on board with a shawl over her head so she was sent down to the Wardroom. But 'she' did not last long there as the other women immediately knew 'she' was a man and he got shot out on his ear.[4]

The *Imogen* had no doctor and the Coxswain had to deal with the injured and dress their wounds. It took him, assisted by other crew members, four hours to deal with all their injuries.

Clothing, food, etc was given out as far as possible. Tea and cocoa was made in the ship's galley and I arranged for bully beef and biscuits to be made available for those who wanted them. Apart from a small amount of bread in the wardroom we had none as owing to yesterday's activities the cook had not had time to bake as he normally does at sea.[4]

The two destroyers then switched roles and *Ilex* recovered the survivors from the other four lifeboats. *Ilex* also picked up sixty-eight survivors from the *Lochavon*. At the end of the exercise, a roll call revealed how laden with human cargo the *Ilex* and *Imogen* had become:

	Imogen	*Ilex*
Bretagne	220	94
Louisiane	19	18
Lochavon	nil	68
Prisoners of War	19	2
Total	254	182

It later emerged that four ships, *Bretagne*, *Lochavon*, *L'Oregon* and *Karamea*, homeward bound from the West Indies, had formed together as an unescorted group when they were attacked by U-boats. The two heavily laden destroyers now set course for home: apart from being low in fuel, they were almost immobilised as fighting units by their shipwrecked passengers filling every possible free space, so that movement about the ships was severely curtailed. The journey home was uneventful, but there was a problem when *Imogen* berthed at Plymouth on Sunday 15 October:

Ilex sent over her two prisoners so we have them all now. The Captain landed at once with the U-boat Captain to see the C-in-C, but before he did we had an awful scramble to get him fixed up in uniform. When the Germans were picked up all their clothing was put down in the boiler room to dry and it never entered my head, though I suppose it should have, that this was asking for trouble. Anyway we got it, as when we went to get it back, dry, every badge and nearly every button had been removed as mementoes. Worse still someone had cut off the sleeves of the Captain's coat at the elbow to get the stripes.

It was impossible to give him his coat back in that state so the Captain had to sacrifice one of his monkey jackets and by taking off the top stripe with the curve and sewing on what buttons remained he was more or less alright. What the Prisoner-of-War camp people will say when they see his jacket was made at Gieves for Commander E.B.K. Stevens we do not know or care. The U-boat Captain was not best pleased about all this and said that he was going to complain to the C-in-C, which he no doubt did. But the Captain said that he was going to say that with all those Frenchmen on board he was lucky that nothing worse happened to him.[4]

The battle with the U-boats was by no means confined to losses of merchant ships. Losses of U-boats were also high. One such U-boat sinking was that of *U-35* by the destroyers *Kashmir* and *Kingston* of the 5th Flotilla on 28 November 1939. A German view of this sinking and the treatment of the shipwrecked crew was described in the reminiscences of Engineer Lieutenant Commander Gerhard Stamer, the Chief Engineer of *U-35*:

During the attempt to attack the Home Fleet, should it leave harbour to intervene in the return home of our battleships [sic] *Scharnhorst* and *Gneisenau*, we were picked up by the sonar sets of three British destroyers, *Kingston, Kashmir* and *Nautilus* approximately 60°N, 2°E. Depth charge attacks lasted until noon. There were no direct hits but leaks developed which made it increasingly difficult to hold the boat down and when the last salvo jammed the hydroplanes in the 'hard-up' position the boat could no longer be held and the attempt to force the boat back below the surface through quick flooding of the ballast tanks failed as the main vent jammed.

'All hands abandon ship'. Later, as the last person below deck, I succeeded in clearing the jam and as I reached the bridge the boat sank beneath the Captain's feet and mine. We drifted for some hours in our lifejackets until the British destroyers turned towards us again and threw ropes to us with which we were landed on board. Our treatment was excellent, just like shipwrecked people. It was the destroyer *HMS Kashmir* who took most of the crew, with me as Senior Officer. The rest, with our Captain, were picked up by HMS *Kingston*. All were saved including our two non-swimmers. On board we learned that the Chief of their destroyer flotilla was Lord Louis Mountbatten, cousin of the King. At my request we were allowed to speak with our men. Lieutenant-Commander Scatchard gave up his cabin for me.

Before we were turned over to the Army…he told me to sign the visitors book. To my reply 'There is a war on you know', he said 'That has nothing to do with it. The first name in the book is that of our Chief's cousin, His Majesty the King. You are the second.' I could never get over this.

The difference between our treatment on board and on land we found very great, we were transferred to London and put up at the Tower. We were not very happy with our treatment. That became sensationally better after a visit announced to us by the sergeant: 'The cousin of the King comes'.[7]

The circumstances and consequences of this unconfirmed visit to the Tower of London in early December 1939 by Lord Louis Mountbatten, Captain (D) of the 5th Destroyer Flotilla, are set out in the translation of a letter written by Lieutenant- Commander Stamer to Lord Mountbatten in July 1974:

It so happened that I was escorted into the Tower of London on my 32nd birthday, 3 December 1939. Heavily guarded by the Scots Guards I was put in a prison cell down in the basement with a rusty bedstead as its only furniture. It was a cold winter and there was a fireplace but there was no fire in it...I asked to see an officer with the only result that a sergeant would appear with the monotonous answer 'I'll see what I can do for you'. Thereupon I decided to go on hunger strike until I came to see an officer – with very little effect, I must say. But I was lucky. As I was slowly beginning to doubt the wisdom of my decision, there was suddenly a commotion in front of my cell and when the door opened no lesser a person appeared than Lord Louis Mountbatten, Flotilla Chief of the destroyers which sank our submarine. I shall never forget the expression on your face and the four words to the sergeant 'Where is the commandant?' It did not take long until a red-faced major from the Scots Guards appeared and explained that it was all a horrible misunderstanding and that I should soon be moved into more comfortable quarters. This really happened and I was most grateful for the turn events had taken.[7]

Destroyer losses were high in the first winter of the war. There were two such losses, close together, at the beginning of 1940. The First Lord of the Admiralty, Winston Churchill, reported to the War Cabinet on 20 January 1940[6] that *Granville*, a flotilla leader returning from a 'seek and search' operation against neutral and enemy shipping, had been sunk. Three officers and seventy-six ratings were casualties or were missing.

Then two days later he had to report the loss of another flotilla leader. *Exmouth* had been torpedoed and from the evidence available it was thought that she had sunk with all hands. He explained that on the previous day the Danish vessel *Tekla*, 1,469 tons, bound from the Firth of Forth for Horsens with a cargo of coal, had been torpedoed fifty miles north-east of the Moray Firth in close proximity to MV *Cyprian Prince* which, carrying valuable stores for the defence of Scapa, was being escorted from Aberdeen to Kirkwall by *Exmouth*. At 1239 *Exmouth* was ordered by the Commander-in-Chief, Rosyth, to hunt the submarine. At 1546 and at 1723 *Exmouth* was told to report her position, but no reply was received. At 1752 *Cyprian Prince* arrived at Kirkwall alone and reported that at 1644, when following *Exmouth*, an explosion had been heard which the Chief Officer had thought to be depth charges dropped by *Exmouth*. Four minutes later a second explosion had occurred. The master had altered course and had then passed through some light wreckage. He had heard voices in the water and had seen flashes, possibly from torches. When clear, he had stopped his engines but, in view of the importance of his cargo, had subsequently decided to go on to Kirkwall. It was a dark night with no moon and faint visibility. An anti-submarine striking force, aircraft, minesweepers, two lifeboats and subsequently a destroyer, had been sent to search the vicinity. One lifebuoy from *Exmouth* had been picked up and floating debris had been sighted but no survivors found."[6]

The pendulum of the battle between the allied destroyers and the German

U-boats swung the other way in the next month, February 1940, when five U-boats were destroyed: *U-41* by *Antelope* on 5th February; *U-33* by *Gleaner* on 12th February; *U-53* by *Gurkha* on 14th February, with *U-54* mined in the North Sea on the same day and *U-63* sunk by the combined efforts of the destroyers *Escort, Narwhal, Inglefield* and *Imogen* on 25th February. It was a battle that would swing to and fro for the rest of the war.

Besides the torpedo danger from beneath the sea, naval and merchant ships operating in convoy within range of German bomber bases were also subject to bombing from the air. This was a threat which they were ill-equipped to deal with. On Saturday 25 November it had been the turn of the convoy escorts *Imogen, Inglefield* and *Imperial*:

Our turn came just before 12.30p.m. when we sighted three bombers on our port quarter flying NW. We sounded the alarm and closed up at 'Repel Aircraft' stations. They crossed our stern and we thought that maybe they had not seen us or were after bigger and better game which we knew they could find. But they altered course and flew up from right astern. They seemed to be going very slowly, taking plenty of time to get a good aim, we thought. Each machine took one ship, and it was quite exciting watching for the release of the bombs which one could plainly see all the way down. They must have been at about 4,000 feet. One wondered not so much as to whether they were going to hit, but whether somehow the Captain had altered course in the right way and in time. Two aircraft dropped four bombs in their first attack; one air-craft then went off for good; the second one did another attack and the third, a persistent bastard, did a fourth run. No hits, although several dropped close to Imperial and none were more than 150 yards away. In the first attack, as some of the bombs exploded, we took a green sea over the forecastle and seeing a man go over the side and hearing the explosion I thought that we had been hit and so dashed forward, rather gallantly I thought seeing that all the danger was over, to see what had happened. The rating, Able Seaman Tadgell, was floating well up in the water with an air life-belt on, which was inflated and [with] another cork jacket which had been thrown to him as he swept aft. We had therefore every hope that when we could return we should be able to pick him up as there was no sea and only a low swell.

But after the attacks were over we searched for an hour, finding the life buoy which had been thrown overboard to him but there was no sign of the man himself. So we reluctantly had to abandon the search. On looking back on the matter I remember he was right in the grain [sic] of Imperial who was following astern and almost as he reached the bow, a stick of bombs went off nearby so one must assume that he was either hit by the ship or by the explosion of the bombs.

In all we fired 28 rounds of 4.7-inch and a thousand rounds of 0.5-

inch. The 4.7- inch were set to short range barrage, which is the only thing catered for in the regulations, and it is infuriating to know that we had little or no chance of retaliating as the planes were so high that when in range they were at too big an angle of sight for our guns. The 0.5-inch were quite useless, but it is very hard to expect sailors to just sit and wait for it. In fact one may say that we fired our guns for the sole purpose of keeping our courage up. The close range barrage does, if nothing else, keep the aircraft up and acts as a deterrent to dive bombing and machine gunning, which latter none of us relish the thought of very much.[4]

The destroyers' battle to protect the convoys was one that was to continue, with fluctuating fortunes to both sides, for the remainder of the war.

NOTES TO SOURCES

1. Vian, Admiral of the Fleet, Sir Peter. *Action this Day* (Frederick Muller: London, 1960).
2. Knight, J. 'Memories of a Miscreant'. Papers 87/15/1. Imperial War Museum, London.
3. Ziegler, P. *Mountbatten: The Official Biography* (William Collins: London, 1985).
4. Ewing, Vice Admiral, Sir Alistair. Papers 65/19/1-3. Imperial War Museum, London.
5. Connell, G.G. *Jack's War* (William Kimber: London, 1985).
6. Gilbert, M. *The Churchill War Papers, Vol 1: At the Admiralty Sept. 1939– May 1940* (Heinemann: London, 1993).
7. King, Captain H.A. Papers 90/23/1. Imperial War Museum, London.
8. Kennedy, L. *On my Way to the Club* (Collins: London, 1989).
9. Whinney, Captain, R. *The U-Boat Peril* (Blandford Press: London, 1986).
10. Churchill, W.S. *The Second World War, Vol 1: The Gathering Storm* (Cassell: London, 1948).
11. Hill, R. *Destroyer Captain: Memoirs of the War 1942–1945* (William Kimber: London, 1975).

IV

The Menace of the Magnetic Mine

The German Navy did not rely entirely upon U-boats with their torpe-does and gunfire or the Luftwaffe on its bombs in their attempt to cut off Britain's vital sea-borne supplies in the first year of war. Another deadly weapon introduced in the Autumn of 1939, which for some worrying months threatened to paralyse Allied shipping movements around the British Isles, was the magnetic mine. In October and November 1939 a number of merchant and naval ships were sunk in what were thought to be swept channels, or close to the entrance of harbours.

The first naval casualty from this new weapon was the destroyer *Blanche*, sunk in the Thames estuary near to the Tongue lightship on 13 November, although the V and W class destroyer *Vega* had been damaged by a mine off Harwich on 7 November. Then, on 21 November, the destroyer *Gipsy* was mined, also off Harwich.

Jerzy Tumaniszwili, then a young Sub-Lieutenant on the *Burza*, some two hundred yards astern of the *Gipsy*, recalls:

> The time was a few minutes to midnight. Suddenly the sky flared up and an ear-splitting roar shook all around. It became as bright as in the daytime. The whole horizon was glowing in flames. HMS *Gipsy* had struck a mine which exploded underneath with devastating force. It looked to me as if the whole ship was blown into the sky. The exploding ammunition and other explosives stored on board created most colourful fireworks far outdoing anything I ever saw on the 4th of July. The ship was ablaze with fire and smoking and sink-ing fast. The men were jumping overboard trying to save their lives. Commander Nahorski turned *Burza* towards the sinking *Gipsy* with the searchlights illuminating the swift running current and bobbing heads of survivors...[1]

The naval diary of Robert Franks, then First Lieutenant of *Gipsy*, recalls events on board that fateful day:

On November 21st, in better weather, we were sent over to the German side of the North Sea. On the way we picked up three German airmen in a rubber dinghy; they had been downed by someone else. On our way back we engaged our first German aircraft with marked lack of success. The skipper wouldn't turn to allow the director to bear and X and Y guns in local control were very poor. I was particularly incensed with Petty Officer Shackell at X gun who fired impact fused shell instead of time fused. Poor chap was killed a few hours later and my anger has always been on my conscience.

We got back to Harwich about 5 o'clock and Chief took the German prisoners ashore. We hoped for a night in but unexpectedly, about 8 o'clock, we were told to proceed with the rest of our division "with all despatch". The skipper was having supper so I took the ship away from the buoy and followed *Griffin* out. Nigel Crossley [Captain of HMS *Gipsy* was a good decentraliser and I was used to this. Soon he came up and stood the other side of the binnacle leaving me to conn the ship out. It was pretty dark but we could see *Griffin's* wake and followed down the channel. The strong ebb tide was probably pushing us down tide of her track. We were just discussing the new mine laying and the skipper was saying we seemed pretty lucky when there was a roar and there was a gigantic mine explosion amidships. All of us on the bridge were shot into the air; I could vaguely remember sailing through the air but not landing. This I did on "B" gun deck in company with the heavy wooden binnacle which I had my hand on. I must have been stunned a while but soon came round and started to crawl about as my back felt broken, having landed on my tail. I also had a cut over my right eye which was therefore covered in blood and I thought I has lost my eye, à la Nelson. I was just thinking vaguely that I ought to do something when a sailor asked me whether he should jump over the side. The sense of responsibility came through my scattered wits.

Many of the sailors had already gone but I soon realised that, although we were blown in half, the bow part wasn't sinking and was probably on the bottom. I stopped any more jumping and looked around for the captain. I found him down on the deck lying awash, with the deck at a steep angle and slippery with escaping oil fuel. With great difficulty and the help of A.B.s Fry and Stevens we carried him further up the deck. Boats now began arriving and the whole scene was lit up by our coast defence searchlights. We got the skipper down to the first boat, a little civilian motor boat, and sent him straight off as he had obviously landed on his head instead of his bottom like me.

The other occupants of the bridge had all been more or less damaged. Rigg, our RNVR Lieutenant… had a twisted arm and broken fingers but did great rescue work. The Captain's cabin hand, A.B. Everatt, was badly wounded and died later. The main casualties were from amidships, the engine and boiler room crews and also our seaboat's crew who were standing by at the time. Many boats soon arrived and we loaded the injured in first and then the remainder which didn't seem many. In fact I found afterwards that the majority had jumped over the side and swam to boats or a nearby ship at anchor. I had a last look round, climbing with difficulty back to the bridge, and then went off in *Brazen*'s boat. We were transferred to a Ganges steamboat and taken to their sick quarters. By the time I got there I was very shaken, cold, wet and dirty and morale had slumped. However after cleaning up and a night's sleep I woke more or less O.K.

I stayed on at Shotley for some days, clearing up things and trying to regain the use of my stern. The captain seemed to be getting better though he was terribly damaged; they tried an operation but he died. He had a big funeral at Shotley in the wind and the rain and we all felt terrible.

We found that most of the superstructure of the ship was above water at low tide and some of it at high tide. All the boats and carley floats had been destroyed in the explosion and our experiences led to many new safety measures and the wearing of life belts all the time. We also tried to instil the principle of sticking to the ship to the last moment. I think some of our chaps were unnecessarily drowned. Altogether we lost about 30 chaps. [2]

That same day, in the Firth of Forth, the brand new cruiser *Belfast* had her keel almost ripped away by a magnetic mine laid by *U-21*, commanded by Lieutenant Fritz Frauenheim. [3] She was under repair and out of action for many months. Equally damaging was the explosion of another magnetic mine which holed the battleship *Nelson* as she entered Loch Ewe on 4 December. That mine, one of eighteen strung across the entrance to the loch, had also been laid by a submarine, *U-31*, commanded by Lieutenant Johannes Habekost, during the night of 27 October. *Nelson* was out of action for seven months.

Although U-boats were involved in the laying of considerable numbers of mines,* the major magnetic mine threat and damage to Britain's merchant fleet in late 1939 and early 1940 came from those mines placed

---

* Up to 1 March 1940 the German U-boats carried out thirty four mine-laying operations around the coasts of Great Britain, using 250 ton Type II boats which, because of their small size, were ideal for this dangerous inshore work. The locations of this U-boat mine laying included: West Coast of Britain (Loch Ewe, Clyde, Liverpool, Swansea, Bristol Channel); Channel Coast (Falmouth, Portland, Weymouth, Portsmouth, Dover); East Coast (Cromarty, Invergordon, Dundee, Firth of Forth, Blyth, Newcastle, Hartlepool, Great Yarmouth, Flamborough). Two U-boats, *U-16* and *U-33*, were lost on these operations; *U-16* was lost while trying to pass through a British-laid minefield.

by German destroyers at the mouths of estuaries and entrances to harbours along the eastern seaboard of Britain. Between September 1939 and March 1940, 128 merchant ships, totalling 430,000 tons,[3] were sunk within sight of their own coast and the safety of harbour, with the bulk of these losses coming from the then seemingly undetectable magnetic mine.

Ironically, the British Admiralty knew the basic technology behind the new weapon, having developed an early prototype as long ago as 1918, but had no way of detecting their presence on the sea-bed. Normal practice with conventional percussion mines was to sow them at a depth of twelve to eighteen feet, anchored to the sea-bed, and floating freely under their own buoyancy. They were designed to explode when struck by the hull of a passing ship. With the magnetic mine entirely different sowing and detonation principles were involved. Here the magnetic mines were sown in a pattern on the sea bed at a depth of between sixty and ninety feet. They were thus designed, and ideally suited for use in, shallow waters, in the narrow sea passages between sandbanks and at the mouths of estuaries and harbours. The mines exploded when activated by the magnetic field of a ship passing over them.

To begin to detect them, British mine specialists needed to know the exact details of the magnetic sensing device which set off the mine when a ship passed over it. Only then could they think about counter measures to eliminate the threat. Meanwhile the mines sown by the German destroyers were creating havoc. To increase the hazard, the enemy also mixed the mine-laying, sowing pairs of tethered conventional percussion mines interspersed at intervals with sea-bed-sown magnetic mines. This complicated mine-clearing and increased the hidden danger.

The number of mines laid by the German destroyers along Britain's eastern seaboard ran into the hundreds. They were normally laid on moonless nights by small flotillas of destroyers, with the operations carried out over several weeks under the noses, and without the knowledge, of the British authorities. Grand Admiral Raeder, Commander-in-Chief of the German Navy until 1943, reported to Hitler on the mine-laying achievements of the German destroyer force on 22 November 1939: "During the last new-moon period it has laid 540 in the mouths of the Thames and the Humber."[4]

Raeder had sent his destroyers on mine-laying expeditions on no less than eleven occasions: four times into the Thames estuary, resulting in the sinking of forty one allied ships; three times off the coast of Cromer, resulting in the loss of eight allied ships; twice to the mouth of the Humber, resulting in fourteen sinkings; and twice to the mouth of the Tyne outside Newcastle, with the consequent sinking of thirteen ships.[3] In addition, many other ships were damaged. The total of these losses were sixty-seven merchant ships, totalling 252,237 tons, together with three British destroyers and six escort vessels.

Kelly was to fall foul of a mine sown at the mouth of the Tyne. She had been under repair at Hebburn following the wave damage received in November 1939 when she was ordered, together with *Mohawk*, to go to the assistance of two tankers reported to have been attacked and sinking off the mouth of the Tyne. Captain Mountbatten, ordered to proceed at full speed, rightly suspected that the two merchantmen might have been mined rather than torpedoed; and once on the scene approached the ships with some caution. His concern was justified: *Kelly* struck a tethered mine. The mine grated along *Kelly*'s bottom, progressively bumping heavily under the forebridge, engine-room and wardroom before exploding against the propellers, wrenching her stern badly out of line. Towed back, *Kelly* was again in dry-dock under repair for eleven weeks:

> We had a look at one [tanker] and then turned to inspect the other which was on fire a few miles away. When we were about half way the *Kelly* hit a mine which exploded by the stern and when she was back in dry-dock at Hebburn and measured she was found to be about a foot shorter than when she was built. The mine had squashed the stern up and there were two fairly big ripples in the side about ten feet and twenty feet from the stern.[5]

Carrying out these clandestine mine-laying operations put great physical and psychological strain upon the German destroyer crews. They were very risky ventures. There was the perennial problem of boiler tube failure, also the consequence of being found immobile at daybreak only a few miles off the English coast. In addition, the destroyers had to risk going aground from having to operate close inshore in shallow waters amid a maze of sandbanks at night and without lights, all the while avoiding lightships and patrols. There was also the ever-present danger, if found and engaged in gunfire by British warships, of a massive on-board explosion from a deck full of highly sensitive mines.

Of the twenty two destroyers available to the German Navy at that time, seventeen participated in at least one mine-laying operation. The *Friedrich Eckoldt* took part on five occasions and the *Hermann Kunne* and *Wilhelm Heidkamp* on four. Lieutenant-Commander Friedrich Kothe, Captain of the *Hermann Kunne*, who carried out three of her four mining operations between 12 and 19 November 1939, commented: "It was enough to give one a nervous breakdown."[4] Up to that time, it would appear that the British authorities had no idea that these clandestine mine-laying operations were going on:

> The British Navy clearly had no idea of the real origin of this mine-laying, for on every single mine-laying operation the German destroyers returned home without loss or damage from enemy action. [4]

For its part the British Navy had been equally busy with mine-laying operations, both offensive and defensive, during the early months of the war. As early as the night of 9–10 September 1939, with the war barely a week old, the British destroyers *Esk* and *Express* had laid an offensive mine barrage in what was suspected to be the exit channels of cleared passages through German defensive minefields laid off their own coasts. Then, between 25 September and 23 October, 3,636 mines were laid by British ships in a deep defensive anti U-boat barrage in the Straits of Dover between Folkestone and Cap Griz Nez. The mine-laying operation proved to be an effective deterrent in preventing the passage of U-boats through the Channel and out into the North Atlantic. On 8 October *U-12*, on 13 October *U-40* and on 15 October *U-16* were all lost trying to make their way through the minefield.[6]

The destroyers *Esk* and *Express*, together with *Intrepid* and *Ivanhoe*, were again on mine-laying duty on the night of 17–18 December, laying 240 mines off the Ems estuary.

The German clandestine mine-laying operations, which had been going on for seven weeks, were very nearly detected on the night of 6–7 December 1939. Two German destroyers, the *Hans Lody* and the *Erich Giese* were laying mines off Cromer. There should have been three destroyers taking part: the *Erich Giese* and the *Bernd von Arnim* laying mines with the *Hans Lody* acting as escort. However, the *Bernd von Arnim* had suffered boiler tube troubles early in the evening of 6 December and had been forced to remain behind, leaving the *Erich Giese* to lay her seventy six mines with *Hans Lody* standing by on guard. The *Erich Giese* began sowing her mines at 0212 on 7 December, laying four miles off the Cromer lighthouse in the narrow shipping lane between sandbanks and the Norfolk coast. There was an early panic when one mine exploded prematurely on striking the bottom, but surprisingly the two ships were not detected or challenged. Instead the British, apparently suspecting an air raid, began probing the night sky with searchlights instead of directing them to the dark waters off the Norfolk coast.

Then at 0254 lookouts on the starboard side of *Erich Giese* reported two blackened ships at a distance of some five miles. The leading blacked out ship was showing a stern light. The two ships, which turned out to be the brand new British destroyers *Juno* and *Jersey*, were on patrol and travelling at high speed. Increasing speed to match that of the British ships, and turning onto a parallel course, the *Hans Lody* and *Erich Giese*, still undetected, prepared to launch a torpedo attack, each German destroyer targeting its oppositely-positioned British counterpart. Both pairs of ships were travelling in line on a course approximately 325 degrees, almost due north-west.

At 0315 the two German destroyers fired a combined spread of seven torpedoes at a range of 5,800 yards. After a torpedo running time of nearly four minutes, a huge sheet of flame some 500 feet high erupted from the second-in-line British destroyer, which had been struck in the fuel bunkers on the port side by a torpedo from *Erich Giese*.[6] The torpedoed ship was *Jersey* – only commissioned eight months earlier in April 1939. Her colleague *Juno* turned and, laying a smokescreen, went to her aid. With dawn approaching, the two German destroyers, close to the English coast and fearing retaliatory air attacks, made off to the east and home. *Jersey*, badly damaged, was towed back to port for repairs. She remained under repair until late September 1940, while the Germans' clandestine mine-laying continued undetected.

> The British Admiralty, either out of ignorance or embarrassment that the public should know that German destroyers were operating so close to the East coast of Britain, announced that the *Jersey* had been torpedoed by a German U-boat. [4]

Although the mine-laying German destroyers might have escaped detection and damage from British destroyers on this occasion, a fortnight later their light cruisers consorts, sent out to escort returning destroyers home from their mine-laying operations, were not so fortunate. Contrary to conventional naval practice where destroyers were expected to escort larger and more valuable warships, the German naval authorities had been sending a force of light cruisers to escort mine-laying destroyers home from their night time operations off the coast of Britain. The apparent reason for this tactic was to give additional protection to the destroyers and a greater sense of security to their crews, tired after a night of nervous stress and physical labour. The destroyers and their crews were considered invaluable for their mine-laying role, and were carrying the fight against Britain and her allies with some considerable success.

Thus, on the night of 12–13 December, the German destroyers *Hermann Kunne, Friedrich Ihn, Erich Steinbrinck, Richard Beitzen* and *Bruno Heinemann*, had been laying mines off the mouth of the Tyne under the command of the Officer Commanding Destroyers, Commodore Bonte. After carrying out the operation, the returning destroyers were to rendezvous with the light cruisers *Nurnberg, Leipzig* and *Köln* (under the command of Rear Admiral Gunther Lutjens, Commander Scout Forces) coming out to meet them.

At 1124, only a few minutes after the cruisers had met up with their own escort of two Heinkel 115 planes, the *Leipzig* was hit amidships by a torpedo fired by the British submarine *Salmon* (Lieutenant-Commander E. O. Bickford). The *Nurnberg* and *Köln*, taking evasive action, turned to be bow-on to the direction from which the torpedo had come. In mid-turn the *Nurnberg* was hit on the starboard beam by another torpedo. Two hours later the five destroyers, which the cruisers had been sent to escort, arrived on the scene and, forming a screen around the two damaged cruisers, escorted them home. The damage received by the *Leipzig* was so bad that she could only be used thereafter as a training ship. Two months later, Grand Admiral Raeder wrote: "The use of cruisers as an escort for destroyers or other light forces in the form provided for on 13 December has proved inexpedient and wrong."[4] The unorthodox practice was stopped.

By the end of 1939 it had become of paramount importance for the German Navy to maximise the threat of their magnetic mine, so as to cut off Britain's sea-borne supplies before the British could find an effective counter-measure. The technical secrets of the mine could not be concealed forever; it had become a race against time for both navies. Seeking to maximise the mine's impact, Grand Admiral Raeder sought Luftwaffe assistance to lay the German Navy's small quantity of some 120 air-borne type magnetic mines. The Luftwaffe high command, whose relations with their naval counterparts were not especially close, thought it not worth their time and effort to divert resources for such a small quantity of mines. Instead they proposed a policy of waiting until some 5,000 air-borne type mines were available and then saturating, over a very short period of time, all the mouths of the estuaries and the entrances to British ports.

In the meantime Raeder, fearing discovery of the mine's secrets and impatient to maximise its already considerable impact upon British shipping movements, decided to lay his supply of 120 mines using planes under the control of the German Navy. Thus, on the evening of 20 November 1939, nine Heinkel 59 float planes took off on a mine-laying operation to the mouth of the Thames estuary, each plane carrying two mines. It was possibly a mine from this operation which destroyed HMS *Gipsy*. Because of navigational problems, only four of the obsolete planes found the target area, laying seven mines in total. Ten mines were laid on a second raid, and twenty-four on a third and final operation on 22 November. It was all something of a piecemeal operation which, from a German point of view, was to have disastrous consequences.

On the night of the final operation, shortly before 2200 hours, a Heinkel 59 was seen by men of the Observer Corps to drop two mines off Shoeburyness on the north bank of the Thames estuary. These mines fell, not into the intended shallow waters of the estuary, but on to tidal mudflats and were exposed to view at low tide. Royal Navy personnel from HMS *Vernon*, the shore-based naval establishment responsible for developing underwater weapons, were sent, at extreme personal risk, to examine the mines. Lieutenant-Commander J.G.D. Ouvry, assisted by Chief Petty Officer Baldwin, tackled the first mine. Lieutenant-Commander R. Lewis and Able Seaman Vearncombe were at a safe distance, observing and recording the progress and technical details of the dismantling, with information being passed to them by Lieutenant Commander Ouvry. This procedure was standard demolition practice. In case of premature explosion, the information gathered up to the point of explosion would have been used by Lewis and Vearncombe in tackling the second mine. However, all was well: the dismantling of the mine was safely completed and the Germans' secret weapon was no longer secret.* Counter-measures were developed, and British and Allied ships were soon effectively demagnetised or 'degaussed' by means of a current-carrying cable around the hull of the ship. Later minesweeping procedures, which detonated mines lying on the sea-bed at a safe distance from the ship, came into use, and the menace of the magnetic mine from the Allied point of view was effectively over and under control.

Grand Admiral Raeder, having tried to lay his magnetic mines by air, and in doing so having given away the mine's secrets, resumed night-time mine-laying with destroyers into the early weeks of 1940. On the night of 6–7 January the destroyers *Friedrich Eckoldt*, *Erich Steinbrinck* and *Friedrich Ihn* laid mines off the Thames estuary. It was mines from this operation which resulted in the loss of the destroyer *Granville* on 19 January 1940 and the sinking of a further six merchant ships totalling 21,617 tons.[6]

The continuation of night-time magnetic mine-laying operations with destroyers was hampered by worsening weather conditions in late January and early February 1940, with many of Germany's surface vessels icebound and inactive in the Baltic.

As a consequence, little offensive activity took place across the North Sea, although on the night of 9–10 February the *Friedrich Eckholdt*, *Richard Beitzen* and *Maas Schultz* laid 110 magnetic mines off the Shipwash, and the *Bruno Heinemann*, *Wolfgang Zenker* and *Erich Koeller* laid 157 contact mines off Cromer. Both operations were screened by the destroyers *Wilhelm Heidkamp*, *Theodor Reidel* and *Hermann Schoemann*. It is an indication of the importance and urgency being placed upon maximising the impact of the magnetic mine's secrets that nearly half of the entire German destroyer fleet was committed to this one night's operation.

When conditions improved and more intensive German destroyer operations were again possible, any intended resumption of night-time mine-laying operations received a serious setback in late February. It was a self-inflicted setback that would further reduce the already relatively small number of available German destroyers, shake morale, and further inflame the mistrust and antagonism between the German Navy and the Luftwaffe.

Cajus Bekker[4] recounts how, on the evening of 22 February 1940, six German destroyers were passing through the six-mile-wide cleared channel in their own defensive minefield in the Heliogoland Bight. In line ahead, they were heading north-west on a course of 300 degrees. Their task on this operation was not mine-laying but to intercept and harass boats fishing in the Dogger Bank. Any British boats found in this disputed

---

* Lieutenant-Commanders Ouvry and Lewis were each awarded the DSO and CPO Baldwin and Able Seaman Vearncombe the DSM for their bravery.

mid North Sea area would be sunk or captured and taken as prize vessels; any neutral boats searched for contraband and allowed to continue if free of any contraband contravention. It was all part of the ongoing tussle for control of the North Sea, and the German pursuit of economic warfare for the curtailment of British food supplies by deterring British trawlers from fishing too far from their coastline. There was also a concern that British naval intelligence was gaining vital information on German shipping movements from their fishing fleet operating in the disputed area.

The six destroyers were led by the *Friedrich Eckholdt*, followed at 200-metre intervals by the *Richard Beitzen, Erich Koeller, Theodor Reidel, Max Schultz* and *Leberecht Maas*. In command, on the *Friedrich Eckholdt*, was Commander Fritz Berger. There was a low mist beneath a clear sky and a full moon. Then at 1913 lookouts on the bridge of the lead ship heard the sound of an aircraft which suddenly appeared some 2,000 feet above the ships. They had obviously been seen: the unidentified aircraft flew alongside the line of ships on a reciprocal course before turning in towards them.

Unclear as to the identity or intentions of the aircraft, the destroyers reduced speed to seventeen knots in order to reduce the glistening of their wakes in the bright moonlight, and their crews prepared for anti-aircraft action. At 1921 the twin-engined plane re-appeared swooping low over the flotilla, and the *Richard Beitzen* and *Erich Koeller*, second and third in the line of ships, opened fire with their light anti-aircraft weapons. The plane replied with machine gun fire. What followed in the confusion and fog of war was a catalogue of misunderstandings, mistakes and, in the end, utter disaster for the German destroyers and their crews. By the exchange of gunfire the crews of both ships and aircraft had it wrongly confirmed in their minds that the other was an enemy, although some observers on the ships later claimed to have seen at this point identification crosses on the wings of the aircraft in the flashes of gunfire. The aircraft moved away only to reappear some twenty minutes later, assuming it to be the same aircraft, astern and on a bombing run.

At 1944 two bombs fell astern of the last ship in the line: the *Leberecht Maas*. The destroyer replied with anti-aircraft fire, only seconds before a huge explosion occurred amidships from a bomb which had struck between the bridge and the forward funnel, followed by a pall of black smoke. The stricken ship signalled: "Am hit. Require assistance."[4] Ordering the other destroyers to stay clear, the flotilla leader, the *Friedrich Eckoldt*, cautiously closed on the smoking ship. As it did so the *Leberecht Maas*'s anti-aircraft guns again commenced firing and a further two bombs were thought to have fallen on the stricken ship – one astern and the other apparently striking near the after funnel – causing an explosion which engulfed the destroyer in flames and smoke. When this cleared the *Maas* was seen to be broken into two sinking halves. Rescue boats were sent from the *Erich Koeller* and *Richard Beitzen* to assist those of the *Eckholdt* in attempting the rescue of any survivors, while the *Theodor Riedel* and *Max Schultz* circled the scene as an anti-submarine/anti-aircraft screen. In all the confusion there was great uncertainty as to the source of the attacks. Suddenly at 2004 an explosion, followed by a fireball similar to the one that had signalled the end of the *Maas*, was seen some 1,000 yards from the *Reidel*. As the *Reidel* turned towards the explosion to investigate, submarine soundings were reported to starboard and the crew of No. 1 gun reported seeing torpedo tracks. Lieutenant-Commander Gerhard Bohmig on the *Reidel* ordered a depth charge attack on the suspected submarine. Four depth charges were dropped, one of which did not explode. However, the other three did, and in doing so did considerable damage to the slowly moving *Reidel*: her gyrocompass, rudder motor and all command controls were temporarily put out of action by the explosions. The captain ordered all hands to put on life-jackets because of the suspected presence of a submarine and the temporary lack of control and manoeuvrability of the *Reidel* until repairs could be effected.[7]

There was by now considerable confusion as to what exactly was happening and who were the attackers: planes, submarines or both. Reports were still coming in of submarine soundings, and the *Koeller* prepared to ram what turned out to be the still-afloat bows of the *Maas*. By now it had been established that the explosion and second fireball had come from the *Max Schultz*, with whom all contact had been lost. Amid all the confusion Commander Berger, the Flotilla Leader on the *Friedrich Eckoldt*, was in a considerable quandary. He had lost two destroyers in mysterious circumstances; an unknown number of survivors from these two ships were in the water and needed to be rescued; submarine contacts had been claimed and torpedo tracks reported; and they had been attacked by aircraft. He did not know if the original aircraft attack would be continued, or if it had been replaced by attacks from submarines or other aircraft drawn to the area. Commander Berger's first responsibility was the safety of the remaining destroyers in his depleted force. He therefore had little option but to withdraw from the immediate danger area in the confines of the swept minefield channel: "I could no longer hazard my ships in rendering further assistance to the men from the Maas and Schultz. I was obliged to beat a retreat."[4] Accordingly, at 2036 he gave the order: "All ships to proceed on a course 120 degrees, speed seventeen knots."[4] The four destroyers withdrew, leaving behind them 578 of their comrades. There were only sixty survivors from the combined crews of the *Maas* and *Schultz* totalling 638 men. All sixty came from the *Leberecht Maas*. There were no survivors from the 308 men and crew of the *Max Schultz*.

There never were any British or Allied aircraft or submarines in the vicinity. A subsequent German Commission of Enquiry into the disaster concluded that both ships had been sunk in mistake by a German plane:

a Heinkel III of X Air Group sent to seek out and attack British shipping across the North Sea. The crew had mistaken their destroyers for British ships, which the aircraft crew assumed to be confirmed when they were fired on as they flew towards the ships. The Commission of Enquiry decided: "We are of the opinion that a salient cause of the disaster was the fact that the aircraft crew were not briefed about the possibility of encountering German warships."[4] The Luftwaffe had not been told beforehand that German ships would be operating that night across their own planned area of operations. Grand Admiral Raeder had to admit to Adolf Hitler, as Supreme Commander of the German Armed Forces: "The failure of Navy Group West to inform X Air Corps in good time concerning the proposed destroyer operation contributed to the unhappy outcome..."[4]

More detailed post-war analysis of the two sinkings concluded that while the *Maas* had undoubtedly been attacked by the *Heinkel* and badly damaged, its subsequent sinking (and that of the *Schultz*) had probably been caused when the two ships ran into a mine barrage newly laid by two British destroyers on the night of 9–10 February in the narrow mine-free path in the Germans' own minefield.

There was one further incident on that unhappy night to cause yet more acrimony between the German Navy and the Luftwaffe. Just four hours after the sinking of the two destroyers, another Heinkel III of X Air Corps, returning from its North Sea mission, flew over the island of Borkum at a height of 800 feet. The naval anti-aircraft guns on the island opened fire and at 0033 hours the Heinkel, with its three-man crew, crashed in flames.

Following the loss of the two destroyers, the coming of Spring reducing the hours of darkness that had helped conceal the destroyers' mining operations, coupled with preparations for their destroyers involvement in Germany's planned April campaign in Norway, the mine-laying operations of the German destroyers off Britain's East coast came to an end. German mine-laying using new models of mine laid by U-boats continued however, and despite the Royal Navy's counter measures against the magnetic and other types of mine, allied ships losses from mines continued until the end of the war. Thus the British battleship *Warspite*, veteran of Jutland in the First World War and of numerous scrapes in the Second, was badly damaged by a mine, thought to be acoustic- or pressure-activated, some 30 miles off Harwich on 13 June 1944.[8]

NOTES TO SOURCES

1. Tumaniszwili, J.P. Correspondence with author. 5 June 2001.
2. Franks, Captain R.D. Naval diaries, correspondence with author. October 2002.
3. Doenitz, Grand Admiral J. *Memoirs: Ten Years and Twenty Days* Lionel 4. Leventhal Ltd., London, 1990.
4. Bekker, C. *Hitler's Naval War* Trans. Ziegler, F. Macdonald, London, 1974.
5. Knight. J. 'Memories of a Miscreant' Papers 87/15/1. Imperial War Museum, London.
6. Rohwer, J. and Hummelchen, G. *Chronology of the War at Sea: 1939–1945: The Naval History of World War Two* (Greenhill Books: London, 1992).
7. Whitley, M.J. *German Destroyers of World War Two* (Arms & Armour Press: London, 1991).
8. Plevy, T.A.H. *Battleship Sailors: The fighting career of HMS Warspite recalled by her men* (Chatham Publishing: London, 2001).

V

Collisions and Other Catastrophes

With the war barely a week old Winston Churchill had had to report to the War Cabinet on collisions involving, and badly damaging, three of the country's precious stock of destroyers.[1] The *Vanquisher* and *Walker* had been in collision while escorting an outward bound convoy. *Vanquisher* was reported to be in a sinking condition and *Walker* had been badly damaged. The destroyer *Wrestler* had also been in collision with a merchant ship.

Fortunately the damage sustained by the ships was not as bad as was first feared. The next day the First Lord was able to report that both *Vanquisher* and *Walker* were now proceeding to Plymouth, *Vanquisher* under tow and *Walker* under her own steam. They joined the growing numbers of destroyers in the repair yards.

Admiral Sir William James, Commander-in-Chief, Portsmouth, took a tolerant view of the early destroyer mishaps. In a letter to a friend dated 19 September 1939 he wrote:

> ...our main job here has been organising and sailing the convoys to Cherbourg, Havre and Brest. All has gone well. One or two minor mishaps to destroyers, and I was asked if there were to be Boards of Enquiry in accordance with the Regulations. I had decided on my policy – no Boards of Enquiry unless the Captain (D) tells me that the fellow concerned is a slacker or of no use. These Boards, though not intended to be of a punitive nature, are invariably looked on as such by a young officer hauled before one, and are very apt to take the confidence out of him. I cannot have that here. They will be crossing in all weathers, in fog, and with no shore lights, and it will be a miracle if we do not have some 'incidents'.[2]

Winston Churchill was also inclined to take a benign view of these early collisions. He knew from his previous tenure as First Lord of the Admiralty twenty-five years before that it would take time for the destroyer captains to adapt to wartime operating conditions. He did not want them to be judged by peacetime standards. In a minute to the First Sea Lord and Board of Admiralty on 24 September 1939 he commented:

> A lot of our destroyers and small craft are bumping into one another under the present hard conditions of service. We must be very careful not to damp the ardour of officers in the flotillas by making heavy weather of these occasional accidents. They should be encouraged to use their ships with wartime freedom, and should feel they will not be considered guilty of unprofessional conduct if they have done their best and something or other happens. I am sure this is already the spirit and your view, but am anxious it should be further inculcated by the Admiralty. There should be no general rule obliging a court martial in every case of damage. The Board should use their power to dispense with this, so long as no negligence or crass stupidity is shown. Error towards the enemy – i.e. to fight – should be most leniently viewed, even if the circumstances are not pleasant.[3]

Later the number of collisions involving destroyers was to become a greater concern, and the need to conserve the overworked stock of them was recognised as being crucial to Britain's continuing survival in the autumn of that first year of the war. A stock-take on 18 October 1939 showed that Britain had at its disposal a maximum of 187 destroyers including those of the Australian, Canadian and Polish Navies. Ninety-eight of these (approximately one half) were in home waters, of which twenty-four, (or one quarter) were unserviceable, refitting, damaged or otherwise out of commission. The country was becoming desperately short of these ships.

A large number of the available destroyers not in home waters were in the Mediterranean. Towards the end of 1939, with Italy still remaining neutral, and the German naval offensive with submarines and surface raiders inflicting increasing losses among Britain's merchant shipping, many units of the Mediterranean Fleet were recalled home. They were to be deployed on convoy escort duties or sent off to hunt for German commerce raiders, including the pocket battleship *Graf Spee*, operating in the Indian Ocean and the South Atlantic. Among those recalled was the First World War veteran battleship *Barham*, with her screening unit made up of units of the D class destroyer flotilla recalled earlier from the China Station. Up until that time, following its recall, the flotilla had been engaged on contraband patrol and escort duties in the Red Sea and the Mediterranean, with the flotilla split between Malta (*Diamond, Defender, Decoy* and *Dainty*) and Gibraltar (*Duncan*, the flotilla leader, *Diana, Daring* and *Delight*).

During the passage home the destroyers were deployed around *Barham* to act as an anti-submarine escort. They were in a fan-like shaped screen about a mile ahead of the battleship. The flotilla had not practised this formation, nor operation at night under wartime conditions with all the ships completely darkened and showing no lights. It was before the widespread availability of radar on ships, and there were considerable difficulties and dangers involved in keeping station and estimating distances between ships.

On 15 December, on a particularly dark night off the north-west coast of Ireland, the time came for *Barham* and her escorts to alter course towards their destination on the Clyde:

> The alteration was to be made by what was known as a Red Pennant Turn. In simple terms, it meant that when the battleship altered course the fan-shaped screen of destroyers would have to be ahead of her on her new course. What was in doubt, however, was when they should move. Should they move before the battleship altered course so as to be in position when she did alter – or should they wait until she altered and then move over? With this ambiguity, the destroyers usually started to move gradually in advance of the battleship's alteration course.[4]

It was a manoeuvre which was to bring tragedy:

> It happened that at the critical time on that night, I was on watch in the flotilla leader, HMS *Duncan*… At the vital time I went to the back of the bridge to watch the other ships of the screen through the binoculars, especially those ships on the outside of the turn. Suddenly in the middle of the manoeuvre, *Barham* switched on her navigation lights. Then she switched on a searchlight. In the searchlight's beam was, apparently, a submarine. The assumption was that the battleship had rammed a U-boat. At first no signal was made to say what had happened. The Captain was, of course, on the bridge by this time so I, as First Lieutenant, went down to lower a boat to pick up survivors from the U-boat – or so I thought. As the boat was being lowered there were several loud explosions. There must be a second U-boat which had fired torpedoes and hit *Barham*. As an immediate reaction, I thought we should release a life saving raft for the survivors for the time being, and seek and attack this supposed second U-boat.
>
> Back on the bridge however I saw through binoculars what seemed at first to be a fire on the rammed vessel. Then, with horror, I realised it was the red anti-fouling on the bottom of the destroyer and that the imagined conning tower was, in fact, the Asdic dome.* It became clear that what earlier were thought to be torpedoes from a second U-boat were the depth charges of the capsized destroyer which had

---

* The Asdic dome, containing the oscillator which emitted a sound wave when seeking a submarine, was housed inside the hull and could be raised when not in operation or lowered to protrude below the hull when searching for submarines.

been primed and had fallen out of their storage racks and reached the depth at which they were set to explode.

The unhappy ship was, we learned, *Duchess* (1,375 tons), the ship on the outside wing. She must have turned late, underestimating the distance, cut too fine across the bows of *Barham* (31,000 tons) been rammed and capsized...Casualties were very heavy. The Commanding Officer, Lieutenant Commander Robin White, an up-and-coming chap and one very well liked, was among those lost. He should have been on the bridge. As it was, the sliding door of his sea cabin, just below the bridge, jammed. He could not escape. A number of men in the water were killed by the ship's own depth charges, bringing to light another ambiguity in orders; whether depth charges should or should not be primed to fire before an attack on an enemy submarine commenced. One moral might be said to be that there was a painfully clear need for practice of such obvious manoeuvres by darkened ships, and this should have been realised in peace-time.[4]

The collision had occurred at 0427 hours. On the *Barham*, Seaman Frank Loy saw that *Duchess* was turned completely over and floated for a short time bottom up:

There were terrible scenes as *Barham* lost way and rescue attempts were made. Sea boats were turned inboard, hampering life saving operations. Men screamed as they drowned in the cold waters, choked by spreading oil fuel. In these early days of the war no escape ports were provided in ships' sides and the capsized for'ard half of the destroyer presented stark horror as men screamed through the small scuttles [portholes] as they passed astern to their deaths. *Barham* struck *Duchess* between the forward funnel and the galley flat. Depth charges, not set to "Safe" exploded in the after part of *Duchess* adding to the night's carnage. A young midshipman and Leading Seaman Charlie Bishop both dived into the icy cold water to rescue several men; they were the heroes of the night. Other *Duchess* men survived by walking down their ship's side and stepping onto the side of *Barham* by the 6-inch starboard battery. It took until we reached Greenock to clean off the oil from the survivors whom we had plied with hot drinks liberally laced with rum."[5]

Only one officer and twenty-two ratings survived the collision. Six officers and one hundred and twenty three ratings of the *Duchess* died.*

---

* The D class destroyers suffered grievously. Of the original nine ships in the flotilla, only HMS *Duncan*, the flotilla leader, and HMS *Decoy*, transferred to the Royal Canadian Navy in 1943 and renamed *Kootensay*, survived the war. Four were sunk by bombing, one by U-boat and two in collisions.[6]

Duncan, present at the demise of her sister ship *Duchess*, had her own near escape from disaster less than a month after that sinking. Early in January 1940, *Duncan* sailed from Methil on the Firth of Forth to Bergen in Norway as senior convoy escort. The weather was foul: very cold with a strong head wind, a rough sea and intermittent snow.

...the Ship's company was at cruising stations, with half the men closed up at the armament and the other half off watch. During the night, the sea and the head wind increased so much that the merchant ships, slow at the best of times, could make little headway. To prevent *Duncan* getting too far ahead of them, to lose ground so to speak, the Officer of the Watch decided with the Captain's permission, to turn one or more circles occasionally! In one of these circles the ship was caught in a heavy snow shower with visibility almost nil. Suddenly, up the voice-pipe from 'X' gun, the 4.7 inch gun at the after end of the ship, there came a report: 'Please, Sir, voice in the dark!'

The Officer of the Watch had no time to find out what this astonishing and apparently irresponsible report might mean. There came a heavy, shuddering thump amidships, violently shaking the whole ship. The engine room-boiler room bulkhead, a particularly vulnerable spot, had been hit. I was sleeping forward in the sick bay that night, and I dashed out in stockinged feet and fell straight on my backside on the snow-covered deck – never again to take off my boots when turning in at night at sea till the war ended! I tried to estimate the angle at which the torpedo might have been fired so that some other ship might get the U-boat. After a slight delay, the Captain made it clear that we had been rammed.

The voices in the dark had come from a Norwegian merchant ship which was out of position. I went to the engine room and the boiler room to make sure that there was no one trapped below and then reported this. The Captain then ordered the placing of the collision mat, a peacetime remedy designed to deal with all holes that might be caused when ships were hit by the enemy's shells or in minor collision. This mat was a rug-like object with lines attached to all four corners. The twenty foot hole in the ship's side was plainly far, far too big for the collision mat to be of the slightest use and some minutes were lost in persuading the Captain that this was so. It remained to make sure that all water-tight doors, hatches and outlets to the sea were quickly closed. An outlet drain normally above the water line, in the Ward Room, was found to be choked open with wet newspapers so that the whole compartment was progressively flooding.

Volunteers were needed to go down into the unlit compartment – all electric power was, of course, off. This was going to be a dangerous and difficult job and I was pleasantly surprised when two men – two of the ship's 'black sheep' volunteered. The morale of the ship was not after all so bad, I began to think. Leaving the scene to inspect other parts of the ship where water might be coming in, I took a torch and eventually went aft, below again, to look at the progress. There, in the dark were two men, both horizontal, rolling happily unconscious – very drunk on the flooded deck and surrounded by bottles. They had drunk the lot from the Wardroom cupboard – beer, whisky, port, sherry, brandy – all of it. Hoisted onto the upper deck, they recovered sufficiently to fight, until the Torpedo Coxswain, the senior rating on board a destroyer, rendered both harmless with a convenient wooden mallet and then had them lashed up in strait-jackets. He, above all others, was excellent throughout. He had a third case, a young rating who became uncontrollably hysterical, similarly treated.

The ship did not sink. She settled with six inches of freeboard on one side and eighteen inches on the other and, with the upper deck awash, was towed slowly by another destroyer to Invergordon. All the ship's store rooms were, of course, flooded or inaccessible during the long, cold tow and we existed on tea, ship's biscuits and, for lack of anything else available, cold tinned Irish stew. Even the seagulls tired of what we threw away.

When *Duncan* berthed on the wooden pier at Invergordon, there were a number of civilian fire engines awaiting us. With speed and efficiency, they had their pumps working and kept the ship afloat until a salvage firm had put a wooden patch, about twenty-five feet long, over the hole in the ship's side. In the meantime, the destroyer leader *Exmouth* came alongside to help remove the ammunition and thus lighten the ship. Next came a minesweeper to help carry on the good work. Both these ships then went to sea and were lost, *Exmouth* with all hands.[4]

Two months later there was to be another collision and one that was to cause some hilarity among other destroyer crews in the fleet. Given the flamboyance and attention-seeking nature of her Captain, and the accident-prone nature of his ship, it was perhaps inevitable the Captain Lord Louis Mountbatten's ship *Kelly* would be one of the ships involved and the butt of the amusement. By the beginning of March 1940 she had been repaired following her mining in the North Sea the previous December, and was back at sea. At dawn on 9 March 1940, in a raging snowstorm, *Kelly* collided with the Tribal class destroyer *Gurkha* which resulted in a thirty-foot gash to *Kelly*'s bow.

The resultant amusement in the fleet was generated by an order that Captain Mountbatten had given following the earlier mining of the *Kelly*. He had apparently given instructions to his radio operators that following a crash or explosion they were immediately, without further ado, to send out the signal: "Have been hit by mine or torpedo. Am uncertain which."[7] It was a commendable intention, to inform the Admiralty immediately of an incident, and eminently sensible following the loss of a number of ships, including the *Exmouth*, from unknown causes.* Unfortunately the signal did not envisage the possibility of a collision, and particularly a self-inflicted one. The collision was *Kelly's* fault and prompted the cheerful, and perhaps gleeful, response from the Captain of the Gurkha: "That was no mine but me."[7] The repairs to *Kelly* took another six weeks.

Mountbatten's glamour, good looks, wealth and above all Royal connections made him a controversial destroyer captain. He was a favourite below decks, particularly among his crew, but other aspects of his character made him less popular in other quarters of the Navy:

> The lower deck thought him wonderful. Among the officers…there were those of us who were in the war [with him] and knew that as a captain in command he was consistently unfortunate, with one glorious defeat after another. That he was courageous and dashing with very outstanding charm was beyond question; ambitious – yes, most certainly and with a powerful driving force; conceited – well, yes, no ducking it; scheming – yes and ruthless too, but then every senior officer must be within limits; successful showman – par excellence…[4]

Not all the collisions occurring in that first winter of the war resulted in the loss of a ship, lives, or serious damage. There were other minor scrapes resulting in amusement, at least for the officers and men of the ships not involved, to relieve the tedium of life in the destroyers. Lieutenant A. Ewing, serving on the destroyer *Imogen*, records in his diary entry of 18 November 1939 one collision story going the rounds at the time: "One of the Tribals going up a searched channel [cleared of mines] at night at 27 knots passed an armed trawler. She was only in sight from the trawler for 18 seconds and she took some paint off her…[8]"

As well as collisions, groundings were another fairly frequent cause of damage – usually minor – and of delay for the destroyers and other small ships working under wartime conditions. The same 18 November diary entry of Lieutenant Ewing records the amusing side of such a grounding:

---

* It was later established that HMS *Exmouth* had been sunk by a torpedo from *U-22* (Lieutenant Commander Jenisch).

...the sloop *Weston* had the misfortune to run aground on a shoal in the Firth of Forth. She was duly repaired but on the very first day of going to sea she ran aground on the same shoal. When called for his reasons the Captain merely replied 'see my letter No..., dated...', this being the report of his original grounding. I doubt if he is still in command.[8]

An infinitely more serious incident – perhaps the most serious grounding during the first year of the war – leading to the total loss of the Hawkins class cruiser *Effingham* and damage to the Tribal class destroyer *Matabele*, occurred during the Norwegian campaign in the spring of 1940.*

The immediate situation in Norway on 21 May 1940 was that *Effingham* was to be pressed into service as a makeshift troopship to transport several hundred British troops of the South Wales Borderers to new positions.

The *Effingham*, loaded with troops and their equipment, was to be escorted by the *Matabele* and the smaller destroyer *Echo*:

It seems probable that *Matabele's* Captain and Navigator would have visited *Effingham* the previous night to discuss the programme for the following day. *Echo*, unfortunately was absent and so was entirely unprepared for the unexpected manoeuvres that occurred.[9]

At 0600 *Effingham*, which had been the flagship of the Commander-in-Chief of the Campaign, Admiral of the Fleet The Earl of Cork and Orrery, signalled that the trio of ships was to proceed out of harbour independently and to form up outside, with the *Matabele* three cables (600 yards) ahead of *Effingham* and with *Echo* abreast of the *Matabele* and 2 cables (400 yards) to her starboard. Their speed was to be seventeen knots.

The account of Commander S.H.K. Spurgeon, captain of *Echo*, details the critical happenings of the ships' passage that day:

At about 2000, after we had entered a wide fjord, station keeping on *Matabele* became more critical, particularly when my navigator, Lieutenant Warrington-Strong (pilot) pointed out that two alternative openings lay some distance ahead either of which we might be called upon to take. I checked the very small-scale chart with him and commented on the lack of flexibility our position ahead of *Effingham* entailed.

About this time he pointed out a rock marked "Faksen" on the chart, somewhere well ahead, also a wide opening off to starboard

---

* See Chapter Ten

down which I felt surely we must turn. In anticipation we reduced speed to lose bearing on the two ships to port and started turning to starboard expecting *Effingham* to hoist a new course signal. Instead she hoisted *'Echo* take up your appointed station'. This immediately created a situation amounting to an order for the three ships in company to continue on what I considered, according to our chart, a very hazardous route, especially at high speed in the vicinity of one charted submerged rock marked "Faksen" and other visible outcrops dispersed over the area.

By this time *Echo* had dropped back to a position close on *Effingham's* beam so I ordered a high speed of 28 knots to catch up. I told our pilot "Take a fix", and by eye set *Echo* on a course that would, in due course regain station on *Matabele*. Meanwhile pilot had fixed our position on the chart – a very quick and difficult job in the circumstances and together we checked our present course for danger. We agreed that, with any luck, deep water should continue under *Echo* for several miles so long as we remained within about 50 to 100 yards of the rocks to starboard. We estimated that we would pass the "Faksen" about 3 to 400 yards to port. Both *Effingham* and *Matabele* should have seen *Echo's* high stern wave breaking dangerously over the adjacent rocks as we raced closely by. I could not understand their signal to us and the necessity to run so close to danger at high speed and presumed they must have had some very strong reason unbeknown to me.

I was watching *Matabele* as she was gradually coming on to correct bearing for reducing [our] speed to 17 knots. Suddenly her masts and yards commenced waving, indicating one or both propellers had touched. *Effingham* must also have seen this as she started to turn away. Almost immediately a great puff of smoke billowed from her funnels as she also hit the Falsen Rock on to which she had followed *Matabele*.

Matabele moved slowly away, obviously not under proper control and we never saw her subsequently.* *Echo*, now very much occupied, went alongside *Effingham's* starboard bow, got lines secured, and tried to take her in tow. She was already making water and a slight scend [sic] from the ocean started parting all wires. Neither was there any time to spare as we feared we were sitting targets. Fortunately she remained on an even keel but had settled in the water a few feet.[9]

The diary of the Rev'd Meredith Dewey, Chaplain on *Effingham* at that time, records the on-board impressions of the grounding:

---

* HMS *Matabele* was repaired and returned to service. She was torpedoed and sunk in the Barents Sea, 17 January 1942.

...Now drawing near to Bodo – our destination where a small section of Scots Guards are holding the road north against quantities of Huns. Entering the fjord at 6.00pm with Coventry ahead. and *Echo*, two destroyers, and *Cairo*, another A.A. ship astern...Just finished dinner at 7.50 when a colossal bump, ship heeled over to port 20 degrees. Rushed to close the scuttles near to me thinking at first a torpedo. Ship righted herself and by the time out of the Ward Room fairly easy to get up on deck. Apparently some little panic among the soldiers in the recreation space to get out, otherwise strangely orderly. Ship on quite even keel, black smoke and steam belching out of funnel and making gasping sounds as though in the effort to get off the rock on which we had charged at 20 knots [sic].

Did not know at the time extent of damage, heard afterwards 200 feet rent in bottom from forward magazine to after engine room. All the plates of the engine room heaved up and apparently ship broke her back. Pearce, a pleasantly broad Cornish man, engineer sub lt., turned off the valves just in time to prevent blowing up. The lower decks soon flooded.

Destroyer *Echo* came along starboard side and removed 1200 troops without any kit and some seemed in a hurry to get off. Only two fell into the water, a very neat operation otherwise.[10]

From the recollections of the Captain of *Echo*:

The 2nd Battalion of South Wales Borderers soon commenced streaming on board, an unending orderly crowd. We estimated about one thousand troops. In addition *Effingham's* Captain asked if we could also take two watches of her ship's company – about another 400, which were squeezed on board. I doubt if any destroyer ever had so many survivors on board before. After a few uneasy rolls as we left from alongside, with a promise to return for the Captain and third watch later, we cautiously steamed towards two A/A cruisers, who were lying about 15–20 miles away, and we transferred our passengers and shared them between the two cruisers...With the departure of the cruisers *Echo* returned to the wreck of the *Effingham* at speed...

We went alongside, and whilst the one watch of ship's company who had remained on board, about 200, were busy with jobs necessary before she could be abandoned, her Captain invited a few of us on board, perhaps as a gesture of appreciation for returning before the Luftwaffe had spotted and dealt with the "sitting duck". He gave pilot a charthouse watch and myself a stylus barometer, as, together, we left the *Effingham* a deserted ship and boarded *Echo*...Perhaps his only comfort at that moment was that not a single casualty had occurred amongst the sixteen hundred aboard at the time that she was wrecked. [9]

Some of the necessary jobs that engaged the crew before evacuation of their ship could best be described as 'salvage operations':

Everyone quite placid on board and distributing the contents of canteen, people going off with one hundred packets of cigarettes. Rashley, the Wardroom wine steward, having seen to the safety of the ship's cat, ascended into the Wardroom with a basket of half empty gin and brandy bottles and tried to talk to me full of gin and bad R.C. religion. By now had decided to collect some possessions of my own. Quite dark between decks as all dynamos had stopped, preventing the launching of the ship's boats. Strange paralysis prevented me from collecting gear...However, put change of clothes into suitcase, two razors and sermon notes, and camera into pocket and cheque book, and took case up in time to heave it on to Echo as she sailed away with the soldiers...Went down again to open up two large boxes of chocolates from Effingham Girl's School to hand around to the troops... Found a boy with bronchitis from the sick bay without anything on except a jersey and trousers and so went aft of quarterdeck where everyone was looting quantities of sheepskin coats belonging to S.W. Borderers. Like Gehazi overcome with covetousness...took at least a change of raiment for myself as well as the boy. Ship still upright but slowly settling down. Everyone full of jokes and good humour and dressed up in an astonishing variety of miscellaneous gear belonging to soldiers' equipment." [10]

Back on *Echo:* "We moved about a mile away. Her Captain had been told she was to be destroyed at his discretion so, at his request, two torpedoes from Echo ended her life."[9]

The subsequent Board of Enquiry found that *Effingham* had been using a larger scale Norwegian chart than *Echo*'s smaller scale Admiralty chart of the area. She had chosen the course taken in order to shorten the journey and so minimise the risk of air attack upon the ship, handicapped as she was with over one thousand troops on board. In the event the course drawn on the Norwegian chart went directly through the centre of "+ Faksen". This word 'Faksen' was not understood by *Effingham* to mean 'rock'. The "+" had been accepted as a simple crossing of latitude and longitude degree lines only, when in fact it showed the exact position of the rock.[9]*

Collisions with destroyers continued to occur throughout the rest of

---

* Groundings continue to occur to ships in passage, even in times of peace and with the general availability of much more sophisticated navigational aids than was the case in the 1940s. On Saturday 6 July 2002 the Type 42 destroyer HMS *Nottingham* struck a submerged rock off Lord Howe island, some 200 miles north east of Sydney, Australia, and was badly holed below the waterline.

the first year of the war, and indeed until the cessation of hostilities in 1945. On 19 March 1940 Winston Churchill reported to the War Cabinet[1] that the destroyer *Jervis* had collided with the Swedish SS *Tors* and had sustained extensive damage both above and below the waterline. There were two dead and fifteen missing.

Ship losses, battle damage and collisions among destroyers were by the Spring of 1940 a cause of increasing concern to the First Lord. On 1 April 1940 he sent a minute[1] to Rear Admiral B.A. Frazer, then Third Sea Lord and Controller, enquiring about the present status of the forty destroyers undergoing repairs and wondered if something could not be done to speed up the delivery of new destroyers by leaving out, for the time being, some of the more non-essential improvements and additions. He stressed the need to have available the maximum number of destroyers in the forthcoming months.

Churchill sent a further memorandum the following day, requiring a highly detailed monthly progress report on destroyer availability. He demanded a monthly return showing, *inter alia*, the number of destroyers lost, number available for service, under repair, repaired since the previous report, sent for repair, new vessels received and the number expected in the next month. He also asked to see the proof of the returns form before it was printed, which illustrates the degree of detailed control that Churchill was by now exerting upon the day-to-day operation of naval affairs. One week later, Captain Ralph Edwards, then Deputy Director, Operations Division of the Admiralty, wrote in his diary:

> Winston Churchill is taking a great personal interest and tends to interfere with the sailors' business. He is an extraordinary man and has an astonishing grasp of the situation, but I wish he would keep to his own sphere. [11]

Collisions and groundings were not the only calamities to deplete the Allies' precious collective stock of destroyers. On 30 April the battleship *Warspite*, by then participating in the Norwegian Campaign* was reammunitioning, at Greenock. On board *Warspite*:

> ...we were ammunitioning ship one day with hatches open. After a large bang, bits of metal fell around the ship; we automatically thought of an Air Raid. However, it was the French destroyer the *Maille-Breize*, which had blown up. My girlfriend heard the noise in the town centre where she was working in Woolworth's. The French, we were told, used rarefied air in their torpedoes, and one, upon being charged, shot along the deck, exploded in the

---

* See Chapter Eight

entrance to the forward mess-decks, and trapped all the ratings there. The portholes of all destroyers at that time were too small to climb out of…

All the small boats in the harbour converged on the destroyer to assist, and an Engineer and Stoker from the Warspite were sent over with oxy-acetylene cutting gear to try to weaken a patch by the portholes to enable the trapped men to force a way out. However, the heat was terrific, and eventually rescue attempts were abandoned and she sank.[12]

There was heavy loss of life, although the War Cabinet minutes for 1 May 1940 only record that fifty casualties had been taken to hospital.[1]

Less than two months later the British Navy was also to lose a destroyer, *Khartoum*, by an inboard torpedo explosion. The loss occurred on 23 June 1940 in circumstances following action against Italian submarines in the Red Sea, Italy having joined the German side on 10 June 1940. An account by Ordnance Artificier A. Johns, then serving aboard *Khartoum* explains how:

We had got back to our allotted position on Perim Patrol and just had our dinner when there was a terrific explosion aft of the Officers Gallery in the after superstructure. I thought we had been bombed, but soon found out what it was. The Engineer Officer who had had his lunch and was sitting aft of the Gallery in the superstructure with all the doors open to catch the breeze which the moving ship may have given to him, suddenly found a torpedo warhead passing over his body. He was lying out on a deckchair. He was terribly burned as the galley was oil fired and the warhead had broken through all the pipes [which] caught fire instantly. The warhead having passed over the Engineer Officer, carried on aft and passed through the hydraulic pipe system of 'X' gun turret so we had a situation where approximately ninety gallons of hydraulic oil all burning fiercely nixed with the galley fuel oil catching everything alight inside the after superstructure, pouring down the hatch to the Wardroom and the after cabin flats. Meanwhile the warhead had passed through the after bulkhead of the after superstructure and comes to rest, white-hot, on the stern. I've never seen steel catch fire and heat up so quick. It burnt right through the deck and down into 'X' turret magazine and depth charge magazine, but the speed of the fire amazed me…it blew the stern off the ship.[13]

Khartoum was a total loss. Later, Able Seaman G. Sear, on board *Kingston* recorded:

We last saw the *Khartoum* lying on the bottom of Perim harbour as we called there before proceeding to the Red Sea and Suez Canal to join the Mediterranean Fleet in April 1941.[13]

Yet another valuable destroyer was lost by mishap at about midnight on 16 July 1940 when *Imogen*, returning to Scapa Flow from an operation, collided with the cruiser *Glasgow* in thick fog off Duncansby Head. The *Imogen* was extensively damaged in the collision, caught fire and had to be abandoned. She later sank. One hundred and thirty five of her crew were picked up by the *Glasgow* and safely landed at Scapa Flow, but nineteen of their shipmates lost their lives in the accident.

NOTES TO SOURCES

1. Gilbert, M. *The Churchill War Papers, Vol 1: At the Admiralty, Sept 1939 to May 1940* (Heinemann: London, 1993).
2. James, Admiral Sir William. *The Portsmouth Letters* (Macmillan: London, 1946).
3. Churchill, W.S. *The Second World War, Vol 1: The Gathering Storm* (Cassell: London, 1948).
4. Whinney, Captain R. *The U-Boat Peril* (Blandford Press: London, 1986).
5. Jones, G.P. *Battleship Barham* (William Kimber: London, 1974).
6. Haines, G. *Destroyer War* (Ian Allan: Shepperton, 1982).
7. Ziegler, P. *Mountbatten: The Official Biography* (William Collins: London, 1985).
8. Ewing, Vice Admiral Sir Alistair. Papers 65/19/1-3. Imperial War Museum, London.
9. Spurgeon, Commander S.H.K. Papers 90/23/1. Imperial War Museum, London.
10. Grimstone, A.V., Lyons, M.C., and Lyons, U. *Meredith Dewey: Diaries, Letters, Writings* (Pembroke College: Cambridge, 1992).
11. Edwards, Admiral Sir Ralph. File REDW Churchill Archives Centre, Churchill College. Cambridge.
12. Earridge, Stoker F.W. Papers 85/35, Imperial War Museum, London.
13. Johns, Ordnance Artificier, A. In the papers of G. Sear, 91/17/1, Imperial War Museum, London.

VI

"The Navy's here":
The Altmark Affair

Unable in 1939 to match the Royal Navy, and aware that Britain's ability to fight a prolonged war was dependent upon her being able to keep open her vital sea lanes, the German planners proposed to concentrate their naval offensive upon Britain's mercantile fleets bringing supplies of food and raw materials to Britain. They intended to do this by means of surface commerce raiders and underwater U-boat attacks. The threats from both were to persist almost until the end of the war; but perhaps surprisingly in the light of the subsequent success of U-boats and mines in sinking Allied merchant ships, the threat posed by German surface raiders was considered by some sections of the Admiralty in 1939 to pose the greatest threat. Shortly before the outbreak of hostilities the First Sea Lord, Admiral Sir Dudley Pound, wrote: "Nothing would paralyse our supply system and seaborne trade so successfully as attack by surface raiders."[1]

The reason for this concern is not hard to find. The surface commerce raider, in addition to the damage it can cause by the number of ships that it can sink, poses its threat by simply being there, roaming the high seas at will, able to prey unhindered upon unarmed merchant ships. In the days before long-range air or satellite surveillance and present-state detection technology, the spectre of powerful German ships roaming the oceans, picking off lone merchant ships and attacking convoys, was an unending nightmare for the Admiralty. It meant the Allies withdrawing capital ships and other heavy units from other duties and deploying them, albeit thinly, to protect the many convoys against possible attack or using them on searches to try to find and sink the raiders.

The surface raider threat that the Admiralty most feared on the outbreak of war came from five German ships. These were the two battle-cruisers *Scharnhorst* and *Gneisenau* and the three so-called 'pocket battleships', *Admiral Graf Spee*, *Deutschland* and *Admiral Scheer*. All were of modern build, fast and powerful,* which made them ideal 'hit and run' raiders

---

* See Chapter One.

against convoys of merchant ships. The three pocket battleships were something of an unknown quantity. The ships, of a class novel to British naval thinking and design, and ostensibly built in compliance with pre-war treaty 10,000 ton construction limits, were in fact of more than 12,000 tons. For their size they were very fast, capable of 26 knots, and their diesel engines gave long endurance at sea. The speed of all five ships meant that, in theory, they could escape from any warship which they could not overcome with their own heavy guns.

However, the German surface raider had a number of obstacles to overcome which threatened any potential success. Geographically bot-tled up in their Baltic and North Sea ports, they first had to break out into the Atlantic Ocean and thereafter remain, undetected, at sea for a long period, without the security of succour, replenishment or repair at some friendly overseas naval base – comforts enjoyed by their Royal Navy opponents at their British Empire bases. Grand Admiral Doenitz, the German Commander of their U-boat fleets, was a stern critic of his country's surface raider strategy and plans:

> The plan did not give due consideration to our geographical position vis-à-vis Britain. Britain's vital arteries, which had to be attacked, lay to the west of the British Isles on the high seas of the Atlantic. And it was essential that German naval forces should be able to break out into those areas and maintain themselves there, if they were to have the slightest effect. It was then absolutely essential that the naval forces we proposed to create should be capable of adequately fulfill-ing these vital prerequisites.[2]

Grand Admiral Doenitz, naturally enough, thought that the emphasis should be put upon the use of the U-boat arm of the German Navy.

The German planners did not need to overcome the breakout problem with their first commerce raiding venture. Before war was declared on 3 September, and before Britain could put fully into place its Northern Barrage of patrolling ships in the narrow seas between the Shetlands and Norway, the two pocket battleships *Admiral Graf Spee* and *Deutschland* were already at sea, on station, ready to sink merchant ships. Their replen-ishment and maintenance was entrusted to two supply ships also on sta-tion when war broke out.

The *Admiral Graf Spee*, under the command of Captain Hans Langsdorff, had left its base at Wilhelmshaven at 2000 hours on Monday 21 August. Her destination was the vast expanse of the South Atlantic. She was to be kept supplied by the tanker *Altmark*. Captain Heinrich Dau, her Master, had been ordered to store his ship by 2 August with enough supplies to last the *Graf Spee* for three months, and then to sail to Port Arthur in New Mexico to take on 9,400 tons of diesel fuel oil to replenish, as required, the tanks of the pocket battleship. After loading the fuel oil she was to make for an area off the Canary Isles and await further instructions from *Graf Spee*.

The *Deutschland* sailed on Thursday 24 August for the North Atlantic. She was followed by her supply ship, the *Westerwald*, with instructions to rendezvous with her pocket battleship south of Greenland.

Graf Spee and her crew had a short war. She sank her first merchant ship, the 5,050 ton steamer *Clement*, on Saturday 30 September. *Clement* was first machine gunned by the spotter plane of *Graf Spee*, and her wheelhouse destroyed, before being stopped. Her crew took to the boats; but her Master, Captain F.C.P. Harris, and her Chief Engineer, Mr W. Bryant, were taken prisoner onto the *Graf Spee*. They were courteously received and well treated. Captain Harris later recounted:

> ...We followed an officer up the ladder and on to the bridge. When there, we met the Captain [Langsdorff] and ten officers. He saluted me and said "I am sorry, Captain, I will have to sink your ship. It is war." Shortly afterwards he said "I believe you have destroyed your confidential papers?" I said "Yes". He answered "I expected it. That is the usual thing."[3]

Graf Spee then sank the merchantman with gunfire after two unsuccessful attempts to sink her by torpedoes. Later Captain Langsdorff, speaking in good English to his two prisoners, said:

> "If you will give me your word not to attempt any sabotage or espionage, and do exactly as we tell you, you will be left free, otherwise I will have to put a guard on you." I said "You can take my word. Neither the Chief nor I will attempt anything." He said "All right, shake hands."[3]

They were given cigars and beer, followed by a meal, and two and a half hours later were transferred to a neutral Greek merchant ship which *Graf Spee* had stopped and searched. *Graf Spee* then lost herself again in the vastness of the South Atlantic.

For nearly three months she led the Royal Navy a merry dance, crisscrossing the South Atlantic and even sailing into the southern Indian Ocean to sink unescorted merchantmen. In many ways it was a gentlemanly battle, free from the bitterness of later sea warfare. There was no wanton killing of merchant crewmen, who were allowed to take to their boats or be taken prisoner before their ships were sunk. The prisoners where thereafter periodically transferred to *Altmark* whenever the pocket battleship and her supply ship rendezvoused.

The contrast between captivity on the two German ships could not have been more different. Second Engineer H. Saville was captured and taken on board *Graf Spee* when she sank his ship, the 4,651 ton *Newton Beech*, carrying a cargo of maize, on 5 October 1939. He and his fellow ships' officers were well treated: "We were not at any time called prisoners, but were referred to as 'The Englishmen'."[4]

Moved to the *Altmark* on 18 October, his diary records the change in their circumstances:

> Transferred to German oil tanker *Altmark* at 4pm. Living in between decks had a restless night. Eighty foot ladders to climb to get on deck. We were not ill-treated on the *Altmark*. We were sleeping on the iron deck with carpets to keep us warm and we were definitely referred to as "The Prisoners"...Our exercise on the ship was very limited. We were only allowed three-quarters of an hour every forty eight hours, and often not that. Very rarely did we see the light of day.[4]

His diary entry for 26 December records: "Not allowed to wash or go on deck at all. Worst we have to suffer was the monotony."[4] Second Engineer Saville was to spend a total of 135 days as a prisoner on board *Graf Spee* and *Altmark*.

In all, *Graf Spee* sank nine ships totalling 50,089 tons, an almost insignificant tonnage when compared with the tonnage sunk by U-boats in one night in one convoy in the later years of the war in the appropriately named Battle of the Atlantic. What *Graf Spee* did do, however, was to tie down a significant number of Allied warships in their search for her. On 5 October the Admiralty, in conjunction with the French Naval Authority, formed eight 'hunting groups' to carry out this task. At the time of her eventual discovery, no less than three Allied battleships, three aircraft carriers and fourteen cruisers were looking for her. She was found on 13 December 1939 off the mouth of the River Plate, South America, by one of the weaker hunting groups, comprising the 8,390 ton cruiser *Exeter*, with six 8-inch guns, and the 7,000 ton light cruisers *Achilles* and *Ajax*, each armed with eight 6-inch guns. Although outgunned and outranged by *Graf Spee*'s 11-inch guns and themselves badly damaged in the process, the cruisers succeeded in inflicting heavy damage on the pocket battleship, driving her to seek refuge in Montevideo harbour in neutral Uruguay. Given seventy-two hours to repair her damage, treat or offload her wounded and leave, and fearing that heavier British units were waiting for her over the horizon, Captain Langsdorff chose to scuttle the *Graf Spee* outside Montevideo harbour on Sunday 17 December. Her crew were interned and Captain Langsdorff committed suicide in his cabin.*

Graf Spee's supply ship, the 10,000-ton *Altmark*, meanwhile remained undetected to the south. The Admiralty had only confirmed her involvement

---

* The funeral of Captain Langsdorff took place the following afternoon at the German cemetery in Buenos Aires. Among those attending was Captain Pottinger, Master of the *Ashlea*, one of the ships sunk by the *Graf Spee*, who represented the captains of British merchantmen who had been prisoners in the pocket battleship.[3]

with the pocket battleship when questioning the sixty-one British Merchant Navy officers released when *Graf Spee* entered neutral Montevideo harbour. Only then did they learn that she probably had some three hundred British merchant seamen on board. Other than that, they were only able to glean the scantiest information about her: her tonnage, likely speed capability and last known appearance and profile. It was thought that *Altmark* might carry concealed deck guns and that she had last refuelled the *Graf Spee* at an unknown position on 6 December 1939. Her master, Captain Dau, was thought to be an ardent Nazi who would do his best to avoid capture and return home, with his ship and prisoners intact. A wide-ranging search was put in hand by the Admiralty for the prison ship, with orders to find and shadow the ship, but not to sink her because of the British seamen aboard.

The *Altmark* succeeded in evading all the searching warships for nearly two months. She made her way undetected from the South Atlantic, through the North Atlantic and the channel between the Faroes and Iceland, before finding temporary sanctuary in the Norwegian neutral waters of the Inner Leads, the chain of islands running almost the length of Norway.

From radio interceptions and intelligence sources the Admiralty knew by mid-February 1940 that she was nearing home, reaching Norwegian waters on 12 February. On 13 February men from the cruiser *Aurora*, being fitted with degaussing equipment at Port Edgar in the Forth, were detailed off in groups of twenty men to temporarily join ships of the 4th Destroyer Flotilla under the command of Captain P. Vian. One group joined the destroyer *Cossack*, arriving just before 2200 hours carrying rifles, bayonets, steel helmets and webbing equipment. Other similar groups joined the cruiser *Arethusa* and the destroyers *Sikh*, *Nubian*, *Ivanhoe* and *Intrepid*. They were under immediate sailing orders and the overall command of Captain Vian.

As it turned out there could not have been a better choice to lead the force. Determined and decisive, Captain Philip Vian was already a somewhat controversial figure. A fellow destroyer captain, who had served under Vian, remembers:

> ...Vian, as a Captain, was unbelievably rude, hot tempered and frequently needlessly offensive; one had to stand up to him and be right – or make him think so. In action, he was quiet, calm and very, very quick; anyone who raised his voice unnecessarily at any time did not do it twice. Otherwise, some distance beneath his ferocious exterior, he could be man of surprising kindness. In some ways he was a genius. He had no surfeit of false modesty and yet his written reports were brief to the point of being self-effacing.[5]

Captain's Vian's official orders were for the ships to carry out an ice reconnaissance into the Skagerrak, but the "buzz" (on-board gossip) was that they were going to look for the *Altmark*. The fact that the men transferred from the *Aurora* were given boarding instruction and training once on board their temporary postings only reinforced the rumours.[6]

On 15 February 1940 the *Altmark* was reported to be off Trondheim and, one day later, off Bergen. She would soon be able to shelter under the umbrella of Luftwaffe protection and be able to call upon German warships to escort her and her crew to a triumphant homecoming. For the British merchant seamen locked up below, there was only the prospect of a long sojourn in a German prisoner-of-war camp.

The Government of neutral Norway was naturally aware of her passage through their territorial waters, and sent patrol vessels to intercept her and escort her through their Inner Leads, widely used as sea passages by non-Norwegian merchant shipping. On the morning of 14 February *Altmark* was stopped by the Norwegian patrol vessel *Trygg*. A Norwegian officer boarded and requested to search the ship. He was taken to the bridge, but when Captain Dau insisted that his ship was an unarmed tanker, the officer left without conducting his search. The Norwegians were in a difficult position, caught between two warring nations, neither of whom they wished to offend. The Norwegian authorities were fully aware of Britain's view that the *Altmark* was carrying British seamen as prisoners in Norwegian waters and therefore breaching her neutrality, but were also in fear of antagonising Germany and creating an incident which would give the excuse for Norway to be invaded.

Altmark requested a pilot to assist in the continuation of her passage, but as one was not available, *Trygg*'s captain lent *Altmark* two Norwegian sailors who knew the local waters. These two makeshift pilots boarded *Altmark* together with another officer from *Trygg* who looked around the deck but did not search the ship. *Altmark* was asked to anchor overnight because of the risk of collision with the many fishing boats operating within the Inner Leads. The alternative was for *Altmark* to leave Norwegian territorial waters altogether. Captain Dau said he was unable to anchor because the anchor winch was frozen. The tanker turned towards the sea and another Norwegian patrol vessel, *Snoegg*, took up escort position. Her commander boarded *Altmark* and questioned Captain Dau and his officers, but left without searching the ship. *Altmark* proceeded on her way and was again stopped, this time by the Norwegian destroyer *Garm*. Her captain went on board to search the ship but was refused permission. *Altmark* was therefore told to leave Norwegian waters, and the two makeshift pilots left the tanker, together with *Garm*'s captain.

Below decks, the British prisoners were doing their best to attract attention. In his diary entry for Thursday 15 February, when he had been in captivity for 133 days, Second Engineer Saville records: "Stopped by Norwegian patrol. We made all the noise we could in the hope of attracting attention, allowed to proceed on our way."[4]

In an interview with newspapers after his rescue, Second Engineer Saville elaborated on the incident:

> We forced the door open a little way and nearly yelled ourselves hoarse. The Norwegian officers must have heard us, and although they say they searched for us, we know that that is not true. The door we had forced was lashed by the German guard with wire.[4]

The Norwegians saw to it that somehow word was got to the British Embassy in Oslo and the Naval Attaché there signalled to the Admiralty in London that *Altmark* was steaming off the Norwegian coast north of Bergen. The hunt intensified. Hudson aircraft of Coastal Command took off from Thornaby on Tees Bay at 0825 on 16 February, to inspect all shipping in the reported area. Now *Altmark*'s good fortune deserted her: she was spotted by one of the Hudson aircraft at 1250. A member of the aircrew later gave his account of the discovery to newspapers:

> We set off...Visibility was not good, but later it became a beautiful day...[and]... visibility increased to more than forty miles. Near the coast we found the sea frozen over. We proceeded to comb most thoroughly an area from the extreme south point of Norway northwards. Flying well outside territorial waters, I examined every mile with binoculars. Then fifteen miles ahead, I saw a smudge of smoke and a minute later a ship with a black hull and cream upper works steaming directly towards us. We swung out slightly to get a broadside view of her. My heart sank when I recognised her from her lines that she could not be our quarry. But fifteen seconds later I spotted something else – a grey ship, with funnel aft, the distinctive feature of the *Altmark*. We flew up to her at 1,000 feet and inspected her through glasses at a mile range. Then we turned in on top of her for a closer inspection. Just as we had turned to dive low on the ship I saw another aircraft of our formation also sweep down. He was going 'hell for leather' and I thought for a moment he would hit the sea. But he flattened out over the stern and I came in on his stern two seconds afterwards. At the same moment I saw that the third aircraft was also diving.
>
> As we dived my eyes were riveted on the stern, searching for a name. I saw letters about a foot high. Because of the speed at which we were diving the letters seemed to dance in a jumble. I expected that when they could be read they would spell a Norwegian name. I could not suppress a whoop of joy when I saw that they read *Altmark*...All the members of my crew saw the word *Altmark*. They were not holding a thumb up – a signal of success. Each man had two thumbs up. For a few moments we 'went wild' as we swept across the *Altmark*'s decks at funnel height. I could see only one man on deck. There was

no other sign of life aboard. Not a shot was fired from the *Altmark's* hidden guns. We took note of the *Altmark's* position and, having accomplished the task of finding her, we headed for home.[7]

The three aircraft returned safely after an eight-hour flight and another Coastal Command aircraft was dispatched from Leuchars in Scotland to shadow the *Altmark*.

Meanwhile, Captain Vian and his erstwhile 'ice reconnaissance' force were at sea, south of *Altmark's* reported position. He divided his force: the cruiser *Arethusa*, with the destroyers *Intrepid* and *Ivanhoe*, were dispatched to search a zone to the north of the reported position; while Captain Vian in *Cossack*, in company with fellow Tribals *Maori* and *Sikh*, moved to cover the southern zone. They had little idea of *Altmark's* last known appearance and were forced to stop and question a number of neutral ships in their search for the prison ship.

> We had, in fact, no firm information even about the appearance of our quarry. The best clue we could find was in a wardroom copy of an *Illustrated London News*. This showed a picture of two vessels, the caption of which read "German raider *Altmark* examining a neutral merchant ship in the Atlantic". Which of the two was the *Altmark* it did not say, and we assumed it was the four-masted ship in the foreground, rather than the tanker-type further away. So when a four-masted freighter was sighted making south along the coast, I thought we had found our intended victim. Meanwhile the long night approached.[8]

It was not until mid-afternoon, under darkening skies, that *Altmark* was finally found:

> Salvation was provided by a young officer in *Arethusa*. His keen eyes detected, far away, a shadow passing close to and interrupting the black and white land background, and, significantly, the mast and funnels of a torpedo boat, which must be a Norwegian escort. Identity became certain as *Arethusa* closed: the ship was wearing the German ensign, and soon the name *Altmark* was visible on her counter.[7]

The German ship was accompanied by two Norwegian torpedo boats. The Captain of *Arethusa* ordered *Altmark* to stop and sent in the destroyers *Intrepid* and *Ivanhoe*. Not surprisingly, the German ship chose to ignore the order and proceeded on her way with the two Norwegian torpedo boats ranged on either side of her. Their presence, and the evasive actions of the *Altmark*, prevented any boarding by parties from the two British destroyers. German newspaper reports subsequently quoted Captain Dau:

Another destroyer then tried to come between the Altmark and the coast, but this the *Altmark* prevented by an adroit manoeuvre. At 4.56 the *Altmark* defeated an attempt of the *Intrepid* to lay herself to starboard and the destroyer was thrown back by the wash of the screws.[7]

Then, abreast of Josing Fiord, *Altmark* turned sharply to port, increased speed and passed through the narrow entrance into the fiord. The two Norwegian torpedo boats *Kjell* and *Skarv* followed her in, effectively blocking the entrance. This was the position when *Cossack* arrived just as darkness fell.

The Captain of the senior Norwegian vessel, *Kjell*, was invited aboard *Cossack* to discuss the situation. Through a British junior officer on *Cossack*, Paymaster Sub-Lieutenant G. Craven, who could speak both Swedish and German, the Captain of *Kjell* informed his British counterpart that *Altmark* had been examined on three occasions since entering Norwegian waters, the last time off Bergen on 15 February. She was unarmed, nothing was known of the presence on board her of British prisoners of war, and she was to be allowed to proceed unhindered through Norwegian territorial waters. His instructions were to resist any attempted entry into Josling Fiord to board *Altmark*, using force if necessary. His ship's torpedo tubes were trained on *Cossack*. Given the difficult diplomatic circumstances, the British naval force held off, and requested further instructions from the Admiralty in London.

Back in London there was frantic activity at the Admiralty and the Foreign Office. The First Lord of the Admiralty, Winston Churchill, was all for boarding the *Altmark* and rescuing the British seamen thought to be on board, using whatever force was necessary. Though the ship was in neutral Norwegian territorial waters, in his view she forfeited any entitlement to protection by carrying prisoners-of-war through neutral waters on her way to Germany. Aware that such action might well have unfavourable repercussions, and sensitive to world opinion – particularly in America and among unaligned neutral countries – he consulted with Lord Halifax, the Foreign Secretary. With the latter's agreement a signal was sent directly to Captain Vian in *Cossack* at 1725:

Unless the Norwegian torpedo-boat undertakes to convey *Altmark* to Bergen with a joint Anglo-Norwegian guard on board and a joint escort, you should board *Altmark*, liberate the prisoners, and take possession of the ship pending further instructions. If the Norwegian torpedo-boat interferes, you should warn her to stand off. If she fires upon you, you should not reply unless attack is serious, in which case you should defend yourself, using no more force than is necessary and ceasing fire when she desists.

> Suggest to Norwegian destroyer [sic] that honour is served by submitting to superior force.[9]

Cossack closed on *Kjell* once more, and Sub-Lieutenant Craven explained his Captain's orders and proposals:

> It was explained to him that time had become a factor of importance, since the intervention of German aircraft might be expected at daylight. Having placed *Cossack* in a position from which our pom-poms could play upon Norwegian decks, whilst their torpedo tubes were no instant menace to us, I said we could parley no longer, and must board and search *Altmark* forthwith, whether we fought them or not. *Kjell's* Captain decided that honour was served by submitting to superior force and withdrew. On rounding the bend in the fiord, *Altmark* at last came into view. She lay bows inshore, encased in ice, her great bulk standing black against the snow-clad mountains."[8]

Captain Dau was determined however not to tamely submit to being boarded. He trained his searchlight on *Cossack's* bridge, intending to dazzle her commanding officers. In an attempt to ram *Cossack*, where a boarding party of three officers and thirty ratings were making ready, he then came astern on full power through the channel in the ice which *Kjell's* entry passage had made.

> There followed a period of manoeuvring in which disaster, as serious collision must have entailed, was avoided by the skill of my imperturbable navigator, Maclean, and by the speed with which the main engine manoeuvring valves were operated by their artificers.
>
> Lieutenant Bradwell Turner, the leader of the boarding party, anticipated *Cossack's* arrival alongside *Altmark* with a leap which became famous. Petty-Officer Atkins, who followed him, fell short, and hung by his hands until Turner heaved him on deck. The two quickly made fast a hemp hawser from *Cossack's* forecastle, and the rest of the party scrambled across.[8]

One of those across was Paymaster Sub-Lieutenant Craven, who had leapt from the torpedo davit just moments before it was demolished by contact with *Altmark*.[6]

When Lieutenant Turner reached *Altmark's* bridge he found the engine telegraph set to full astern in an attempt to force *Cossack* ashore. Turner set the telegraph to 'stop'. Captain Dau and others on the bridge accepted this take-over of the ship's command, except for the Third Officer, who attempted to re-set the telegraph, but "Turner forbore to shoot him."[8]

As it was apparent that the momentum of *Altmark* would inevitably take her aground by the stern and *Cossack* with her, having transferred all her boarding party the destroyer cast off and moved away. *Altmark* duly grounded, to the consternation of the men imprisoned below. One of the prisoners, Stanley Pemberton, reported:

> When the *Altmark* grounded there was a crash on one side, and the stern lifted nearly out of the water. There was a bit of panic among us below, for we knew nothing of what was happening.[(10)]

It was anticipated that the surrender of Captain Dau and control of the bridge would signal a general capitulation by the rest of *Altmark*'s crew without resort to further violence, but this was not to be the case. Armed German sailors, transferred from the *Graf Spee* to guard the prisoners, resisted, opened fire, and severely wounded Gunner J.J.F. Smith, one of *Cossack*'s boarding party. The boarders returned fire, whereupon some of the German guards left the ship and fled across the ice, from where they commenced sniper action against the boarding party. In the resulting exchange of fire the Germans, silhouetted against the snow, had six men killed and a further six wounded. There were no further British casualties.

With resistance overcome, the boarding party broke open the locked hatches to the holds below and Lieutenant Turner shouted down: "Any British down there?"[(8)] His shouts were greeted by yells of acknowledgement and shouts back, to which he replied: "Come on up then. The Navy's here."[(8)] Second Engineer Saville, held below, remembered the moment:

> On Friday we saw that a searchlight was playing on the ship. Again we started shouting and a voice shouted down to us "Are you prisoners?" We were taken up to the deck and waited while the *Cossack* came into the fiord again.[(4)]

By this time, as *Cossack* was edging her way forward to come alongside the *Altmark* preparatory to taking off the prisoners, a figure was seen to be struggling in the water alongside *Cossack*:

> A signalman on the bridge was sure it was a messmate who had somehow fallen over. The ship was manoeuvred to bring the man alongside. Then, as he seemed incapable of holding on to the line thrown to him, two officers of my staff, Lieutenant-Commander Ormsby and the Secretary, Paymaster-Lieutenant Burkitt, promptly jumped into the freezing water to rescue him.
>
> They were lucky to survive this gallant act. So cold was the water that the man, when helped on board, was found to be already dead from exposure. Furthermore, far from being one of our company, he was a German. He had not been wounded, but had fallen through the

ice as he tried to escape ashore. Ormsby and Burkitt were fortunately little the worse for their swim.[8]

As *Cossack* came alongside *Altmark*, her searchlight trained on the deck scene, the prisoners started to emerge from the holds, laughing, cheering and waving: "They were white and debilitated after their long spell below but not, as had been expected, stretcher cases."[8]

By midnight all 299 liberated prisoners were safely on board *Cossack*, who then cast off, moved past the silent Norwegian torpedo boats *Kjell* and *Skarv*, and headed out to sea. It was only when safely out of the fiord that Captain Vian found that two of his destroyers, waiting outside Josing Fiord, had intercepted a fully laden German iron-ore ship whose crew had scuttled her.

Cossack landed her rescued seamen the next evening at Leith, where they received a tumultuous welcome. Ken Robinson, at his action station on *Cossack*'s 'X' gun, remembers:

> There was not too much room to move about on the messdecks but everyone was in high spirits, including the released prisoners who did not seem much the worse for their experience. We headed back to Leith at a fair speed and landed the freed prisoners amidst a lot of cheering. I remember going to some sort of reception, which I think was at the Town Hall. There was food and drink and speech-making and the incident was in all the newspapers and on the radio. The British Government made the most of the propaganda value.[6]

The treatment of the British seamen while held prisoner on the *Altmark* had been basic and living conditions very unpleasant; but there had been none of the ill-treatment which the Government had anticipated. In Britain the episode aroused a great surge of national pride and Captain Vian* and his crew were treated as heroes by the public and the press. With an eye to world opinion and the importance of positive propaganda on their respective home-fronts, both sides subsequently gave their own version and interpretation of events, and rebuttals of those of their opponent, to the world. The British Government, conveniently forgetting its own violation of Norwegian neutrality, sent a communication to

---

* Captain Philip Vian, 1894–1968, went on to have an illustrious naval career. Awarded the DSO following the *Altmark* affair, he was promoted Rear Admiral in 1941. Commanded the 15th Cruiser Squadron in the Mediterranean 1941–42, including the escorting of convoys to Malta, for which he was knighted Commanded the Eastern (British) Task Force, Normandy invasion 1944. Vice-Admiral, commanding the Carrier Force, British Pacific Fleet, including taking part in the assault on Japanese held Okinawa, April 1945. Fifth Sea Lord 1946 Commander-in-Chief, Home Fleet, 1950–1952.

the Norwegian Government complaining of the perfunctory manner in which the search of the *Altmark* had been conducted and claiming that the Norwegian Government had failed in its obligations as a neutral. The Norwegian reply repudiated these charges and counter-accused both Britain and Germany of violating its territorial waters. It later became more apparent that the Norwegians may have to some extent been duped by German assurances and tactics during the visits of their naval officers to the *Altmark*. While the evacuation of the prisoners was taking place, Paymaster Sub-Lieutenant Craven was questioning Captain Dau on the bridge of the *Altmark*:

> The Captain...told him that on every occasion the ship had been visited ("besuchen"), not searched ("untersuchen"). Each time the winches had been worked to make a clatter and hoses had been played into the holds to drown out the efforts of the prisoners to make their presence known.[8]

For its part, the German propaganda machine put out some startling claims to be picked up and reported by the world's press and radio. According to Captain Dau, *Cossack* had come alongside and boarded *Altmark*, firing wildly and driving the crew into groups. Six of the German sailors had been shot down like cattle. One of the British boarding party had been shot by one of his comrades, and while the *Altmark*'s Fourth Officer was running chivalrously to fetch bandages for him, he had been shot down. It was further claimed on German radio:

> The British shot wildly at the German sailors. The points of egress of the shots found on the dead had a diameter of five to six centimetres which showed that the British used 'dum-dum'* bullets.[10]

One claim made by Captain Dau was more credible. In an interview given to German newspapers and reproduced in the British press,[7] he claimed that the British boarding party, when they had control of *Altmark*, had proceeded to steal everything they could lay their hands on before returning to *Cossack*. The same British newspaper, in attempting to repudiate German claims that *Altmark* was an unarmed ship, reported:

> One of the British sailors brought back from the melee the cap of a German naval rating, proving conclusively that active service personnel of the German Navy were on board the *Altmark*.[7]

---

* Bullets with nose sawn off or flattened. Prohibited by the then internationally accepted Geneva Convention.

Even Winston Churchill became involved. On 25 March 1940 he sent a reproving personal note to Admiral Sir Dudley Pound, First Sea Lord, and to Admiral Tom Philips, Deputy Chief of the Naval Staff:

> I see charges of looting preferred against our men in the German Press. I should not think it necessary to mention this but for the fact that it has come to my notice that the Captain of the *Altmark's* watch, chronometer and Iron Cross were stolen, and are now in the hands of some sailors as souvenirs. Anything of this kind must be stopped with the utmost strictness. No souvenir of any value can be preserved without being reported and permission obtained. Personal property of enemy's [sic] may be confiscated by the state, but never by individuals.[9]

It is interesting to conjecture how such a minor matter may have come to the First Lord's attention. Lieutenant Rolf Dau, the former commander of *U-42*, was captured and made a prisoner of war when his submarine was sunk by the destroyers *Ilex* and *Imogen* on 13 October 1939.* It is conceivable that a complaint contained in a letter – sent via the Red Cross from his older brother Captain Heinrich Dau of the *Altmark* – was passed on to Churchill. It was Lieutenant Rolf Dau's coat that had been mutilated by souvenir hunting sailors when onboard the destroyer *Imogen*. The Dau brothers had some reason to regard British destroyer men as thieving pirates.

This view was also that of the German authorities. When they occupied Norway two months after the *Altmark* affair, the Germans erected a commemorative board in Josling fiord. Translated, it read:

> Here on the 16 February 1940, the *Altmark* was set upon by a British sea-pirate.[6]

The sign, which was double-sided, was duly 'liberated' – not on this occasion by sailors, but by British airborne troops in 1944. One side was given to Admiral Sir Philip Vian, the former Captain of *Cossack*. The other side is now on display at Airborne Forces Museum, Browning Barracks, Aldershot.

Neither *Cossack* nor *Altmark* survived the war. *Cossack* took part in the Second Battle of Narvik on 13 April 1940** and the attack on and sinking of the German battleship *Bismarck* on 27 May 1941. She was badly damaged by a torpedo from *U-563* off Gibraltar on 27 October 1941 while on convoy escort duty, eventually sinking. Her then commander, Captain E.L. Berthon, and 158 officers and men were lost.

---

* See Chapter Three.
** See Chapter Eight.

The *Altmark* was refloated following her grounding, repaired and renamed *Uckermark*. She became engaged in blockade running between Bordeaux, in Occupied France, and Germany's ally Japan. Her role was to fuel U-boats and surface raiders on the outbound trip and go on to Japan to pick-up palm oil, rubber, wolfram and tin for the home run. The *Uckermark* left Bordeaux on such a voyage on 9 August 1942 but was forced to return to port by British sea and air surveillance activity in the Bay of Biscay. She finally left Bordeaux on 9 September 1942 and arrived at Yokahama, Japan on 24 September, having refuelled the German surface raider *Michel* in the South Atlantic en route. On 30 September, while her crew were cleaning out the fuel oil from her tanks prior to taking on board a cargo of edible oils, something went wrong with the operation and there was an explosion with the highly combustible mixture. *Uckermark* blew-up, killing fifty-three of her crew.[11]

NOTES TO SOURCES

1. Roskill, Captain S.W. *The Navy at War, 1939-1945* (Collins: London, 1960).
2. Doenitz, Grand Admiral K. *Memoirs: Ten Years and Twenty Days* (Lionel Leventhal: London, 1990).
3. Pope, D. *The Battle of the River Plate* (William Kimber: London, 1974).
4. Saville, H. Papers 85/50/1, Imperial War Museum, London.
5. Whinney, Captain R. *The U-Boat Peril* (Blandford Press: London, 1986).
6. *HMS Cossack: Some Survivors' Narratives.* HMS Cossack Association, 1998.
7. *The Times*, Tuesday 20 February 1940.
8. Vian, Admiral of the Fleet Sir Philip. *Action This Day* (Frederick Muller: London, 1960).
9. Churchill, W.S. *The Second World War, Vol 1: The Gathering Storm* (Cassell: London, 1948).
10. *The Times*, Thursday 22 February 1940.
11. Brice, M. *Axis Blockade Runners of World War II* (B.T. Batsford: London, 1981).

VII

The Beginning of
the Norwegian Campaign

The *Altmark* affair confirmed beyond all doubt that the Germans were making illegal use of neutral Norwegian territorial waters. It also served to rekindle one of Winston Churchill's pet schemes – to cut off German iron ore supplies obtained from Sweden via the Norwegian port of Narvik and transported through the Norwegian territorial waters of the Inner Leads back to Germany. As early in the war as 19 September 1939 he had warned the War Cabinet[1] of the large imports of iron ore, vital for its munitions industry, which Germany imported from Sweden during the winter months via the ice-free Norwegian port of Narvik, with the ore-carrying ships protecting themselves from British naval interference by sailing within Norwegian territorial waters. He had further warned that if the Norwegian Government could not resolve the situation he would be forced to propose mining these territorial waters.

That same day Churchill sent a 'Most Secret' signal to Admiral Sir Dudley Pound, the First Sea Lord, informing him of his warning to the War Cabinet about the perceived Norwegian iron-ore problem and,*inter alia*, instructing that plans for the mining operations should be studied by the Admiralty.[1]

Churchill was hungry for action. In the autumn of 1939 he had protested to Admiral Pound:

> ...we are being driven day by day into an absolute defensive by far weaker forces...I could never be responsible for a naval strategy which excluded the offensive principle and relegated us to keeping open lines of communication and maintaining the blockade.[2]

The problem for the War Cabinet and the Admiralty was that, in Churchill's desire for a more offensive strategy, the Norwegian iron-ore project was only one of the many that Churchill's fertile mind brought forward at this 'Phoney War' period of the early months of the war. Other proposals

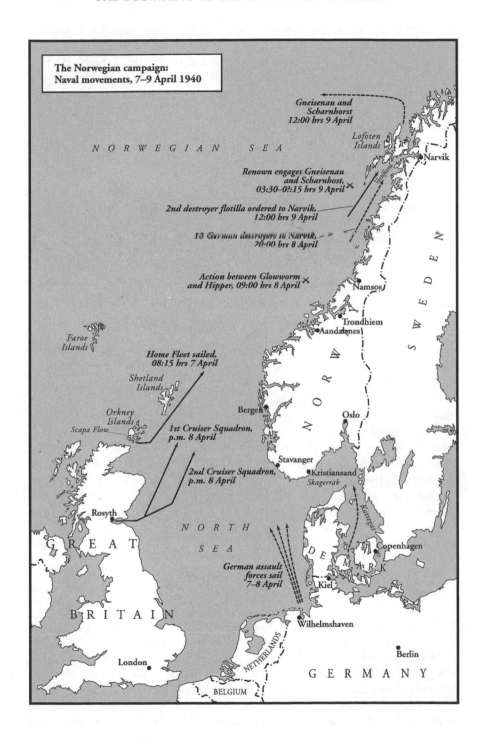

The Norwegian campaign:
Naval movements, 7–9 April 1940

Gneisenau and Scharnhorst 12:00 hrs 9 April

Lofoten Islands

Narvik

NORWEGIAN SEA

Renown engages Gneisenau and Scharnhost, 03:30–0?:15 hrs 9 April

2nd destroyer flotilla ordered to Narvik, 12:00 hrs 9 April

10 German destroyers to Narvik, 20·00 hrs 8 April

Action between Glowworm and Hipper, 09:00 hrs 8 April

Namsos

SWEDEN

Trondhiem

Aandalsnes

Faroe Islands

Home Fleet sailed, 08:15 hrs 7 April

Shetland Islands

NORWAY

Bergen

Oslo

Orkney Islands

Scapa Flow

1st Cruiser Squadron, p.m. 8 April

Stavanger

2nd Cruiser Squadron, p.m. 8 April

Kristiansand

Skagerrak

Rosyth

NORTH SEA

Kattegat

DENMARK

Copenhagen

GREAT

German assault forces sail 7–8 April

Kiel

BRITAIN

Wilhelmshaven

NETHERLANDS

Berlin

London

GERMANY

BELGIUM

included Plan Catherine, to send a British naval force into the Baltic Sea; the establishment of a mine barrage from Northern Scotland to Norway in order to bottle up all German merchant and warships in the North Sea; and the dropping of mines into the River Rhine in order to disrupt the use of that major German waterway. All these proposals came to nothing with changing circumstances and needs, or on practicality or resource grounds; but the Norwegian iron-ore problem nagged away at Churchill.

It was a valid obsession: an all-year-round supply of the rich Swedish iron ores was vital for the maintenance of Germany's armament and munitions industries. In 1938 Germany imported twenty-two million tons of iron ore, with some nine million tons of high-grade ores coming from Swedish sources. Some of this ore came from central Sweden via the port of Oxelosund, but the majority came from deposits at Kiruna and Gallivare in northern Sweden. The ores reached Germany via two routes: from the Swedish port of Lulea at the northern end of the Baltic; and especially from December to April, when Lulea was icebound, from the railhead at the neutral Norwegian port of Narvik. German opinion[3] was that if the Narvik supply was cut off, some 2.5 to 3.5 million tons of iron ore per year would be lost and the even supply of iron ore severely disrupted.

Narvik, situated at the head of the long Ofotfiord, is ice-free in winter. Formerly a small fishing village, its fortunes were transformed in 1902 by the construction of a railway and ore handling facilities for the all-year-round shipping of Swedish ores. The railway ran for twenty-three miles from the port to the Swedish border, and then for a further seventy-seven miles to the iron ore deposits at Kiruna in Sweden. The section of railway on Norwegian territory involved a descent of some 1,700 feet through nineteen tunnels along its length. At the port head was an ore crushing plant, railway sidings, a 1,200 foot long ore-loading quay, and anchorage for thirty ships. By 1939 Narvik was the second largest town in northern Norway and was almost solely concerned with the export of iron ores. Germany was the major importer of the rich magnetic ore, transporting it through the length of the ice-free fiord and on to Germany through the sheltered waters of the chain of islands – the Norwegian Leads – running the length of Norway.

The pushing through of a workable plan of action to stop this flow of iron ore to Germany continued to preoccupy Winston Churchill as 1939 drew to a close.

However, the strategic situation changed with the opportunity or excuse to accelerate action over this supply of iron ore, when on 30 November 1939 Russia, with German acquiescence, attacked Finland. The Allied reaction was for Britain and France to join neutral Sweden and Norway in condemning the attack upon the latter's Scandinavian neighbour. More proactively, the Allies proposed that, with the approval and permission of Norway and Sweden, they send military aid – troops, equipment and supplies – to assist the Finns. The aid would have to pass through Norway and Sweden and would require the establishment of an allied base at Narvik and, *de facto*, the temporary occupation of northern Norway. Scheduled to take place in mid-March 1940, ostensibly to assist Finland in resisting invasion and prevent Russian interference in Scandinavian affairs, it was a proposal with a mixed Allied agenda. The British saw it as a way of cutting off Germany's supply of iron ore. The French were looking for the establishment of a Scandinavian front in order to draw German attention and pressure from their own frontier with Germany. Neutral Norway and Sweden, fearing further alienation of Russia and Germany, wanted nothing to do with what they saw as an ill-thought-out plan. In the opinion of one authority:

> A more hare-brained scheme can seldom have been solemnly concerted by the leaders of a country at war. The Swedes and Norwegians, the fate of Poland vividly before them, would have nothing to do with it. A diplomatic wrangle continued through the winter months while British and French military leaders planned hopefully, gradually convincing themselves that, if landings were made, the Norwegians would accept a *fait accompli* and would thereafter co-operate.[4]

In the event, the Finnish surrender on 13 March 1940 effectively put an end to that particular plan, since there was then no chance of the Swedish and Norwegian governments further risking their delicate neutral positions. Even as all this delicate diplomatic manoeuvring and strategic planning was taking place, Winston Churchill had come up with yet another proposal, fraught with diplomatic difficulty, for stopping German use of Norwegian territorial waters. On Saturday 16 December 1939 John Colville, a member of Downing Street staff, recorded in his diary that the War Cabinet had received:

> A memorandum by Winston Churchill on German iron-ore supplies. He considers it essential to use drastic, and even illegal, methods to prevent ore being shipped from Norwegian ports, and he wants Cabinet authority to lay minefields in Norwegian territorial waters (with the justification that German U-boats are sinking ships in those waters) in order to drive ships carrying iron ore out of territorial waters into the hands of our contraband control.[5]

The issue of stopping German ore supplies rumbled on into the early months of 1940. A political shift in France on 21 March brought in a fresh government there with a more aggressive stance towards the execution of the war, and a renewed call for military intervention in Scandinavia in order to take pressure off the German/French front. The Downing Street diarist's entry for 26 March, reflecting on this renewed French vigour towards the pursuit of the war, observed "this of course suits the book of Winston Churchill whose policy is one of 'action for action's sake'."[5]

It was decided by the Allies to re-examine the original cause of concern in Norway, namely the problem of stopping the passage of Swedish iron-ore through the Inner Leads, and to solve it by a two-step process. Firstly, as Churchill had earlier proposed, the shipping channels would be mined. The operation was christened "Winifred". Norway and Sweden were warned that their neutrality was favouring Germany and that, as a consequence, the Allies had been forced to take this action. It was envisaged that this would provoke German retaliation and possibly their invasion of Norway in order to protect their interests. Then a second preventative Allied measure would be justified – Plan R4 – for the occupation of Narvik, Bergen, Trondheim and Stavanger. The Allies hoped that this occupation, if not welcomed, would at least be received fairly passively by the Norwegian people.

With all the diplomatic activity that had been taking place between the Allies and the Scandinavian countries, and especially given that Norwegian political circles had, within their midst, a small but highly active pro-German group led by Major Vidkun Quisling,* the Germans were naturally not unaware of the Allied interest in cutting off their iron ore supplies. They were also fully alive to the strategic importance of Norway's long coastline. As early in the war as 23 October 1939 Grand Admiral Raeder, Commander-in-Chief of the German Navy, had sent a memorandum to the German High Command arguing the need for bases in northern Norway, north of the narrow strip of water between the Orkneys and the southern tip of Norway, for their surface raiders and U-boats.[6] This narrow gap constituted a bottleneck to German accessing of the Atlantic Ocean, which the British could mine and patrol as they had done in the First World War. Admiral Karl Doenitz, then Commander of the Submarine Arm of the German Navy, supported his superior's proposals. He pointed out that bases at Narvik and Trondheim would have three strategic advantages: the bases were north of the Shetlands and Orkneys and the British naval base of Scapa Flow; they wereice-free throughout the year; and they had adequate rail communications with southern Norway and Germany for logistical support of the two bases.

Persuaded by the arguments, the German High Command also began to plan for their own invasion of Norway. Admiral Doenitz was to later write:

---

* Vidkun Quisling became head of a puppet government in Norway from May 1942 to May 1945. After the war he was tried as a traitor by the Norwegian authorities, found guilty and executed on 24 October 1945.

There were indications that the enemy was also planning military operations against Norway. It was these indications which finally led to the decision to forestall him by means of a counter-stroke. In these circumstances there was, therefore, always the possibility that the enemy might act before we ourselves had had time to complete our operations. He would in any case certainly react with great energy when the German landings had been accomplished. His operations might take the form of attacks on the ports we had occupied, or he might decide to establish new bases for himself. In addition the enemy could with certainty be expected to try and cut the lines of sea communication between Norway and Germany.[7]

Neither the Germans nor the Allies had time on their side in early 1940, as the winter turned to spring. Any invasion of Norway had to take particular account of the geography and climate of the country. Although having a land area greater than that of the British Isles, Norway is very mountainous, with over half of the country lying at a height of over 2,000 feet. The long thin country, running roughly north-south, is intersected by hundreds of deep, steep sized fiords, many of which (particularly in the north of the country) are ice-free in winter due to the favourable influence of the Gulf Stream. Norway is covered by deep snow in winter which, together with frequent blizzards and comparatively poor rail and road communications, make inland movement very difficult. If either side delayed, the melting snows of the spring thaw would only compound the difficulties. Both sides were therefore forced to contemplate a sea-borne intervention against key locations of the country before the thaw set in.

The German Plan, operation "Weserubung", ambitiously staked virtually the whole of her naval strength on a five-pronged simultaneous sea-borne assault upon the major towns and ports of Norway. The make-up of their five naval task forces was to be:

Group One, to Narvik, composed of ten destroyers, each carrying two hundred troops. They were to be escorted by the battle-cruisers *Scharnhorst* and *Gneisenau*. Once the destroyers were safely in Narvik fiord, the two battle-cruisers were to form part of a diversionary plan to draw off any Allied heavy units that were opposing the landings.

Group Two, to Trondheim, consisting of the heavy cruiser *Hipper* and four destroyers, carrying some 1,700 troops between them. After landing the troops, *Hipper* was to join up with *Scharnhorst* and *Gneisenau*, under the command of Admiral Gunther Lutjens, for the joint diversionary excursion northwards.

<u>Group Three,</u> to Bergen, comprising the light cruisers *Köln* and *Konigsberg,* the older training cruiser *Bremse,* and a convoy of miscellaneous merchant ships carrying some 1,900 troops between them.

<u>Group Four,</u> to Kristiansund and Arendal, made up of the light cruiser *Karlsruhe,* three small escort vessels, and some torpedo boats.

<u>Group Five,</u> to Oslo, the capital of Norway, composed of the heavy cruiser *Blucher,* the pocket battleship *Lutzow,* the light cruiser *Emden* and transports carrying 2,000 troops.

The German planning was meticulous. In addition to the sea-borne forces, they had in place some specialist troops and technicians hidden on board supposedly merchant ships – 'Trojan horses' – at Narvik, Trondheim and Stavanger, and had laden oil tankers waiting to sail to replenish the tanks of the task force ships at Trondheim and Narvik. They also arranged for a laden ship to arrive at Narvik in time to re-supply that invading force. Theodor Broch, a Norwegian civilian, visited the British merchant ship SS *Romanby,* also in Narvik, on the morning of 8 April, as the representative of Lloyds of London:

> As I left I observed the huge Nazi whaling ship, *Jan Willem,* riding at anchor at some distance. An oversized swastika flew at the fore-mast...It had arrived from the north and had exceptionally large food stores for being southward bound.[8]

In contrast, the Allied planning was sketchy yet over-elaborate. Operation "Winifred", the mine-laying operation[9] eventually pushed through the War Cabinet by Churchill, called for a force of four mine-laying destroyers, *Esk, Icarus, Impulsive* and *Ivanhoe,* to lay a minefield across the southern side of Vestifiord, which led into Narvik, between the Lofoten Islands and the Norwegian mainland. They were to be escorted by four destroyers of the 2nd Flotilla, *Hardy, Havock, Hotspur* and *Hunter,* who, when the mine-laying operation was completed, were to patrol the area to warn off neutral shipping. The cover the mine-laying, and another simulated mine-laying operation further south, Vice Admiral W.J. Whitworth had the battle-cruiser *Renown* and a destroyer screen of the destroyers *Hero, Hyperion, Glowworm* and *Greyhound. Hero* and *Hyperion* were to simulate the laying of a minefield in a position off Bud, while yet another mine-laying force, of the mine-layer *Teviot Bank* and the destroyers *Inglefield, Ilex, Imogen* and *Isis,* were to actually lay mines off Stadlandet.

On 3 April the War Cabinet finally took the decision to proceed with the mine-laying which, originally planned for 5 April, was rescheduled to take place on 8 April. The whole mine-laying force – the battle-cruiser *Renown,* minelayer *Teviot Bank*, and the sixteen destroyers assigned to either lay mines or provide escorts – sailed from Scapa Flow on the evening of 5 April and the morning of the following day.

Henry Lemmon, a member of the crew of one of Scapa's boom-defence vessels remembered the departure of the force.

> Being on a 'gate' boat, I saw many ships leave never to get back, and the most outstanding memory of all was to see Captain Warburton-Lee lead his flotilla of destroyers [*Hardy, Hotspur, Havock,* and *Hunter*] out one day. He was standing alone on the top bridge, legs astride, and waving his cap to all as they left the boom. On the ship's hailer was played an old gramophone record of 'A hunting we will go'. Truly a wonderful sight of a great man, marred a few days later on hearing he had died on the beach in Norway and had been awarded the VC.[(10)]

The proposed Allied military operations, 'Plan R4', called for troops to be prepared and made ready to occupy the ports of Bergen, Stavanger and Trondheim, and for other troops to be ready to land at Narvik. However it was not intended to actually land troops in Norway "until the Germans have violated Norwegian neutrality, or there is clear evidence that they intend to do so".[(9)] It was envisaged that forces to accomplish R4 would sail so as to arrive at the targeted ports in a co-ordinated manner. The varied objectives of the force were: to occupy Narvik and seize and hold the twenty-three miles of ore-carrying railway line running up to the Swedish border; to occupy Bergen and Trondheim; and to seize and hold Stavanger. To achieve these ambitious objectives, the cruisers *Devonshire, Berwick, York* and *Glasgow* embarked four battalions of troops, to be split between Bergen and Stavanger, while a single battalion intended for Trondheim was to travel in an escorted transport ship. A larger scale operation was planned for the Narvik part of the operation. There, the initial landing was to be carried out by a battalion of troops sailing in transports escorted by two cruisers. These were to be followed by an oiler, the rest of the British troops, plus some French troops: in all a total force of some 18,000 men.

A striking force of two cruisers and three destroyers was to be held in readiness at Rosyth to deal with any sea-borne expedition which the Germans themselves might send against Norway, and capital ship cover against any German interference by their capital ships against the various R4 expeditionary forces was to be provided by the battleships *Rodney* and *Valiant* and the battle-cruisers *Renown* and *Repulse*. No aircraft carrier was available at that time to supplement the naval forces. Overall it was to prove an ill-planned, poorly equipped and badly co-ordinated operation.

While the Admiralty and War Office planned their initiatives, the Germans pressed on with their invasion. They had started embarking troops on 6

April, and the first of these groups – those intended for the invasion of the northern Norwegian ports of Narvik and Trondheim – left their home ports that night. Assembly point for the invasion ships was a lightship at the mouth of the River Weser at 0200 on 7 April 1940. By that evening, the German ships were running into a Force 7 south-westerly gale and the fourteen destroyers of Groups One and Two were particularly suffering from the heavy seas which, sweeping in from astern, were causing the destroyers to yaw badly, making it difficult for the ships to hold course. Many of the soldiers being carried below decks were by now suffering badly from seasickness. Engine room difficulties, still euphemistically termed "teething troubles", were also occurring in some destroyers. The *Eckoldt* had an early temporary engine failure while the *Thiele* had its port cooling water pump fail. The engine room crew, working in appalling weather conditions, managed to dismantle and repair it as *Thiele* struggled to keep up with the rest of the destroyers, using only her starboard boilers.[12]

Overnight, the gale worsened, and by next morning the fourteen German destroyers heading for Trondheim and Narvik were scattered and out of position. It was the gale that brought about the first meeting and clash of the opposing forces. The British destroyers, out in the same area at the same time, were also suffering the effects of the weather – albeit to a lesser extent than their German counterparts. With better sea-keeping characteristics, and untrammelled by having up to 200 troops per ship on board, the British destroyers ploughed on with their appointed mine-laying and escort duties. Then *Glowworm*, one of the destroyers screening *Renown*, lost a man overboard and turned back in the forlorn hope of finding him. She failed to do so, but on the morning of 8 April found destroyers of the invading German force.

At 0830 on 8 April Admiral Whitworth in *Renown* received a signal from *Glowworm* reporting and giving the position of two enemy destroyers, some 140 miles distant from *Renown*. Further signals from *Glowworm* that she was engaging a superior force prompted the Commander-in-Chief Home Fleet, Admiral Sir Charles Forbes, some 300 miles to the south west with his capital ships, to detach the battle-cruiser *Repulse*, the cruiser *Penelope* and four destroyers to go to *Glowworm's* assistance. It was too late and she was too far away; the last signal from the destroyer was timed at 0855. It was not until after the war, five years later, that details of her fate became known.

The two enemy destroyers reported by *Glowworm* (Lieutenant Commander G.B. Roope) had lost contact in the bad weather and heavy seas with their heavier consorts *Scharnhorst*, *Gneisenau* and *Admiral Hipper*. The first destroyer to come into contact with *Glowworm* was *Hans Ludemann*. *Glowworm* fired off recognition signals followed by two salvos of 4.7-inch shells as the *Hans Ludemann*, under orders to avoid conflict and encumbered with her sea-sick troops, made off to the north-west at high speed.

Shortly afterwards *Glowworm* sighted *Bernd von Arnim* on her starboard bow, approached the German destroyer on a reciprocal course, turned and came in to attack from astern. She was manoeuvring and weathering the heavy seas better than her top-heavy, yawing opponent. A running gun fight ensued, with the Captain of the *Bernd von Arnim* attempting to escape rather than fight, encumbered as he was like the *Hans Ludemann* with 200 by now very sick soldiers. When his getaway speed reached thirty knots, the bows of the ship were driving under, the forecastle was buried in the heavy seas, and two men were swept overboard.[14] Her captain reduced speed and at 0910 signalled his predicament to Vice-Admiral Gunther Lutyens, in command of the German naval force.

The Vice-Admiral, at 0920, ordered the heavy cruiser *Admiral Hipper* to detach from his force and deal with the British destroyer. At 0957 the heavy cruiser found and opened fire on *Glowworm*, hitting her amidships with the first salvo of her 8-inch guns. The British destroyer fired a return salvo of two or three torpedoes, which *Admiral Hipper* avoided. Considerably damaged, *Glowworm* made smoke in an attempt to avoid further damage. *Admiral Hipper*, unable because of the heavy seas to answer her helm, passed through the smokescreen and found herself in the path of *Glowworm*. Both ships turned towards each other with the intention of ramming. It was to be an ill-matched joust: *Glowworm*, 1,345 tons and armed with four 4.7-inch guns; against the 13,900 tons of the *Admiral Hipper*, ten times her size and armed with eight 8 inch guns. Racing in, *Glowworm* struck the heavy cruiser abaft of her starboard anchor at 1013 hours. The effect of the impact was to fatally damage *Glowworm*, forcing her down in the water, with her own bows crushed from the impact. Scraping along *Hipper*'s armoured side, *Glowworm*, now in her death throes, nevertheless tore open the German cruiser's outer armour plating for a length of 130 feet and ripped away her starboard torpedo tubes. *Admiral Hipper* immediately took on over 500 tons of water through the gash in her side. *Glowworm* broke clear and at 1024 she capsized, blew up and sank. Despite her damage, the heavy seas, and the urgent need to keep to the rigid invasion timetable, the German heavy cruiser gallantly stopped and desperately tried to rescue *Glowworm*'s survivors. Thirty-eight of her complement of some 145 men were saved, including just one officer, Sub-Lieutenant Ramsey. Her captain, Lieutenant-Commander G.B. Roope, was being hauled on board and had just reached the cruiser's deck when, exhausted, he let go, fell back and was drowned.*

The damage to *Admiral Hipper*, although severe, was not sufficient to prevent her from regrouping with her four destroyers and proceeding to invade Trondheim. Meanwhile, the remaining ten German destroyers

---

* When details of *Glowworm*'s gallant action became known her captain, Lieutenant-Commander Roope, was awarded a posthumous Victoria Cross.[11]

strove to catch up with the *Scharnhorst* and *Gneisenau*, their covering force for the remainder of their journey to Narvik. The weather conditions continued to deteriorate, and all the destroyers were in difficulties. One of them, *Erich Giese*, fell well astern after damage from heavy seas, losing oil and suffering a compass failure. Because of the heavy seas and the long distance covered all the heavily laden destroyers had by now consumed much of their fuel oil and, as a consequence, were riding higher in the water, yawing and pitching as their sea-going properties worsened. Heavy seas constantly broke over their decks, smashing the ships' boats and washing military equipment and stores overboard. Below, the "land-lubber" soldiers were in a bad state: sea-sick and lacking adequate ventilation, sleep or comfort in their cramped and wet accommodation. Finally, at 2100 on 8 April, the ten German destroyers were ordered in to Vestfiord, with Narvik, their destination, at its head.

Further south, the warships *Blucher*, *Lutzow* and *Emden*, plus the remainder of the German Group Five task force, were just outside Oslo fiord at midnight on 8/9 April. In the capital the Norwegian Government, in all-night session, was trying to decide, in the face of German threats and demands, whether or not to peacefully accept a German occupation and avoid bloodshed to its people. There was virtually no time for due consideration of the ultimatum: invading troops would begin landing, whatever the Norwegian Government decided, at 0430 hours. The Norwegian Government declined to accept the demands and decided to resist invasion as best it could, given the uncertainty of the situation across their country as a whole and the ambiguity of allegiance of some pro-German factions in political, military and naval circles.

Although the Norwegian Government was forced to accede to the invader's demands, the German take-over of Norway was not accomplished without stout resistance and examples of great Norwegian gallantry. In Oslo fiord that day, the Norwegian naval forces were to defiantly proclaim their patriotism and allegiance. As the German ships entered the mouth of the German fiord the small armed whaler *Pol III*, armed with one small gun and commanded by Lieutenant Wielding Olsen, a naval reservist, attacked the *Lutzow*, *Blucher* and *Emden* and their escorts. The small whaler was quickly set on fire by the German guns but sinking, and with Lieutenant Olsen mortally wounded, she succeeded in ramming the Mowe class torpedo boat *Albatros*. The Force Five group of ships continued up the fiord, until they reached the narrows guarded by the forts of Rauer and Bolaene. After firing warning shots across the bows, the German ships were allowed to proceed up the fiord. Lack of orders and information was the reason later given by the two battery commanders.[6]

The Germans continued to progress up the fiord until they reached the naval base of Horten. Here the commander of the base led out his three small warships to oppose the vastly superior German force: the 2,000 ton mine-layer *Olav Tryggvason* and the two smaller minesweepers *Oltra* and *Ramma*. With the commander leading in the *Oltra*, they came upon the German ships, transferring troops to small ships for landing ashore, and opened fire. The four 4.7-inch guns of the *Olav Tryggvason* sank the German minesweeper *R.17* and further damaged the *Albatros*, forcing it ashore as a total loss. The other German ships then drove off the three Norwegian ships, badly damaging the *Ramma* and killing her captain and some crew, before landing and capturing the forts of Rauer and Bolaene and the naval base of Horten.

The Force Five ships then continued up the fiord towards the capital Oslo before reaching the formidable obstacle of the Drobak Narrows. On the western side of the Narrows the Norwegians had a battery of fifty-year-old 8-inch guns. On the eastern side they had a battery of 11-inch guns, plus some torpedo tubes set in the rocks.

Admiral Kumnetz, in command of Force Five and perhaps encouraged by the non-resistance of the two earlier forts and a belief that pro-German factions were in control of the guns of the Dvobak Narrows, decided to force the Narrows. His 13,900-ton heavy cruiser *Blucher*, sister ship of *Hipper*, led the way. The admiral had been mistaken. At point blank range, the Norwegian 8-inch and 11-inch guns fired into *Blucher*. The first salvo started a major fire on her deck, and another salvo smashed her steering gear. Then two torpedoes were fired into the ship, causing a magazine to blow up. The crew and troops on board were forced to abandon ship and over a thousand lives were lost. The *Lutzow* received three hits, and her foremost turret was put out of action.

The ships of Force Five were forced to pull back and land their troops and equipment below the Narrows, some fifteen miles short of Oslo. The capital was only taken the following day, by German airborne troops. In two hours, Force Five had lost the *Blucher*; the *Lutzow* was damaged; three torpedo boats had been sunk; and another, the *Albatros*, was beached and a virtual wreck.

Elsewhere during the night of 9 April however, the Germans were taking and consolidating their hold on the major ports of Norway. At Stavanger, just after midnight, the Norwegian destroyer *Sleipner* sank the inbound German collier, *Roda*, later found to be loaded with anti-aircraft guns and other armaments, when the destroyer became suspicious of the German ship's intentions. Later the town was captured by German airborne forces landing at a nearby airbase. At Bergen, the German Group Three force passed the outlying coastal fortifications in the darkness without resistance, but then came under fire from two forts which damaged the light cruiser *Konisberg** before they and the town of Bergen were bombed and overcome by German troops.

---

* *Konisberg* was attacked and sunk the next day by sixteen Skua dive bombers of the Fleet Air Arm, on a round trip of 560 miles from their UK base.[11]

At Trondheim, Group Two (consisting of the heavy cruiser *Hipper* and her four destroyers) forced their way in the darkness at a speed of 25 knots past the two forts at Brettingen and Hysnes, some thirty miles from Trondheim. Their dash was assisted by good fortune when an early salvo of their gunfire destroyed the electricity supply to the forts' searchlights. By 0700 Trondheim was in the hands of German troops, although the forts were not subdued until the late afternoon of the next day.

However, the main and most bitterly fought actions were to take place at Narvik. The Norwegian authorities there were made aware at 0312 on 9 April of the presence of the German destroyers in the Vestifiord by the pilot station at Tranoy. One hour later the ships passed Baroy island and entered Ofotfiord, with Narvik lying at its head. As he passed up the fiord, Commodore Freidrich Bonte, in command of the German force, detached his destroyers in ones and twos to secure the smaller side fiords leading off the main Ofotfiord. On board his flotilla leader the *Wilhelm Heidkamp*, and accompanied by the *Arnim* and *Thiele*, he pressed on to Narvik. Here, the town was defended by two ancient 4,000-ton Norwegian ironclads: the flagship *Norge* and the *Eidsvold*. Each, dating from 1900, was armed with two 8.2-inch and six 5.9-inch obsolete guns.

Due to the bad weather and poor visibility, there was initially some uncertainty on the Norwegian side as to the nationality of the destroyers. To further complicate matters, literally minutes before the sighting of the destroyers as they approached Narvik the Norwegian Senior Naval Officer, Commodore Askin, had received instructions from his Government in Oslo that British forces were not to be opposed. He ordered the *Eidsvold* to meet and challenge the intruders. On sighting the three destroyers, Captain Willoch, commander of the *Eidsvold*, ordered a shot to be fired across the bows of the leading ship and ordered them to stop. The leading *Wilhelm Heidkamp* slowed and signalled that a boat was being sent across. The other two destroyers continued on to Narvik.

In the boat was Lieutenant-Commander Gerlach, one of Commodore Bonte's staff officers sent to parley. He told the *Eidsvold*'s captain that the German ships were there to help Norway against Allied occupation and that, as agreed by the Norwegian Government, he was to hand over the *Eidsvold* to the Germans. Captain Willoch declined, and replied that his orders were contrary to this and asked for time to consult his superior, Commodore Askin, on the *Norge*. Lieutenant-Commander Gerlach refused to allow time for this consultation and left the *Eidsvold*, still under the conditions of truce. As the German boat circled away from the Norwegian ship a red Very light was fired from it. Reportedly on the direct order of General Dietl, commander of the troops being landed at Narvik and the senior German officer present on board the *Wilhelm Heidkamp*, torpedoes were fired at the *Eidsvold*, although Commander Bonte was unhappy and questioned the order: "Musst das sein?" (do we have to do this?).[6]

The torpedoes, at virtual point-blank range against the stationary *Eidsvold*, caused her to sink in less than ninety seconds, taking with her one hundred and seventy four men. Meanwhile the other two destroyers, guided by signal lamps from the German 'Trojan' merchant ships into the harbour, started to land the troops they were carrying. The *Norge*, at anchor inside the harbour, opened fire, awkwardly and inaccurately as her inexperienced crew tried to operate her ancient guns, on the *Bernd von Arnim*. The German destroyer returned fire with her more accurate and rapid-firing 5-inch guns and fired two torpedoes into the *Norge*. The Norwegian flagship turned on her side and sank within two minutes, taking with her over one hundred of her crew.* In contrast to the devotion to duty of the officers and men of the *Einsvold* and *Norge*, the garrison at Narvik, on the orders of Colonel Sundlo, a follower of Vidkun Quisling, did not resist and surrendered to the Germans, although his orders were not universally accepted by the Norwegian troops. An eye-witness in Narvik later wrote:

> ...I ran to the City Hall. A swastika flew there also. In the City Council room I found the caretaker. He said he had witnessed a strange performance in the Market Place a few minutes earlier. Hundreds of Germans had marched up from the piers and had hustled the Norwegian soldiers together in the Market Place. Then Colonel Sundlo and the Norwegian forces had marched over to the school on the other side of the town. But some of the Norwegian officers and half of the soldiers had fallen out of the lines before they reached the bridge and had gone up the street leading towards the Railway Station. He had heard rifle shots from that direction. It appeared that Sundlo had surrendered his men and had ordered them to their quarters. Obviously some of them had refused to obey the order and had bolted.[8]

By 0500 on 9 April, one hour after the expiry of the German ultimatum to the Norwegian Government, the German forces had control of Narvik. It was a similar story elsewhere. Thus by the morning of 9 April the Germans had landed and had occupied, or were in a position to do so, Narvik, Trondheim, Stavanger, Bergen, Kristiansand and Oslo. The surprise of the strikes had bewildered and overwhelmed the Norwegian

---

* Commodore Askim went down with the ship but was rescued, unconscious, from the water. He escaped from Norway when the Allies withdrew in June 1940, and became the Naval Attaché to the USA of the Norwegian Government in Exile in London. On the night of 8/9 May 1945, as a Naval Member of the Allied Supreme Commission, he was deputed, as representative of General Eisenhower, to hand to the German General Bohme at Lillehammer the written orders for the surrender of all German naval units in Norway.

Government and its people. In a single swoop, with simultaneous strikes, the Germans had secured all the strategically-placed Norwegian ports and towns. They were, *de facto*, in control of Norway. While the Allies had dabbled in diplomacy, doubted and delayed, the Germans had taken Norway with a Teutonic blend of dash, daring and duplicity.

Meanwhile, in the days immediately preceding Germany's sudden strike, the Allies were methodically going ahead with their own limited mine-laying operation and the projected 'R4' plans for the occupation of the ports of Bergen, Stavanger, Trondheim and Narvik. Then on 7 April came the rude awakening for the Allied War Cabinet and the realisation that Germany had struck first. Allied air reconnaissance reports started to come in which indicated that the German Navy was at sea in some force. The reports were sketchy and contradictory. They were belatedly communicated; and their significance, and that of other diplomatic intelligence, was perhaps greeted with scepticism in the early hours of 7 April. Valuable hours in which to react to the German offensive were lost. The first direct warning came as early as 0800 on 7 April, when a Coastal Command Hudson aircraft, on patrol over the Skagerrak, sighted a large German warship accompanied by at least six smaller warships steaming in a northerly direction. This information was not received by Admiral Sir Charles Forbes, Commander-in-Chief of the Home Fleet at Scapa Flow, until 1150.

Further aircraft sightings of German ship movements, generally taking place in a northerly direction, continued to come in during the late morning and early afternoon. The initial Admiralty interpretation of German intentions was that a mass break-out of surface raiders into the Atlantic was being attempted. Then, at 1420, the Admiralty sent Admiral Forbes what turned out to be a misguided and misleading message:

> Recent reports suggest a German expedition is being prepared. Hitler is reported from Copenhagen to have ordered unostentatious movement of one division in ten ships by night to land at Narvik, with simultaneous occupation of Jutland (Denmark). Sweden to be left alone. Moderates said to be opposing the plan. Date given for arrival at Narvik was 8 April.
>
> All these reports are of doubtful value and may well be only a further move in the war of nerves.[11]

Doubtful value or otherwise, the Copenhagen reports turned out to be substantially correct.* Still uncertain of the extent of the threat posed by

---

* The Commander-in-Chief subsequently remarked that in the light of later events "it was unfortunate that the last paragraph was included."[11]

the reported German sea movements, Admiral Forbes took the precaution of ordering all his available ships to go to one hour's notice to raise steam. Then at 1727 came a further message from the Admiralty to the effect that an early afternoon bombing raid on a German force* consisting of *Gneisenau, Scharnhorst, Admiral Hipper* and at least twelve destroyers, by RAF light bombers, had been unsuccessful. It was the first real confirmation that Admiral Forbes had received that heavy German units were at sea in strength. He immediately ordered to sea all his available Home Fleet ships. Among them he had nearly sixty destroyers plus French destroyers newly arrived at Scapa Flow.

At 2015, 7 April, the battleships *Rodney* and *Valiant*; battle-cruiser *Repulse*; cruisers *Sheffield, Penelope* and the French cruiser *Emile Bertin*; and the ten destroyers *Codrington, Griffin, Jupiter, Electra, Escapade, Brazen, Bedouin, Punjabi, Eskimo* and *Kimberley* set sail.[11] They left at high speed for the north-east. One hour later the cruisers *Galatea* and *Arethusa* and the eleven destroyers *Afridi, Gurkha, Sikh, Mohawk, Zulu, Cossack, Kashmir, Kelvin,* ORP *Grom*, ORP *Blyskawica* and ORP *Burza*, all under Vice-Admiral Sir G.F. Edward Collin, left Rosyth to take up position some eighty-five miles off Stavanger. They arrived there at 1700 on 8 April, and commenced to sweep northwards.

They were already too late. At about the time that the Home Fleet left its bases at Scapa Flow and Rosyth, *Scharnhorst, Gneisenau* and the ten destroyers of Group One with their 2,000 troops were some 200 miles to the east, off Stavanger and heading for Narvik. Already at sea, covering the four destroyers laying the agreed minefield, were the battle-cruiser *Renown*, the cruiser *Birmingham* and fourteen destroyers under the command of Vice-Admiral Whitworth. It was one of those destroyers, *Glowworm*, that was to make the first, fatal contact with the enemy warships the next morning, 8 April. The signals from the doomed *Glowworm* pinpointed the position of the main German force. They also showed that the bulk of the Home Fleet was out of position for preventing the German invasion of Norway, deployed as they were to intercept an anticipated German breakout into the Atlantic. Some three hours after *Glowworm*'s signal the Germans' real intention, the invasion of Norway, became abundantly clear. At 1145 the Polish submarine *Orzel*, on patrol in the Skagerrak, intercepted the German SS *Rio de Janeiro*, registered by Deutscher Lloyd as a passenger vessel out of Hamburg, bound for Bergen. She was just outside territorial waters and, when challenged by the *Orzel*, declined to stop. The submarine, having unsuccessfully tried to stop and inspect the 9,800 ton steamer, ordered the crew to take to their boats and torpedoed and sank the ship. Among the floating debris of the sunken ship the crew of the

* This naval force was the combined German Groups One and Two, heading for Narvik and Trondheim.

Orzel observed numerous floating bodies in German army uniforms.[13] Following the sinking, a Norwegian destroyer and local fishing boats rescued hundreds of German soldiers in uniform, who stated that they were on their way to Bergen to protect it against the Allies.[11] The sunken ship was only one of the armada of German vessels in the process of sailing into Norwegian ports and occupying them without any declaration of war. This information, although vital to the C-in-C Home Fleet, was not passed to him by the Admiralty until 2255 on 8 April.

The realisation that the Germans were about to take over Norway and that there was now, at this eleventh hour, very little that could be done about it, threw the Allied War Cabinet and its planners into total disarray. No-one seemed to have a clear view over the next few days of the overall situation, or of how the German invasion might be countered. Ad hoc decisions were made, often without consulting or adequately informing each other, by the Admiralty and War Office. Commanders-in-Chief were bypassed or told belatedly of decisions. The Admiralty, abandoning now their "break-out" predictions, decided to concentrate the naval effort upon the parts of Norway which appeared to them to have most strategic importance. Driven on by Winston Churchill and Admiral Sir Dudley Pound, the Admiralty increasingly interfered with the tactical deployment and operation of the ships at sea. General Sir Ian Jacob, Military Assistant Secretary to the War Cabinet 1939–1946, was later to write of this time: "It is always difficult to disentangle Winston and Pound when the former was the First Sea Lord."[2]

At 1045 on the morning of 8 April, with the German invasion now apparent, the Admiralty cancelled the mine-laying operation and ordered the eight destroyers taking part to join Admiral Whitworth's force. This decision left the Vestfiord without any British ships in the vicinity, at a time when their continued presence could have reported and interfered with the German destroyers' entry into that fiord some eighteen hours later. Then, early in the afternoon, Plan R4 was cancelled. At Rosyth the four cruisers of the First Cruiser Squadron, *Devonshire, Berwick, York* and *Glasgow,* under Vice-Admiral John Cunningham, had troops on board waiting orders to sail for Stavanger and Bergen as part of Plan R4. The troops and their equipment were unceremoniously dumped on the quayside and the four cruisers left at 1400 and headed north. In the Clyde the cruiser *Aurora* and other ships were awaiting orders to sail for Norway, again as part of Plan R4; when the plan was cancelled the ships were ordered to Scapa Flow. It was a time of utter confusion. On board *Aurora* was a recalled Admiral, elderly hero-veteran of the First World War, Admiral Lord Mountevans, who had been put in command of this particular task force with no clear role or mandate:

> …I was not at all surprised when I was summoned to the Admiralty by the then First Lord, Mr Winston Churchill, and made use of on

1 The Polish destroyer ORP *Grom* undergoing sea trials in the Solent in 1937.

2 Lieutenant Commander G.B. Roope, VC, Captain of the destroyer HMS *Glowworm*. (IWM A29585)

3 Captain B.A.W. Warburton-Lee, VC, Captain of the destroyer HMS *Hardy*. (IWM HU809)

4 The German destroyer *Friedrich Ihn* which took part in the laying of the magnetic minefield in the Thames Estuary on the night of 6–7 January 1940 which resulted in the loss of HMS *Granville*. (IWM HU3271)

5 The German prison ship *Altmark* in Josingford, Norway. (IWM HU45272)

6 Wrecks of merchant ships in Narvik harbour following the First Battle of Narvik. (IWM A25A)

7 The Tribal class destroyer HMS *Eskimo*, bows and 'A' gun destroyed by a torpedo during the Second Battle of Narvik. (IWM A25A)

8 The German destroyer *Georg Thiele* beached and on fire in Rombaksfiord following the Second Battle of Narvik. (IWM A24)

9 HMS *Kelly*, barely afloat, towed back to Hebburn-on-Tyne after being torpedoed by a German E-boat. (IWM A1960)

11 The crew of 'X' gun, HMS *Ardent*. A/B Hooke is top left in the photograph. (IWM Doc 740)

Above: **12** HMS *Acasta*, lost with her sister ship HMS *Ardent* while trying to defend the aircraft carrier HMS *Glorious*. (IWM Q104287)

Opposite: **10** Able Seaman R. Hooke, the sole survivor of the destroyer HMS *Ardent*. (IWM Doc 741)

13 HMS *Venomous*, the V and W class destroyer launched in 1919. At Dunkirk, over a four day period, *Venomous* evacuated 4,410 men. (IWM 56091)

14 The French destroyer *Bourrasque* loaded with evacuated troops, sinking after striking a mine off Dunkirk. (IWM HU2280)

15 Double-banked destroyers delivering evacuated Dunkirk troops at a British port. (IWM H1645)

16 HMS *Vivacious*, another V and W class destroyer, evacuating troops from the Mole at Dunkirk. The sunken trawler outside the destroyer had received a direct hit. (IWM HU1149)

17 Royal Navy officer who had been at sea since leaving school aboard an ex-American destroyer on counter U-Boat operations in the Atlantic Ocean. This photograph was of a kind used for propaganda purposes by Washington as part of the psychological preparation of the US for entry into the War. (LOC)

18 British seamen aboard the destroyer *Vanoc* preparing to load a torpedo tube. Although destroyers did not carry many, torpedoes were a vital weapon when engaging German U-boats. (LOC)

19 French destroyers capsized and sunk next to burning cruisers. Taken by the Royal Air Force on November 28 1942, the day after the French scuttled and fired their fleet in Toulons harbour. The so-called 'Phoney War', with all its sacrifices, was a fading memory. But the British Navy had suffered no such terrible fate. (LOC)

account of my knowledge* of Norway ...Soon after the German expeditionary force sailed from Stettin I found myself on board HMS *Aurora* in the Clyde, where we were joined by the battleship Warspite with an escort of four destroyers, and also two Tribal class destroyers and the famous Sixth Flotilla destroyer *Foxhound*. Hoping that I might have a chance of going into Narvic, Trondheim, or other port as directed by the Admiralty, I drew up plans for attack, visited the assembled ships and talked to their officers and men, explaining my intentions and imparting what I could fairly tell them regarding the situation. To my great disappointment I was ordered to haul down my flag on Monday 8th April, but I was allowed to proceed to sea and towards the Norwegian coast in HMS *Aurora*. We intercepted wireless messages from which we learned that the Germans had in fact invaded Norway under a well thought out pre-arranged plan. In my opinion the golden days for attacking the Germans at Narvik, Trondheim, Bergen and Stavanger were Tuesday the 9th April and at dawn on Wednesday 10th, when, alas, the Home Fleet was patrolling to the north-west of the Shetlands.[14]

Alas indeed: the Home Fleet, led to believe that the German naval activity had as its objective a break-out of heavy units into the Atlantic to harass Allied convoys, was wrongly positioned to prevent the German landings. Admiral Sir Charles Forbes, the Home Fleet Commander-in-Chief, was thereafter cruelly nicknamed "Wrong-way Charlie", and unfairly blamed. His then Fleet Gunnery Officer, in his memoirs, stoutly rebutted this unjust slur on his commander's reputation:

The failure of the Home Fleet to intercept enemy surface vessels gave rise to the derogatory reference to the Commander-in-Chief as "Wrong-way Charlie". This reflected frustration but, *inter alia*, showed the ignorance of the poor quality of the intelligence and the confusion in the orders received from the Admiralty, particularly during the Norwegian Campaign 1940. The use of this tag, or its condonation, was both unjust and disloyal. It was only in post-war years that it became known that the Germans had broken our Naval General Cypher and were, therefore, aware of our many dispositions and intentions during the period of Sir Charles' command.[15]

---

* Admiral Lord Mountevans had been on four polar expeditions to the Antarctic prior to the First World War and had connections, through his wife, with the Norwegian monarchy. He had served as a dashing First World War captain of the destroyer HMS *Broke* and was affectionately known thereafter as 'Evans of the *Broke*'.

Thus by the morning of 9 April, with the Germans in control of the key ports, towns and airfields of Norway, the Allies had been totally outmanoeuvred. With their armies and air forces impotent it was up to their navies to try to dislodge the Germans or to make their continued occupation of Norway untenable. Destroyers were again to play arguably the major, and unquestionably the most gallant, role in the battles to remove the Germans from Norway.

NOTES TO SOURCES

1. Gilbert, M. *The Churchill War Papers, Vol. 1: At the Admiralty Sept 1939 - May 1940* (Heinemann: London, 1993).
2   Roskill, Captain. S.W. *Churchill and the Admirals* (Collins: London, 1977).
3   Derry, T.K. *The Campaign in Norway* (HMSO: London, 1952).
4   Macintyre, Captain D. *Narvik* (Evans Bros: London, 1959).
5   Colville, Sir John. *The Fringes of Power: Downing Street Diaries 1939– 1955* (Hodder and Stoughton: London, 1985).
6   Brookes, E. *Prologue to War: The Navy's part in the Norwegian Campaign* (Jarrolds Publishers: London, 1966).
7   Doenitz, Grand Admiral K. *Memoirs: Ten Years and Twenty Days* (Lionel Leventhal: London, 1990).
8   Broch, T. *The Mountains Wait* (Michael Joseph: London, 1943).
9   Smith, P.C. *Hit Hard, Hit First: HMS* Renown *1916–1948* (William Kimber: London, 1979).
10 Brown, M., and Meehan, P. *Scapa Flow* (Penguin: London, 1968).
11 Brown, D. (Ed). *Naval Operations of the Campaign in Norway: April–June 1940* (Frank Cass: London, 2000).
12 Bekker, C. *Hitler's Naval War* Trans Ziegler, F. (Macdonald: London, 1974).
13 Peszke, M.A. *Poland's Navy, 1918–1945* (Hippocrene Books: New York, 1999).
14 Mountevans, Admiral Lord. *Adventurous Life* (Hutchinson & Co: London, 1946).
15 Searle, Rear Admiral M. W. 'Reminiscences of the Fleet Gunnery Office, Home Fleet' File SRLE. Churchill Archives Centre, Churchill College, Cambridge.

VIII

The First and Second Battles of Narvik

At 1915 on 8 April 1940 Vice-Admiral W.J. Whitworth in the battle-cruiser *Renown*, accompanied by nine destroyers, had received the signal: "Most immediate. The force under your orders is to concentrate on preventing any German force proceeding to Norway."[1]

The signal was too late and *Renown* and her destroyers were too far away. Ten German destroyers were already being detached at the mouth of the Vestfiord, en route for Narvik, less than two hours after the signal was sent. The German battle-cruisers *Gneisenau* and *Scharnhorst*, having discharged their escort responsibilities for the ten destroyers, then continued on a north-westerly course to take up a patrolling position in the Arctic and in the hope of drawing off British heavy units from the scenes of the German landings in Norway. Admiral Whitworth, because of the extreme weather conditions, was unable to proceed immediately to Narvik from his position off the Lofoten Islands. From his diary:

> From midnight onwards the weather improved, but knowing that the destroyers would be widely strung out on account of the weather I decided to wait until the first sight of dawn and sufficient light to make the turn to the south-eastward without losing touch with them…the squadron turned at 0230, the 9th, snow squalls making the visibility variable.[1]

One hour later the British Force met up with *Gneisenau* and *Scharnhorst* travelling in a roughly reciprocal direction, and a running battle ensued. The British force, travelling at 20 knots, hauled round onto a parallel course to the German ships and opened fire at 0405 at 18,600 yards range. A fierce exchange of gunfire then took place over the next ten or so minutes, with the British destroyers joining in with their 4.7-inch guns but to little effect at the extreme ranges of firing. *Renown* was hit twice but without serious damage. The *Gneisenau* was hit in the foretop at 0417 at a range of 14,600 yards, which destroyed her main fire control equipment and temporarily

115

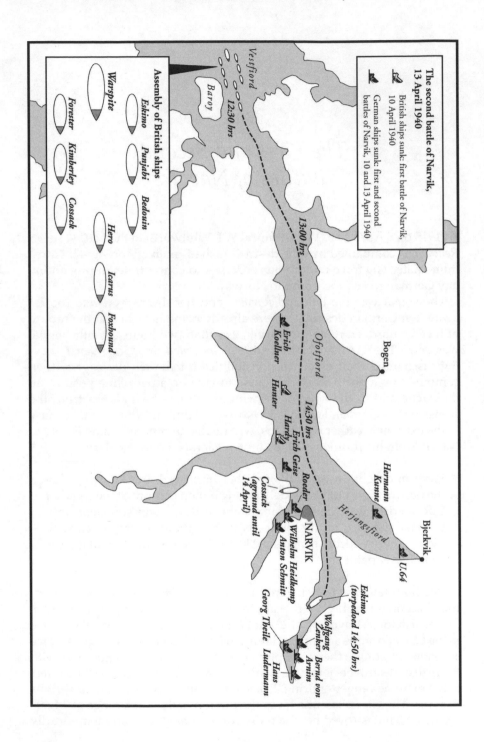

The second battle of Narvik, 13 April 1940

British ships sunk: first battle of Narvik, 10 April 1940

German ships sunk: first and second battles of Narvik, 10 and 13 April 1940

Assembly of British ships

Eskimo   Punjabi   Bedouin

Warspite

Forester   Kimberley   Cossack

Hero   Icarus   Foxhound

Vestfjord

Baroy

12.30 hrs

13.00 hrs

Bogen

Erich Koellner

Ofotfjord

14.30 hrs

Hunter

Hardy

Erich Geise

Cossack (aground until 14 April)

Roeder

NARVIK

Wilhelm Heidkamp
Anton Schmitt

Hermann Künne

Herjangsfjord

Bjerkvik

U.64

Eskimo (torpedoed 14.50 hrs)

Wolfgang Zenker
Bernd von Arnim

Georg Thiele

Hans Lüdemann

put her main armament out of action. The high-speed chase continued for some ninety minutes but the British destroyers were gradually forced by the rough seas to drop back out of the fray. Meanwhile the battle-cruisers ploughed on, and although *Renown* reached a speed of some 28 knots the heavy head-on seas meant that above 24 knots the two foremost turrets of the chasing British battle-cruiser became submerged by the high seas and unable to fire. The rear turrets of the retreating German battle-cruisers were not so handicapped. At 0434 the *Gneisenau* received two further hits, one of which put out of action her 'A' turret, but gradually the two German battle-cruisers drew away out of sight in the snow and rain squalls and *Renown* was forced to abandon the chase.

Renown and her destroyers now turned their attention to the given task of preventing the occupation of Narvik by German naval forces. Vice-Admiral Whitworth ordered his destroyers, left astern in the chase after *Gneisenau* and *Scharnhorst*, to reform and patrol the mouth of the Vestfiord. He arranged a rendezvous of all his forces in the area for 1800 on 9 April at 67°N, 10°30'E. The Admiralty and the Commander-in-Chief Home Fleet, Admiral Sir Charles Forbes, now took a hand in the dispositions. At 0952 Sir Charles Forbes ordered Captain Warburton Lee in *Hardy*, and senior officer of the destroyers accompanying *Renown*, to "Send some destroyers up to Narvik to make certain that no enemy troops land."[1]

The Commander-in-Chief was obviously unaware that Narvik was already occupied by German troops. Then at 1200 the Admiralty in London sent a signal directly to Captain Warburton-Lee:

Press reports state one German ship has arrived Narvik and landed a small force. Proceed Narvik and sink or capture enemy ship. It is at your discretion to land forces if you think you can recapture Narvik from number of enemy present. Try to get possession of battery if not already in enemy hands: details of battery to follow.[1]

With only this flimsy, and indeed totally erroneous, intelligence to go on Captain Warburton-Lee decided upon the make-up of his force to penetrate into Narvik. Previous orders had called for a patrol to be maintained in the vicinity of the minefield at the mouth of the Vestfiord, and Vice Admiral Whitworth would need some destroyers to screen *Renown* and *Repulse* when they rendezvoused later that day. Captain Warburton-Lee therefore decided to leave behind under Captain Bickford the *Esk*, *Icarus* and *Ivanhoe* (mine-layers with no torpedoes and mounting only two guns) and the *Greyhound*. Another destroyer, the *Impulsive*, had been forced to return home with a damaged paravane boom that morning.[1] For the intrusions into Narvik Captain Warburton-Lee had the *Hardy*, the *Hotspur* (Commander H.F.H. Layman), *Havock* (Lieutenant Commander R.E. Courage) and the *Hunter* (Lieutenant Commander L. de Villiers).

117

There was an unexpected bonus when *Hostile* (Commander J.P. Wright), unexpectedly released from escort duties with the cruiser *Birmingham*, turned up in time to join the force as it set off up the Vestfiord.

At 1600 Captain Warburton-Lee stopped off the pilot station at Tranoy to try to gather more precise intelligence of recent enemy movements. Unwelcome news came that Germans held the town of Narvik in some strength. Captain Warburton-Lee was informed that six large warships – in actual fact, ten German destroyers – had gone up the fiord, together with a a submarine, and in addition the entrance to the Olotfiord was probably mined. The Norwegian pilots estimated that the British would need twice as many ships to deal with the situation. This information was signalled at 1751 to the Admiralty by Warburton-Lee, who added "Intend attacking at dawn."[2]

According to the naval historian S.W. Roskill,[3] naval convention is that when a junior officer has decided upon a certain course of action and wishes to inform his senior officer of his decision, but is not specifically seeking the approval of the latter, then the junior officer will preface his message with the word 'Intend'. A message so worded not only does not seek the senior officer's approval but makes clear no reply is expected unless the senior officer disapproves.

Captain Warburton-Lee's stated intention of attacking at dawn had a two-fold purpose: it would then be high water in the fiord, which would better allow his ships to pass over tethered mines should they blunder into a minefield in their passage up Vestfiord; and dawn was the classic time for a surprise attack, in half light against an enemy possibly not fully awake or at full manning of defensive positions. The signalled intention also reached his immediate superior, Vice-Admiral Whitworth on *Renown*. He was later to say that he contemplated reinforcing Warburton-Lee's five destroyers with the cruiser *Penelope* and Captain J.G. Bickford's four destroyers, but this would have left *Renown* and *Repulse* without any screening destroyers and at a greater risk of the U-boats known to have accompanied the German invasion forces. It would also have meant, in the prevailing bad weather, seriously delaying Warburton-Lee's planned attack, giving the still-unknown quantity of the German force in Narvik more time to prepare their defences. Vice-Admiral Whitworth decided to leave things as they stood and not interfere since, he reasoned, the plan "had been made with the forces ordered by the Admiralty...the addition of other forces, involving delay and revision of the plan, was liable to cause confusion."[1]*

Having signalled his intention, Captain Warburton-Lee took his ships

---

* In retrospect Admiral Whitworth reproached himself bitterly on this account, writing that his decision arose from: "...the Admiralty's intolerable action in communicating direct to ships under my command and entirely ignoring my presence."[1]

back down the fiord in order to kill some time so that they would not arrive in Narvik before dawn. During this turn to seaward, on a south-westerly course, their passage was spotted by *U-51* at 2100. This was reported to Narvik, which must have given some relief and breathing space to the ten German destroyers there, hurriedly preparing to depart again for home before they were caught and trapped in the fiord. The British force turned back again at 2330 so as to arrive at Narvik at dawn.

At 2100 the Admiralty had replied to Captain Warburton-Lee's intention signal, ordering him to patrol during the night in the entrance to Ofotfiord in case the enemy should attempt to leave Narvik by turning north through the Tjelsundet channel and thus escape to the northward. Fortunately, Warburton-Lee did not receive, or chose to ignore, the instruction. If he had done so it is now known that he would have run into the German destroyers from their Narvik force deployed there on patrol, and all advantage of surprise would have been lost. Whether or not he received the message, it had ended with "Attack at dawn; all good luck."[1][2] Captain Warburton-Lee's plan had been approved by the Admiralty; he and the men of his five destroyers were on their own.

Then, as more intelligence information came in, and the scale and success of the German invasion became more apparent, the Admiralty started to have doubts and second thoughts. At 0136 on 10 April, with the dawn attack scheduled for 0400, the Admiralty dropped any idea of directing tactical operations from London and sent Captain Warburton-Lee a signal:

Norwegian coastal defence ships *Eidsvold* and *Norge* may be in German hands; you alone can judge whether, in the circumstances, attack should be made. We shall support whatever decision you take.[1]

The decision had been dumped on the Flotilla Captain. It put Captain Warburton-Lee in an invidious position: his information was sketchy, incomplete and mostly proving to be wrong. He would be damned if he did and damned if he didn't. He decided to press on with the planned attack. Captain Warburton-Lee had very little concrete information to go on. He had received Admiralty signals warning of a three-gun battery on a hill to the west of Narvik and the possibility of other German manned batteries facing across the narrows of the Ofotfiord. The Norwegians at the Tranoy pilot station had told him that he faced at least six larger German warships plus a U-boat, when in fact he faced ten plus additional U-boats. He was told he might meet minefields and that he might be opposed by German crews manning the *Norge* and *Eisvold*, when in fact these two ancient ironclads had already been sunk.

His plan was to ignore the dangers and attack any German ships he found, whatever their number and size. *Hardy*, *Hunter* and *Havock* would attack the ships inside Narvik harbour. *Hotspur* and *Hostile* would stay outside to engage any shore batteries that fired upon the force, to keep watch for any other German ships, to be ready to cover the withdrawal of the British force with smokescreen and gunfire, and to take any disabled ships in tow. If the operation was sufficiently successful to warrant it, the *Hardy's* first lieutenant would lead a landing party to carry out demolitions on the iron ore quay. The destroyers made their way cautiously up the Ofotfiord in continuous snowstorms, with visibility at time reduced to two cables (approximately 400 yards). In the bad visibility, stern lights had to be used to keep ahead formation, but the bad visibility did help the British ships escape detection by German U-boats stationed in the outer Ofotfiord.

What Captain Warburton-Lee did not know were the depositions of the German ships opposing him. The German destroyers had disembarked their troops during 9 April and by midnight on 9–10 April were distributed in and around Narvik harbour and the nearby side fiords and inlets of Ofotfiord. The *Zenker, Giese* and *Koeller* were lying in Herjangsfiord, off Elvegaard. The *Heidkamp, Schmitt, Ludemann* and *Kunne* were tied up alongside the pier in Narvik harbour, with two of them refuelling from the whale depot ship *Jan Wellem*, serving as a tanker to the German force. The non-arrival of a second tanker was seriously hampering the refuelling and delaying the turnaround of the German destroyers for their return to their home ports. The *Roeder*, which had been patrolling the western end of the Ofotfiord, joined the four destroyers in Narvik at dawn, anchoring at 0420 off the eastern shore. The remaining two German destroyers, *Thiele* and *Bernd von Arnim*, were anchored off Ballangen some fifteen miles to the west of Narvik.

Shortly after the *Roeder* had anchored, the British destroyers arrived at Narvik – to the complete surprise of the Germans there. The sky had cleared and visibility had increased to about one mile. At 0430 *Hardy* entered the harbour, closely followed by *Hunter* and *Havock*. The three destroyers made a circuit of the harbour, firing off torpedoes and engaging targets with their 4.7-inch guns. A torpedo from the *Hardy* caused a large explosion on board the *Heidkamp*, the German flotilla leader, which killed Commodore Bonte, the German Captain (D) in charge of the German force; his First Officer, Lieutenant Commander Heyke; and the flotilla's Chief Engineer, Commander Maywald.[5] The *Heidkamp* capsized twenty four hours later, with the loss of eighty-one men. The *Anton Schmitt* was hit by one torpedo in the forward engine room and by a second in the after boiler room. She broke in two and sank on the spot, with the loss of fifty men. The *Roeder* was hit five times by shells, which set her on fire and destroyed a boiler room and her fire control system, and so severely damaged her side as to render her unseaworthy. She also lost thirteen men. The two other destroyers in the harbour, the *Ludemann* and the *Kunne*, were both put temporarily out of action by shell fire. *Hotspur* was then sent in to fire her torpedoes, which sank two more German merchant ships. All five British destroyers fired their 4.7-inch guns from the harbour entrance against the ships anchored inside, and although the German warships had returned fire with their 5.1-inch guns, and German troops ashore had used small arms fire against the attackers, the British ships at this stage remained essentially undamaged.

Captain Warburton-Lee considered his position. It was thought that not more than two German destroyers still remained somewhere nearby in the fiords outside of Narvik harbour, and that four of the six destroyers reported by the pilot station at Tranoy to have entered the Vestifiord were inside the harbour. In fact it was five out of a total force of ten German destroyers. Unbeknown to the British, five German destroyers were unaccounted for in the fiords outside the harbour. The British flotilla went in for one more attack, this time keeping outside the harbour except for HMS *Hostile*, which fired in her torpedoes from the entrance. The British ships fired their 4.7-inch guns into the misty, smoke-filled harbour. Six German merchant ships had by now been sunk in the congested harbour, but the 11,776 ton *Jan Willem*, with her precious cargo of oil fuel, miraculously survived the bombardment.

Towards 0600, after an engagement lasting nearly two hours and having expended nearly all their torpedoes, the British flotilla prepared to withdraw. It was at this point that they sighted three German destroyers, the *Zenker*, *Giese* and *Loeller*, coming to join in the gunfight. These were the three ships that had been anchored to the northwest of Narvik at the head of the Herjangsfiord, and which had been alerted to the battle taking place in Narvik at 0515. A crew member of the *Hardy* later recounted:

When we had circled three parts of the way round, three German destroyers came out of the mouth of the fiord behind us, firing at a distance of about 3000 yards. First they shot wide, then they got on the target. Things got hot. The Germans got direct hits on us.[6]

Able Seaman Wilkinson, a gunner on one of the *Hardy*'s 4.7-inch guns, told how:

Our guns started to work and we gave them all we had got. After a while they scored several hits and one shell burst near my gun. Shrapnel was flying all around the gun shield; seven of us were manning the gun and three of my chums were killed.[7]

Then two more German destroyers, the *Thiele* and *Bernd von Arnim* which had been in Ballangenfiord and been bypassed unseen by the British flotilla on their way up Ofotfiord, appeared out of the mist, coming up the fiord and cutting off the British destroyers' line of withdrawal.

There then developed a fierce gunfight as the five British destroyers of

121

1340 tons displacement and each armed with four 4.7-inch guns,* tried in poor visibility to force their way past the five larger German destroyers, each of 2,200 to 2,400 tons displacement and armed with five 5.1-inch guns. Captain Warburton-Lee signalled "Keep on engaging the enemy."[8] It was his last signal to his flotilla. Commander H.F. Layman, captain of *Hotspur* and the senior surviving officer of the First Battle of Narvik, described how:

> Shortly afterwards a shell burst on Hardy's bridge and he (Captain Warburton-Lee) was mortally wounded. Everyone on *Hardy's* bridge and in the wheelhouse was either killed or wounded. The ship, not under control and on fire forward, was making at high speed for the shore of the fiord. The Captain's Secretary, Paymaster Lieutenant G.H. Stanning, was wounded, but struggled down from the bridge to find an empty wheelhouse. He took the wheel himself for a short time but, on relief by an Able Seaman, returned to the bridge. By this time the ship had practically lost steam and the Captain's Secretary directed her to be beached. The Torpedo Officer, Lieutenant G.R Heppel, thinking that bridge steering was out of action, had gone aft to connect tiller flat steering but, finding the bridge still controlling, had returned there in time to agree to the beaching of the ship. The action taken at a critical time by Paymaster Lieutenant Stanning may well have resulted in saving many lives...
>
> He showed great initiative in an unaccustomed role.[8]

On board the *Hardy*:

> Our steam pipe was burst by a shell and the main feed pipe as well. Soon the steering wouldn't work. We ran into shallow water and grounded on the rocks about 300 to 400 yards from the shore. It was then that we got our last order on the ship. It came from Captain Warburton-Lee and it was the last order he was ever to give. It was "Abandon ship. Every man for himself and good luck."
>
> We piled overboard as best we could and swam ashore. It was so cold that a moment after we got into the water there was no feeling in our hands or feet. We had 100 yards to swim and at least another 200 yards to wade before we got ashore. And all the time we were under fire. German shells were dropping around us. They had seen we were in trouble and they let us have it..
>
> Our torpedo officer, Lieutenant Heppel, was a real hero. He saved at least five men by swimming backwards and forwards between the ship and the shore, helping those who could not swim. Finally we got

---

* HMS *Hardy*, the flotilla leader, had a slightly larger displacement of 1,455 tons and was armed with five 4.7-inch guns.

ashore, about 170 of us. Seventeen of us had been killed in the fight and another two were missing.[6]

The *Hardy* and her crew were not alone in their trouble.

Shortly after *Hardy* had been hit, *Hunter* was seen to be on fire and her forward torpedo tubes were missing, indicating some explosion. She was seen to lose steam just ahead of *Hotspur* at the moment the latter's steering and all bridge communication were put out of action. While not under control *Hotspur* collided with the damaged *Hunter* and these two ships, locked together, drew all the enemy's fire. By means of verbal orders to engine room and tiller flat, given from X gun deck, Hotspur was able to extricate herself from this predicament but the combined effects of the collision and damage caused by the enemy caused *Hunter* to sink.[8]

Commander Layman's concise account does not tell the full drama of the disentanglement of the two crippled ships. Hardly had Commander Layman left the bridge to run to where he could give verbal orders from the super-structure where X gun was mounted, than another German shell exploded on *Hotspur*'s bridge, bursting against the pedestal of the gun director and killing everyone on the bridge and in the director tower. Reaching the 'X' gun platform deck, from where the two after 4.7-inch guns were being controlled and kept in action by the wounded Sub Lieutenant L.J. Tillie, Commander Layman was able to control *Hotspur*'s engines by verbal orders passed down the engine room hatch. He succeeded in disentangling the ship from the sinking *Hunter* by passing messages down to the tiller flat in the stern of his ship, and steered a wavering course down the fiord amidst heavy German gunfire. Commander Wright, captain of *Hostile*, later reported that the German destroyers were "zigzagging across Hotspur's rear, doing target practise at her at a range of about 8,000 yards, surrounding her with splashes."[1]

Hotspur was under fire from at least four enemy ships, and seeing her plight the remaining two British destroyers, *Hostile* and *Havock*, immediately turned back up the fiord to cover *Hotspur*'s retirement. *Hostile* and *Havock*, relatively undamaged, were retiring to the west after engaging the *Thiele* and *Arnim*, at point blank range, as the two German ships passed them on a reciprocal course to join their three companion destroyers from Herjangsfiord. The leading British destroyer, *Havock*, turned back. However, finding his forward guns temporarily out of action, Lieutenant Commander Courage turned westward again, screening *Hotspur* with smoke so that his two after guns could be brought to bear on the enemy while his forward guns were cleared. That done, he then turned again, following *Hostile* around, to go to *Hotspur*'s aid. By now the German destroyers were showing little inclination to carry on the fight. They were damaged, short of fuel, and needed to regroup with their fellow destroyers and merchant ships back in Narvik harbour. The *Thiele* had received several hits; her two forward guns were out of action, she was on fire and had a flooded magazine. The *Bernd von Arnim* had received five hits and had a boiler room out of action.

The firelight thus ended at 0630, with three of the original five British destroyers retiring westwards towards the open sea. Behind them they left *Hunter*, which had sunk in mid-fiord. Most of her crew had been killed or died of exposure in the freezing waters of the fiord. Some fifty of her crew were picked up by German or Norwegian ships, but ten of these died later. A number of the rescued survivors of the *Hunter* later managed to escape their captors during the confusion of the next few days and made their way to nearby neutral Sweden, from where they were eventually repatriated back to the United Kingdom. The other destroyer, *Hardy*:

> ...had been last seen aground and on fire with men clambering over the side. One gun was still firing and it seemed likely that the enemy would close and finish her off. In the event the enemy held off and 160 men got ashore.[8]

Once ashore, the survivors found themselves still in desperate straits:

> We were freezing cold. Most of the men had discarded clothing to swim ashore, and the remainder who had arrived with some clothes on had torn them off when they landed because they were so icy cold. Two hundred yards away there was a house. We ploughed our way through nearly six feet of snow to it and found that it had been evacuated when the battle started. But soon the woman of the house and her daughter came back and did all they could for us. There were eighty of us in that house and it only had five rooms.[6]

Their mortally wounded commanding officer, Captain Warburton-Lee, had been brought ashore on a stretcher strapped to a float by Lieutenant McCracken, but was found to be dead on reaching land.* The *Hardy's* Navigating Officer, Lieutenant Gordon-Smith, had a bad head wound and it was decided to leave him on board for the time being rather than risk subjecting him to the shock of being moved through the icy seas. Chief Stoker Stiles and the doctor, Surgeon-Lieutenant Waind, had both been badly wounded. They were got ashore together and the injured doctor, one arm shattered, stayed to tend the chief stoker on the beach while shelter was sought.[2] *

---

* Captain Warburton-Lee, posthumously awarded the Victoria Cross for his gallantry and leadership, is buried along with eleven other officers and men from the *Hardy* and the *Hunter* in Ballangen New Cemetery, Norway.[9]

Meanwhile, a Norwegian girl set off on skis to fetch a local doctor, who arrived and summoned help, ambulances and doctors from the nearest town of Ballangen. While awaiting their arrival, Lieutenant Heppel led a party back on board the beached *Hardy*.

> About an hour after landing, *Hardy's* Torpedo Officer made his way back on board and with a 9lb TNT charge from the detonator tank blew up the steel chests in the Captain's cabin. He was also able to rescue the Navigating Officer who had been too badly wounded to abandon ship. The action of Lieutenant G.R. Heppel in returning to the ship, which was still on fire forward, is most creditable.[8]

By mid-day all the wounded, except for three badly injured men and the ship's doctor, had been evacuated to Ballangen hospital. When, some time later, the ambulances had not returned, and fearing that the German troops from Narvik must soon arrive to take them prisoner, *Hardy's* First Lieutenant, Lieutenant-Commander Mansell, sent off the unwounded survivors to walk to Ballangen under Lieutenant Heppel. "Then came a report that the Germans were coming. We had no arms, and thought it best to get out so we started on a fifteen mile hike to Ballangen."[6] It was to be an arduous march for the already exhausted and ill-shod survivors:

> We walked twelve miles to the village of Ballangen where the Norwegians gave us a hot meal and we slept on the floor in the school-house. We stayed in the school-house for three days and the local people went out and got food for us although they themselves were short.[7]

Lieutenant-Commander Mansell and the rest of the officers remained with their wounded comrades. When a party of men was seen approaching it was first thought that it was a German patrol out searching for them, but it turned out to be a party of British Merchant Navy officers and seamen from the *North Cornwall*, a British merchant ship caught in Narvik harbour at the time of the German invasion. Escaping from their captors, they were trying to make their way westwards looking for Allied forces. They were directed on to Ballangen to join *Hardy's* crew.

By 1500 the promised ambulances had still not arrived and with the temperature dropping and the condition of the wounded men deteriorating, Lieutenant-Commander Mansell succeeded in procuring a horse and sledge to take the remnants of *Hardy's* crew to Ballangen. They arrived there at 2100, and for the time being the battle was over for *Hardy's* survivors.

---

* Chief Stoker Stiles died of his wounds during the afternoon and is buried with his Captain at Ballangen.

For the three retiring British destroyers, their battle was still not finished. Commander Layman in the badly damaged *Hotspur*, without the means of signalling and still having to control the ship from an aft position, had passed command of the remnants of the flotilla to Commander Wright in *Hostile*. As the three ships made their way down the fiord on the way to the sea they met the large German supply ship SS *Rauenfells*, bringing much-needed supplies and ammunition to their beleaguered compatriots at Narvik. In his report of the subsequent action the captain of *Havock*, Lieutenant-Commander R.E. Courage, wrote:

> On the way down the fiord a merchant ship was sighted which proved to be the German SS *Rauenfells*, and *Hostile* stopped her with a shot and ordered me to examine her. I fired another round into her bow and she stopped and her crew hurriedly abandoned ship. I stopped and picked them up while the ship slowly drifted on to the beach. I sent an armed boat over but she was burning fiercely and I was uncertain as to whether she had used her W/T to call her friends. I decided not to risk the loss of my party and ordered them to return. When the boat was hoisted I fired two H.E.s into her to hasten the fire and went ahead. The result was certainly startling as the German ship literally erupted and a column of flame and debris rose to over 3000 feet as testified by both the *Hostile and Hardy's* survivors to the west who saw it over the mountains that height. Fortunately no casualties were sustained in *Havock* but some damage to the hull was done. Judging from the fragments picked up she contained all the reserve ammunition and torpedoes for the destroyer flotilla, and also the Narvik minefield.[8]

The officer in charge of the boarding party sent over from *Havock*, Lieutenant J. Burfield, was rather closer to the action:

> On the way over we met the German crew pulling like mad and gesticulating in a highly excited manner. Of course we ignored them. We got on board and eyed the plumes of smoke coming out of her holds with some suspicion. As well we might; she carried ammunition. We pulled back to *Havock* a bloody sight faster than the Germans in time to get peppered with ironmongery as she went up.[10]

This finally ended the First Battle of Narvik. It had been hard fought, and both sides had suffered heavy losses. Of the five-ship British force, two destroyers had been lost and another badly damaged. German losses from their ten destroyer force were two ships sunk and five seriously damaged such that at least one of them, the *Roeder*, was no longer seaworthy. They had also lost five merchant supply ships anchored in Narvik harbour, as well as the ammunition supply ship SS *Rauenfells*. Both forces had lost their commanders (Captain Warburton-Lee and Commodore Bonte) but it was the German force, caught surprised by the naval assault and now bottled up at the head of Ofotfiord with the British Navy blocking their exit to the open sea, that was the ultimate loser.

> The success of the British coup was due to the German destroyer leader relying for protection against such a surprise attack on the U-boats stationed in the outer fiord. Two of them – the *U-51* under Lieutenant Knorr and the *U-25* under Lieutenant Schutze – did in fact attack the British force on both its entry and exit, only to discover that their torpedoes were duds. Now the fate of the remaining German destroyers at Narvik was sealed. Most had been damaged in battle, their ammunition was nearly exhausted and their fuel tanks almost empty. Only one tanker, the *Jan Wellem* had got through to Narvik and her contribution was far from adequate."[5]

While the German Navy might have been surprised, and was now in some disarray at Narvik following their setback there, their overall success in establishing several footholds in Norway had equally surprised and created some disarray at the War Office and the Admiralty in London. There, a series of hasty and ill-thought out decisions and senior staff appointments were being made, and then countermanded. Thus the elderly Lieutenant General Sir Adrian Carton de Wiart, who had first seen action in the Boer War in 1901, nearly forty years earlier, was one unlikely and surprised appointee:

> Shortly after the Germans made their first landing in Norway, we responded by gallant failure at Narvik. In the middle of the night there was a telephone message for me to report to the War Office. It dawned on me the reason might be Norway, especially as I had never been there and knew nothing about it.[11]

It *was* Norway, and he was to command a landing force. Naval appointments were made in equal haste. Rear Admiral Maund recalled in his memoirs:

> One morning early in April, the tenth I think, a telegram was received directing me to report to the Admiralty at once. On arrival at Plans Division I learnt that plans to land at Narvik were under discussion and I was to be available to advise, as a landing operation would have to be staged.* There were two meetings that afternoon and evening, and I learned that a meeting was to take place in the First Sea Lord's room to

discuss the operation. At a quarter past midnight I was called in. It was a sadly overworked and tired group of officers that sat around the table. I was told that I was to go as Chief of Staff to the Naval Commander for the attack on Narvik and that I was to join the Army Commander, who was on a ship at Scapa, at once. I asked for information about the enemies [sic] forces and what the plan for the operations was to be. I was told it was no time to talk of these things. My job was to get packed and catch an aeroplane that left Hendon for Scapa at 4.30am, or roughly in four hours time. It was nothing if not an imperial pier-head jump."[12]

The previous day, 10 April, Admiral of the Fleet Lord Cork and Orrery had been appointed Flag Officer, Narvik. His appointment, for what was a relatively junior post, was surprising in view of his age, rank and past experience. He was sixty-seven years old and had last served in command of the Home Fleet between 1933 and 1935.

Lord Cork was of course senior to Admiral Forbes, the C-in-C Home Fleet, but although his last sea-going command had ended five years earlier his personality had proved attractive to Churchill as an "offensive-minded" officer. But he received only the most perfunctory briefing from the First Lord and the First Sea Lord before he left London, was given no written instructions, and had not met the military commander Major General P.J. Mackesy until both arrived – in different cruisers – at Harstad. Thus were sown plentiful seeds for muddle and confusion.[4]

While the planning for the attack on Trondheim and the execution of the plan for the recapture of Narvik were proceeding, there was a further proposal for the retaking of the port of Bergen. As early as the morning of 9 April, when the full extent of the German invasion was becoming clearer, a signal had been sent to the C-in-C Home Fleet at 0820 telling him to prepare for attacks on Bergen and Trondheim. Admiral Forbes asked the Admiralty for an assessment of the German strength at Bergen, as he proposed to send in a force of two cruisers with a screen of destroyers.

The Admiral had considerable force at his disposal; so too had he considerable responsibility as to the effective disposition of these forces. He still needed to keep the Home Fleet together, as there was continuing uncertainty as to the intentions, and hence threat, posed by the German battle- and heavy cruisers at large in the North Sea. There was also some uncertainty as to the strength of the German naval force at Bergen and the

---

* Rear Admiral Maund was at the time on the staff of the Inter-Service Training and Development Centre (ISTDC) formed two years earlier to advise, among other things, on tactics and equipment for sea-borne landings.

status of the coastal batteries guarding the port. Given the uncertainty, the cruiser force was strengthened and the cruisers *Manchester, Southampton, Glasgow* and *Sheffield*, with a screen of seven destroyers from the 4th and 7th flotillas, were detached just before noon, under Vice-Admiral G. Layton. His orders were "to attack enemy forces reported in Bergen, these include one Kola class cruiser. Defences may be in enemy hands..."[1]

Vice-Admiral Layton's position was some eight miles to the south west of Bergen. With a gale blowing and heavy head-on seas the destroyers in his force could only maintain a speed of sixteen knots. Then at 1408 allied aircraft reported at least two German cruisers at Bergen. This information, together with the continuing uncertainty as to whether the coastal defences were now in German hands and the increasing delay in the British ships' passage due to the head winds and heavy seas, meant that the British force would not now reach Bergen before nightfall. This caused the Admiralty in London to call off the attack. Admiral Layton's force was ordered to rejoin the Fleet. It later transpired that the German ships in Bergen, from their Group 3 force, consisted of the light cruisers *Koln* and *Konigsberg*, each armed with nine 5.9-inch guns, and the old training cruiser *Bremse*, armed with four 5.1-inch guns. The shore batteries, although under German control, were not operational at that time. What was also not appreciated by the Admiralty at that time was the operational capability of the German air-force. The Luftwaffe, flying from captured Norwegian airfields, demonstrated this capability with continuous air attacks upon ships of the Home Fleet between 1430 and 1800 on 9 April. Initially these attacks were concentrated upon Vice-Admiral Layton's returning cruisers and destroyers, and the *Southampton* and *Glasgow* were damaged by near-misses. The Tribal class destroyer *Gurkha* was less fortunate. Captain Vian, in the flotilla leader *Afridi*, described the loss of the *Gurkha*:

> In the destroyer conditions were very unfavourable, since our forward guns were washing down and spray was breaking over the gun-directors above the bridge. Their fire, which should have helped protect the cruisers, the main focus of attack, was largely ineffective. One destroyer of the flotilla, *Gurka*, was commanded by a noted gunnery officer, Commander Sir Anthony Buzzard. After years of training, presented at last with live targets, he was excessively annoyed by his inability to hit them, and turned his ship away from wind and sea, to better the conditions for the control and fire of the guns.
>
> This involved leaving the cruiser screen, and I should have recalled him at once, but in those very early days of air attack upon ships, the tactics to be pursued by surface forces were still being worked out, and there was no set policy. Buzzard's manoeuvre cost him his ship and very nearly the lives of his crew. Since he was now steering 25 knots in one direction whilst the cruiser squadron and screen were

steaming at high speed in another, he was quickly over the horizon and so became a detached ship. As such he attracted immediate attention from the Luftwaffe who naturally preferred such a target rather than a compact force with many guns.

Gurkha was overwhelmed by the weight of the assault, hit, stopped, and left in a sinking condition. As night drew on, and the moment came nearer when the ship must inevitably go to the bottom, Buzzard's predicament became serious. The situation was saved, and only just in time, by his firing high explosive shells into the sky. One of the bursts was observed by the cruiser *Aurora* who closed from a distance to investigate, found *Gurkha*, and took off her crew.[14]

The timely rescue of *Gurkha*'s crew was observed by Admiral Mountevans who, having had his hasty appointment to command a force under the now-abandoned Allied 'R' plan for Norway cancelled, found himself in a supernumerary position, without official appointment other than as an observer, on the rescuing *Aurora*.

While near the Norwegian coast bomber after bomber attacked the *Aurora* and patrolling destroyers; one dive bomber hit *Gurkha* so badly that we heard she was on fire and sinking. However, *Aurora* closed her and managed to rescue 190 of her crew of 207. It was a good bit of work, and I wrote to the Commander-in-Chief Home Fleet and told him how well her Captain, L.H.A. Hamilton, had handled his ship in bad weather and saved nearly all of *Gurkha*'s crew.

On the 10 April 1940, after looking at the Norwegian mountains at dawn, I wrote in my diary "I went down to my cabin and literally cried at not being allowed to go in with the force of cruisers and destroyers then in sight and smash up the German forces, then disembarked at Trondheim, Bergen and Stavanger."* Late that day we returned to Scapa and landed the *Gurka*'s survivors, and at nine o'clock that night I left Scapa and flew to Inverness in a Henley aeroplane, and next day returned to London...[15]

Besides the loss of the *Gurkha* and the near-miss damage to the cruisers *Southampton* and *Glasgow*, the *Rodney* was also hit by a bomb but only slightly damaged.

The ferocity of the Luftwaffe attacks on the allied ships, the rapid build-up of German air forces in southern and central Norway, and the consolidation by the Germans of the coastal defences of the ports that they had occupied, was to cause a rethink of Allied strategy for Norway.

---

* At that very moment, dawn on 10 April, that was precisely what the destroyers under Captain Warburton-Lee were attempting to do at Narvik.

Admiral Forbes, the commander on the spot, was forced to conclude:

> The scale of air attack that could be mounted against our military forces on shore and our naval forces off the Norwegian coast was grievously underestimated when the operations were undertaken.[3]

Captain Vian, commanding in the *Alfridi* one of the destroyer flotillas in the heat of action, was to write in his memoirs:

> The air assault on the cruiser taskforce, plus the bomb hit, which did no damage on *Rodney*, convinced Admiral Forbes that, in the absence of fighter protection from land based aircraft, the Fleet could not operate as far south as Bergen. An attack on Bergen would need to be left to aircraft, while even further south our submarines would have the task of disrupting the enemy shipping routes across the Skagerrak and Kattegat.[14]

Their vulnerability to concerted dive-bomber attack was confirming that the defensive anti-aircraft armament of destroyers in particular was inadequate. However, not everyone back in Britain and at the Admiralty was yet convinced of the threat posed by the dive-bomber. Destroyer captains in particular received cold comfort from their commanding officer, the Rear-Admiral (D), with regard to air attacks at this stage of the war. This particular Rear-Admiral:

> ...formed the opinion that whether a ship was struck or was not struck by bombs was purely a matter of competence of individual commanding officers in taking avoiding action, and so informed them at a subsequent meeting in his flagship at Scapa Flow.[14]

The Rear-Admiral (D)'s opinion also found support at the Admiralty, as Captain Roskill confirms:

> ...the Norwegian campaign brought many new troubles, and heavy losses to the fleet; and it was there that the Navy learnt the hard lesson that, so long as adequate air cover was lacking, control of coastal waters by warships in support of military operations was impossible. Forbes himself became very critical about the ineffectiveness of his ships' A.A. gunnery, and it was in those months that the mistakes made by the Admiralty before the war in the design of such weapons and their control systems came home to roost. Rear Admiral Tom Phillips, the Deputy Chief of Naval Staff, who had no first-hand experience of the deadly effect of unopposed dive bombers on warships, insisted that all that was needed to deal with them effectively

was greater courage and resolution; and he took it very badly when told that such ideas were unjust to those officers who had the experience, and were in fact far from the truth.[4]

Commenting upon Admiral Phillips' strong views on the adequacy of ships' anti-aircraft protection, Captain J.H. Godfrey, at that time Director of Naval Intelligence at the Admiralty, was to write:

This view was not shared by the Navy, the Naval Staff or Admiral Chatsfield. Unfortunately Churchill was supported by Admiral Phillips (DCNS and later VCNS) who during the Norwegian Campaign clung tenaciously to the view that anti-aircraft fire without fighter cover would provide adequate protection to surface craft against air attack…I have never been able to understand why such a clever and able man as Phillips should have had this deeply rooted obsession, so evident to those who attended the VCNS morning meetings during the brief Norwegian campaign.[16]*

At Narvik, in the north of Norway, following the destroyer battle of 10 April, the Admiralty finally decided to send in a second, stronger naval force to finish off the cornered German warships there. The British were still unsure as to whether other warships than those encountered by Captain Warburton-Lee's force were in the Narvik fiords. There were also delays caused by changing Admiralty priorities; the non-availability of the cruiser *Penelope*, earmarked to lead the second attack when she struck a rock and was rendered unserviceable; and by the need to refuel and reposition ships due to take part in the second attack. Three valuable days were lost.

The Germans used the three days respite to try to get their destroyers into some sort of seaworthy condition. They had taken a terrible mauling from Captain Warburton-Lee's destroyers and were in a desperate state, cut off from supplies and immediate help. All that the German Navy could do was to try to send supplies by U-boat, and report to the German Supreme Command in Berlin: "Every available ship in the German Fleet has been committed. All available U-boats are in action. Three U-boats are in Vaagsfiord, five in Westfiord, three are proceeding to Narvik with ammunition and stores."[17]

The succour would not arrive in time to help the beleaguered ships. *Wilhelm Heidkamp* had lost eighty-one of her crew before capsizing and

---

* Admiral Phillips' strong views on this matter are considered by many to have been a factor in the subsequent loss of the new battleship *Prince of Wales* and the battle-cruiser *Repulse*, with Admiral Phillips in command, which had sailed from Singapore with only a light destroyer screen and without air cover, and were overwhelmed in massed attacks by Japanese bombers in December 1941.

sinking on 11 April. *Anton Schmitt* had also been lost, together with fifty of her crew. *Dieter von Roeder* had been hit five times by British shells; her side was so severely damaged as to render her unseaworthy, boiler room No. 2 was out of action and thirteen of her crew were dead. *Hans Ludemann* had her forward No. 1 gun out of action and a fire in one compartment; two of her crew had been killed. *Hermann Kunne* – besides receiving shell splinter damage – had been so badly shaken by the torpedo which had sunk *Anton Schmitt*, moored alongside her, that her main and auxiliary engines were out of action following the battle. She had also lost nine of her crew. *Georg Thiele* had received seven shell hits. Her fire control and No. 1 gun were disabled, her magazine was flooded, and there were fires both fore and aft of the ship. Thirteen of her crew were dead. The *Bernd von Arnim* had received five shell hits, putting boilers 2 and 3 out of action, and she was unseaworthy due to damage to her side and forecastle. Two of her crew had perished. Only the *Wolfgang Zenker*, *Erich Guise* and *Erich Koellner* had received neither damage nor crew losses, but had used up approximately 50% of their ammunition,[1] which could not be replaced following the sinking of the ammunition supply ship *Rauenfells* by the retiring British force.

The German force had not only suffered loss and damage to its ships: among its dead were its Commanding Officer, Commodore Bonte, and the flotilla's Chief Engineer, Commander Maywald. Their combined experience and knowledge was to be sorely missed over the three days of respite. The second in command, Captain Bey, took command of a force that was in a fatalistic mood. They knew that they were on their own, and Captain Bey faced a difficult task in trying to reorganise and revitalise his force. The crews of the German destroyers responded by working tirelessly to try to get as many ships as possible into a seaworthy condition for a desperate attempt at a breakout, carrying out what local repairs they could, and sharing out oil, fuel and ammunition.

Orders were received from the German High Command to put to sea on the night of 10–11 April with as many ships as were seaworthy. Only the *Guise* and *Zenker* were ready to go, and set off down the Ofotfiord and got as far as Tranoy. There the two destroyers sighted the cruiser *Penelope* and two patrolling British destroyers. They could have tried to fight their way out, but:

> … Bey's heart failed him, his nerve shaken by the disastrous events of the morning. He turned back to Narvik. At noon on the 11th, though more of his ships were by then fit for sea, he signalled to his Commander-in-Chief that a breakout that evening was impossible.[2]

The position of Captain Bey's trapped force took a further turn for the worse that night when two of his three undamaged ships, the *Zenker* and the *Koellner*, ran aground while manoeuvring in the narrow harbour confines. The *Zenker* damaged her propellers, restricting her to a top speed of 20 knots, but the *Koellner* fared far worse: she was so badly damaged as to have become unseaworthy. Meanwhile, *Penelope*, intended to play a leading role in the planned British attack but disabled when striking a rock, had to be towed back to Skjelfiord by the destroyer *Cossack*. Thus mistakes and misfortune were not the sole property of either side at Narvik.

The British finally settled upon mounting a morning attack on 13 April, and Admiral Whitworth transferred his flag from the battle-cruiser *Renown* to the battleship *Warspite*,[18] veteran of the Battle of Jutland nearly a quarter of a century before. At 0730 the *Warspite* (Captain V.A.C. Crutchley) rendezvoused with nine destroyers – the four 'Tribals' *Bedouin* (Commander J.A. McCoy), *Cossack* (Commander R. St. V. Sherbrooke), *Eskimo* (Commander St. J.A. Micklethwaite), *Punjabi* (Commander J.J. Lean), plus *Hero* (Commander H.W. Biggs), *Icarus* (Lieutenant-Commander C.D. Maud), *Kimberley* (Lieutenant-Commander R.G.K. Knowling), *Forester* (Lieutenant-Commander E.B. Tancock) and *Foxhound* (Lieutenant-Commander G.H. Peters) – just inside Westfiord, some one hundred miles from the town of Narvik. This force assembled for the second attack was capable of dealing emphatically with whatever German ships remained in Narvik and its environs.

At Narvik, Captain Bey had some inkling of the time and likely strength of the attack from U-boat reports and German intercepts of British signals, and deployed his trapped and battered destroyers in defensive positions in side inlets and bays, so that the British might conceivably be ambushed and forced to pay dearly before the German ships were overwhelmed and sunk. His more battle-worthy destroyers were to be stationed in the side fiords at Ballengen and Herjans. The crippled *Koellner* was to be placed in an ambush at Taarstadt.

The British force steadily made its way, in heavy snow showers, up the fiord. *Warspite* was screened by *Foxhound*, *Icarus* and *Hero*, with mine-clearing sweeps streaming out to clear a path through any minefields. On *Hero*, Able Seaman A.H. Turner wrote in his diary entry for that day:

> *Hero*, with *Icarus*, *Foxhound* and *Forester* swept the channel for mines starting about 0530. All hands closed up at action at 0515. Weather was very cold, slight mist, and snowing at intervals. The entrance to the fiord was very narrow with snow covered mountains on either side.[19]

Bedouin, *Punjabi* and *Eskimo* were off *Warspite*'s starboard bow and *Cossack*, *Kimberley* and *Forester* off the port bow. Battle ensigns were hoisted at 1050, and at 1100 the squadron passed Tranoy and entered Ofotfiord. The Second Battle of Narvik was about to commence.

Visibility was poor, with frequent snow showers, and the lookouts needed all their concentration if they were to avoid the expected torpedo attacks from lurking U-boats as well as from the damaged, but still highly dangerous, destroyers waiting for an opportunity to sink the ultimate prize of the battleship *Warspite*. The Admiralty and Admiral Whitworth were well aware of the threat posed by torpedo attacks in the narrow confines of the fiord. There was little room for manoeuvring or the taking of evasive action by the 31,000 ton battleship. Everyone was on full alert. At 1100, as they were entering Ofotfiord, the presence of a submarine had been reported by *Eskimo*:

> Depth charges were dropped to keep her down as we passed. The hills were scanned for land batteries but the only sign of life onshore was a group of Norwegians waving their caps and cheering.[19]

Telegraphist R.W. Lush on *Icarus* remembered: "Once or twice we saw torpedo tracks heading towards her (*Warspite*), but quick signalling from our bridge enabled her to avoid them."[20]

Admiral Whitworth did not rely entirely on reactive measures to combat torpedo attack. At 1152 he ordered off *Warspite*'s Swordfish floatplane, L9767 "Lorna", after briefing the observer, Lieutenant-Commander W.L.M. Brown, and the pilot, Petty Officer Airman F.C. Rice, to:

> Carry out a general reconnaissance for the fleet advancing up Ofotfiord, with particular reference to the presence of German warships inside fiords, the movement of German forces, and the positions of shore batteries. Bomb any suitable targets.[21]

At about midday the *Koellner*, on her way to take up her ambush position at Taastadt, and escorted by the *Kunne*, sighted the British force emerging through the narrows. On *Hero*: "1225. Enemy in sight, one destroyer coming towards us out of the mist...*Forester* and *Foxhound* opened fire and enemy destroyer withdrew."[19]

The *Kunne* exchanged fire at the limit of visibility with the greatly superior British force some six miles away, before signalling the alarm and retiring back towards Narvik. The *Koellner*, badly damaged by her grounding and unable to participate in any running battle, made for Djupvik Bay on the southern side of Ofotfiord. Here she hoped to remain undetected until the British ships steamed past, when she could launch a telling torpedo attack, at a range of 3,000–4,000 yards, before being overwhelmed. It would be an act of supreme gallantry and sacrifice by the German destroyer's crew. Her captain's hopes were dashed when she was spotted by *Warspite*'s Swordfish plane and her ambush position reported. Thus when the *Warspite*'s starboard bow destroyers rounded the point of

Djupvik Bay their torpedo tubes and 4.7-inch guns were already trained to starboard waiting to fire. The torpedoes of the British *Bedouin* and *Eskimo* and the German *Koellner* left their respective tubes almost together, and the guns of the three destroyers similarly opened up together. The *Koellner* and her gallant crew stood no chance. She only managed to fire one salvo from her guns before the combined salvoes from *Bedouin* and *Eskimo* crashed into her, to be followed by a torpedo which blew off her bow. The *Warspite* rounded the point and fired her 15-inch shells at point blank range into the stricken ship. The *Koellner* rolled over and sank. Her own torpedoes had missed.

Meanwhile *Warspite*'s Swordfish aircraft and crew were carrying out the second part of their orders: "bomb any suitable targets". They had flown on some twenty miles to Herjangsfiord where they spotted *U-64*:

> *U-64* was seen on the surface at the top of Herjangsfiord near Bjrevkvik. I selected two anti-submarine bombs and put the Swordfish in a dive and released the bombs at 200 feet. I couldn't see the bombs fall as we pulled out, but [Leading Airman Maurice] Pacey saw the starboard bomb fall close alongside and the port one hit just abaft the conning-tower: the U-boat was already sinking when I could see her again. She hit us in the tail with one shot. I think it was from her 37mm gun.[21]

U-64, the first German U-boat to be sunk from the air in the Second World War, was a brand new Atlantic class submarine and had had her sea trials curtailed to take part in the Norwegian operation. Thirty-six of her crew, who had put up a spirited resistance to the Swordfish attack, survived.

When the *Kunne* reported the oncoming British flotilla, the remaining six German destroyers were still in Narvik harbour, desperately trying to raise enough steam to sail. Captain Bey ordered the ships to leave harbour as soon as they had sufficient steaming power.

The immobilised *Roeder* was left behind as, one by one, the five destroyers departed. The *Hans Ludeman* sailed first, followed by the *Wolfgang Zenker* and *Bernt von Arnim*. The less prepared *Thiele* and *Giese* sailed sometime afterwards.

After leaving Narvik harbour the *Hans Ludeman*, *Wolfgang Zenker* and *Bernd von Arnim* met up with the returning *Kunne*, and the four destroyers turned and fired off torpedoes at the British ships. On *Hero*: "the mist lifted and more enemy destroyers were sighted and engaged by our destroyers...1255. Torpedo fired at us – missed."[19]

The ensuing brisk action was both intense and confused, with the German ships rapidly changing course to put off the British gunners and the British ships having to take violent evasive action to avoid torpedoes. With the ships of both sides firing independently, the shellfire was erratic and the fall of shot difficult to estimate. The captain of the *Hero*, Commander Biggs, summarised the exchanges:

From 1300 to 1355, *Hero* engaged three separate enemy destroyers with her two foremost guns at ranges between 10,000 and 15,000 yards. During this period it is estimated that only six hits were obtained on enemy ships. This was largely due to the large number of ships firing at a few enemy destroyers from practically the same bearing which made the picking out of (our) own fall extremely difficult. It was also due to the fact that only the two foremost guns could be brought to action, owing to the restriction imposed on *Hero* being guide of the fleet and also employed on sweeping duties.

Owing to her duties as guide to the fleet, which necessitated long periods on a steady course at a steady speed, *Hero* appeared to be practically continuously under fire, but the ship was not hit except for one small splinter.[1]

Punjabi was not so lucky and was forced to temporarily retire from the action. She was hit by a veritable shower of German 5.1-inch shells. The first, striking just below the bridge, had exploded between her decks, killing one man and wounding three others in the Transmitting Station controlling the guns. As two of the wounded were being attended to on the nearby messdeck, they were even more seriously wounded by the second shell which burst on the upper deck, near the locker containing ready-use cordite charges for the guns. Shell splinters killed two of the ammunition supply party and wounded others. The cordite charges were ignited, starting a fierce fire.

Simultaneously, *Punjabi* took a third shell forward, which shattered a bulkhead and started flooding compartments. A bursting shell started a fire between the funnels, and a further shell struck aft, plunging into a storeroom and, starting a blaze, threatened a magazine which had to be rapidly flooded. A further hit bursting on the starboard motorboat set it alight and, more seriously, fractured a steam pipe main, engulfing the engine-room in roaring clouds of steam. Shell splinters from the various hits, scything across the decks, killed two on the pom-pom gun and three on the torpedo-tubes, as well as injuring others.

Commander Lean, *Punjabi*'s captain, received the message from the engine-room that engines would have to be stopped in order to repair the burst steam-main – just as he had to deal with torpedoes heading towards his stricken ship. Captain Lean had just sufficient time, and steam, to evade the torpedoes before turning his attention to his ship's predicament. *Punjabi* had fires raging forward, amidships and aft. Compartments were flooding and fire-fighting equipment damaged so that the gun's crews had to be put on to helping to fight the fires with buckets of seawater.

The ship's guns were in any case largely ineffective and on local control because of the shell damage in the Transmitting Station.

The engineer officer arrived on the bridge to make his report, but was immediately badly wounded in the back and arms by a further shell bursting on the upper deck below. He was able to make his accident damage report on the fractured steam main before collapsing. This last shell also killed the stoker in charge of the party fighting the fire amidships and wounded others in the group. *Punjabi* had a lot of casualties and, to complicate matters further, one of her casualty clearing stations had also been put out of action:

> ...at 1400 HMS *Punjabi* was in close action with the enemy for some fifteen minutes. The ship sustained much damage and was on fire in three separate places when she retired from the action. The value of the [medical facilities] dispersal system with alternative dressing stations was well illustrated, as one became untenable owing to fumes from calcium flares in a flooded compartment nearby.[22]

Punjabi reported herself to Admiral Whitworth on *Warspite* as fit for service one hour after her temporary withdrawal.

It was about this time that ten Swordfish planes from the aircraft carrier *Furious*, under Captain Burch, Royal Marines, attacked the German destroyers. They had flown through the Ofotfiord narrows at 500 feet in snow squalls and poor visibility. The weather cleared when they reached the more open fiord, and they dived from a height of 2,000 feet to release their mix of 250lb and 20lb bombs from a height of 900 feet. The open-cockpit Swordfish biplanes, designed as a torpedo bomber and already obsolescent, were not at all suited to this type of bombing attack and no direct hits on the enemy were obtained. There were near-misses on the *Hermann Kunne* and the *Bernd von Arnim* which did little damage. Two of the attacking aircraft were lost.

In the continuing battle in the approaches to Narvik, the *Erich Giese*, which had by now raised enough steam to leave harbour – the last German destroyer to do so – was quickly pounced upon by the British ships and rapidly set on fire, close inshore, north of the harbour. Her captain gave orders to abandon ship. The remaining German destroyers, joined now by the *Thiele*, were forced back up the fiord, and at 1350 were ordered by Captain Bey to retire up the Rombaksfiord. The *Hermann Kunne* made for Herjangsfiord, and was followed by *Eskimo*, who torpedoed her. Out of ammunition, *Kunne*'s captain beached his ship to allow his crew to escape ashore. They later joined up with the 139th German Mountain Regiment, who were defending an area to the north of Narvik.[1]

In response to the German withdrawal into Rombaksfiord, the British destroyers divided: some went into Narvik harbour, and the remainder followed the German ships into Rombaksfiord. *Cossack*, followed later by *Foxhound* and *Kimberley*, went into Narvik harbour, where the crippled *Diether von Roeder* lay in wait. Captain Sherbrooke, in *Cossack*, recounted what followed:

> On the way up the fiord, the *Warspite's* aircraft reported a large German destroyer at the inner end of Narvik harbour and McCoy, the senior officer in destroyers, ordered me to take care of it, while the other tribals went on to Rombaks and Herjangs after the other Germans. On approaching the harbour I saw the numerous sunken ships and I knew that if I was to penetrate to a position from which I could see the German destroyer without running on a wreck, I would have to go slow. Owing to the headland...I could not get a visual sighting of the German...but by the time the director was on, the German had several seconds to aim at *Cossack's* large forepart coming round the point. The net result was that he scored several hits before I could get in a shot at him, and in the process cut my main steampipe, so killing one boiler-room crew and temporarily cutting off steam to the main engines. The way I had on carried me to a point where *Cossack* grounded,* but by this time I was going very slow, and so in due course after lightening the forepart and having the nasty experience of being fired at much too accurately by a German mortar, which we could not see, we got off. We were very close to dry land and I remember a Norwegian coming down on skis and giving us some helpful information about the strength of the German garrison and their movements.[23]

The immobilised *Roeder* put up a stubborn resistance and did much damage to *Cossack* before being overcome:

> In HMS *Cossack* there were heavy casualties. The ship was struck by eight shells and most of her casualties occurred through explosions around the guns and boiler-rooms.[22]

Nine of *Cossack's* crew were killed and another twenty were wounded. So spirited was *Roeder's* fightback that her gun flashes led the Admiral on *Warspite* to believe she was a coastal gun battery. The immobilised destroyer was subjected to salvoes from *Warspite's* 15-inch guns, but without being hit.

Kimberley and *Foxhound* had followed *Cossack* into Narvik harbour, and Commander Sherbrooke on the grounded *Cossack*, seeing *Roeder* on fire

---

* According to Vice-Admiral Whitworth: "*Cossack* fouled and got caught up in the wreck of a merchant vessel, and was not grounded in the ordinary sense of the word." [24]

and now apparently abandoned by her crew having expended all her ammunition, ordered *Foxhound* to go alongside and board the destroyer. As *Foxhound* closed, her Captain, Lieutenant-Commander Peters, saw a number of Germans suddenly emerge from below on *Roeder*, leap ashore and quickly drive off in a waiting car. Suspecting a trap, Lieutenant-Commander Peters held off and stopped *Foxhound* some fifty yards short of the German destroyer. There was indeed a trap. It was sprung when there was a sudden burst of machine gun and other rifle fire from positions along the quay. Directed on *Foxhound*'s decks, it killed one man and wounded others before the German guns were silenced by return fire from *Foxhound*, just as the *Roeder* erupted in two shattering explosions.

A Norwegian civilian, Theodor Broch, then the Mayor of Narvik, gave his account of the end of the *Roeder*:

It really was true that the broken mosaic by the pier that afternoon was made up of parts from one of the ten [German] destroyers. She had been the last in line of the German squadron and they themselves had called her "The Tactical No. 10". She had been mortally wounded in the harbour battle of April 10th and had not been able to participate in the death struggle this fateful Saturday. When the naval battle began in the outer fiord she had been left deserted and tied to the pier. All things removable had been brought ashore and her crew and officers had taken up position in the railroad tunnel above the pier.

The destroyer had been changed into a huge floating mine loaded with depth charges ready to explode. From the observation point up in the tunnel the Germans had followed the battle outside. They saw a British destroyer [HMS *Cossack*] enter the harbour. She had obviously been hit during the battle and proceeded at slow speed, listing badly. Cautiously the crew manoeuvred her between the wrecked ships until they could beach her in shallow water at Ankenes, to the south of the harbour, in full view of the town. The sea bottom was even there and it was low tide.

Then a second British destroyer [HMS *Foxhound*] entered the harbour. She was in battle trim and looked as though she were hunting more opponents. When she discovered the silent German destroyer along the pier she approached cautiously. A dynamite expert stole down from the tunnel. He started the timing device and escaped to safety. The mine was set for ten minutes. The British destroyer continued to approach. The distance to "The Tactical No 10" was now only about two hundred yards and grew constantly less. Suddenly a shot burst from a German machine-gun nested planted among the wooden pillars beneath one of the iron-ore piers. The soldiers there had not been informed. The British changed their course and were out of danger when the German ship exploded. It was this terrifying explosion that we had heard earlier in the afternoon...I kept watch on the beached British destroyer across the harbour, not more than a mile or so away. She was not so badly damaged that she could not fire and she kept sending shells against the German machine-gun nest beneath the iron-ore pier. I could see the propellers whip the water and I hoped each moment that she would get off again."[23]

Cossack was to remain grounded until 0315 on the next day. She was eventually able to make her way, stern first and escorted by *Forester*, to Skjdfiord for sufficient repairs to be carried out for her to return home on 23 April.

Foxhound stopped to rescue survivors from *Erich Giese*, which lay burning outside the harbour, then with *Kimberley* rejoined the rest of the flotilla. Eighty seven men had been killed on *Erich Giese* and many more wounded. The abandoned German ship drifted off the harbour entrance, burning fiercely, for many hours before sinking.

The British squadron still had to deal with the remaining four German destroyers: *Bernd von Arnim, Hans Ludemann, Georg Thiele* and *Wolfgang Zenker*, which had retreated into Rombaksfiord. Five British destroyers, led by *Eskimo*, with *Forester* and *Hero* later joined by *Bedouin* and *Icarus*, followed them in. *Warspite* remained outside, prepared to engage the retreating German ships with indirect fire guided by her Swordfish plane, which had already reported the position of two German destroyers at the far end of Rombaksfiord. Five miles up, the fiord narrows to a neck only a quarter of a mile wide, strewn with rocks, opening beyond the neck but still only half a mile wide in places. Two of the German destroyers, *Hans Ludemann* and *Georg Thiele*, had turned into a small bay three miles beyond the narrows. As the British destroyers rounded the bend at the narrows, both sides commenced firing with hits being scored on *Hans Ludemann*. Before retiring further up the fiord this destroyer fired off three torpedoes, while *Georg Thiele*, much more seriously damaged and on fire, managed to fire off four torpedoes. Her ship's captain, Lieutenant Commander Max-Eckart Wolff, described *Thiele*'s last minutes:

Shortly afterwards the first enemy destroyer pushed through the narrows, and we opened fire at five kilometres. This destroyer was followed closely by a second, then at short intervals, by a third and fourth. They concentrated their fire exclusively on the *Georg Thiele*, the other three German ships in the fiord being now inaccessible to the enemy. The stationary Thiele was hit again and again.

Our last torpedo, aimed and fired personally by the Torpedo Officer, Lieutenant Sommer, from an after-tube, ran on the surface at reduced speed towards the enemy and struck a destroyer of the Alfridi class level with the bridge, severing the forward part of the ship. The after part of the ship, which was towed away, was said later to have sunk. It is believed the destroyer was the *Cossack*.*

Our gunfire had become irregular and weak, consisting largely of single shells fired at random. Gun No. 2, with which telephone communication had failed, received orders by shouting from the bridge. Nos. 2 and 4 had suffered interruption in their ammunition supply, and No. 5 was running out. The forward position received a hit, killing one man and wounding two. With the Gunnery Officer lying momentarily stunned on the deck, the fire-signaller ordered rapid fire on his own initiative. When nothing happened, the Gunnery Officer called the bridge and reported "Am receiving no more ammunition. At about this time further hits were sustained in the W/T office, the bridge and the after structure.

The captain gave the order "Stand by to sink ship!" and setting the engine room telegraph to "full speed ahead" – the operator being dead and the coxswain badly wounded – ran his ship against the steeply rising rocks, the bows lodged against them. He then gave the order "Abandon ship!" Part of the crew then jumped into the water from the port side, while the rest landed directly over the forecastle. The captain himself left the ship after destroying the last secret documents (depth of water 105 metres). The wounded were carried to land and taken to cover....Our ship was now burning brightly fore and aft...Later she capsized, the stern broken off at the forward funnel, and sank after heavy explosions.[5]

The German destroyer had sixteen killed and twenty eight wounded.

The torpedo from *Georg Thiele* struck *Eskimo* just forward of her bridge, blowing away the whole forepart of the ship which hung down in a tangled mass of wreckage. Between decks there was fearful damage and loss of life:

The explosion carried away the bows of the ship and the forward medical station disappeared with its staff. The ship remained afloat and turned in uncontrolled circles while her Medical Officer crawled about in water and oil fuel to attend the casualties trapped in the wreckage. The casualties from HMS *Eskimo* were taken on board HMS *Forester* which already had a small number of casualties of her own. HMS *Eskimo* was towed to the Lofotens by HMS *Punjabi*. Later she was towed to safety by HMS *Vindictive*. It was not until June 5, at Barrow-in-Furness, that it was possible to remove many of the dead from her wreckage.[22]

From *Hero*, A.B. Turner observed the behaviour and devotion to duty

---

* It was in fact the *Eskimo*, and she did not sink.

of 'B' gun crew on *Eskimo*, who had seen 'A' gun, only a few feet in front of them, disappear with the rest of her bow when the torpedo struck:

> A sheet of flame shot up from the *Eskimo* and her bows disappeared. 'B' gun crew, with the bows shot away from beneath them, continued to fire. They deserved the cheer we gave them.[19]

The commanding officer of *Forester* also commended 'B' gun crew's conduct:

> Her 'B' gun's crew, though badly shaken by the explosion, magnificently continued firing as if nothing had happened. It looked as if the *Eskimo* would sink immediately.[1]

Eskimo did not sink. After a short delay she steamed, stern first, back through the narrows to allow her companions to pass through until the wreckage of her bow struck the bottom and she grounded. *Forester* stayed with her and took off her wounded, while *Hero*, *Icarus* and *Kimberley*, which had come round from Narvik, went on up the Rombaksfiord towards its head. The time was now 1510.

> Aircraft from *Warspite* reported three more German destroyers round the corner. *Hero* took the lead to investigate, being cheered by *Eskimo* and *Forester* as we passed them.[19]

At the far end of Rombaksfiord the British force came upon the last three German destroyers. Out of ammunition, they had been run ashore and evacuated by their crews, who could be seen on shore making their way inland towards a railway line.

> One destroyer [presumably the beached *Georg Thiele*] was sighted which we immediately engaged. No reply came from the enemy so we went right round the bend, *Icarus* and *Kimberley* coming up astern in support. After a few rounds the ships were observed to be sinking and their crews abandoned ship and commenced to climb the hills. Shortly afterwards two of the three destroyers turned over and sank. The third remained afloat, with fire raging beneath her depth charges.[19]

This third destroyer, *Hans Ludemann*, was on an even keel, and whalers with armed boarding parties were sent from *Hero* and *Icarus* to examine her:

> *Hero* sent a boarding party to the remaining destroyer. She was the

Hans Ludemann. Many articles of German kit were brought back. One of the boarding party entered the wireless office of the enemy ship and saw two operators sitting by their desks with their heads blown off. He decided not to examine the office further. One wounded man was brought back to *Hero* but he died later and was buried at sea.[19]

When the boarding parties returned to their respective ships, *Hero* fired a torpedo into the *Hans Ludemann* which broke her back and set her on fire forward.

That effectively ended the Second Battle of Narvik. The Germans had lost a total of ten destroyers and one U-boat in the two battles, and the British two destroyers with another half a dozen badly damaged but repairable. The loss of life at Narvik – civilian and naval, neutral and belligerent – had been heavy: 435 Norwegians, 321 Germans and 188 British.[26] On the British ships there were many wounded to be helped. The three Tribals *Cossack*, *Eskimo* and *Punjabi* had received heavy casualties. The other destroyers that had taken part in the action had fared better:

HMS's *Foxhound*, *Icarus*, *Bedouin*, *Hero* and *Kimberley* all escaped with a comparatively light list of casualties, which is accounted for, to some extent, by the fact that the action was fought at very close range, so that many shells passed clean through a number of destroyers without exploding. In HMS *Foxhound* there were a few casualties from rifle bullets fired from the shore by German snipers. HMS *Warspite* had no casualties, but she took on board casualties from HMSs *Eskimo*, *Cossack*, *Punjabi*, *Foxhound* and *Forrester*. *Warspite's* sick bay had been damaged, so the forward medical flat was converted into an operating theatre in which fifty-nine major surgical casualties were treated. In due course the walking casualties from HMS *Warspite* were transferred to the SS *Franconia*. Cot cases were kept on board for twelve days and were then transferred to HMHS [His Majesty's Hopital Ship] *Isle of Jersey* on April 26. In due course, these casualties arrived at the Royal Naval Auxiliary Hospital, Kingseat, Aberdeenshire…in this action HMS *Warspite* virtually performed the duties of a hospital ship for some time, which meant that numerous casualties were subjected to far less handling and hardship that those in the First Battle of Narvik when there was no major ship present to perform such duties.[22]

The presence of so many wounded comrades on board had a profound effect upon *Warspite's* crew:

The ship has stopped and *Forrester* and *Bedouin* are secured alongside with their bows to our quarterdeck. A little further up the fiord can still be seen three big fires, the remains of enemy destroyers burning away, and the smell of burning paint and flesh is horrible. *Forrester* and *Bedouin* are now transferring wounded and prisoners to us; the wounded are mainly from *Eskimo*; some nasty sights.[27]

Twenty-one-year-old Stoker Earridge remembers:

They were laid out on our mess decks, and we heard that there had been over forty operations performed that night. To us young stokers, who had to step over them to reach the hatches to our own boiler or engine rooms etc, you knew this was definitely for real, especially when a young fellow asked me to cover his legs as they were cold, and you had to make believe, as he had lost both of them.[28]

The two Narvik battles had taken a heavy toll in the destroyers of both sides, but there was to be one unexpected happy outcome for the British side. Survivors from *Hardy*, lost in the first battle, were being sheltered and cared for by kindly Norwegians in Ballengen. Three days later came the second battle, and the excited Norwegian hosts told their British guests from both *Hardy* and the merchant ship *North Cornwall* that a German destroyer (which turned out to be *Koellner*) had been sunk not too far away. Two small boats set out from Ballengen, one manned by Norwegians and the other by British naval and merchant seamen from among the survivors, to investigate. They returned in some triumph with an undamaged motorboat from the *Koellner* which they had found abandoned on the shore. In it was a signal lamp, which *Hardy*'s Yeoman of Signals set up in the attic of the school house where some of the survivors were billeted. Lieutenant Heppel of *Hardy*, together with the captain and the first officer of *North Cornwall*, set out in the motor boat to seek help from the British flotilla which they had seen passing up the fiord. They made contact with the British ships, and at dusk the Yeoman of Signals up in the schoolhouse attic, was able to take a signal from the *Ivanhoe* that an armed party was coming to their rescue. By 0100 on 14 April all the survivors of *Hardy* and *North Cornwall* – except for the most severely wounded who had to be left in hospital, later to become prisoners-of-war – had been embarked on British ships.

Having achieved an overwhelming naval victory, Admiral Whitworth now found himself in something of a dilemma as to his next course of action. The Germans had no surface warships left in the fiord. He had at his disposal overwhelming firepower, even if a lot of his ammunition had been expended. However, to make good the capture of Narvik he could, at best, only muster a landing party of some 200 sailors and marines to take on the 2,000 German troops already established ashore and augmented by the sailors who had escaped the sinking of their ships. To use his naval guns to try to drive out these entrenched troops could only result in many more civilian casualties and cause heavy damage to the town, far more devastating and widespread than that already caused in the harbour and its surrounds. Theodor Broch, Narvik's mayor, visiting the harbour area immediately after the battles, reported:

> The harbour itself was a ship graveyard with wreckage wherever one looked. The pier itself was a tragic sight. The new cold storage vault that we had built was gone except for some falling brick walls. The installation of the heavy equipment had never been completed. We had planned the dedication for the last days of April. The creamery on the other side of the square had also been hit. One wall had a gaping hole and all the windows were blown out, but the building itself might perhaps be repaired. The piers looked hopeless. The wooden planks of the old pier had been blasted away. The wooden pillars projected from the water like so many stumped teeth. The new pier was torn apart. The huge concrete block at the end had been cut in two as by a huge axe. Everywhere was strewn with wreckage. Parts of ships were thrown ashore among timber, logs and cleft rocks. Whole parts of warships lay in silent testimony to the terrific force of naval artillery fire.[25]

Admiral Whitworth was aware of two particular threats that his flotilla faced. An air attack could be imminent: a dozen German aircraft had flown over at 1800. And, in the confined space of the fiord, he feared torpedo attack from the U-boats known to be in the area. The Allies were not then aware that the magnetic torpedoes being used by the U-boats at that time were completely useless. It was a major disaster for the Germans and extremely fortunate for the Allies, who throughout the Norwegian campaign only lost one ship from a torpedo fired by a U-boat. Grand Admiral Raeder, reporting to the German High Command on the abysmal performance of the U-boat arm in Norway, admitted that the new magnetic torpedoes had proved a failure, and declared: "The torpedo crisis is a national disaster."[17]

Before pulling his ships back from their increasingly exposed position, and believing that the arrival of Allied troops was imminent, Admiral Whitworth signalled to his Commander-in-Chief and the Admiralty late in the evening of 13 April:

> My impression is that enemy forces in Narvik were thoroughly frightened as a result of today's action, and that the presence of the *Warspite* was the chief cause of this. I recommend that the town be occupied without delay by the main landing force.
> I intend to visit Narvik again tomorrow Sunday (14th), in order

to maintain the moral effect of the presence of the *Warspite*, and to accept the air and submarine menace involved by this course of action.[1]

Next morning the Admiral confirmed his confident belief Narvik could be taken relatively easily, and advised the Commander-in-Chief and Admiralty:

> I am convinced that Narvik can be taken by direct assault without fear of meeting serious opposition on landing. I consider that the main landing force need only be small, but it must have the support of Force B* or one of a similar composition; a special requirement being ships and destroyers with the best available A.A. armaments.[1]

The squadron then moved back into Vestifiord, leaving the destroyers *Ivanhoe* (who had joined the evening before) and *Kimberley* at Narvik, with orders to prevent the discharge of cargo – which might have included ammunition and military stores – from any of the merchant ships still afloat in the harbour. The squadron awaited further orders to be, in Admiral Whitworth's words, "ready to operate against Narvik when required."[1]

The call did not come. The Allied land forces were not ready to seize the initiative and take Narvik when it was at its most vulnerable, and the chance was lost.

NOTES TO SOURCES

1. Brown, D. (Ed). *Naval Operations of the Campaign in Norway: April–June 1940* (Frank Cass: London, 2000).

2. Macintyre, Captain D. *Narvik* (Evans Brothers: London, 1959).

3. Roskill, Captain S.W. *The War at Sea: 1939–45* (HMSO: London, 1954).

4. Roskill, Captain S.W. *Churchill and the Admirals* (Collins: London, 1977).

5. Bekker, C. *Hitler's Naval War*. Trans Ziegler, F. (Macdonald: London, 1974).

6. Hardy, A.C. *Everyman's History of the Sea War* (Nicholson and Watson: London, 1948).

7. *The Times*. April 20, 1940.

8. Supplement to the *London Gazette*. 1 July 1947, paras 21 – 27.

9. Communication, Commonwealth War Graves Commission. November 2000.

10. *Daily Telegraph*. 15 February, 1999.

11. Carton de Wiart, Lieutenant-General Sir Adrian. *Happy Odyssey* (Jonathan Cape: London, 1950).

12. Maund, Rear Admiral L.E.H. *Assault from the Sea* (Methuen: London, 1949).

---

* His present squadron of *Warspite* and the destroyers.

13. Colville, Sir John. *The Fringes of Power: Downing Street Diaries 1939–1955* (Hodder and Stoughton: London, 1985).
14. Vian, Admiral of the Fleet Sir Philip. *Action This Day* (Frederick Muller: London, 1960).
15. Mountevans, Admiral Lord. *Adventurous Life* (Hutchinson: London, 1946).
16. Godfrey, Admiral J.H. Memoirs. Ref GDFY, Vol VII, 1903 – 1946: A Naval Miscellany, Part II. Roskill Archives, Churchill Archives Centre, Churchill College, Cambridge.
17. Brennecke, J. *The Hunters and the Hunted* (Burke Publishing: 1958).
18. Plevy, T.A.H. *Battleship Sailors: The Fighting Career of HMS Warspite Recalled by her Men* (Chatham Publishing: London, 2001).
19. Turner, Able Seaman A.H. Papers. 96/22/1. Imperial War Museum, London.
20. Lush, R.W. Telegraphist. Letter to author, June 1986.
21. Rice, Lieutenant-Commander F.C. Letter to author, August 1986.
22. Coulter, Surgeon Captain J.L.S. *The Royal Naval Medical Service: Vol VII* (HMSO: London, 1956).
23. Sherbrooke, Captain R.S. Letter to Captain Roskill, January 1950. Roskill Archives, Churchill Archives Centre, Churchill College, Cambridge.
24. Whitworth, Admiral W. Whitworth Correspondence, June 1950. Roskill Archives, Churchill Archives Centre, Churchill College, Cambridge.
25. Broch, T. *The Mountains Wait* (Michael Joseph: London, 1943).
26. Rohwer, J. *War at Sea 1939–1945* (Chatham Publishing: London, 1996).
27. Parker, Chief Petty Officer F. Account, Imperial War Museum, London
28. Earridge, Stoker F.W. Account: biographical details. Imperial War Museum, London.

IX

The Battle for Central Norway

With the Germans in control of the main towns and ports of Norway, and a strong pro-German faction in the country's governing establishment, the Allies now had the choice of abandoning their Norwegian campaign or of trying to eject the Germans from the country. The Allies chose the latter course, although they were ill-prepared and equipped to do so. The First Lord of the Admiralty summarised the position:

> The Norwegian Government, hitherto in their fear of Germany so frigid to us, now made vehement appeals for succour. It was from the beginning obviously impossible for us to rescue Southern Norway. Almost all our trained troops, and many only half trained, were in France. Our modest but growing Air Force was fully assigned to supporting the British Expeditionary Force,* to Home Defence, and vigorous training. All our anti-aircraft guns were demanded ten times over for vulnerable points of the highest importance. Still we felt bound to do our utmost to go to their aid, even at violent derangement of our own preparations and interests. Narvik, it seemed, could certainly be seized and defended with benefit to the whole Allied cause. Here the King of Norway might fly his flag unconquered. Trondheim might be fought for, at any rate as a means of delaying the northwards advance of the invader until Narvik could be regained and made the base for the army. This, it seemed, could be maintained from the sea at a strength superior to anything which could be brought against it by land through five hundred miles of mountain country. The Cabinet heartily approved all possible measures for the rescue and defence of Narvik and Trondheim.[1]

Churchill and his Cabinet colleagues were only too well aware how the practical realities differed from the political rhetoric – what they did not

---

* On the northern flank of the Franco-German border.

appreciate at the time was the magnitude, in military terms, of the difference. The Allied troops would lack:

> ...aircraft, anti-aircraft guns, anti-tank guns, tanks, transport and training. The whole of Northern Norway was covered in snow to depths which none of our soldiers had ever seen, felt, or imagined. There were neither snow-shoes or skis – still less skiers. We must do our best. Thus began this ramshackle campaign.[1]

The reactive plan to cancel Germany's success therefore envisaged attack on two fronts: upon Narvik in the north of the country and upon Trondheim in central Norway. Following the British naval victory at Narvik the Allies – Churchill and the Admiralty in particular – were keen to regain Narvik, with its strategically ice-free harbour, and in doing so cut off much of Germany's iron-ore supplies from Sweden. The Norwegian Government, pushed north, urgently wanted the recapture of Trondheim because of its symbolic, political and strategic importance. Trondheim, the third largest town in the country, was the ancient capital of Norway and the crowning-place of its kings. It was also the meeting point of the two main routes from Oslo, a main route from Norway into Sweden, and the only road and rail link to Narvik and the north. It had in addition a large, well-equipped and sheltered harbour.

The Germans themselves regarded Trondheim as of vital importance. Intercepted Allied signals indicated the probability of allied landings in the Trondheim area, and on 14 April, the German High Command issued the directive:

> (a) The Army (Group XXI) was to reinforce the garrison at Trondheim as soon as possible, taking possession of the railway Oslo-Dombaas and Aandalsnes.
> (b) The navy was to concentrate U-boats in the waters around Trondheim and Aalesund, and to arrange for the transport of the most important supplies by U-boats to Trondheim.
> (c) The Luftwaffe to destroy enemy troops already landed; to prevent further landings in the Aandaslsnes area; to occupy Dombaas with paratroops and to send airborne reinforcements to Trondheim.[2]

The Germans were obviously determined to hold Trondheim as a first priority. With their troops at Narvik cut off from sea-borne succour, the fate of their hold on Narvik and northern Norway depended upon them holding Trondheim. Meanwhile, the Allies' initial first priority was still Narvik. On 11 April a major Allied landing force, Convoy NPI, had left the Clyde in three liners – *Empress of Australia*, *Monarch of Bermuda*, and *Reina del Pacifico* – to be joined later by two further liners: *Batory* and *Chrobry*, sailing from Scapa Flow. In addition to their close screen of destroyers, their escort was reinforced by Admiral Layton's two cruisers *Manchester* and *Birmingham*, joining at 1900 on the 13th off Cape Wrath. They were then further strengthened by the battleship *Valiant*, the fleet repair ship *Vindictive*, and six destroyers *Codrington, Acasta, Ardent, Fearless, Griffin* and *Brazen*. This powerful taskforce then set sail for Vestifiord and Narvik at a speed of 14 knots.[2]

One of the convoy's close screen of destroyers was *Echo*. The account of her captain, Commander S.H.R. Spurgeon, indicates the potential for offence inherent in a mixed nation campaign, and the delicate diplomacy needed when working with allies:

> *Echo* arrived unaccompanied at Scapa Flow on April 12, 1940, when we received a signal from the C-in-C Home Fleet from his flagship to repair on board with my navigation officer...The C-in-C instructed that Echo was to take over as 'Senior Officer of Escort' from a French destroyer commanded by a four ringed Capitaine who had somehow slipped into the screen of British destroyers ahead of the convoy before its departure.
>
> I explained, in kindergarten French, that *Echo's* take-over as 'Senior Officer of Escort' was necessary because we were fitted with Asdic and he was to take station astern; which, very courteously, he somehow understood and did. The Admiral voiced the hope that there would be no difficulty in this move. [3]

The troops on board the liners, all destined for Narvik, were under the command of Major-General P.J. Mackesy, who had left Scapa Flow on 12 April aboard the cruiser *Southampton*. Admiral of the Fleet Lord Cork and Orrery, appointed Flag Officer Narvik in charge of the naval side in the Narvik area, also left Rosyth in the cruiser *Aurora*, also on 12 April. This ship was to remain as his flagship for much of the Narvik campaign.

Then, as the convoy was on its way, the Government decided upon a two-pronged response to the German occupation of Norway, taking on the liberation of Trondheim as well as Narvik. The Norwegian Government was keen to concentrate on Trondheim, and their Commander-in-Chief, General Ruge, had asked for a British division to attack Trondheim from the north while he attacked it from the south. The convoy received changed orders. On *Echo*:

> By daylight on April 14 the mountains of the Lofoten Islands, at the entrance to Vestfiord and the approaches to Narvik were in sight. From then on Echo proceeded on her course towards Narvik as ordered, before departure from Scapa Flow, until sighting three destroyers approaching from the starboard bow. They identified

themselves as 'friend' and signalled 'Convoy to Split'; *Chobry* and *Empress of Australia* proceed to Namsos.[3]

With the convoy and task force now split, for one attack upon Trondheim and another upon Narvik, this narrative will deal first with destroyer actions and activities in the Trondheim campaign. Bearing in mind Admiral Whitworth's unaddressed proposal to attack and retake Narvik immediately after the annihilation of the German destroyers there on 13 April, *Echo* was to proceed with the other three liners to Vaagsfiord, north of Narvik. The observations of Commander Spurgeon, with the convoy task force as Captain of *Echo*, are of interest:

> On the morning of April 14 Lord Cork in *Aurora* could not have been aware that *Echo* with convoy N.P.I. was in sight of the entrance to Vestfiord, otherwise *Echo* would well have been employed with its overwhelming force of troops and destroyer escort, to make a successful assault and landing at Narvik itself...when every enemy ship had been sunk and the Germans were isolated and demoralised and without stores.[3]

The Allies' immediate response to the Norwegian Government and its Commander-in-Chief's plea for assistance in retaking Trondheim was to order, on 13 April, Vice-Admiral Edward-Collins, with his cruisers *Galatea* and *Arethusa*, to escort the troopship *Orion*, carrying the 148th Infantry Brigade, "Maurice Force", under Brigadier Morgan, to Namsos. This was a small town sixty miles north of Trondheim, at the head of Namsenfiord. Brigadier Morgan's force had originally, under Plan R4, been earmarked for Stavanger, but was dumped ashore on 8 April when that plan was cancelled. They were soon to have their orders changed once again. The War Cabinet now decided, following news of the success of the Second Battle of Narvik, that that town could be taken relatively easily by half of the N.P.I. convoy taskforce and accordingly split it, with half the force in the liners *Chobry* and *Empress of Australia*, taking the place of Brigadier Morgan's force at Namsos. His force would now form the southern arm of a pincer movement against Trondheim by landing at Aandalsnes, a small town at the head of Romsdalfiord, to join up with Norwegian forces under General Ruge.

In preparation for the landings north and south of Trondheim the cruisers *Glasgow* and *Sheffield*, under the command of Captain F.H. Pegram in *Glasgow*, with destroyers of the 4th and 6th flotilla, scoured the Stadlandet area for enemy warships and searched for suitable small ports where troops could be landed. In the words of Captain P. Vian, on *Afridi*:

While the cruisers searched for the enemy warships – whose presence proved to be imaginary Captain Pegram sent the six destroyers to Aalesund, near the entrance to the Romsdalfiord, where merchantmen had been reported. *Somali*, Captain R.S. Nicholson, who was the senior destroyer officer, led us in, but we found that the ships were all Norwegian.

The two flotillas separated, to visit and inspect possible landing ports. In doing so we came under heavy air attack from a succession of Junkers 88, which were conveniently based on the Stavanger airfield nearby.

It became clear at once that in an attack from the air in narrow waters flanked by mountains, the cards were held by the aircraft. There was too little sea-room for full freedom to manoeuvre, and the aircraft's approach was screened by the rock walls. As often as not, when they did come in view it was at such an angle that our 4.7-inch guns, whose maximum elevation was only forty degrees, could not reach them.[4]

Captain Vian's experience was to be shared over and over again by ship's companies throughout the Norwegian Campaign, which would ruthlessly expose to the Allies what German bombers, and particularly dive-bombers, could do to warships operating close inshore with inadequate or no fighter cover. It also confirmed the limitations of the RAF's heavy twin-engined bombers, which were essentially designed (and their crews trained) for strategic bombing against land targets, and not for tactical support operations against sea targets. The RAF planes were also having to operate from United Kingdom bases at the extremes of their range and their attacks were largely ineffective; while naval carrier-borne aircraft, largely obsolescent in design and performance, were markedly inferior to their German land-based counterparts and were not always available or, because of technical problems and severe weather conditions, not operational.

Since little was known about the presence of German troops in the Namsos area, Royal Marine detachments from the two cruisers, together with armed naval parties, were transferred to destroyers and landed ashore to reconnoitre. Namsos was found to be free of German presence, and the town was occupied by the landed detachments. Here, Captain Nicholson in *Somali* awaited the arrival of the military commander and the main force, due to arrive on the *Empress of Australia* and *Chombry*. The military commander, Major General Carlton de Wiart, arrived by air in typically spectacular fashion:

General de Wiart had left his home in the Masurian Lakes in Poland in face of Russian invasion; the War Office lost no time in pouncing; here was a man whom nothing could deter and nothing could frighten; ideally suited to command forces organised at forty eight hours notice to drive the Germans out of Norway!...The General arrived characteristically, his flying boat being shot up by a German fighter as it landed in the fiord. His A.D.C. was wounded but he himself reached *Somali* undamaged.[4]

General Carton de Wiart's own account makes light of the desperateness of his appointment and arrival in Norway:

Having got my orders, I collected my kit and flew up to Scotland the next day, April 13th. We were to fly across to Norway the same night but were delayed by a blizzard, and took off the next morning in a Sunderland. We did not seem set for victory from the start as poor Elliott was sick the whole way over, and on arrival at Namsos we were attacked by a German fighter. Captain Elliott was wounded and had to return to England in the same plane to spend several weeks in hospital.

While the German plane was attacking us we landed on the water and my pilot tried to lure me into the dinghy which we carried. I refused firmly, having no intention of allowing a Hun plane the pleasure of pursuing me in a wobbly and clumsy rubber dinghy when the Sunderland was still on top of the water.* When the German had fired all his ammunition he flew off, and one of our Tribal Class destroyers, the *Somali*, sent a boat over to take me on board.[5]

Captain Nicholson had quickly concluded that Namsos would not be suitable for the berthing of the two liners and the envisaged disembarkation of their troops. Namsos lay at the seaway end of a long narrow fiord, with steep snow-covered hillsides running down to the water's edge. Its disembarkation facilities consisted of a single stone quay and a smaller wooden pier. There was also a small wooden pier at the hamlet of Bangsund on the other side of the Namsen river. The troopships and the disembarking soldiers would be extremely vulnerable to air attacks in the confined area. He recommended that the *Empress of Australia* and *Chobry* not be sent directly to Namsos, but that their troops be disembarked onto destroyers away from enemy air attack, for transfer ashore at Namsos. General Carton de Wiart agreed with this assessment, and the Admiralty ordered that the two troopships be berthed in a remote anchorage at Lillesjona, some one hundred miles north of Namsos.

Somali was by now completely out of ammunition. The destroyer had undergone three sustained air attacks and had successfully evaded sixty bombs. During her final hours at Namsos she had had to resort to firing practice shells at the attacking German bombers "for morale effect", [6] but travelled up to Lillesjona (Lillehammer) with General Carton de Wiart, so that he could join up with his troops disembarking from the liners to ferrying destroyers. The General and his staff transferred to the *Afridi*, and *Somali* returned home to re-ammunition.

> ...I had a conference with Admiral Sir Geoffrey Layton on his flag-ship, after which I was taken on board the *Afridi*, commanded by Captain Philip Vian of *Cossack* fame, who showed me every consideration and kindness, though I must have been an inconvenient guest.[5]

Captain Vian assumed command of the destroyer force which, in addition to *Afridi*, consisted of *Sikh, Matabele, Mashona* and *Nubian*, the latter having escorted the oiler *War Pindari* to Lillesjona. The destroyers refuelled, not without incident:

> The destroyers were ordered to refuel from an oiler which had been provided. *Afridi* was hardly alongside before the Junkers arrived, an uncomfortable position to be in during the bombing attacks, since we could only fire on one side.[4]

After refuelling, the destroyers commenced disembarking troops of the Lincolnshire and York and Lancaster Regiments, but had to depart hurriedly with their soldiers for Namsos when enemy bombers again found them.

> As we lay immobilized at Lillesjona alongside the transports, embarking two of the three battalions carried, enemy aircraft again attacked us. They scored some near misses, which did no considerable damage. Lillesjona at this time was out of reach of the Stuka dive-bombers, which could hardly have failed to score some hits had they been employed.
>
> The lack of air cover, which was to prove fatal to the success of the whole campaign, was already a depressing feature. The effect of even a token fighter protection, which at one stage took the form of an occasional old Gladiator or Skua, was most remarkable. So long as even one of these aircraft was about, every enemy bomber kept clear."[4]

The five destroyers arrived at Namsos during the night of 16 April. By daylight, the troops had been landed and dispersed into the wooded

---

* General Carton de Wiart does not mention that he was one month short of his sixtieth birthday and had lost an arm and an eye during forty years of active service in many wars and skirmishes, going back to the Boer war in 1900. The General had style.

hillsides. To hide their presence, evidence of quayside activity was covered over to keep it from the prying eyes of German reconnaissance planes constantly flying overhead during the daylight hours.

The two liners and their escorts at Lillesjona were now being subjected to continuous air raids, which was causing concern to the inexperienced and helpless soldiers on board the troopships. To relieve the troops of this morale-sapping ordeal and to avoid the risk of the troopships being sunk, Admiral Layton withdrew the ships and escorts out to sea. It was also decided to transfer the troops from the large and unwieldy *Empress of Australia* to the smaller *Chrobry*, which also carried the bulk of the soldiers' stores and equipment. *Empress of Australia* was sent back to the United Kingdom, escorted by the cruiser *Birmingham* and two old V and W destroyers, taking with her some 170 tons of stores which it had not been possible to unload. The plan was now for *Chrobry* to sail for Namsos so at to arrive at 1745: sunset. She was to be escorted by the anti-aircraft cruiser *Curlew* and the five Tribal class destroyers ferrying troops. This plan was successfully accomplished and by 0200 on 18 April the troops were ashore, hidden away with any evidence of their arrival removed.

On the evening of 19 April four French troopships, the *Eld' Jezair, El Mansour, El Kantara*, each of 5,000–6,000 tons and the 10,000 ton *Ville d'Oran*, arrived with three battalions of French Chasseurs-Alpin troops. They were escorted by the anti-aircraft cruiser *Cairo*, who had replaced *Curlew*, the French cruiser *Emile Bertin*, and four French destroyers. Up to this time it had been possible to keep knowledge of the landing of troops from the Germans; but, following the arrival of the French contingent, it became no longer possible to keep the landings secret and the ships, harbour and troops were soon subjected to very heavy air attacks:

> Although far better trained than we were, and experienced at looking after themselves, they did not obliterate the traces of their landings. The next morning the Germans saw that troops had been put ashore, and the French made themselves still more noticeable by loosing off their machine guns at them, which succeeded in making matters much worse. The Germans responded with more and more bombs and in a matter of hours Namsos was reduced to ashes.[5]

During the raids *Emile Bertin* was hit by a bomb and retired from the scene, leaving *Cairo* and the four French destroyers to try to fight off the bombers. The Luftwaffe virtually obliterated the town and its harbour facilities, destroyed stores and made the re-supply and reinforcement of "Maurice Force" by sea well nigh impossible.

When *Nubian* returned to Namsos during the night of 20 April to give some anti-aircraft fire support to the beleaguered garrison, her Captain,

Commander R. W. Ravenhill, found "The whole place was a mass of flames from end to end."[6]

The next day the sloop *Auckland* relieved *Nubian* who, out of ammunition, left for home. Her Captain later described:

> ...the very great strain imposed on personnel of these anti-aircraft ships. Owing to the high mountains no warning can be obtained of the approach of aircraft...
>
> Ships must be kept under way day and night and when attacks come there is little room for manoeuvre. There is continued tension and the knowledge that...nothing can come to your assistance is trying on the nerves.[6]

One final body of French troops was landed at Namsos on 22 April, but their troopship, the 10,000-ton transport *Ville d'Alger*, was unable to land her cargo of heavy stores, anti-tank guns and an anti-aircraft battery. They were the last troops to be landed at Namsos. Their situation was desperate and their ebullient commander, General Carton de Wiart, was forced to concede that for "Maurice Force", "I see little chance of carrying out defensive or, indeed, any operations, unless enemy air activity is considerably reduced."[2]

Some two hundred miles to the south of Namsos in the Romsdalfiord area, a hastily mobilised and partially trained Norwegian Army under its Commander-in-Chief, General Ruge, was trying to prevent the Germans reinforcing by land their garrison at Trondheim. It had been planned that while the Allied northern pincer attack on Trondheim would go via Namsos, their southern pincer would land at Aandalsnes, at the head of the Romsdalfiord, to assist the Norwegians and close the pincer grip on Trondheim. Romsdalfiord appeared to offer a suitable southern base for the Allies: Aandalsnes was some forty miles from the fiord entrance, where there were two small timber exporting ports with suitable landing quays, at Molde on the northern side and at Aalesund on the southern. This latter small town, opposite Molde, was selected as the site for a battery of naval 4-inch guns, intended to dominate the approaches to the fiord and prevent any German attempt at the sea-borne reinforcement of Trondheim.

The drawback with the selected landing area was that, like Namsenfiord and the town of Namsos to the north, the steep-sided Romsdalfiord would become a trap for any ships entering its narrow confines. The steep sides of the fiord, rising in places to over two thousand feet, enabled dive-bombers from the nearby German occupied Stavanger airfield to approach unseen before diving almost vertically onto the ships confined below before any anti-aircraft fire could be brought to bear against them.

As a first step, the Allies set about securing the landing sites. The four sloops *Auckland*, *Black Swan*, *Flamingo* and *Bittern* had sailed from Rosyth on the 14 and 15 April, with some seven hundred ill-prepared marines and sailors hastily collected together from the battleships *Nelson* and *Rodney* undergoing repair and refit at that naval base. They were under the command of Colonel Simpson, Royal Marines. These small 1,200 to 1,350-ton sloops, overcrowded and overloaded with seven hundred and twenty five marines and sailors, three 3.7-inch howitzers, eight anti-aircraft pom-pom guns and two 4-inch guns, met fierce seas and were forced to seek shelter at Invergordon. While there they were redirected by the Admiralty from their original destination of Namsos to Aandalsnes, and left for there on 16 April, arriving late on the following evening. By 0700 on 18 April, Aandalsnes, Molde and Aalesund had been occupied without resistance and, seemingly, without German knowledge.

The naval landing parties remained ashore awaiting reinforcements and were absorbed into the short-lived "Operation Sickle". The first reinforcements, some 1,000 troops, had left Rosyth in the early hours of 17 April, in the cruisers *Galatea* and *Arethusa*, the two anti-aircraft cruisers *Carlisle* and *Curacoa*, and the destroyers *Arrow* and *Acheron*. They were landed at Molde and Aandalsnes on the next evening, 18 April. The two cruisers left the following morning. The presence of the Allied force was soon detected by the enemy, and from 20 April onwards the three towns were subjected to almost daily attacks from the Luftwaffe as the Allied intentions became clear.

The warships bore the brunt of the bombing, with the two anti-aircraft cruisers being picked out for specific attention. *Curacoa* was hit and badly damaged on 24 April. There were no heavy anti-aircraft guns ashore, and the warships positioned at Romsalfiord, together with those bringing troop and stores reinforcement, had to act as floating gun batteries to form the only anti-aircraft defence. Ammunition expenditure was extremely high and, as there were virtually no stocks available locally, warships had to return home to Scottish bases to re-ammunition. Fortunately for morale, the sailors and the troops ashore did not know how serious was the anti-aircraft ammunition supply position. On 20 April Admiral Pound, the First Sea Lord, signalled to Admiral Forbes, the Commander-in-Chief, Home Fleet:

Recent expenditure of destroyer long range anti-aircraft ammunition has been heavy if the total size of the reserve held is appreciated. This is now reduced to 13,000 rounds of which 6,000 rounds are abroad. Deliveries in the next three weeks should reach 6,000 rounds after which further supplies are not immediately in sight. Although I am unwilling to suggest restriction in the use of any anti-aircraft gun, it is obvious that expenditure of this nature at the recent high rates must be curtailed. Action has been taken to accelerate supply to the maximum and you will be informed when the margin is ample.[2]

Admiral Forbes chose not to pass on this depressing news to his ships' captains; they had troubles enough with the German bombers. The cruiser *Suffolk* had attempted to disrupt the Luftwaffe bombing attacks by closing in and bombarding the German-held Stavanger airfield on 17 April. She endured nearly seven hours of continuous bombing during the operation and subsequent withdrawal and, badly damaged, arrived back at Scapa Flow the following day with seventy casualties and her quarterdeck awash.

Conditions in Romdsalfiord, like those at Namsos and Namsenfiord, further north, were becoming increasingly difficult as the daylight hours of mid- to late April grew longer and the bombing attacks became almost continuous. The unloading of troops and supplies could only take place in the few hours of darkness between about 2100 and 0200, to enable the transports and supply ships to get clear of the narrow fiord confines before the bombers returned with the daylight. Further reinforcements arrived at Aandalsnes on 21 April. Six hundred men were landed from two small transports, escorted by the destroyers *Jackal* and *Javelin*, but the merchantman *Cedarbank* was sunk by a U-boat. Because of the Germans' defective torpedoes, she was the only Allied ship to be torpedoed during the Norwegian campaign. Nevertheless it was a serious loss, since she carried a cargo of anti-aircraft guns and lorries.

On 21 April the cruiser *Arethusa* returned with stores, anti-aircraft guns, ammunition and an advance party of RAF personnel, hoping to establish a makeshift fighter airfield on the nearby frozen Lesjaskog Lake. *Arethusa* left immediately after discharging her consignment to be replaced by the cruisers *Galatea*, *Sheffield* and *Glasgow* and the destroyers *Vansittart*, *Campbell*, *Ivanhoe*, *Icarus*, *Impulsive* and *Witch*. This force, under Admiral Edward-Collins, took in over 2,000 troops, anti-aircraft guns and search-lights. On 24 April, Admiral Layton left Rosyth for Romsalfiord with the cruisers *Manchester*, *Birmingham* and *York*, plus the destroyers *Arrow*, *Acheron* and *Griffin*. They took with them a further 1,600 troops and 300 tons of stores. They also carried General Paget and his headquarters staff to take over command of "Sickle Force".

Meanwhile the Luftwaffe onslaught during the lengthening daylight hours continued. Any anticipation of relief from bombing by the RAF fighters operating from the frozen lake proved to be short lived. The obsolete Gloster Gladiator fighters, transported from the United Kingdom by the aircraft carrier *Glorious* and flown off from her flight deck between 1730 and 1800 on 24 April, were destroyed by German bombers within a few hours.

Despite the air bombardment, the Royal Navy continued to supply "Sickle Force". On the afternoon of 27 April four supply ships escorted by the destroyers *Afridi*, *Withington* and *Amazon* were so fiercely attacked that only two ships were unloaded, one at Molde and the other, partially, at Aandalsnes. Captain P. Vian on the *Afridi* recalled how:

Returning to Scapa Flow to refuel and replenish ammunition, Afridi was ordered, when this was done, to take certain destroyers under her command and to escort ships carrying supplies to Aandalsnes; one of these was a small tanker loaded with petrol, whose maximum speed was five knots! Aandalsnes is approached through Romsdalfiord, and lies forty miles from the entrance, off which we arrived on 27 April. The daylight passage of the convoy and escort through this waterway, speed five knots, on a steady course and with mountains rising steeply either side, presented an alluring invitation to enemy aircraft. Junkers attacks persisted to the end, but the fire of the destroyers, though limited to an elevation of forty degrees, was enough to keep the enemy just too high for their standard of marksmanship. Not a ship received a direct hit, though some were damaged by the splinters from near misses.

We found Aandalsnes on fire, and were met by the smoke-blackened Naval Officer in Charge. He informed us that the decision had been taken to evacuate: there was no need, therefore, for the supply ships, least of all the petrol tanker, to remain; would we please take them away? Having given fresh supplies of ammunition to the sore beset guard ship, *Black Swan*, take them away we did, not without the thought that the ordeal through which we had just been, and that which faced us during the return passage of Romsdafiord, seemed unnecessary. However, luck was with us; the scale of attack was less than before; night was drawing on; and we reached the open sea without serious damage.

By now, Able-Seaman Gammon, who, as my cabin hand, was stationed on the bridge in action, had developed a flair for picking out, from aircraft approaching, those which had *Afridi* in their sights; he was nearly always right, and often reported the moment of bomb release. This information was a great assistance in making the decision when, and in which way, to swing the ship to avoid the bombs.[4]

This "dodging the bombs" seemed to become the standard, and indeed the only, way for the destroyers to counter the German bombers during the Norwegian campaign. There were modifications to the practice, as described by Commander S.H.K. Spurgeon, then captain of the destroyer *Echo*:

The Luftwaffe seemed to concentrate on the anti-aircraft cruisers whose guns soon wore out through overuse. The destroyers then became attractive targets for the bombers because the destroyer guns were limited in elevation and by flying high they were immune from short range weapons. We were, in other words, defenceless. Several times, day after day, we were bombed by these aircraft and, as daylight extended to little less than twenty four hours in that latitude, the whole ship's company had little rest. As soon as an aircraft was seen approaching, our evasive action was to increase speed and alter course immediately following the release of the bomb. This could be seen easily enough, with its wobbly trajectory towards the targets. When it exploded a white column of spray would rise, leaving a black and dirty-looking soapy patch on the surface.

Echo's Yeoman of Signals was a very efficient companion on the bridge; his name was Yeoman Paul and he well knew what effect this rather gruelling endurance test had on the morale of the ship's company, because there was always the chance that the next bomb might score a hit. One day Paul suggested that, whilst the aircraft was making its approach, he would like to make a signal to its pilot on the very bright ten-inch lamp, of a rude four letter word repeatedly. This would, he said, be a useful lesson of the ship's company to polish up their morse and, in addition, would give the pilot of the aircraft an opportunity of knowing exactly what we thought of him. Paul had a good vocabulary and, from then on, the silent suspense of the bomb drop was broken by laughter; he assured us later that the not uncommon complaint of belly ache amongst them had been cured. This then was *Echo's* unusual method of maintaining its high standard of morale.[3]

With conditions ashore becoming untenable and supply difficulties increasing, the decision to evacuate was taken. The whole Allied campaign in Central Norway was disintegrating, as the Germans became increasingly determined to consolidate their hold on strategically vital Trondheim. The proposed frontal naval assault upon Trondheim – "Operation Hammer" – to accompany the two land pincer movements from Namsos and Aandalsnes, had been abandoned. Admiral Forbes had had to tell the War Cabinet that "to carry out an opposed landing...under conditions of continuous air attack was hardly feasible."[7] The Navy was simply too stretched for such an assault, lacking in particular serviceable cruisers and destroyers. Furthermore, there was growing German activity on the Western Front in Europe, threatening France and the Low Countries and possibly threatening England directly with invasion; and Italy, following the full flood of German conquests, was becoming increasingly belligerent in the Mediterranean theatre, threatening our supply lines to the Middle and Far East. These circumstances combined to draw off warships from the Home Fleet to meet these new challenges. The Royal Navy simply did not have enough serviceable ships to fulfil all the calls upon it.

The abandonment of "Operation Hammer" spelt the end for "Operation Maurice" at Namsos and "Operation Sickle" at Aandalsnes. On 28 April the War Cabinet took the decision to abandon its campaign in Central

Norway completely, and to re-embark the forces landed at Namsos and Aandalsnes as soon as possible. In explaining to Admiral Forbes the reason for abandoning Aandalsnes in particular, Winston Churchill, First Lord of the Admiralty, wrote "It is impossible for 3,000 to 4,000 men without artillery or air superiority to withstand advance of 70,000 or 80,000 thoroughly equipped Germans."[2] The Allied navies had done all that had been asked of them in putting the men ashore in the first place; now they had to get them off again, and destroyers would again be in the forefront.

It was originally planned to take off the troops on the nights of 1–2 May and 2–3 May. There were thought to be some 5,500 men to be re-embarked from the Aandalsnes district and 6,200 from the Namsos area. They were to be evacuated regardless of the loss of equipment. At Aandalsnes, Vice-Admiral Edward-Collins would be in charge of the evacuation on the first night, and Vice-Admiral Layton on the second night, while Vice-Admiral Cunningham would be in command at Namsos on both nights. In the event, the Aandalsnes evacuation took place on the nights of 30 April–1 May and 1–2 May; Namsos troops were evacuated on the night of the 2–3 May as planned. Surprisingly, no German surface ships tried to interfere with the withdrawal operations.

Prior to the evacuation of the troops it was planned to evacuate the King of Norway, the Crown Prince, members of the Norwegian Government loyal to the Allied cause, and the Allied delegations in Norway, from Molde to a place of safety further north. The task was entrusted to the cruiser *Glasgow* and the destroyers *Jackal* and *Javelin*. They arrived late in the evening of 29 April and sailed again almost immediately, with their 280 passengers and twenty three tons of gold bullion from Norway's gold reserves. As the ships cast off from the burning quayside at Molde, under attack from German bombers, Captain M. M. Denny, the naval officer in charge at Aandalsnes, saw them off, "with fire hoses playing, the whole scene brilliantly lit by the flames of the burning town."[2]

The warships in the Romsdafiord, still trying valiantly to defend the towns and troops from the constant air attacks, were becoming overwhelmed. On the night of 29–30 April the Luftwaffe began attacking throughout the hours of darkness as well as in the daylight hours. The guard ship *Black Swan* had fired off 2000 rounds of 4-inch and 4,000 rounds of pom-pom ammunition in two days before she was hit on 28 April and forced to return to Scapa Flow. She was relieved by another small sloop, *Fleetwood*, 990 tons, who likewise fired off all her anti-aircraft ammunition within two days and had to return home to re-ammunition on 30 April. Heavily overloaded for so small a warship, she brought with her 340 evacuated troops.

Vice-Admiral Edward-Collins arrived at Aandalsnes at 2230 on 30 April for the first night's evacuation with the cruisers *Galatea*, *Arethusa*, *Sheffield* and *Southampton*, the destroyers *Somali*, *Mashona*, *Sikh*, *Wanderer*,

Walker and *Westcott* and the troop transporter *Ulster Monarch*. A further destroyer, *Tartar*, and the troop transport *Ulster Prince*, were sent to evacuate from Molde. The ships, apart from *Sheffield* and *Southampton* who had joined from the Narvik area, had come direct from Scapa Flow. With the conditions ashore at Romsdalfiord deteriorating by the hour there had been no time or intelligence for any planning and the Admiral made his arrangements and issued his orders at sea. Brigadier Hogg, Commander, Army Base ashore, in reply to the Admiral's request for information on evacuation possibilities, had signalled "Probably unsafe to berth transports, but worthwhile trying with destroyers; if this fails, propose using destroyers' boats along south shore eastwards of Aandalsnes."[2] Since it would have been impossible for the destroyers' boats to have embarked, in the short hours of darkness, the envisaged numbers of troops to be evacuated, Vice-Admiral Edward-Collins risked berthing his ships, placing the *Galatea* alongside the concrete quay, the only serviceable berthing spot. The destroyer *Walker*, placed alongside *Galatea*, ferried troops back to *Sheffield* while *Galatea* loaded. When *Galatea* was full, *Arethusa* took her place. When the last party of troops assembled at Aandalsnes that night had been embarked, the three cruisers had successfully taken off some 1800 troops. The men were exhausted and ravenously hungry, but embarked on board in an orderly and disciplined manner, although many were without arms or equipment.

Meanwhile *Tartar* and *Ulster Prince* had gone to Molde to embark the last of Captain Denny's base staff and the Commander of the Norwegian Army, General Ruge, and his staff. Lieutenant Ludovic Kennedy recalled:

> We were ordered to evacuate any troops that had made their way to Molde, and for me this moment meant a return journey along the fiord where once my parents and I sat on the deck of the *Sigurd Jarl*, listening to Norwegian folk songs on the gramophone as we made our leisurely way from Bergen to Trondheim. I remembered Molde as an attractive little fishing port; but the night we reached it in *Tartar* it was burning from end to end, having been attacked by German dive bombers for the past five days.[8]

It was a bitter time for General Ruge, who felt betrayed by the Allies in his struggle to free his country from the invading Germans. Brigadier Clarke described the General's reaction when General Paget, the Allied Commander of "Maurice Force", had broken the news of the Allies' intention to withdraw from Central Norway:

> There was silence, and quietly he said, almost to himself: "So Norway must go the way of Czechoslovakia and Poland." Then he looked up.

"But why?" he asked. "Why withdraw when your troops are still unbeaten?" Once again he repeated how he had staked all his hopes upon British aid, and how it was from his advice alone that the Government had decided to fight on...

When next he spoke he was his own self once more. "But these things are not for us to decide, General," he said, "we are soldiers and we have to obey. Let us return to our plans. Please tell me what help I can give you to carry out your orders." The tension was over and we never heard another hint of bitterness. [6]

General Ruge at first agreed to be evacuated, in the mistaken belief that he and his staff would be taken to continue the fight in northern Norway. When he found that this was not so, and that he was being evacuated back to England he refused to leave his troops. The Captain of *Tartar* sent Lieutenant Kennedy to find him and try to persuade him to change his mind:

> After making fast alongside the jetty, word reached us that the Commander-in-Chief of the Norwegian Army, General Ruge, was in the town, and the Captain sent me ashore to find out if he would like to come to England and join the Norwegian forces there. I finally tracked him down in a wood above the town, standing with his staff officers in a clearing in the snow. There were perhaps a dozen of them and I have never seen a more dispirited-looking group, saying nothing and looking down at the burning town with glazed eyes. The light from the fires lit up their blue-grey cloaks and peaked caps...
>
> I gave the General the Captain's message; his response was to smile and shake his head. Weeks later he was captured and sent to a concentration camp.* [8]

Vice-Admiral Edward-Collins also sent the destroyers *Wanderer* and *Sikh* to pick up troop remnants from Alfarnes, set at the mouth of a small fiord six miles north of Aandalsnes. Overloaded with 150 troops, *Wanderer* grounded and had to be pulled clear by *Sikh*. Altogether some 2,200 men were safely taken off from Rombalsfiord on the first night's operation, the only German opposition coming from an ineffectual bombing raid between 0300 and 0400 hours on 1 May, as the ships were leaving the outer reaches of the fiord.

The next night's evacuation, taking off the remaining Allied troops (put at 1500, plus an unknown number of Norwegian troops and

---

* General Ruge survived the war. He was liberated from Luckenwalde prison camp in Germany by advancing Russian troops on 22 April 1945. [9]

refugees), was entrusted to a force under Vice-Admiral Layton. It consisted of the large cruisers *Birmingham* and *Manchester*, and the destroyers *Inglefield, Delight, Diana, Somali* and *Moshona*, the latter two destroyers, not having taken troops on board the previous night, being pressed into a second night's service. The anti-aircraft cruiser *Calcutta* and the sloop *Auckland* had arrived during the day to provide some anti-aircraft cover for the withdrawal force, and met up with them as they approached the outer reaches of Rombalsfiord. On nearing their destination, *Somali* was detached to Aalesund to collect troops there and *Diana* was sent to Molde to take General Ruge and his staff to Tromso in the north of the country where he wished to lead the remnants of the Norwegian Army continuing their fight there. Measuring just under 600 feet,[10] the *Birmingham* and *Manchester* were too long to berth alongside the concrete quay, and had anchored off Aandalsnes at 2300 on 1 May, while the remaining destroyers went back and forth to the quay ferrying the troops to the cruisers. In an hour 1,300 men had been transferred. The force then sailed for home, leaving *Calcutta* and *Auckland* to pick up a supposedly 200-strong rearguard. In fact 700 men turned up, and Calcutta took them on board in 15 minutes. The gallant *Auckland* waited, and took on board the final rearguard of 240 men, who "embarked with such commendable promptitude that the ship was alongside for only seven minutes."[2] They were obviously keen to leave the calamitous campaign in central Norway behind them. In total, over 2,200 men were taken off that night without a single casualty.

There now remained the final and perhaps most difficult – indeed desperate – stage of the evacuation: that of extricating some 5,400 troops from Namsos. It was probable that the Germans by now realised that the Allies were pulling out of Central Norway, and would do their utmost to make the Namsos evacuation impossible or at least as bloody and damaging as possible. The man in charge of the evacuation, Vice-Admiral J.H.D. Cunningham, had sailed from Scapa Flow on 29 April with the cruisers *Devonshire* and *York* and the French cruiser *Montcalm*, the destroyers *Afridi, Nubian, Hasty,* and *Imperial*, and the French destroyer *Bison*. He also had the French troop transports *Eld' Jezair, El Kantara* and *El Mansour*. He intended to bring off half the troops in the transports on the 1–2 May and the second half in the cruisers the following night, but had contingency plans to try to carry out the whole operation in one night if necessary. Four other destroyers, *Kelly, Grenade, Griffin* and *Maori*, under Captain Lord Louis Mountbatten in *Kelly*, had been sent on ahead. As the evacuating ships approached the Norwegian coast on 1 May, they ran into dense fog, which prevented the cruisers and transports from venturing into the outer reaches of the Namsos fiords. However, Captain Mountbatten's destroyers groped their way up the fiord leading to Namsos using the echo of their Asdics off the steep sides to fix their position. It took all night and it was not until 0500 in the morning of 2

May that Captain Mountbatten reached Namsos and was able to report it clear of fog.

> He was set upon at once by enemy bombers. Namsos harbour was untenable by warships during daylight. The frigate *Bittern* had already been heavily damaged, and the anti-aircraft cruiser *Carlisle* had been forced to go to sea during the day.[4]

None of Mountbatten's ships were hit, but *Maori* received a near miss and was damaged, suffering twenty-three casualties. With conditions ashore deteriorating, the increasing intensity of the German bombing, and his transports low in fuel, Admiral Cunningham realised that his best hope of a successful withdrawal was to try to accomplish it in one night. General Carton de Wiart, in command ashore, believed that he could not disengage and collect together his troops in time and that the evacuation would need to be spread over two nights. The General later wrote of the evacuation in his memoirs:

> Gradually we retired towards Namsos, where we were to embark. The evacuation was to take place on two consecutive nights. I intended sending the French troops off the first night, and they had all gone down at dusk to be ready to embark. We waited – no ships turned up. There was no word from the Navy, and I must admit to feeling anxious. Just before dawn I had to move the troops into their positions again, leaving them, depressed and disappointed, to await another night.
> I was getting more and more anxious as Mr Neville Chamberlain had told the House of Commons that General Paget's force had been evacuated from Aandalsnes, which left me the only unenvied pebble on the beach. Alone against the weight of Germany.
> In the course of that last endless day I got a message from the Navy to say that they would evacuate the whole of my force that night. I thought it was impossible, but learned a few hours later that the Navy do not know the word. Apparently there was a dense sea mist quite unsuspected by us off shore and this had prevented their coming in the night before...[5]

The attempt at evacuation in one night was agreed. Captain Vian in *Alfridi* led in the three French transports, followed by the cruiser *York* and the destroyer *Nubian*. They were joined in the fiord by *Kelly*, *Grenade* and *Griffin*. At 2230 *El d'Jezair* tied up at the stone pier and *El Kantara* secured alongside her. For safety and lack of docking space, both *El Mansour* and *York* stayed in the fiord, and had troops ferried to them by destroyers and trawlers from the wooden pier.

As the night wore on, it became clear that, although it would be possible, except for the rear-guard, to load the transports before daylight, they could not be sailed together in time to make a worthwhile offing [position at distance from shore]. The troopships were therefore sailed one by one as they were ready, escorted by warships.[4]

El Mansour, the last transport to leave, cleared the pier at 0230 on 3 May, escorted by *York* and *Nubian*. Only the rear-guard was left to be evacuated.

Alfridi remained to embark the General and the rear-guard, who were held up by the snow bound roads leading to Namsos. General de Wiart, when he arrived, found that his baggage had been sent to the cruiser *York*, and told me he would travel with it, but was very sorry not to be coming with us. So were we at the time, but later we thought otherwise. The rear-guard, the Colonel and thirty five other ranks of the York and Lancaster Regiment eventually arrived and were duly embarked. There was a mass of abandoned motor transport on the jetty, on which *Alfridi's* guns were turned before she sailed. We expected a rough passage as it was becoming light, but in the event reached Admiral Cunningham's force by 5.30am without being attacked.[4]

It was only a temporary reprieve. The first transport and its escorts reached Scapa Flow without incident, but the latter groups were subjected to air attacks which began at 0845 and went on for nearly seven hours until 1530 when the ships were two hundred miles off the Norwegian coast.

When the air attacks began, it soon became evident that the Junkers 88, which we knew by now so well, had been reinforced that morning by the Stuka dive-bomber, which we knew not at all. Up to that time they appear to have been used almost exclusively against troop formations ashore, and against the guard ships stationed at the ports.[4]

The *modus operandi* of the Junkers 87 Stuka dive-bomber was soon to become all too familiar to the ships of the Royal Navy: the arrival of a formation of the gull-winged, single-engined, fixed-undercarriage planes; the sequential peel away of the aircraft to port; the near-vertical 70° dive; and the application of its air brakes to limit its accelerating speed, with the accompanying stomach-churning howl reaching a crescendo as the bomb was released and the Stuka pulled out of its dive:

Almost at once a Stuka scored a hit on *Bison*; the bomb exploded the forward magazine, and the whole forepart of the ship blew up, including the bridge with its officers. The hulk listed heavily to port and *Grenade*, Lieutenant-Commander R.C. Boyle, went quickly alongside to take off survivors while *Montcalm* and the transport went on.

I could see through my glasses that, owing to the angle of *Bison's* deck, and on account of the number of wounded, the transfer was going to be a slow business. It was apparent that *Grenade* was awkwardly placed; she was isolated, stopped, alongside another vessel, and could make little use of her guns – a very obvious target. I therefore asked Admiral Cunningham if *Alfridi* might leave him, to join *Grenade* and *Bison* and provide air protection. He agreed at once and off we went.

On arrival it seemed to me that on balance it would be better to go alongside *Bison's* free side and assist *Grenade* in the embarkation of survivors, rather than to lie off, standing by for attack. This we therefore did, hopefully playing hoses on a depth charge, mounted on the side of *Bison's* deck, which was burning, and on exploding small arms ammunition.

It quickly became clear that whether one lay alongside the up or the down side of a heavily listed ship, the transfer of personnel was an extremely awkward job. Time was important, because the fire burning in the fore part of the hulk was spreading aft, where the survivors were mustered.

Soon flames were seen coming up the after hatch, and it was reported that the fire had reached the compartment adjoining the after magazine. The survivors began to take to the water. This I encouraged them to do, as it was clear that *Grenade* and *Alfridi* would be uncomfortably placed if the after part of *Bison* blew up while we were alongside; it would be easier and quicker to get men out of the water with our boats and those of *Imperial*, who had now joined us, than to take them off the hulk.

Up to this time the air attacks which had been made on the group had been warded off; with the ships cast off and free to manoeuvre, it appeared reasonable to suppose that the rescue would be completed, despite a further attack. Then there occurred an unforeseen calamity. The surface of the water was covered with oil fuel, which had escaped from *Bison's* forward tanks. This now ignited, making the situation for the swimmers a terrible one, and adding greatly to the difficulties of the boats' crews. But, despite two further air attacks, the rescue proceeded, and by eleven-thirty it was completed. The hulk was sunk and the destroyers proceeded to overtake the convoys. Of the survivors, *Alfridi* had sixty-nine on board.[4]

However, the ordeal of *Bison*'s rescued men and of *Alfridi*'s own crew was not yet over:

> On reaching Admiral Cunningham's force at 2pm, we expected to be able to relax, since good offing had been made, and the convoy would, we hoped, be outside the range of dive-bombers. This was not so; a formation of Stukas arrived simultaneously with us. One of them went into a dive at our starboard side, its target obviously *Alfridi*. The vital action was taken, a violent turn towards, to make the angle of descent too steep for the pilot. At this point Gammon reported a second Stuka coming at us from the port side. Maurice suggested reversing the rudder, but I thought this would bring the ship up steady just about the time the bombs arrived, and I asked him to continue the turn to starboard.
>
> This was fatal. The first bomb hit us just behind the bridge, exploded in the foremost boiler-room, and started a devastating fire at the after end of the mess decks. The second hit us just ahead of the bridge and blew out a large portion of the port side. Through this aperture (until the gradual flooding of the ship carried it below the water-line) some men escaped from the mess decks with the help of Petty Officer L.T. Bell, who went down over the forecastle side to pull them out. Lieutenant W.G. Wheeler, Chief Electrical Artificier A.P. White and Engine Room Artificier W.A. Scott worked indefatigably in smoke and darkness to save others who had been overcome by the fires.
>
> It was soon clear that the ship was sinking, and Imperial was called alongside to take off survivors. At a quarter to three *Alfridi*'s stern reared up, and the ship slid under the water by the bows. We lost forty nine officers and men, thirteen soldiers and more than thirty of the twice unlucky *Bison*'s crew.[4]

There was a further air attack – the last – at 1530 on the destroyers *Griffin* and *Imperial*, but no damage was done and all the ships arrived safely at Scapa Flow. The thirteen soldiers of the York and Lancaster Regiment rear-guard lost on the *Alfridi* were the only army casualties in the entire evacuation. It had been a magnificently executed operation by the Royal Navy. Admiral Forbes, Commander-in-Chief, Home Fleet, immediately sent the message to all the British, Polish, French and Norwegian war-ships, small boats and merchant ships attached to his fleet:

> During the last three weeks you have been engaged upon two of the most difficult operations of the war that naval forces are required to undertake. You may be proud that you have carried out these opera-tions with the loss at sea of only about twelve officers and men of the Army in the face of heavy air attacks. I am proud to command a fleet

that has shown itself capable of meeting the heavy demands made upon it with such determination and success.[2]

General Carton de Wiart, doughty commander of the ill-fated "Maurice Force" at Namsos and a many-times wounded veteran of forty years' active service added his own tribute:

On my sixtieth birthday, May 5th, we arrived back at Scapa Flow exactly eighteen days after we had set forth. Captain Portal, who commanded the York, thought it was a most fitting occasion for a bottle of champagne. He must have known that to me the taste is extra good after a surgical operation or a major disaster. Norway had given me my first opportunity of seeing the Navy at work, and working with them my admiration for them had grown with the days. We caused them endless trouble, and forced them to do extra and unusual jobs, but instead of showing any signs of resentment they gave us the freedom of their ships.[5]

NOTES TO SOURCES

1. Churchill, W.S. *The Second World War, Vol 1: The Gathering Storm* (Cassell: London, 1948).
2. Brown, D. (Ed). *Naval Operations of the Campaign in Norway: April–June 1940* (Frank Cass: London, 2000).
3. Spurgeon, Commander. S.H.K. Account 90/23/1. Imperial War Museum, London.
4. Vian, Admiral of the Fleet Sir Philip. *Action This Day* (Frederick Muller: London, 1960).
5. Carton de Wiart, Lieutenant General Sir Adrian. *Happy Odyssey* (Jonathan Cape: London, 1950).
6. McIntyre, Captain D. *Narvik* (Evans Bros: London, 1959).
7. Roskill, Captain S.W. *The War at Sea: 1939-1945* (HMSO: London, 1954).
8. Kennedy, Sir Ludovic. *On My Way to the Club* (Collins: London, 1989).
9. Gilbert, Sir Martin. *The Day the War Ended* (Harper-Collins: London, 1995).
10. Young, J. *A Dictionary of the Ships of the Royal Navy of the Second World War* (Patrick Stevens: Cambridge, 1975).

X

The Abandonment of the Norwegian Campaign

With the withdrawal from the central sector, the only foothold that the Allies still had in Norway was in the north in the approaches to Narvik; the town itself being firmly in the hands of the Germans. As explained earlier, Convoy NP1, originally intended for Narvik, had been split on 14 April and some of the ships and their troops sent off on the ill-fated expedition to Namsos in central Norway. The remainder of the convoy, with troops in the three liners *Monarch of Bermuda*, *Reina del Pacifico* and *Batory* had proceeded towards Narvik. From the start it was to prove as ill-conceived and badly conducted as the campaign at Namsos and Aandalsnes. The ships of the Royal and Allied Navies were again to be called upon to perform heroically in support of the land forces.

Serious differences quickly emerged between the Army and Navy commanders as to the conduct of the campaign. This arose partly from the differences in the orders given to Major General Mackesy and to Admiral of the Fleet Lord Cork and Orrery, the respective land and sea commanders, and partly due to their different characters and thus their interpretation of their orders.

Furthermore, the two men had never met prior to their separate arrivals in Norway. Mackesy – cautious and methodical – had received written orders from the War Office which, *inter alia*, ruled out any idea of attempting an opposed landing, and laid down that:

> Your initial task will be to establish your force at Harstad, ensure cooperation of Norwegian forces that may be there and obtain the information necessary to plan your further operations.[1]

The War Office obviously foresaw a steady build-up of the poorly trained and equipped Allied troops, and a methodical approach to the recapture of Narvik. Lord Cork on the other hand – decisive, impulsive and greatly superior in rank to his opposite number – had not been given compatible orders by the Admiralty. He had been briefed by Churchill and Admiral Sir Dudley Pound and:

> ...my impression on leaving London was quite clear that it was desired by H.M. Government to turn the enemy out of Narvik at the earliest possible moment and that I was to act with all promptitude in order to achieve this result.[2]

Any such quick proactive initiative by the Allied military was ruled out by the chaos of the convoy arrival, and the time taken to land the troops and their equipment. The selected military base from which to mount the campaign to recapture Narvik was Harstad. This small port, with limited facilities, was the only town of any size in the area apart from Narvik itself. Harstad was situated on the eastern shore of the island of Hannoy, the largest in the chain of the Lofoten Islands which form the western shore of Vestifiord, leading on to Narvik. Harstad was some thirty miles 'as the crow flies' to the south east of Narvik, but some seventy-five miles by the nearest sea route. The overland routes, over very difficult terrain, were approximately the same distance.

The transports and their escorting warships were initially directed to the Tromso area, at the northern end of the Lofoten Islands, which caused some confusion among the Allied troops. On the destroyer *Echo*, one of the escorts:

> First one boat, then another, then a small procession arrived alongside *Echo*, the passengers representing all the various nationalities of the troops carried. After much heel clicking and saluting at the gangway, they were ushered below to the wardroom where formalities, of course, ceased. There were French Foreign Legionnaires, including snow-trained Alpine regiments, senior Polish officers, all keen to get at the Germans, some British Guards and Norwegian troops, wondering how they could get ashore. "Is this Narvik?" was the general question. "If not, why not?"
>
> Needless to say we could offer no explanation as to why we were in Tromso and not Narvik, except that the urgency of our arrival was not so great as first anticipated and we were now awaiting further instructions. The variety of languages did not facilitate general conversation but, despite this language problem, discussion became livelier as tongues were loosened, aided by naval hospitality and a universal understanding of what the word 'beer' meant. They then turned to some of their own problems. They had, apparently, spent long periods aboard the troop ships before departure from the U.K. The British had discovered that one of their Brigadiers had gone off to Namsos in one of the detached troopships; fodder for mules

on board had nearly run out – where, in deep snow, could they get grass?[3]

The convoy and escorts were ordered back to Harstad, and by 17 April the troops were offloaded. Then it was found that the transports had not been 'tactically loaded': that is, the stores and equipment had not been loaded so that the items which were needed first were the most easily accessible, and the least-needed items were at the bottom of the holds. The system of 'efficient' loading had been employed, based upon the concept of best use of the hold space. The stores and equipment all had to be unloaded and then sorted out.

Because of the confines of Harstad, the three liners had to anchor, ten miles away across the fiord, from whence the troops were ferried ashore by destroyers and "puffers", small local boats.

> Soon after our arrival *Echo*, as were all the other destroyers, was mainly employed on transporting troops and supplies to the various little ports in the seemingly unending fiords in the approaches to Narvik.[3]

There was one diversion. An attempt was made by a German U-boat to disrupt the landings, but she was depth charged by the destroyers *Fearless* and *Brazen*, "which literally blew the U-boat to the surface in the middle of the pattern. The crew abandoned their vessel, *U49*, and started screaming in the most dreadful fashion."[2]

Nearly all the German crew were picked up, and during the rescue *Brazen* picked up confidential papers which revealed the whole U-boat disposition for their Norwegian campaign.

Back in London, the War Cabinet, still reeling from the shock of the ease of the German take-over of Norway a few days earlier, were in a state of some confusion over their Norwegian strategy, the problems likely to be encountered and the level of resources that would be needed.

The subsequent events in central Norway, described earlier, and then later at Narvik and the north of the country, were to conclusively demonstrate the inadequacy of Allied responses to German ambitions and power in this first year of the war. The confusion on the Allied side extended to the respective naval and military commanders in Narvik. Despite a number of meetings, they were unable to agree any plan for the rapid recapture of Narvik and its surrounding area. Admiral of the Fleet Lord Cork and Orrery wanted to press ahead with an early naval-led assault upon Narvik, while General Mackesy considered this unduly hazardous and probably impossible, because of the deep snow ashore and because the very few landing craft that were available would mean that most of his troops would have to be ferried ashore, probably in the face of heavy machine gun fire, in open naval boats. To this he was totally opposed. In a message to General Sir Edmund Ironside, Chief of the Imperial General Staff, the British Commander-in-Chief, he expressed the view that a naval bombardment would not wipe out German gun emplacements and machine gun nests, and that any attempt to do so would also produce heavy civilian casualties and severe civic damage to the town and port of Narvik. Only if the bombardment itself induced the enemy to surrender would he countenance his troops going ashore in open boats. General Mackesy's alternative plan, an unopposed landing of the shores of Rombaksfiord and an advance overland to envelop Narvik, was not possible through the heavy snow, and would have to wait until the thaw set in.

On 21 April, the War Cabinet placed Lord Cork and Orrery in supreme command of the expeditionary force, and on 24 April, following three days of heavy snow which prevented any action, naval or military, orders were given for a naval bombardment of Narvik, with the aim of forcing the surrender of the German garrison there. The assault was carried out by the battleship *Warspite*, cruisers *Effingham* and *Enterprise* and the destroyer *Zulu*.

An escort screen was provided by the destroyers *Hostile*, *Havock*, *Hero* and *Foxhound*, while the repair vessel *Vindictive* embarked a battalion of the Irish Guards, ready to land if the bombardment succeeded in its aim of forcing a German capitulation. The three hour bombardment, against targets difficult to locate under their blanket of deep snow and carried out under conditions of recurring snowstorms, produced little observable damage. A wireless station was destroyed, together with small railway buildings and rolling stock, and a ferry steamer was sunk. It did not result in the evacuation or surrender of the German garrison, and the Irish Guards were disembarked.

Thereafter, although the Government at home and Lord Cork and Orrery on his flagship *Aurora* continued to press the army commander for a decisive attack, the military activity was confined to the garnering of reinforcements and the gradual investment of the Narvik peninsula in preparation for a land assault upon the town when the weather conditions improved. Three battalions of French Chasseurs Alpins arrived on 27 April, followed the next day by General Bethoart as military commander of the French forces. Early in May, two battalions of French Foreign Legionnaires and four battalions of Polish troops arrived, together with a battery of 25-pounder guns.

The demands upon the Allied destroyers at this time were very heavy, particularly since the increasing German land activity in the Low Countries and Northern France necessitated the withdrawal of numbers of Allied destroyers as cover against the threat of invasion of Great Britain. The destroyers – jacks of all trades – were in constant demand for fetching and carrying, ferrying troops and bombarding land targets. The Polish destroyers *Blyskawica* and *Grom*, with their seven 4.7-inch guns, were assigned bombarding duties. On *Blyskawica*:

> On arrival at Narvik we took up our patrol. We were guarding a tunnel through which the Germans were entering Narvik. We fired frequently into the tunnel to keep the Germans out. Then one fine morning the Germans opened fire with small arms. We were hit several times but damage was slight. Then the Germans opened fire with larger guns and we were hit several times but damage was again slight and there were no casualties. Then the [German] air force took over and we were bombed at frequent intervals. We managed to avoid the bombs...We were relieved by ORP *Grom*.[4]

From early May onwards the Allies' naval problems in the Narvik area were worsened by increased German air activity following the evacuation of Allied troops from central Norway. The Luftwaffe was then able to move not only to airfields nearer to the Narvik theatre but also to reinforce its high-level bombers with the much more deadly Stuka dive bomber. The effect of the much increased Luftwaffe activity was not slow in coming. On 5 May the Polish destroyer *Grom* was shelling railway tracks and a road-bridge leading to Narvik used by German troops when, at the entrance to Rombaksfiord, she was hit by German bombs. She was very unlucky, and the German success was regarded as something of a freak happening. The bomber dropped a stick of six bombs from a height of some 17,000 feet. At that stage of the war bomb aiming accuracy was not very precise, but out of a stick of six bombs two struck *Grom*, one amidships among the deck torpedoes, exploding them and the compressed air container the other the side of the ship. It was a devastating strike: the ship broke in two and sank in two minutes. Although boats from *Aurora*, *Faulknor* and *Bedouin* were quickly on the scene, fifty-nine of *Grom*'s crew were killed and another twenty-four wounded out of a total crew of 180 officers and men. Lieutenant J. Tumaniszwili remembered:

> At the time of the sinking of *Grom*, I was a Sub-Lieutenant...aboard the Polish destroyer ORP *Burza*. I witnessed the transfer of survivors from the British battleship HMS *Resolution* to the hospital ship *Atlantis*...
> We stood at anchor in the sleepy town of Harstad...To my surprise up the gangplank came a Rear-Admiral. He informed our captain, Commander W. Francki, of the sinking of the ORP *Grom* and offered condolences. No details were known yet, including how many may have died. He relayed that the survivors were on board HMS *Resolution* and were to be transferred by us to the hospital ship *Atlantis*. We were to proceed immediately. Needless to say we were

very saddened and somewhat shook up by the news. We had lost one of the three destroyers that left Poland a day before the war began. I was worried about my close colleague Victor Szabunia who was serving on board the *Grom*. Had he survived?

We left Harstad and set course for Narvik…When we came closer, through my binoculars, I could see the ship's company lining the decks. On the main deck aft I noticed some strangely dressed civilians. I recognised some…they were men from the *Grom* and there was Victor with his smiling face.[5]

The transfer of the *Grom*'s wounded and survivors from *Resolution* to *Burza* was emotional. Lieutenant Tumaniszwili has written:

In the meantime the lines were being dropped and we were shoving off. The officers and crew of HMS *Resolution* were standing to attention and suddenly we heard the Polish National Anthem played by the battleship band. I felt a lump in my throat and had to clinch my lips to stop my unmanly sobbing. Looking round I saw some men with tears running down their cheeks. *Burza* was slowly and majestically leaving its friends. Friends who were paying their respects to those who perished. We were all under a magical spell at that moment and I was sure our hearts were beating so loud that they could be heard a thousand miles away in Poland. The last chords of the "Dabrowski Mazurka" died away. The spell was broken by the loud shouts of the battleship crew "Hurrah! Hurrah! Hurrah!". We responded shouting "Niech zyje Royal Navy! Niech zyje Wielka Brytanja" [Long live the Royal Navy! Long live Great Britain]. Now some distance away, we could hear the melody of the "Beer Barrel Polka" ["Roll out the Barrel"], one of the most popular tunes among the British sailors. The brisk winds of the fast moving destroyer swept away the remaining emotions and unmanly tears.[5]

The efforts and devotion to the Allied cause of the popular Polish sailors on the destroyers had not gone unnoticed or unappreciated. Lord Cork and Orrery, in a signal to the Admiralty reporting the loss of the *Grom*, included the proposal: "I hope that the manning of a British destroyer by the crew of the Polish destroyer Grom may have favourable consideration, they are excellent material."[4] The proposal was seized upon by the Admiralty: by the war's end in May 1945, the Polish Navy consisted of one cruiser, six destroyers, three submarines and five motor torpedo boats, all manned by Polish officers and seamen, operating under Admiralty control.

The withdrawal of Allied forces from central Norway in early May, together with fears of an imminent German assault against the Low

Countries and northern France that would bring Britain face-to-face with German forces across the narrow Straits of Dover, galvanised public opinion in Britain and brought to a head the growing criticism of the Conservative Government's handling of the war. Even the Royal Navy, valiantly as it had performed throughout the war, was implicated in this hurtful attack. The Labour Opposition called for a debate on the war situation, which took place on 7 May. It was an angry confrontation, and the Government – especially the Prime Minister, Neville Chamberlain – were bitterly attacked from all sides, including their own back-benchers.

It was obvious that the Government could not go on: it had lost the confidence of the House and of the Nation. On Friday 10 May 1940 Neville Chamberlain resigned and a new Coalition Government was formed with Winston Churchill as its Prime Minister. That same day German troops invaded Holland and Belgium and began their push into northern France. It was against this background of political and national crisis back home that the Allied forces in Norway continued their struggle to take Narvik.

On land, no significant progress was being made. General Mackesy continued to insist upon the build-up of his forces in keeping with a strategy of envelopment, as against an opposed landing by a direct attack in order to take the town. Meanwhile, with Allied abandonment of central Norway, strong German forces were beginning to advance up the coast from the south to reinforce their Narvik garrison. In order to counter this threat the destroyer *Janus* had landed a hundred French Chasseurs-Alpins troops at Mosjoen, the terminus of the railway running from Namsos, some hundred miles to the south, on 2 May. At about the same time, a company of Scots Guards was landed at Bodo, the small port at the entrance of the Vestifiord astride the main road to the north, with the objective of preventing it from being taken by German paratroops. A further small force, "Scissorsforce", in five independent companies under Lieutenant Colonel C.M.V. Gubbins, was sent to the area to harass and delay the advance up the sole useable road to the north.[6]

Colonel Gubbins and his force arrived on 4 May. One company was positioned at Mo, a small township at the head of Ranfiord, some fifty miles north of Mosjoen. The other companies were spread across the German lines of advance. Once again, the forces deployed by the Allied command proved totally inadequate to the allotted task. The Germans responded with dash, and completely outmanoeuvred the Allied initiative with a daring sea-borne operation. A crew made up from the German destroyers at Trondheim manned the Norwegian coastal vessel *Nord-Norge* and took 300 German troops by sea through the Inner Leads to land at Mo and cut off "Scissorsforce". By the time the only available British warships, the cruiser *Calcutta* and the tribal destroyer *Zulu*, arrived on the scene, the German troops had been landed and reinforced by a further forty troops, with mortars and machine guns landed from Dornier sea-planes.

Although the *Nord-Norge* was sunk before her stores could be landed, the German troops ashore were able to drive out the company-strength and lightly-armed Allied troops opposing them, and secure the township. They also effectively cut off the line of retreat of "Scissorsforce", and Colonel Gubbins was forced to evacuate his men in small locally secured boats and retire to the north.

The long-awaited attack on Narvik was scheduled for 13 May. It would involve a landing at Bjerkvik at the head of Herjangsfiord to the north of Narvik, and a formidable naval force was assembled to enable the landing. In the cruiser *Effingham* was Lord Cork, General Bethouart, Commander of the French land forces, and General Auckinleck, who had arrived from the United Kingdom the previous day to relieve General Mackesy.

> Then came the assault upon Bjerkvik. At nine o'clock in the evening we began the approach through Ofotfiord and into Herjangsfiord. *Havelock* led the way, with *Fame* to starboard and *Somali* to port. We arrived at our bombarding position shortly before midnight, but there was still some daylight. Behind us were tank and armoured landing craft ,and the *Aurora,_Protector,_Effingham_*and *Vindictive,* all packed with British, French and Polish troops.
>
> On our fo'castle a small detachment of Foreign Legion had mounted trench mortars and these opened fire as we closed the beach. The enemy offered some resistance with light weapons and some machine gun bullets flattened against our windscreen. All ships put up a terrific bombardment and our troops had little trouble once they got ashore. In the background, silhouetted against the snow, was the mighty *Resolution* and her escorts *Basilisk* and *Wren*. It must have been a forbidding sight to the enemy ashore.[7]

The attack on Bjerkvik was successful and the town quickly taken at a cost of thirty-six casualties. The contribution made by the naval bombardment is debatable: the targets ashore were difficult to locate and destroy. Captain Stevens of the destroyer *Havelock* explained:

> Enemy machine gun posts were immediately, but only temporarily, silenced by a few rounds of 4.7-inch shell. These posts were heavily concealed and probably equipped with light automatic guns, which could be lowered and raised as easily as a rifle.[2]

The Allied ships in the fiord were not such difficult targets to find, and were subject to heavy air attacks. Between 11 and 27 May the anti-aircraft cruiser *Cairo* engaged enemy aircraft on all but two days, expending 5,700 rounds of ammunition in the process. So heavy was the wear on her guns that half of them had to be taken out of commission because of the danger of premature shell bursts from the barrels, whose rifling had been worn almost smooth.[1] While the preliminaries for the eventual attack on Narvik from the north were proceeding more-or-less to plan, the Allied position south of Narvik was rapidly deteriorating in the face of the steady German advance northwards from the Trondheim area. To try to stem this German threat, General Auckinleck sent a large proportion of the British force in the Narvik area south on 13 May. The Irish Guards, the Brigade Headquarters, a troop of 3rd Hussars and their tanks, some anti-aircraft guns and other military stores sailed on the evening of 14 May in the troopship *Chrobry* escorted by the destroyer *Wolverine* and the sloop *Stork*. About midnight, they were attacked by German dive-bombers when in the middle of Vestfiord *en route* to the southern flank, and *Chrobry* was set on fire and badly damaged. Several army personnel were killed, including a number of senior officers.

Wolverine took off 700 troops and the ship's crew, and the *Stork* a further 300, before returning them to Harstad. The smoking but still afloat *Chrobry* was sunk by aircraft from the carrier *Ark Royal* on 16 May; her cargo, anti-aircraft guns, tanks and equipment sinking with her.

On 17 May another attempt to reinforce the southern flank was made, and the South Wales Borderers sailed for Bodo from Harstad in the cruiser *Effingham*. They were escorted by the cruisers *Coventry* and *Cairo* and the destroyers *Echo* and *Matabele*. Approaching Bod, *Effingham* attempted a short cut and, together with her close escort *Matabele*, struck rocks.* Although there were no casualties and *Matabele* was not badly damaged, *Effingham* was firmly aground and could not be towed off. She became a total loss, together with her cargo of machine-gun carriers and military stores. The rescued Irish Guards and South Wales Borderers were eventually transported to their southern flank destination in destroyers and small coastal craft.

Since the bulk of the British troops were now committed to trying to stem the German advance on the southern flank, the delayed attack upon Narvik, after the fall of Bjerkvik, would now be made by forces composed mainly of French and Polish troops under the command of General Bethouart. However, by now the focus of Allied concern was not Norway, but elsewhere. John Colville, a member of the Prime Minister's staff at No. 10 Downing Street, recorded in his diary entry for 13 May:

> Another crisis is brewing in the Mediterranean and it begins to look as if Italy may come in against us. Winston apparently thinks so, but I feel much will depend upon events in the Low Countries.[8]

With Allied interest and activity now increasingly focused on France and the Low Countries, the Norwegian Campaign was relegated to that of a

---

* See Chapter Five.

minor, and expensive, sideshow. Ships were drawn away from northern Norwegian waters either to reinforce the Mediterranean Fleet against any Italian entry into the war, or to prepare for the increasingly likely withdrawal of the British Expeditionary Forces from France and the defence of the United Kingdom. Such RAF fighter aircraft that the aircraft-carriers of the Royal Navy had been able to ferry to improvised airfields in the Narvik area were deemed to be more urgently needed back home. For the French forces stranded in Norway, preparing for the attack on Narvik at must have been a most worrying time. Like their Polish allies, they could soon be homeless.

On 21 May Churchill told the Cabinet that the forces in the Narvik area might have to be withdrawn, and the next day the Allied Chiefs of Staff agreed with this view. On 24 May Lord Cork received a telegram from the War Cabinet:

> HMG has decided your forces are to be evacuated from Northern Norway at the earliest possible moment. Reason for this is that the troops, ships and certain equipment are urgently needed for defence of the United Kingdom.
>
> We understand from military point of view operation of evacuation will be facilitated if enemy forces are largely destroyed or captured. Moreover destruction of railway and Narvik port facilities make its capture highly desirable.
>
> Norwegian Government have not, repeat not, been informed and greatest secrecy should be observed.[6]

The attack upon Narvik began on the night of 27–28 May – about the time that the evacuation of the British Expeditionary Force troops from Dunkirk began.* Under cover of a naval bombardment, French and Polish troops, together with some Norwegians, stormed ashore and drove the Germans from the town. The naval forces gave what gunfire support they could with their now depleted and thinly deployed ships. The cruiser *Southampton* fired her 6-inch guns at selected targets ashore from a range of 4,000 yards, while the anti-aircraft cruisers and destroyers, with their smaller calibre main armament, closed in to about 1,000 to 2,000 yards. The primary objective of the naval gunfire was to prevent the enemy from reinforcing their garrison in the town.

At 0500 on 28 May, some thirty German bombers arrived overhead. They had the sky to themselves: the RAF fighters designated to provide air cover for the daylight hours of the landing were fogbound at their base at Bardufoss. More dive bombers arrived. Lieutenant John Mosse, on *Havelock*'s bridge during the atttack, recounted the scene:

> Above the general din, we heard the scream of a dive bomber as it roared out of the sky and dropped two bombs just astern of

Southampton. Arriving in formations of fifteen or twenty planes at a time, they bombed us incessantly for two hours. Everyone increased to full speed and manoeuvred independently within the narrow limits of the fiord which was only three miles wide. The valley reeked with the bitter stench of cordite fumes from the guns. Time and again the ships were hidden from one another by vast columns of water. For a few moments a curtain of water completely bridged the entrance to Rombaksfiord. The conversation on the bridge went:

> "One's coming in on the starboard side sir"
> "He's diving, sir."
> "Hard astarboard. Three hundred revolutions"
> "Bombs dropped, sir."
> "Three coming from astern, out of the sun, sir."
> "Port thirty."
> "Southampton's getting a bit close, sir"
> "Hard aport."
> "One bearing green nine o. He's diving, sir."
> "I'll kill the next — who says that. Starboard thirty."
> "Down everybody."[7]

The bombarding ships were forced to take what evasive action they could: HMS *Cairo* was unable to avoid all the bombs. From *Havelock* (Cdr E.B.K. Stevens), Lieutenant Mosse noted:

> *Cairo's* hit! She had caught two bombs, one just before the bridge, one just abaft. She stooped for a short time with smoke and flames pouring from her, then, to our intense relief, she got under way again and smothered the fire. Besides carrying the Admiral, she had on board the French General Berthouart, and we were ordered alongside to take off the General and his staff. As we were securing we glanced up at her bridge. There, utterly unmoved and glaring down from the side in a tin hat, was the red monocled face of Admiral of the Fleet, the Earl of Cork and Orrery, better known as "Ginger" Boyle, whom Lawrence of Arabia had once described as "white-hot". "Good morning Steve" he said laconically.[7]

The *Cairo* had thirty casualties, killed and wounded, but was able to make her way back to the United Kingdom.

Almost immediately after the capture of Narvik, plans for the withdrawal of Norway were begun. It was decided to withdraw the hard-pressed forces from the southern flank as soon as possible, and the troops

---

* See Chapter Twelve.

there were successfully evacuated from Bodo between 29 and 31 May. 1,000 men were taken directly back to the United Kingdom in the fleet repair ship *Vindictive,* while the remainder of the force was withdrawn to Harstad in the destroyers *Firedrake, Vanoc, Arrow, Havelock* and *Echo,* and in some small Norwegian coasters.

The Norwegian Government was informed on 1 June of the Allied intention to withdraw totally from their country. Although they were naturally dismayed and upset, the decision, given the parlous state that Britain and France were now in, was accepted as inevitable. Arrangements were made to bring the King of Norway, the Crown Prince, members of the Norwegian Royal Family, Government, French and Polish embassy staff and members of the Corps Diplomatique, in all some 461 men and women, back to the United Kingdom in the cruiser *Devonshire,* which left Tromso at 2030 on 7 June.[2]

By now, on the continent, Holland had fallen, Belgium was about to do so, and German forces were advancing into northern France and seriously threatened to overrun the channel ports and cut off the British Expeditionary Force. The evacuation of Dunkirk took place between 26 May and 4 June; and on 10 June Italy declared war on Britain and France. The 24,500 troops in Norway could expect little outside help. With the help of a dwindling number of Royal Navy warships, they would have to start their journey home as best they could. The Admiralty was able to provide troopships and transports, which left Britain either singly or in small groups to arrive at Tromso and Harstad during the first week of June. Lord Cork had asked for additional destroyers, to provide escorts and a measure of protection for the loaded ships against air and U-boat attacks on their return journey. Other than the three screening the *Ark Royal* (*Diana, Acheron* and *Highlander*) and the two screening *Glorious* (*Ardent* and *Acasta*) he only had six. These six (*Havelock, Fame, Firedrake, Beagle, Echo* and *Delight*) were fully occupied ferrying troops to the evacuating transports and protecting the anchorages against attack. The Admiralty spared him three further ships: *Arrow, Walker* and the sloop *Stork.* On the positive side, the aircraft carriers *Ark Royal* and *Glorious* had arrived on 2 June, and their aircraft were able to provide some air cover for the embarking troops and to attack German airfields and communications.

Lord Cork organised his evacuating troopships into two main groups and his store ships into a separate 'slow convoy', and distributed his few escorts as best he could among them.

Group One, escorted by the fleet repair-ship *Vindictive,* consisted of the troopships *Monarch of Bermuda, Batory, Sobieski, Franconia, Lancastria* and *Geordic.* Between them they carried 15,000 men. This group set off in the early hours of 7 June and, by prior arrangement, were met early the next day by the battleship *Valiant* and her screen of four Tribal class destroyers: *Tartar, Mashona, Bedouin* and *Ashanti.* They were later joined by a close convoy escort of five destroyers: *Atherstone, Wolverine, Witherington, Antelope_*and *Viscount*, which had been delayed by thick fog. As they approached the Clyde, *Valiant* and her destroyers left the convoy, which arrived safely in Scotland.

Group Two, carrying the remaining 10,000 men, left at 2300 on 8 June in the troopships *Oransay, Ormonde, Arandora Star, Duchess of York, Royal Ulsterman, Ulster Prince* and *Ulster Monarch*. The *Vandyck* had been sunk by German aircraft on her way to the rendezvous point. The troopships had an escort made up of the cruiser *Southampton*, the anti-aircraft cruiser *Coventry* and the destroyers *Havelock, Fame, Firedrake, Beagle* and *Delight*. Rear Admiral Vian in *Coventry* was in charge of the convoy, and Lord Cork, accompanied by Generals Auckinleck and Bethouart, sailed in the *Southampton*. The *Ark Royal* accompanied the convoy, and her aircraft and screen of three destroyers, *Diane, Acheron* and *Highlander*, searched for possible enemy submarines, surface ships and aircraft. The convoy duly arrived unscathed at the ports in the United Kingdom.

The 'Slow Convoy', made up of two groups, sailed on 7 June. That from Harstad consisted of the storeships *Blackheath, Oligarch, Harmatton, Cromarty, Firth, Theseus, Acrity, Coxwold* and *Couch*. They were escorted by the destroyer *Arrow*, the sloop *Stork* and ten armed trawlers. The group from Tromso consisted of the *Oil Pioneer, Yermont, Arbroath* and *Nyakoa*, with an escort of four armed trawlers.

The Allied evacuation had been carried out in great secrecy and the withdrawal of troops with great tactical skill – such that it came as something of a surprise to the Germans, who allowed the various convoys to sail home without interference from their Navy. It wasn't until the 7 June that the first report of an Allied convoy being at sea off the coast of Norway reached German ships engaged in "Operation Juno". The object of this enemy operation was to relieve pressure on the German land forces in the Narvik area by attacking Allied transports and warships in the Narvik/Harstad environs, and disrupting Allied supply convoys *en route* there. The German force for "Operation Juno" was a powerful one. It consisted of the battlecruisers *Scharnhorst* and *Gneisenau*, the cruiser *Hipper*, and the four destroyers *Karl Galster, Hans Lody, Erich Steinbrink* and *Hermann Schoemann*.

At 0630 on 8 June the German force claimed its first victims: the 5,000 ton tanker *Oil Pioneer* and her escorting trawler *Juniper*, elements of the slow convoy from Tromso. The Germans picked up twenty-five survivors from the tanker and four from the trawler. *Scharnhorst* and *Hipper* then flew off scouting aircraft to search for other targets. The plane from the *Scharnhorst*, searching to the north, reported two ships. *Hipper* was sent to deal with them. They turned out to be the 20,000-ton troopship *Orama*, returning to the United Kingdom without escort, empty of troops because she had arrived in Norway with insufficient oil or water to await a return, loaded, with the main convoys. She did however have on board some one hundred German prisoners of war. The *Hipper* jammed *Orama's* SOS signals and sank her at 1106, picking up 275 survivors. The other ship was the hospital ship *Atlantis*. In accordance with the Geneva Convention, the *Atlantis* was allowed to proceed on her way, unmolested by the German warship, on the understanding that she did not use her wireless to reveal the German positions. At 1400 Admiral Marschall detached the *Hipper* and his four destroyers to Trondheim to refuel, and continued north with *Scharnhorst* and *Gneisenau* to search for the British aircraft carriers reported to be operating in the Andenes area.

In addition to the escorted Allied convoys returning to the United Kingdom, there was one other British naval force at sea. At 0253 on 8 June the aircraft carrier *Glorious* had been detached from the main group of ships leaving Norwegian waters and sent ahead of the escorting force (the *Ark Royal*, two cruisers and eight destroyers) screening the main convoy carrying 12,000 evacuated troops. The *Glorious* had only a light screen of two destroyers, the *Acasta* (Commander C.E. Glasfurd) and *Ardent* (Lieutenant-Commander J.F.Barker). To this day there is controversy as to why she sailed separately, only a few hours ahead of the other ships.

Officially, she left early because she was short of fuel. However, this explanation has been widely criticised by naval historians[9][10] and others.[11] Winston Churchill, by then of course Prime Minister and no longer First Lord of the Admiralty, was sceptical, later writing:

> The *Glorious* had been detached early that morning to proceed home independently owing to a shortage of fuel...The explanation is not convincing. The *Glorious* presumably had enough fuel to steam at the speed of the convoy. All should have been kept together.[11]

Other explanations have been proposed to account for the separate sailing which was to have disastrous consequences. Central to these explanations is the controversy over the character and behaviour of the captain of *Glorious*, Captain G. D'Oyly-Hughes. Though he had his supporters and friends, many found him authoritarian and ill-tempered. A distinguished First World War submariner decorated for his exploits, he had little carrier experience, having been appointed Captain of *Glorious* only in May 1939. Unfortunately for an aircraft carrier captain, he reportedly had little time for naval aviation or aviators. It was generally agreed that *Glorious* was not a happy ship. The aircraft carrier had been operating in Norwegian waters since 23 April, using her aircraft to assist both the naval operations and the troops ashore. On 14 May she sailed from Greenock, ferrying aircraft for operations ashore in Norway. On board she carried six Walrus aircraft, which were flown off to Harstad on 18 May, and eighteen crane-loaded Hawker Hurricane fighters of 46 Squadron of the Royal Air Force, which were to be flown off the carrier when near the Norwegian coast to operate from a prepared airfield at Bardnfoss. These were duly flown off on 26 May. For her own protection, *Glorious* carried six Sea Gladiators of 802 Squadron and six Swordfish of 823 Squadron Fleet Air Arm. The Hurricane pilots, under the command of Squadron Leader K.B.B. Cross, sailed with their planes. Their ground crews sailed separately in the troop-ship *Batory*. The RAF pilots too found that the *Glorious* was not a happy ship. There had been some trouble over leave allowances when the aircraft carrier had returned from Norway on 4 May, and when the ship sailed again ten days later many of her crew were missing, either through desertion or overstaying their leave. Her captain was also having difficulties in his relationship with some of his senior officers, particularly those of the flying arm of the aircraft carrier. The leader of the RAF Hurricane pilots, Squadron Leader Cross, reported:

> My immediate boss was [Commander] J.B. Heath who welcomed me on board and said come and meet the captain. D'Oyly-Hughes was a very formidable looking man. We got no welcome from him. He looked at me and nodded. He never asked to meet the other pilots. So I thought, well, this is the way they went on in the Navy.[10]

It was during this penultimate trip of the *Glorious* to Norwegian waters that the antagonism between the Captain and the senior officers of the Fleet Air Arm serving on the carrier came to a head. Lord Cork, in overall command of the Norwegian campaign, had suggested that aircraft from *Glorious* might consider mounting an air attack upon the German forces in the area of Mosjoen. Captain D'Oyly-Hughes took this suggestion as an opportunity for some offensive action, after the frustrations of the aircraft ferrying duties upon which *Glorious* had been employed. This was despite the fact – of which Lord Cork was probably unaware when he signalled his suggestion – that *Glorious* had no Skua dive-bombers on board, and was only carrying a token protection force of the six obsolescent Sea Gladiator biplane fighters and the six equally obsolescent Swordfish biplane torpedo bombers, ill suited for the bombing of land targets. Captain D'Oyly-Hughes's two senior Fleet Air Arm officers, Commander Heath and Lieutenant-Commander E.H.P. Slessor, were doubtful of the outcome of an attack with its vague objective: "To bomb anything they find – roads, aerodromes, bridges – anything they can find."[10] The aviators pointed out that the ship carried no appropriate maps of the target area, which was, in any case, well outside the Swordfish's operational range unless extra fuel tanks were fitted, which would have taken some twenty-four hours. There was no information about likely targets or their location, and no intelligence on likely opposition from German fighter aircraft. Furthermore, the Swordfish aircraft, with a top speed of 130 knots, was notoriously vulnerable to machine gun and small arms fire when flying in a low-level attack role in broad daylight. The two Fleet Air Arm officers felt compelled to advise their Captain that the operation was likely to be one of suicidal risk for very little tactical gain.[12] They were ordered to go ahead and plan the attack with its now redefined objective: "To bomb any suitable objectives that can be found, including troops on road between Hemnes and Mosjoen, small bridges or viaducts and enemy aerodromes."[10] When the aviator selected to lead the attack was informed of the plans, he was so concerned about the suicidal nature of the proposal that he asked permission to put his views in person to the Captain. When the three Fleet Air Arm officers returned to the Captain with their plan of attack and again expressed their doubts about its likely outcome, Captain D'Oyly-Hughes reportedly lost his temper and relieved Commander Heath of his duties. The Commander went to his cabin, and the Captain cancelled the plans for the sortie.

Among the crews on board *Glorious* there was mixed support for both the Captain and the Commander; with some feeling that an attack attempt ought to have been made even if it had to be aborted, others that it was foolishly suicidal: "The trouble between the Captain and Commander [Air] was known and talked about by some members of the ship's company and although nobody knew the full facts people took sides in the argument."[13] Commander Heath was put ashore when the *Glorious* returned to Scapa Flow, and steps were put in hand to deal with the incident. At 1755 on 30 May a signal was sent from the Commander-in-Chief to *Glorious*: "Commander J.B. Heath is to be sent from Glorious to Dunblane Castle [the depot ship] tonight, Thursday, and is to be temporarily accommodated there until further notice."[10] *Glorious*, without Commander Heath but with his friend Lieutenant-Commander Slessor somewhat reluctantly in charge of the air-arm of the ship, left again for Norwegian waters, in company with *Ark Royal*, on the evening of 2 June.

That, briefly, is the background to the alleged real reason for the early detached departure time of *Glorious* from Norway on 8 June: so that Captain D'Oyly-Hughes could pursue courts martial proceedings against Commander Heath. This explanation has always been dismissed in official circles as too trivial a reason and unworthy of Captain D'Oyly-Hughes. However, again controversially, Lieutenant Commander E.G. Le Geyt, Captain of the destroyer *Diana*, which had been in close escort company with *Ark Royal* and *Glorious* immediately prior to the latter's departure, has claimed that a signal had passed from *Glorious* to Vice-Admiral Wells in *Ark Royal* at about 0225 requesting permission to depart immediately to Scapa Flow, "for the purpose of making preparations for impending courts martial."[10] The request, if made, was approved: *Glorious* left with *Acasta* and *Ardent* at 0253.

Before leaving, *Glorious* had received back on board what was left of the

RAF Hurricane and FAA Sea Gladiators, sent barely a fortnight earlier to help protect the Allied troops against Luftwaffe attacks, for return to the United Kingdom. The Hurricanes in particular would make an invaluable contribution in the impending Battle of Britain, now only weeks away, over the skies of southern England. Their retrieval back on board was a ground-breaking operation carried out with great skill and daring by the RAF pilots, who otherwise would have had to destroy their aircraft to prevent them from falling into German hands. It was to be the first time that the fast landing-speed Hurricanes had ever attempted to land on the short pitching deck of an aircraft carrier. A sandbag in the tail-frame of the aircraft, to help keep the tail down when full brakes were applied on touchdown was the aircrafts' only hastily improvised safety aid. *Glorious* was to do her part by steaming into the wind at her top speed of 29 to 30 knots. Flight Lieutenant P.G. Jameson, leading the first test landing of three Hurricanes on the evening of 7 June, reported:

> The Captain of the *Glorious* kept his word. When we saw the *Glorious* it was going flat out, with steam pouring out of every rivet hole. While we waited for a signal to land on, Sergeant Taylor went down and made a perfect landing on the carrier. When I tackled him about it later, he said he had engine trouble, but I suspect he really wanted to be the first chap to land a Hurricane on a carrier.[10]

Early the next day, commencing at 0115 hours, *Glorious* landed ten Sea Gladiators and a further seven RAF Hurricanes, the latter led by Squadron Leader Cross – later, Air Marshall Sir Kenneth Cross. When the Squadron Leader went up to the bridge to report to Captain D'Oyly-Hughes, instead of the expected congratulations he found the Captain "complaining about how long we had taken to do it."[10] Clearly the Captain was in a hurry to leave.

Mid-afternoon found the three ships, the destroyers ahead on either bow of the *Glorious*, some two hundred miles from the Norwegian coast and two hundred miles nearer home and safety. The ships were zigzagging about a mean course of 250° and steaming at seventeen knots, presumably in order to conserve fuel but at a sufficient speed to thwart U-boat attack. *Glorious* had only twelve of her eighteen boilers connected up. Visibility was excellent, with a light wind and a northerly swell running. On board the carrier there was a surprisingly relaxed atmosphere; she had no patrolling aircraft aloft, and, although one Swordfish torpedo plane and a flight of three Sea Gladiator fighters from her own skeletal air complement were on ten-minutes stand-by notice, no aircraft were ranged on the flight deck. The embarked twenty Hurricanes and Sea Gladiators were stowed below. There was no look-out in the crow's-nest, although the ship carried no radar to warn of approaching enemy ships or planes, and the ship was at cruising stations, a fourth degree of readiness, with the crew enjoying a 'make and mend' or an officially designated period of rest and relaxation. Then, at 1545, in perfect visibility, *Glorious*'s smoke was spotted by Midshipman Siegfried Goss, stationed on look-out duty high in the top platform of the *Scharnhorst*. Together with the *Gneisenau*, the two German battle-cruisers closed at full speed to investigate. Some twenty minutes later they were spotted from the *Glorious* and the destroyer *Ardent* was sent to challenge, while *Glorious* turned away at her best speed, but with full speed capacity not immediately available due to some of her boilers being disconnected. *Ardent*'s challenge to the oncoming ships was answered by gunfire from the *Gneisenau*'s secondary armament of 5.9-inch guns, and the two destroyers made smoke to aid the carrier's escape:

> The destroyers were magnificent, truly, and they started by laying a smoke screen across our stern. The first didn't lay, you could still see these German ships through the smoke screen or underneath it, then the second destroyer took over and laid a beautiful, marvellous smoke screen, tip-top, copybook.[14]

But there was to be no escape. At 1632 the forward 11-inch guns of the *Scharnhorst* opened fire at a range of some 28,000 yards, or nearly fourteen miles, far beyond the range of the 4.7-inch guns of the Glorious and her two destroyers. *Gneisenau* opened fire at 1645.

> Just after 1600 that day I was having tea in the P.O.'s mess when action stations sounded. On arrival at the starboard director pom-pom platform I saw splashes close to the ship's side. At first I thought they were bombs. Then looking around I saw two ships, hull down. I could see the flashes and smoke from their guns. Our 4.7-inch guns were useless because the enemy was too far away out of our range. We altered course away, the enemy now being on our port side. The destroyers *Acasta* and *Ardent* came in close and made a smokescreen. This was difficult because the weather was still bright and clear.[13]

Glorious desperately tried to send off signals reporting her position and situation, but these were either jammed by the radio operators on the *Gneisenau* or sent on the wrong frequency, and in any case the carrier's main wireless aerial was shot away early in the action. A corrupted message was picked up by the *Devonshire* some one hundred miles away, but the cruiser could do nothing to help the *Glorious* or her escorts, and, carrying the King of Norway and his Government in secrecy to the United Kingdom, controversially decided not to break radio silence to pass on the very faint and garbled message.

The captains and crews of the *Acasta* and *Ardent* did their utmost to fend off their two powerful adversaries. They employed every trick in the destroyer's armoury: they laid masking smoke screens; they exposed themselves to try to draw the enemy's fire, violently changing course and speed to put off the German gunners; they made threatening torpedo runs to try to force the German ships to turn away. Extracts from the log of the *Gneisenau* shows how hard they tried and how well they succeeded:

> 1619. One destroyer reported to be turning towards the *Gneisenau*.
> 1626. Proceeding at 26 knots. Secondary armament opened fire on British destroyer.
> 1635. *Glorious* enveloped in smoke screen laid by the destroyers. Conditions for guns very difficult.
> 1640. Speed 29 knots. The destroyer *Ardent* also enveloped in a smoke screen, now became visible again, and opened fire at a range of 16,400 yards.
> 1642. *Gneisenau* turned hard to starboard to avoid a torpedo attack, but it proved a false alarm and she resumed her previous course.[15]*

The Captain of the *Gneisenau* was particularly impressed by the tactics of the *Ardent*, who was proving an elusive opponent:

> The conduct of the *Ardent* was particularly spirited and clever. She outmanoeuvred the fall of shot very capably, laid smoke and used it with great skill, and varied her speed from 10 to 35 knots. In this way she made the task of our guns very difficult.[15]

At 1647 *Ardent* was sighted from *Scharnhorst*. The destroyer fired off torpedoes and retired into the smokescreen. At 1658 *Gneisenau* sighted *Ardent* to the port of *Glorious* and opened fire with her secondary armament, to be followed by *Scharnhorst* at 1701. Extracts from the log of the *Scharnhorst* record the ongoing battle with *Ardent*:

> 1701. *Ardent* engaged with secondary armament on appearing out of smoke. Range decreasing rapidly and adding to the danger of torpedo attack. Foretop instructed to keep a careful watch.
> 1704. Ardent proceeding rather slowly with a heavy list, received a direct hit. Signal received from C-in-C "*Ardent* has fired three torpedoes".
> 1707. Hydroplane contact reports torpedo approaching on a bearing of 330°. *Scharnhorst* turned 20° to port.
> 1711. Further hit observed on *Ardent*, and the Captain opened fire on her with the anti-aircraft guns, using fuse settings.

---

* There are some discrepancies between the time given in the German logs and those from British sources.

1717. ...The *Ardent* listing more heavily.

1725. *Ardent's* mast broke off, and listing even more heavily, she finally capsized. Secondary armament ceased fire.[(16)]

Ardent's attacks had not been totally ineffective: she secured at least one hit from the 4.7-inch guns on *Scharnhorst's* upper deck abreast of 'B' turret, but without inflicting serious damage. *Ardent* had fought magnificently against all the odds, and no-one recognised this more than her enemy. Commander Schubert, Executive Officer of the *Scharnhorst*, was to write:

> She fought with outstanding resolution in a situation that was hopeless for her. The destroyer received numerous hits and finally went down, her bow armament firing to the last and her engines apparently in order and driving her at high speed.[(10)]

Another member of the crew of the *Scharnhorst* observed the sinking of the Ardent:

> I had the opportunity to see the *Ardent* as it went down and it was an extraordinary feeling because one imagines what the other people are going through. I was on the upper deck and I saw the *Ardent* leaning over, lots of smoke, and it shot and fought right up to the last. It made a great impression on me. They weren't enemies, they were opponents.[(17)]

Ardent capsized and sank at about 17.28, some five miles from the *Scharnhorst*, her last torpedo passing only a few yards in front of the German battlecruiser's bow.

There were only two survivors from the sinking of the *Ardent*, Able Seaman R. Hooke and Ordinary Seaman R. Jones. Roger Hooke was later to write movingly of the last hours of the Ardent and the fate of her crew:

> Things went well all Saturday until about half past four in the afternoon. All of us were enjoying a nice cup of tea when 'Action Stations' was sounded. Everyone was quite taken by surprise, some saying it must be a submarine about. When we were at our stations we could see on the horizon two ships, to whom they belonged we did not know. The *Glorious* then told us to go and investigate and ascertain who they were. We, therefore, steamed off in their direction, until we could see them much more plainer and then challenged them which they also did to us. Then we knew they were German battleships and then the fun started. They very soon began to open fire on all three of us. The very first salvo at us went into No 1 Boiler Room which naturally reduced our speed. We endeavoured to put them off by zigzagging and making a smoke screen, but it was all to no avail,

time after time we were hit, and, considering the range between us, it showed the accuracy of their guns and range finders.

Our guns were really of no great hindrance to the German ships, and we got into position for firing torpedoes to see if there was a chance of putting them off, even if only for a little while. We fired four torpedoes at them, but they did not seem to make any alteration of course at all.* We could see the other two ships of ours off to the westward, and plenty of steam escaping from the *Glorious*...Well, all this time we were being constantly hit, and men were being injured, so that it became a case of every man for himself. The ship was listing well over to port, and still doing about fifteen knots, and there seemed no way of stopping her, so that boats could be lowered to pick up men who had already jumped for it. What with the smoke and steam escaping everywhere, it was impossible to do very much, or see anything. After about half an hour of this ordeal, the ship began to sink and I had given help to get a raft over the side, on which I managed to scramble. From that raft I saw the end of a good ship, officers and men. The other two ships, when I last saw them, were steaming away to the northward, with the German ships in full cry after them.

The Captain, who I am sorry to say was lost with the ship, was a really good man and had done quite a few years in destroyers. Of course at the time we were carrying extra officers to what we really should have been, and that accounts for the loss of nine lives. The crew was mainly Royal Fleet Reservists, with some Royal Navy Reserve and Royal Navy Volunteer Reserve, the latter being very young men. The remainder, of which I was one, were Active Service. Taken all round, we really had a very fine body of men."[18]

After leaving the ship A.B. Hooke and five fellow survivors managed to scramble onto the raft he had helped launch. Three of these died on the raft from exposure during the following days. They had no food or water, and had several hopes of being picked up from a passing convoy and overhead aircraft dashed. For the remaining three survivors:

Things by now were beginning to get a bit agonising. We had to lie down on the side of the raft to get a bit of sleep, as our strength was giving out fast. Once more another comrade passed away. He was a leading seaman. Now there were only two of us left to carry on; for how much longer we did not know.

At last our prayers were answered. On waking up from one of my

* See 1707 entry in *Scharnhorst* log above. In fact, the torpedoes forced *Scharnhorst* to alter course.

short naps, and as I had done before, I had a good look round the horizon and sky. Away on our starboard side I saw a seaplane, but from the distance could not make out who she belonged to. After shaking my comrade and telling him, I found it had by then flown close up to us. Well she turned out to be German, and she had seen us. Flying round into the wind she made a good landing on the choppy sea. Coming towards us, the pilot got our raft between the floats and the navigator gave us a hand into the rear of the plane. I had enough left in me to ask where we were being taken, and he said Trondheim, the time necessary to get there being four hours. Our first words of course were to ask for a drink, and after five days without food or water, we really could not swallow enough. Once we had been given a drink, we both lay down for a sleep, as it was much warmer and one could stretch out quite comfortably. Then we were shaken and told we were at Trondheim. After being lifted from the plane, I saw a German soldier carrying a pot of coffee and I at once asked for some. Straight away I was given a cup and I enjoyed it. Afterwards we were lifted into an ambulance and driven away to hospital. We were given very good treatment and, after nine days, moved on to Oslo...my remaining comrade [Seaman Robert Jones] passed away after a fortnight in Oslo, leaving myself as the sole survivor* of the destroyer HMS *Ardent*.[18]

While the secondary armament 5.9-inch guns of the *Scharnhorst* and *Gneisenau* concentrated upon fending off the attacks of the two destroyers, their main armament of 11-inch guns were pounding *Glorious* into destruction. The aircraft carrier, destroyers and their crews were to be subjected to nearly one-and-three-quarter hours of bombardment, from 1632 to about 1812. In the first salvo, an 11-inch shell penetrated the flight deck and exploded inside the hangar. The blast wrecked the precious recovered Hurricane fighters housed there and started a major fire. In the third or fourth salvo, a shell struck the carrier's island structure, destroying the bridge and killing almost everyone there, including Captain D'Oyly-Hughes. By now, *Glorious* was a mass of smoke and flame but was still moving at high speed and could still possibly affect an escape.

Then a further salvo resulted in a hit to the boiler intakes, which caused a drop in steam pressure and *Glorious*'s speed started to falter. On board, Stoker J O'Neill, a member of a fire control party, later reported:

I could see it was a losing fight as Jerry was hitting hard and heavy and

---

* Mr Hooke was later transferred to a Prisoner-of-War camp in Germany until repatriated back to England on medical grounds on 25 October 1943. Accompanied by his wife, Mr Hooke, then aged 69, attended the commissioning of the new HMS *Ardent*, a type 21 Frigate, on 14 October 1977. The frigate was later lost during the Falklands War.

we could not get close enough with 4.7-inch to return fire...Orders came through for us to go and put a fire out on P.4 gun. When we got to it all about the place were dead bodies. Some played hoses on the flames, others had to throw ammunition overboard. The hoses were washing the remains of some of our shipmates off the bulkheads. Having managed the fire, we were ordered to go below again; some of the young lads were wondering when their turn would come. Then a fire started in the intake to 'C' boiler-room and the boilers had to be shut down.[10]

By now (about 1810) *Glorious* was being hit again and again, with one momentous strike in the region of the central engine room which shook the ship from stem to stern. As flames continued to envelop the ship and she started to list to starboard, an initial order to 'Abandon Ship' was made and then cancelled, because of a temporary lull in the German firing when *Glorious* became totally obscured from the German battle-cruisers by the smokescreen laid by her destroyers. Revisiting *Gneisenau*'s log, "1735. Glorious enveloped in a smoke screen laid by destroyers. Conditions for guns very difficult."[15]

When the smoke drifted away *Glorious* was seen, listing to starboard, and the German bombardment of her recommenced. The final order to abandon ship was passed at 1840 with the ship's list of 15 to 20° steadily increasing. *Glorious*'s end was near.

Acasta, who had been laying a protective smoke screen close astern of *Glorious*, now hauled off to the northwest. From Leading Seaman C.G. "Nick" Carter on board *Acasta*:

We then started making a smokescreen, still being on the starboard quarter of *Glorious*, also very, very close to her. I still had not seen the enemy. The fire on HMS *Glorious* was now, as it seemed to me, out of control, flames could be seen rising to a great height. The enemy then renewed their attack on *Glorious*, and believe me if ever a ship took a lot of punishment she did...I never actually saw her sink.[10]

Acasta for a time steered away from the enemy but she was not retiring: her crew were preparing for a final sally at the two German battle-cruisers, making smoke, launching smoke floats and preparing the torpedo tubes. A message had been passed to her crew from the Captain, Commander C.E. Glasfurd: "You may think we are running away from the enemy. But the Navy never does. The *Glorious* is sinking, and our chummy ship the *Ardent* has sunk. The least we can do is make a show. Good luck to you all. May God be with us."[19] *Acasta* turned onto the enemy warships. From the account of Leading Seaman Carter:

We then altered course into our own smokescreen. I had the order to stand by and fire tubes 6 and 7, we then came out of the smoke screen, altered course to starboard firing our torpedoes from port-side…I fired my two torpedoes from my tubes aft, the foremost tubes fired theirs, we were all watching results. I'll never forget that cheer that went up, on the port bow of one of the ships a yellow flash and a great column of smoke and water shot up from her, we knew we had hit, personally I do not see how we could have missed so close as we were. The enemy never fired a shot at us, I feel they must have been very surprised. After we had fired our torpedoes we went back into our own smokescreen, altered course again to starboard, stand by to fire remaining torpedoes, and this time as soon as we poked our nose out of the smokescreen, the enemy let us have it, a shell hit the engine room, killed my tube's crew, I was blown to the aft end of the tubes, I must have been knocked out for a while because when I came to my arm hurt me, the ship had stopped with a list to port, here is something, believe it or not I climbed back into the control seat, I see those two ships, I fired the remaining torpedoes, no one told me to, I guess I was raving mad. God alone knows why I fired them but I did. The *Acasta's* guns were firing the whole time, even firing with a list on the ship, the enemy then hit us several times, but one big explosion took place right aft, I have often wondered if the enemy hit us with a torpedo, in any case it seemed to lift the ship out of the water. At last the captain gave orders to abandon ship. I will always remember the Surgeon Lieutenant, (H.J. Stammers, R.N.V.R.), his first ship, his first action, before I jumped over the side* I saw him still attending the wounded, a hopeless task, and when I was in the water I saw the Captain leaning over the bridge. Taking a cigarette from a case and light it. We shouted to him to come to our raft, he waved, "Goodbye and good luck", a ridiculous end to a gallant man.[10]

Nick Carter was mistaken in his assumption that *Acasta's* initial torpedo attacks had scored a hit on one of the German ships. The flash that he and his shipmates saw was most probably a shell hit from one of *Acasta's* 4.7-inch guns striking the *Scharnhorst* forward. However, one of the torpedoes he describes firing did find its mark. At 1734, at a range of some 13,000 yards or more than six miles, *Scharnhorst* was hit aft by a torpedo which put the after turret out of action, caused severe flooding and killed forty-eight of her crew. From a Carley float, one of the sinking *Glorious's* crew, Stoker

---

* Leading Seaman Carter was three days and nineteen hours on a Carley float before being picked up, the only survivor from a raft originally full of survivors who had, one by one, all perished. He was picked up by a Norwegian trawler bound for the Faroe Islands. In the event he was the only survivor from the sinking of HMS *Acasta*.

C. Hobbs, saw *Acasta's* torpedo strike: "From the raft to the destroyer, it was no more than three or four hundred feet at the most. I watched that torpedo go and heard the explosion."[10] The torpedo hit caused confusion on the *Scharnhorst* as to its source. From the German ship's log:

> 1734. Violent shudder astern. Suspected torpedo hit. This was confirmed later when pieces of the casing were found by the crew. There was considerable doubt as to whether the torpedo had been fired by the *Acasta* or a British submarine. The C-in-C, Admiral Marschall, was of the opinion that it had been fired by a submarine, as the damage was on the starboard side, and the *Acasta* had been to port. The captain of the *Scharnhorst*, Hoffman, however, considered it more likely to have been the Acasta on account of the intricate turns she had been executing at this time, and it was thought quite possible that she may have been to starboard at this time.[16]

Leading Seaman Carter's account of the *Acasta's* torpedoing of the *Scharnhorst* was not initially believed back in Britain as it was thought, in the confusion of *Glorious's* survivors' accounts, that it was *Ardent* that had done the damage. It was not until after the war that German records and accounts confirmed that the torpedoing was from the *Acasta*.

The two German battle-cruisers continued to fire on the *Acasta* after *Scharnhorst* had been torpedoed, although the German battlecruiser was in increasing difficulty from the damage she had sustained. *Acasta* continued to return fire until the last. Extracts from the logs of the *Scharnhorst* and *Gneisenau*, arranged chronologically, record the final moments of the battle:

Gneisenau
1741   ceased fire on orders from C-in-C, but at 1745 opened fire again on the *Acasta*. Range 14,220 yards. Course 200° altered to 170° in order to close range.

Scharnhorst
1742   *Acasta* engaged by the secondary armament.
1743   The gun's crew was forced to abandon one of the turrets which was later flooded. The ammunition chamber was reported to be flooded. Starboard engine failure. Speed maintained at 26 knots.
1746   Course 260°. List increasing to starboard with flooding in various compartments.
1752   Pumping in progress. The *Acasta* was now outside potential torpedo range, but still in sight and was engaged by secondary armament.

1805   The middle engine slowed down and a minute later stopped completely. A second turbine was flooding, and one propeller limping badly.

Gneisenau

1807   Range 11,490 yards. Hits and heavy explosion observed aboard *Acasta* followed by further hits. Last salvo fired at a range of 10,940 yards silenced the destroyer. The carrier had already sunk.

Scharnhorst

1808   The *Acasta* was observed burning fiercely aft, and secondary armament was ordered to cease fire in order to conserve ammunition. The *Glorious* was no longer visible.

Gneisenau

1808   Permission granted to open fire on the *Acasta* once again with the anti-aircraft guns as she was now within range of these.

Scharnhorst

1808   *Acasta* was continuing to fire. The secondary armament engaged her again. The *Scharnhorst* received another shell in one of her turrets.

1812   Orders received from C-in-C to cease fire. The damage to the engine room was considerable. The middle engine was flooded and out of action. Revolutions on starboard engine had to be reduced due to heavy knocking and shaft vibration.

1813   "Cease fire all guns" as the destroyer was obviously sinking as a result of hits received from secondary armament. [15],[16]

Acasta sank at approximately 1812 hours. For the British, in addition to the loss of three ships, the human cost was appalling.

The Royal Navy lost 1,162 sailors from the *Glorious*, 152 from the *Ardent* and 160 from the *Acasta* – a total of 1,474 officers and men, with only one survivor each from the *Ardent* and *Acasta*. In addition, the Royal Air Force lost 41 officers and men on board *Glorious*. A total of 1,515 men. It was a major – arguably avoidable – Allied disaster.

For the Germans it was a major naval triumph, and they escaped with relatively light losses: they had one battle-cruiser severely damaged and lost 48 officers and men. However, there was little rejoicing at their success on board the German ships.

After the war, crew members of the *Scharnhorst* and *Gneisenau* recalled their feelings immediately after the action:

> The atmosphere after the battle was downbeat. The entire stern crew was dead, and I remember a man from the stern area, he was sitting there really sad because all his friends were gone. There was no celebration or victorious mood…
>
> When the destroyers went down (Admiral) Marschall ordered the flags to be put at half mast. The whole bridge stood to attention.[14]

In spite of this respect shown to their opponents, the two German battle-cruisers did not linger to pick up survivors. Admiral Marschall feared that a British submarine was lurking nearby, and in any case the *Scharnhorst* was in urgent need of dockyard attention. *Acasta*'s torpedo had left the German ship with a hole some 40 feet long and 13 feet wide below the waterline. Both German ships were also low on ammunition, which curtailed any thought of immediate further action against British shipping. Between them, the two battlecruisers had expended 387 rounds of 11-inch and an astonishing 1,148 rounds of 5.9-inch ammunition in sinking the three British ships. The German ships returned to Trondheim,* leaving the shipwrecked British sailors in the water and on a miscellany of lifeboats and floats. The heavy loss of life was undoubtedly made much worse by the long delay in rescuing those men who survived the sinkings. A number of survivors were saved mainly by Norwegian ships such as the 350-ton motor vessel *Borgund, en route* to the Faroes, who picked up a number of men from Carley floats after they had been in the water for over two days.

The efforts and sacrifice of the *Ardent* and *Acasta* had not been totally in vain. By a quirk of fate, the two German battlecruisers – because of their enforced return to harbour – missed intercepting the later-sailing main convoy of relatively lightly-escorted troopships evacuating the Allied force from Norway back to Britain, which returned safely to the United Kingdom.

The tragic circumstances of the loss of the *Glorious, Ardent* and *Acasta* and over 1,500 lives in June 1940 was over-shadowed by even more momentous events and loss elsewhere. The "miracle of Dunkirk" and the evacuation of the British armies from France had just taken place, France was on the verge of capitulation, and the Battle of Britain was about to begin. It was a time when the survival of the nation was at stake. Italy had entered the war on the German side on 10 June – the very day that the few

---

* On 29 June the *Gneisenau* left Trondheim, only to be torpedoed by the British submarine HMS *Clyde* and so badly damaged that she was put out of action for many months.

survivors of the three British ships were still in the waters of the North Sea awaiting rescue or death.

There was a Board of Enquiry into the circumstances of the loss of the *Glorious*, but its report has never been made public. There was no court martial, the Admiralty choosing to post Commander J.B. Heath to be Executive Officer of *Vindex*, a seaplane carrier based at Freetown, Sierra Leone, taking over her command with the acting rank of Captain, in October 1940.[10] Over two years later, in December 1942, Captain Heath was notified:

> Their Lordships have had under review the circumstances which led to your leaving HMS *Glorious* in May 1940, and I am to inform you that in the official view of the Admiralty no charges involving your honour or professional reputation stand against you.[10]

In the immediate post-war years there were attempts made to get the valour of the captains and crews of the *Acasta* and *Ardent* recognised by the award of posthumous decorations for gallantry, but they came to nothing, and there the controversial episode of the sinking of the *Glorious* remains.

With the safe arrival back in Britain of the evacuated Allied troops, the blighted campaign in Norway came to an end. It had not been a successful one, and it had taken a particularly heavy toll on the naval side. The loss of ships to the Allied and German sides was roughly equal, but the proportionate losses of the Germans, with their smaller navy, were more far-reaching. The Allies lost in various ways one aircraft carrier, two cruisers, nine destroyers, one sloop and four submarines. The Germans, in addition to the torpedo damage to the *Scharnhorst* and *Gneisenau* which kept them out of action for some months, lost four cruisers, ten destroyers and three U-boats. Their losses in cruisers and destroyers were such that at the end of June 1940 Germany's naval forces in these categories were reduced to one 8-inch cruiser, two light cruisers and four destroyers.[20] They also lost much valuable merchant shipping in the campaign. The German Navy was thus in no position to participate in any sea-borne invasion of Britain following the fall of France in the summer of 1940.

NOTES TO SOURCES

1. McIntyre, Captain D. *Narvik* (Evans Bros: London, 1959).
2. Brown, D. (Ed). *Naval Operations of the Campaign in Norway: April–June 1940* (Frank Cass: London, 2000).
3. Spurgeon, Commander S.H.K. Account. 90/23/1. Imperial War Museum, London.
4. Witkowski, Petty Officer B. Letter to author, April 2001.
5. Tumaniszwili, Lieutenant J.P. Correspondence with author, March 2001.
6. Warner, P. *Auckinleck: The Lonely Soldier* (Buchan and Enright: London, 1981).
7. Mosse, Commander J.P. 'Half a Lifetime' Account 90/23/1. Imperial War Museum, London.
8. Colville, J. *The Fringes of Power: Downing Street Diaries 1939–1945* (Hodder and Stoughton: London, 1985).
9. Roskill, Captain, S.W. 'The Cantankerous Captain of HMS *Glorious*'. Article, *Sunday Times*, 15 June 1980.
10. Winton, J. *Carrier Glorious* (Leo Cooper: London, 1986).
11. Churchill, W.S. *The Second World War, Vol 1: The Gathering Storm* (Cassell: London, 1948).
12. Slessor, T. Private Papers. Correspondence with author, Nov 2001.
13. Elliott, Petty Officer G.W. Letter. Glorious File, GLOR Box 1. Roskill Archive, Churchill Archives Centre, Churchill College, Cambridge.
14. Leggott, Lieutenant-Commander R. Transcript, television documentary, First Circle Films. Roskill Archive, Churchill Archives Centre, Churchill College, Cambridge.
15. Transcribed Extracts translated from the log of the Gneisenau. Glorious File, GLOR Box 2, Roskill Archives, Churchill Archives Centre, Churchill College, Cambridge.
16. Transcribed extracts translated from the log of the Scharnhorst Glorious File, GLOR Box 2, Roskill Archives, Churchill Archives Centre, Churchill College, Cambridge.
17. Document File, television documentary. First Circle Films. Roskill Archive, Churchill Archives Centre, Churchill College, Cambridge.
18. Hooke, Able Seaman R. 'Survivor of HMS Ardent'. Account, 66/66/1. Imperial War Museum, London.
19. Austin. J. with Leading Seaman Nick Carter. *The man who hit the Scharnhorst* (Seeley Service: London, 1973).
20. Derry, T.K. *The Campaign in Norway* (HMSO: London, 1952).

XI

The Evacuation from France Begins

Even as Allied troops were being withdrawn from Norway, the Allied naval forces there were being whittled down to face other threats. Some were transferred to the Mediterranean to reinforce the British Fleet there in case Italy should decide to enter the war on the side of its Axis partner Germany. Other ships had been moved south to the English Channel and waters around the south of England to counter the growing threat to the British Expeditionary Force in northern France from a German thrust through the neutral Low Countries.

Given all the circumstances, the transfers from the Norwegian campaign were accomplished smoothly and expeditiously. The destroyer *Codrington* (Captain G.F. Stevens-Guille) for example, left Scapa Flow at 0730 on 10 May and at 0800 the next day was tied up alongside an oiler in Dover harbour, having steamed 530 miles in twenty-three hours at an average speed of 23 knots.[1]

The transferred ships, and those that they reinforced, were quickly employed on a range of overlapping operations and counter measures, or engaged in direct actions against the enemy off the Dutch, Belgian and French coasts. They were barely in time. May 10th 1940 was to be a day of destiny for the British Nation and the Royal Navy. It was the day that the Prime Minister (Neville Chamberlain, head of the Conservative Government) was forced to resign, and Winston Churchill became Prime Minister and Minster of Defence of a Coalition National Government. It was also the day that Germany launched its long-expected assault in the west and invaded neutral Holland, and it heralded the start of desperate times for the destroyers of the Royal Navy. Later that day, four destroyers left Dover for Dutch ports with demolition parties, and Admiral G.F. Edward-Collins, with his cruisers *Galatea* and *Arethusa* and an accompanying miscellany of destroyers and two merchant ships, went to Ijmuiden to bring the Dutch gold reserves to England. The next day, 11 May, *Arethusa* and two destroyers escorted back two merchant ships carrying the Dutch bullion. One of the escorts was the old V and W class destroyer *Vimy*

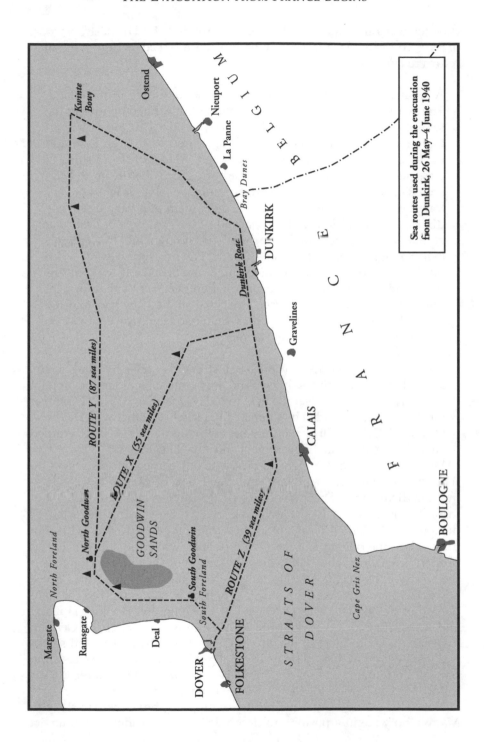

Sea routes used during the evacuation from Dunkirk, 26 May–4 June 1940

(Lieutenant Commander C.G.W. Donald) built in 1918. The destroyer, part of the escort of an Atlantic convoy, had earlier received an urgent signal to return to Dover immediately:

> After arrival there and refuelling we headed for the Hook of Holland. The Germans had swept through Holland but we had no idea of the severity of the situation. On arrival…we picked up the most disreputable old rusted merchant ship that appeared as though it should have been sold for scrap many years ago. Ahead of us a British 'J' class destroyer had slipped out of harbour shortly before us and signalled us to keep close station on our merchant ship. It was not very long before the Luftwaffe attacked, their main aim very obviously directed at the 'J' class destroyer ahead of us. That type of destroyer at that particular stage of the war was ultra modern and its Captain's evasive high speed tactics were superb. The pressure was off when our own air cover arrived and we sailed into Sheerness without further incident…Imagine our surprise when later we were informed, without confirmation of course…[that] we on the *Vimy* had escorted the bulk of all the gold in Holland which had been stowed away on board the disreputable tramp steamer.[2]

On 12 May the destroyer *Codrington*, just one day after her dash south, embarked the Crown Princess Juliana and her family at Ijmuiden and brought them safely to England. Over the next two days *Malcolm*, the 16th Destroyer Flotilla Leader, commanded by Captain T.E. Halsey, together with *Hereward*, brought back Queen Wilhelmena and her entourage, while *Windsor* returned the members of the Dutch Government and Allied Legations.

Meanwhile, the demolition parties sent out earlier on destroyers, to Amsterdam, Flushing, Antwerp and the Hook of Holland, were having a difficult time. Their objectives of destroying strategic stores and installations of value to the invading enemy were being thwarted or denied by the Dutch local authorities and property-owners. One can understand the dilemma of the Dutch people: while the authorities and property-owners might wish to defy the invaders, they had reason to fear the wrath of their conquerors for any collaboration with the Allied cause and to have concern over the future loss of their livelihoods. Thus the completion of demolitions was prevented at Flushing, the Hook of Holland and Antwerp; and it was not until 13 May, three days after the German invasion and with most of the city in German hands, that the oil stocks and installations at Rotterdam were set alight.[1] The next day the resisting parts of Rotterdam were savagely dive-bombed by the Luftwaffe; and the following day, 15 May, the Dutch Army surrendered.

Not all the overrun Dutch people were cowed by the German onslaught. Many who were in a position to do so defied the invaders, as in an act

202

recorded by Lieutenant G. Lumsden, Navigating Officer of *Keith* (Captain D.J.R. Simson):

> As we returned to Dover at dawn one day a very unfinished Dutch cruiser was seen: it was found that a Lieutenant Commander and a few even younger officers with a crew of about a hundred volunteer seamen and stokers had brought her out from Rotterdam, with only a very general chart of the North Sea, and with no knowledge of our own or enemy minefields, to join the Royal Navy. A most gallant piece of work.[3]*

The Dutch Government had warned the Allies that they would have to capitulate the day before doing so, to give as much time as possible for the withdrawal of the demolition parties and other Allied troops and personnel. To this end, the Dutch proposed to hold out as long as possible in the area of the major Schelde waterway. This they did, but on 15 May the destroyer *Valentine* was sunk by German bombers near Terneuzen, and *Winchester* damaged, while shielding a ferry evacuating troops across the Scheldt. *Westminster* was also damaged by German bombers during operations off the Dutch coast during this period.

A few days later, with the Allied land forces being forced westwards by the German onslaught, naval operations commenced along the Belgian coast, with six Royal Navy destroyers operating under the command of Admiral Abrial of the French Navy, based at Dunkirk. Once again veteran V and W class First World War vintage destroyers were to the fore of the action, providing escorts and helping bring back large numbers of refugees from Ostend between 15 and 18 May. The destroyer *Whitley* was lost; bombed and beached near Nieuport on 19 May. Another destroyer veteran, *Vega*, led a force of blockships to attempt the closure of the entrances to Ostend and Zeebrugge harbours on 25 May. The attempt on Ostend was aborted and that on Zeebrugge was unsuccessful. The operation against Zeebrugge was repeated the next day, again led by Commander C.I. Horton in *Vega*, and this time was successful.

In addition to the Royal Navy's operations to assist the Allied land forces being pushed westwards by the German thrust on the mainland, more conventional naval actions against the enemy were being carried out. Thus on 9 May 1940, the destroyers *Kelly* and *Kandahar*, earlier transferred from Norwegian waters to the East coast of England, were:

---

* The cruiser *Jacob van Heemskerck*, one destroyer and seven submarines, with some of the ships new and unfinished, left their Dutch bases soon after the invasion of their country had started and arrived safely at British ports to continue their fight against the invaders of their country.

Ordered to rendezvous with the cruiser HMS *Birmingham* and a force of destroyers, including *Kelly*, commanded by Captain Louis Mountbatten in the *Kelly*. The force was proceeding to intercept a German mine-laying squadron who were homeward bound after laying mines off the east coast of Britain... At dusk the *Kelly* reported a submarine contact by hydrophone. We were at the time doing 28 knots and I was ordered to join her in the hunt while the rest of the force, under the *Birmingham*, continued to intercept the German ships.[4]

They were joined by the destroyer *Bulldog*, who had lost contact with the main force. After a fruitless search, the Captain of *Kandahar*, Commander W.G.A. Robson, urged the abandonment of the U-boat hunt and rejoining the *Birmingham* in their allotted task of searching for enemy minesweepers: "After some twenty minutes we gave up the hunt and tried to catch up with the Birmingham."[4] Then (as recorded by Mountbatten's official biographer)[5] to the consternation of the two accompanying ships, the ebullient Captain Mountbatten sent a light-hearted superfluous message from *Kelly* to *Birmingham* by bright Aldis lamp: "How are the muskets? Let battle commence."[5] This unnecessary, and arguably ill-judged, signal may have alerted nearby E-boats (large German torpedo boats) since:

As night fell, we started to see peculiar green lights. Of course this was before the days of radar, so we only had our eyes to guide us, but it was not long before I realised that these were E-boats and reported this. At about 2200 I saw, by great good luck, the splash of torpedoes being fired on my starboard beam and immediately put the wheel hard over towards the position of the E-boats and was lucky enough to comb the tracks (of the torpedoes). One torpedo passed on either side of us. In fact a stoker Petty Officer in the boiler-room said he actually heard it scrape down the side. The *Kelly* was not so lucky. She was hit by at least one torpedo and there was an enormous explosion.[4]

The torpedo struck *Kelly* in a position under the bridge, tearing a fifty-foot hole in her side and opening up the forward boiler room. Twenty-seven men were killed and many more wounded:

I was in the SDO, [Signal Despatch Office] sitting on the deck when something caught my attention. I stood up to get a better look, and BANG, a tremendous shock on the deck and the doorway was a mass of flames. I unscrewed the clamps holding the port and deadlight down and tried to get out, but my shoulder was caught so I got back in, meaning to take my coat off, when I noticed the flames had gone.

The fact that the tanks had been nearly empty had probably saved me from being roasted, so I went to the upper deck and nearly slid off the ship because she was listing badly and the iron deck was covered in oil.[6]

Kelly was stopped and dead in the water. There was no power and only emergency lighting:

The *Kelly* was taken in tow by the Bulldog, who was astern of us. *Kelly* had miraculously remained afloat, in spite of major damage, and I was ordered to escort her back to the United Kingdom.[4]

So stricken was *Kelly* that it was thought that she would capsize at any moment, but Captain Mountbatten was determined to save his ship.

It was the beginning of a very long haul. First we jettisoned every bit of top weight that we could move. We shot off ten torpedoes and all our depth charges; we cut our boats adrift; we threw ammunition overboard; we unbolted the lockers and threw them out too. And so we were able to remain afloat with a heavy list to starboard – rather unsteady, difficult to manage, but the *Kelly* was afloat, and that was all that mattered to me.[7]

The towing of the yawing *Kelly* was not a straightforward operation:

When the tow was taken up then the next problem was how to steer the *Kelly* to help the *Bulldog*, for the torpedo explosion had not only destroyed all the power, it had also cut the connection between the wheelhouse and the tiller flat. In the latter were four cylinders filled with fluid working on two double-ended pistons connected by a yoke which turned the rudder. In normal working, when the wheel was turned two of the cylinders filled with fluid while the other two emptied, turning the rudder and when the wheel was released the rudder automatically went back to midships. As all the power had been cut off the rudder had to be turned by hand with a lever which had to be pumped to and fro and when the rudder was to be moved the other way, another lever reversed the flow of oil when pumping was resumed. A chain of men was set up to convey the orders from the bridge but it was a very slow job and we never completed one order before the next was received. For instance, the order came "Starboard twenty" and we would pump away, but when we had put on only ten degrees the order "Midships" would be received, then before the rudder was midships it would be "Port twenty", and when we had got it five or ten degrees to port it would be "Midships" again. I had been near the tiller flat hatch when the emergency steering was set up and wasn't sorry to be roped in as it gave me something to do, but after about an hour I asked to be relieved.[6]

Kelly's troubles were not yet over, however. Captain Mountbatten recounts how, shortly before midnight:

> ...we suddenly heard the sound of an E-boat engine, and then she arrived at full speed. She hit the *Bulldog* a glancing blow, bounced off her and came right inboard onto the *Kelly*. Our starboard gunwale was awash, and so she was able to come right onboard us, with a rush, firing her 20mm gun. I remember ducking down behind the bridge screen and thinking to myself "What a damn silly thing to do!" So I straightened up and watched the rest of the action. The E-boat (MTB 40, we now know it was) sheared off davits and guard rails as she passed down *Kelly's* side and then vanished into the night.[7]

Kandahar, who had initially carried on ahead to avoid the same fate as *Kelly* from any lurking E-boats, came alongside to take off wounded. Before doing so her captain, Commander Robson, had signalled "Is Captain (D) alive?" to *Kelly*. "Yes. You are not in command of the flotilla yet," was Captain Mountbatten's tart retort.[5] *Kandahar* came alongside:

> She had a good many wounded, so I put my bow alongside and took the worst of them off for attention by my doctor, who was not only an ear, nose and throat specialist, but also a pupil of Gillies the famous plastic surgeon. With our young sick-berth steward giving the anaesthetic he patched up a lot of these sailors, and he later made up an album of photographs sent by delighted wives who said he had made their husbands much better looking than they had ever been before![4]

The transfer of the wounded was not accomplished without incident:

> And then came the Luftwaffe. We were transferring our wounded to the *Kandahar* when they first appeared. The first attack was driven off, but we knew they would be back, and they were.[7]

The long tow continued:

> Somehow the night passed and in the morning the wind had freshened and the sea, though calm the previous night, now had quite a top on it...With daylight came another hazard. Every hour or so an enemy bomber would come over and drop a few bombs, but as it

stayed rather high none hit the ship. The slight swell put a greater strain on the tow-rope which kept parting, and what with one thing and another we made very slow progress.[6]

It was indeed to be a long haul. It was to take ninety-one hours to tow *Kelly* back across the North Sea from her torpedoed position, some one hundred miles west of Denmark. In the afternoon the Gunner (T), Mr Brownjohn, organised a party for the burial service, which was conducted against a background of helm orders being shouted along the communication chain to the tiller flat as the surviving sailors struggled to keep their ship afloat.

> ...in the afternoon we buried three bodies which had been accessible. A mess table was taken aft and one end placed on the guard rails, then the first body, sewn up in a hammock with cannon balls at its head and feet (so that's what they were for*), was placed on the table and covered with a Union Flag. Louis read the burial service and at the appropriate place two men took hold of the table, making sure they also had a grip on the flag (that was needed for the others), lifted the table so that the body slid out and a volley of rifles was fired.[6]

As the day wore on food and water became increasingly short and a food search party was organised. One result was a large box of liquorice allsorts found by a boy seaman. He and his neighbours gorged themselves on the liquorice. The consequences only added to the seamens' troubles. one sufferer observed: "The difference between these bloody allsorts and a good dose of salts is about ten minutes. We are in action today all right."[8] The tow continued on the day following the torpedoing, 10 May 1940:

> By now there were quite a few ships clustered around us and the Admiral signalled me saying that with Hitler invading the Low Countries this was a waste of force, he suggested that we should open the sea-cocks and scuttle the *Kelly*. To this I replied that I did not want to scuttle my ship; we could dispense with further help and defend ourselves if tugs could be sent to tow us.[7]

The Captain's determination won the day and the tow continued:

> That night two of us slept on the deck of the SDO as no-one was allowed to go on the mess-decks, apart from the fact that they were not easily accessible as the torpedo had blown the deck up to within

---

* See Chapter One, page 7.

three or four feet of the deck-head, and it wasn't until the ship had been docked at Hebburn that we learned that the whole bridge structure was unsafe and might have gone over the side at any moment. Our night might have been more uncomfortable than it was if we had known that…That torpedo broke my nerve. Before, I always slung my hammock and undressed before getting into it, but afterwards I never slung it or undressed when the ship was at sea. I slept as best I could on the lockers, always ready to go down to the flag-deck at a moment's notice should anything happen. What is more I was never happy below decks once the ship had left harbour, at every bump and bang, be it only a wave breaking against the side, I went hot all over… I was always glad that my job kept me out in the open, on the bridge or flag-deck. I don't know what I would have done if my action station had been in a magazine, or if I had been a stoker always in the boiler room when on watch. I wasn't afraid of drowning, but I had a constant fear of being taken down inside a ship. Also I was afraid of being afraid and I was glad I was in the Navy, even if I wanted to run there was no place to run to.[6]

In due course tugs appeared to take over the tow from *Bulldog*:

But the night before they appeared, we were nearly done for after all; the sea got up, and the ship started to develop a very unpleasant slow roll. I could feel that we were very near complete loss of stability… So the whole ship's company was transferred to the escorting destroyers, with the Luftwaffe bombing the open boats as they went across. The next morning the tugs appeared and we were on the last lap. Six officers and twelve men came back on board – just enough to handle the ship and man the close-range weapons. I worked a 0.5 inch machine gun, and I must say that it's much more satisfactory actually firing a gun than just sitting there when you are being attacked.[7]

So *Kelly* came home. She eventually reached the Tyne on the evening of 13 May. The ship was so badly damaged that it took six months to rebuild and repair her.

In naval circles it was a highly controversial episode. It was pointed out that *Kelly* should not have been where she was when she was torpedoed. The primary purpose of the force of which she was a part was to seek out and destroy German minesweepers and their escorts. Mountbatten had allowed himself to be diverted into a prolonged and fruitless search for a suspect U-boat and finally, it was alleged, drawn attention to himself with disastrous results by making unnecessary signals by Aldis lamp. On the other hand he had shown outstanding leadership, seamanship and determination in bringing *Kelly* home. His superior officer, Vice Admiral Layton on board the cruiser *Birmingham*, had wanted him to abandon *Kelly* as the risks involved, particularly for her vulnerable escorting ships, outweighed her salvable value.

To the British Public, drowning in military disasters and defeats first in Norway and now in France and rapidly losing confidence in its Conservative Government, the incident was presented as an epic naval triumph. *Kelly* had fought her way out of a German trap and Captain Louis Mountbatten, cousin of the King, was a hero.*

While the *Kelly* was being towed home and in the following days, the crisis in the Low Countries and northern France was rapidly worsening. The situation on land during the next fortnight, following the German invasion of the Low Countries on 10 May, was as complex as it was confused.

The Germans began their offensive by sweeping through neutral Holland, Belgium and Luxembourg by means of the rapid deployment of armoured columns, supported by the use of dive-bombers and paratroops against strategic targets and key installations. Targets such as Rotterdam were so devastatingly attacked, and such was the speed and ferocity of the German assault, that the morale of the civilians and the fighting spirit of the military were broken, and a state of panic and confusion spread rapidly. With the German effort planned and unified, and in contrast the response of the Allies and their invaded neighbours Holland and Belgium unprepared and uncoordinated, it became very difficult to mount any organised defence against the onslaught. The situation was rapidly worsening. Back at Downing Street on 14 May 1940:

In the evening the military news was disturbing. Holland is to all intent and purposes lost, the French are being pressed on the Meuse, and the Germans look like breaking through at Sedan, and we are besought to send more fighter squadrons to France if the enemy advance is to be checked. The French speak ominously of the lack of defences between Sedan and Paris.[9]

The next day the Dutch Army surrendered and laid down its arms, putting greater pressure on the Belgian Army, left responsible for defending the left flank of the British Expeditionary Force. On 17 May the French

---

* The repaired *Kelly* was sunk by German dive-bombers off Crete on 23 May 1941. Her captain, Lord Louis Mountbatten, went on to become Admiral of the Fleet, Earl Mountbatten of Burma. After the sinking of the *Kelly* he held the wartime posts of Chief of Combined Operations and Supreme Commander, South East Asia Command. After the War he became the last Viceroy of India and later First Sea Lord. He and members of his family were assassinated by the provisional IRA on 27 August 1979.

9th Army's front was broken, with German forces crossing the River Oise, threatening the British GHQ and base supply and support areas to the rear. Only by mobilising all available troops in the area – service and communications troops as well as combatants – was the German thrust held up. In London:

> Winston is depressed. He says the French are crumpling up... and that our forces in Belgium will inevitably have to withdraw in order to maintain contact with the French. There is, of course, a risk that the BEF may be cut off if the French do not rally in time.[9]

By the next day the enemy had penetrated as far as Amiens and had severed rail communications with the Allied bases to the rear. In his 19 May diary entry, General Alan Brooke – later Lord Alanbrooke, Chief of the Imperial General Staff but then a Corps Commander in the BEF serving in France – noted:

> The news on the French front was worse that ever, they were attempting one full counter attack to try and restore the situation. Should this fail it looks as though the Allied Forces would be cut in the centre! The BEF communications to the sea would be completely exposed and so would our right flank. GHQ had a scheme for a move in such an eventuality towards Dunkirk, establishing a defended area around this place and embarking all we could of the personnel of the BEF, abandoning stored and equipment.[10]

20 May saw the line at Arras breached by German armoured columns which had broken through and were sweeping northwards, making for the channel ports and threatening to cut off the BEF In Downing Street, John Colville's diary entry for Tuesday 21 May records:

> The situation in France is extraordinary. Owing to the rapid advance of armoured troops, the Germans are in many places behind the Allied lines. Enemy columns have reached Amiens and are thought to be on the way to Abbeville; it is clear that the main thrust is north-westwards towards the Channel Ports...The German advance is now really dangerous, and it is staggering that France should have so far put up less resistance to invasion than did Poland, Norway or Holland. Preparations are being made for the evacuation of the BEF in case of necessity.[9]

That day, 21 May, an Allied armoured formation largely made up of British tanks, successfully attacked the German forces south of Arras; but the momentum could not be maintained, and it provided only a temporary respite from the German onslaught. Elsewhere, an enemy column was approaching Boulogne, and German forces had crossed the River Somme and cut the rail communication link at Abbeville . The Allied position was rapidly deteriorating, with 250,000 Allied troops now north of the River Somme cut off from their daily needs of 2000 tons of supplies, food and ammunition. General Alan Brook's diary entry for 23 May was stark:

> Nothing but a miracle can save the BEF now and the end cannot be far off... Abbeville, Boulogne and Calais have been rendered useless. We are therefore cut off from our sea communications, beginning to be short of ammunition; supplies still alright for three days but after that scanty... It is a fortnight since the German advance started and the success they have achieved is nothing short of phenomenal. There is no doubt that they are most wonderful soldiers.[10]

By the evening of 23 May Boulogne was completely cut off and German armoured columns were within nine miles of Calais, which was cut off the next day. In and around the port of Boulogne there was chaos, with the Allied soldiers there, mainly base and service personnel, in a state of panic and disarray. Because of the deteriorating position there, two battalions of Irish Guards had been sent over on the previous day in ships escorted by the destroyers *Venetia* and *Whitshed*. *Whitshed* found that there was complete chaos on the quayside due to the panic of a disorganised rabble of base troops.[11]. As evacuation now appeared inevitable, a demolition party under Lieutenant-Commander A.E.P. Welman was sent to Boulogne early on 23 May. With it went "Force Buttercup", consisting of six platoons of sailors and marines, plus machine gun and medical parties, totalling some 235 men. This force, under Major C.F.L. Holford, Royal Marines, was sent to restore order in the immediate dockside area, and to provide cover for the demolition party. They sailed in *Vimy* (Lieutenant Commander C.G.W. Donald). When the destroyer arrived, four French destroyers were bombarding a nearby airfield in German hands and returning fire on enemy tanks and artillery shelling the harbour. Allied base troops, in considerable disorder, were crowding the quayside area clamouring for some means of evacuation.

By 1530 the whole of Boulogne, except for a bridgehead around the quayside area was in German hands; all the Allied anti-tank guns were out of action and half of Major Holford's force had become casualties. The destroyer leader *Keith*, under Captain D.J.R. Simson, Captain (D) of the 19th Destroyer Flotilla, was sent over during the afternoon and at 1750 received orders that all troops were to be evacuated. *Keith* and *Vimy* went alongside the quay and were met by a rush of panic-stricken soldiers and civilian refugees desperate to be evacuated, and by close range enemy mortar, machine gun and rifle fire which very quickly caused damage and casualties to the two destroyers. Lieutenant G. Lumsden, Navigator on *Keith* reported:

> We had begun to embark the mass of people into the ships until they were blocking all gangways and ladders... Thirty Stukas in a single line wheeled to a point about 2000 feet above us, and poured down in a single stream to attack the crowded quay and our two destroyers. The only opposition was some scattered rifle and Lewis gun fire, mostly from soldiers ashore, and the single-barrelled two-pounder pom-poms in each destroyer.
>
> The Captain ordered the crews of the 4.7-inch guns to take cover because they were useless against the aircraft. He also ordered the bridge people below. The bridge was just above quay level and exposed to splinters from bombs bursting there. I stood back to allow him down the ladder to the wheelhouse, as courtesy and seniority demanded, but he signed to me to precede him; no Captain likes to leave his bridge when under attack. I took one or two steps down when he fell on top of me, shot in the chest by a German sniper. The doctor arrived and pronounced him dead. Our First Lieutenant, now in command, was shot in the leg. He ordered everyone in the bridge structure to lie down, because German small arms fire and splinters from mortar bombs fired from weapons sited in houses overlooking our berth, were piercing the sides of the wheelhouse, and hitting frightened men and women struggling to get down the steep ladder to the mess deck below. It seemed a miracle that the ship had not been hit directly by bombs, but lying there she and *Vimy* alongside were open to further air attack and our bridges and upper decks were already swept by small arms fire from positions we could not identify in an area we had understood to be occupied by British troops.[3]

Captain R. Whinney, himself a noted destroyer Captain, paid his tribute to *Keith*'s gallant Captain:

> One good memory of the Royal Naval College was the Term Officer who looked after us when we first joined. Lieutenant Commander (then) Simson was a bachelor. A Scottish trial rugger cap, he was a cheerful, red-haired driver, but friendly and kindly, a man to inspire liking. After leaving Dartmouth as Term Officer, Simson was promoted to Commander and then Captain. In the early days of World War II, he took his destroyer into Boulogne to help evacuate the Army, then in retreat prior to Dunkirk. It was a hot day and the ship

was lying alongside the jetty firing at German tanks up the road. Simson, not untypically, and despite the advice of his officers, was on the bridge, coat off, in his white shirtsleeves; he was an easy target for the German sniper who got him. In different ways, some of us modelled ourselves on David Simson.[12]

The *Vimy* was also in serious trouble. Able Seaman Harris was on her bridge when:

I noticed our Captain, Lieutenant-Commander Donald, train his binoculars on a hotel diagonally opposite, but quite close to our ship. I heard another burst of fire from the snipers in the hotel, and saw our Captain struck down. He fell onto his back and as I leaped to his aid I saw that a bullet had inflicted a frightful wound to the forehead, nose and eyes of his face. He was choking on his own blood, so I moved him onto his side. I received his final order, "Get the First Lieutenant onto the bridge urgently." As I rose to my feet more shots from the hotel swept the bridge. The Sub-Lieutenant fell in front of me, with four bullet holes in a line across his chest.[2]

With their position on the quayside untenable and his Captain mortally wounded, the First Lieutenant took *Vimy* away, followed by *Keith*, also under the command of her First Lieutenant. *Keith* had to come out stern first, with her First Lieutenant looking out of a small porthole in the charthouse:

No communication was possible with men on the upper deck to slip our wires, so after ringing on main engines, I shouted orders to the Signal Officer and Chief Yeoman who were manning the engine telegraphs, to make the ship surge ahead and part the wires. This achieved, it was not too difficult to swing the stern off the quay, and start the ship moving astern. I rushed up to the bridge more than once to increase my view astern, but soon clattered down again, when bullets whistled past as I showed my head. Keeping as close as I dared to the stone pier on the northern side of the channel, I was mightily grateful to round the corner successfully. Knowing the rudder would be more effective at high speed, I increased shaft revolutions to give fourteen knots. Outside the harbour we manned the bridge and sorted out our load of disorderly refugees. Captain Simson and some dozen others were quietly buried at sea as we scanned the skies for enemy aircraft. It was decided to return to Dover to land our refugees and wounded.[3]

Keith had lost her Captain and had seven seamen killed, and another 28 of her crew wounded.

With so many Allied troops clamouring for evacuation further destroy-ers – *Venetia, Venomous, Vimiera, Windsor* and *Wild Swan* – started to arrive during the late afternoon to join *Whitshed* already there. At 1830 the Germans launched another sustained air attack which so added to the opposition as to make the harbour area untenable to ships. On *Whitshed*, Commander E.R. Condor, the senior officer present, signalled Dover that they would not be able to enter until air cover was provided. Some fifty minutes later twelve Spitfires of the RAF arrived and engaged the enemy planes, and by 1955 the destroyers were making their way into Boulogne harbour. *Whitshed* and *Vimiera* entered first, engaging enemy field guns shelling the harbour area as they did so. They berthed and started embark-ing the Welsh Guards who, in contrast to the milling, disorganised base troops who had earlier tried to force their way onto the ships, "marched down to the jetty in perfect order followed by the equally steady Irish Guards and Royal Marines."[1]

Between them the two destroyers embarked about one thousand men and left the harbour at 2020 hours to be replaced by *Wild Swan, Venomous* and *Venetia*. All three destroyers were hotly engaged by the enemy, but gave as good as they got in the close-range battle, their quick-firing 4.0 and 4.7-inch guns and 2-pounder pom-pom guns firing over open sights at enemy tanks and gun positions only 300 yards away. French coastal batteries, taken over by the Germans, also joined in the onslaught on the approaching destroyers. *Venetia* was hit while still in mid-channel, her commanding officer wounded, twenty of her crew killed and a further ten wounded. She was unable to proceed to the quayside and backed away. *Wild Swan* and *Venomous* withstood the onslaught and embarked over nine hundred troops before leaving at low tide at 2130 hours. Although the two destroyers successfully withdrew, it was not without trouble. As *Venomous* pulled away, her wheel jammed and she had to steer with her engines while *Black Swan*, following her, momentarily grounded. However, they reached Dover safely.

By midnight some 3000 troops had been evacuated and although a con-siderable number still remained in Boulogne, further evacuation was by now problematic. *Windsor* had however already left for Boulogne at 2030, arriving there after dark. She was able to lift off some 600 troops under cover of darkness without difficulty or incident. On leaving the harbour, her Captain reported that it was possible that two further destroyer trips could clear Boulogne of all the Allied troops trapped there. Admiral Ramsay at Dover ordered across *Wessex* and *Vimiera*. Only *Vimiera* was able to make the trip and arrived at 0015 on 24 May to find the quayside silent and in darkness. There were still well over 1,000 Allied troops await-ing evacuation, and *Vimiera* quickly embarked all she could, cramming the troops into every corner and only leaving working room around the guns. Even so, she was still obliged to leave some 200 Welsh Guards behind, and left at 0245. Five minutes after leaving shore batteries resumed their bombardment of the harbour area, and five minutes after that *Vimiera* had a lucky escape with a near miss from a German bomber. The over-laden and top-heavy destroyer was very vulnerable to air attack, since she could not readily manoeuvre; even a five degree turn caused the ship to keel over alarmingly. *Vimiera* reached Dover at 0355 and landed some 1,400 British, Belgian and French troops and refugees. It was *Vimiera*'s second trip in less than twenty four hours, and marked the end of the Boulogne evacuation. The Royal Navy's destroyers could do no more; between them, the seven destroyers, *Keith, Vimy, Whitshed, Vimiera, Wild Swan, Windsor* and *Venomous*, had brought off 4,368 troops and refugees.[13]

While the evacuations at Boulogne were taking place, other naval activities – largely involving the same group of destroyers – were simultaneously taking place further along the French coast at Calais. This time however there was to be no attempt at a large-scale evacuation – at least not of the fighting troops of the British Expeditionary Force. The new British Government had been forced to conclude that the complete withdrawal of the BEF from France might be necessary. The Belgian Army on the left flank was in danger of capitulating; the Germans had cut off the BEF from the French Army to the south and were sweeping round to completely isolate the British force, which was withdrawing towards Dunkirk. A crucial element of the withdrawal plan called for the port of Calais to be held in order to delay the German encirclement of the BEF, and allow it to withdraw into a pocket around the port and beaches of Dunkirk. At Calais, the job of the Royal Navy was to reinforce and supply the garrison there, evacuate non-essential base troops, and bombard enemy tank concentrations and artillery positions threatening to over-run the town and harbour.

At 1150 on 22 May the destroyer *Verity* escorted two troopships with a reinforcing battalion of the Queen Victoria Rifles over to Calais to support the British Rifle Battalions and 800 French troops garrisoned there. Later that day *Vimy* and *Wolsey* escorted over a merchant ship from Southampton carrying the tanks and troopers of the 3rd Royal Tank Regiment. The next day *Venomous* sailed for Calais with a demolition party to blow up the harbour installations, and in the afternoon *Windsor* and *Venetia* bombarded German mechanised columns approaching the town. By the evening of 23 May the town was under constant air attack and the harbour under German artillery fire. Back in London on 23 May:

> A dramatic afternoon, mostly spent in the Upper War Room at the Admiralty. It began with the news that the Germans were in Boulogne, that the BEF could not break through southwards to join up with the French, and that they had only two days' food left. It seemed that our army would have to retire

precipitously and try to embark, under Herculean difficulties, for England.[9]

The next day, as the desperate holding action at Calais dragged on, Admiral Ramsay sent the destroyers *Grafton*, *Greyhound* and the Polish *Burza* to support the bombarding destroyers already there. The rampant German dive-bombers extracted a heavy toll: *Wessex** was sunk and *Vimiera* and *Burza* damaged. Despite the air attacks, *Wolfhound* and *Verity* succeeded in landing supplies of ammunition and took off wounded soldiers. The battle raged on, and the military commander in Calais, Brigadier C. Nicholson, received a message from Winston Churchill during the afternoon of 25 May to be circulated among the troops:

> The eyes of the Empire are upon the defence of Calais, and His Majesty's Government are confident that you and your gallant regiment will perform an exploit worthy of the British name.[14]

With the port no longer tenable to larger warships, a small evacuating force of seven trawlers, three yachts and two drifters, escorted by the destroyers *Verity* and *Windsor*, left Dover at 2130 on 25 May for Calais. Then, at 0300 on 26 May, a signal was sent to Brigadier Nicholson telling him that there would be no mass evacuation of his troops and that they were to fight on to the end:

> Every hour you continue to exist is of the greatest help to the BEF. Government has therefore decided you must continue to fight. Have greatest possible admiration for your splendid stand. Evacuation will not (repeat not) take place, and craft required for above purpose are to return to Dover. *Verity* and *Windsor* to cover Commander Minesweeping and his retirement.[14]

The Calais garrison was finally overrun during the evening of 26 May. They had helped to hold up the encircling Germans for three days, allowing more of the BEF to congregate on Dunkirk and ultimately to escape back to Britain, while they were killed, wounded or made prisoners of war. Brigadier Nicholson was later to die in a German Prisoner-of-War Camp.

---

* See page 214.

NOTES TO SOURCES

1.   Roskill, Captain S.W. *The War at Sea 1939–1945* (HMSO: London, 1954).
2.   Harris, Able Seaman D. Papers 87/15/1. Imperial War Museum, London.
3.   Lumsden, Captain G.J.A. Papers 66/24/1. Imperial War Museum, London.
4.   Robson, Vice Admiral Sir William. 'My Naval Life' File RBSN. Churchill Archives Centre, Churchill College, Cambridge.
5.   Ziegler, P. *Mountbatten: The Official Biography* (William Collins: London, 1985).
6.   Knight, Signalman J. 'Memories of a Miscreant'. Account 87/15/1. Imperial War Museum, London.
7.   Mountbatten, Earl Louis. *Mountbatten: Eighty Years in Pictures* (Macmillan: London, 1979).
8.   Poolman, K. *The Kelly* (William Kimber: London, 1954).
9.   Colville, Sir John. *The Fringes of Power: Downing Street Diaries 1939– 1945* (Hodder and Stoughton: London, 1985).
10. Danchev, A. and Todman, D. (Eds). *Field Marshal Lord Alanbrooke: War Diaries 1939–1945* (Wiedenfeld and Nicholson, London: 2001).
11. HMS *Whitshed*. Report M 014793/40. Papers, File: ROSK 4/23. Churchill Archives Centre, Churchill College, Cambridge.
12. Whinney, Captain R. *The U-Boat Peril*. (Blandford Press: London, 1986).
13. Gardner, W.J.R. (Ed). *The Evacuation from Dunkirk: Operation Dynamo, 26 May–4 June 1940* (Frank Cass: London, 2000).
14. Churchill, W.S. *The Second World War, Vol II: Their Finest Hour* (Cassell: London, 1949).

XII

Dunkirk and the Fall of France

The steadfastness of the Calais garrison helped to at least delay the encircling German mechanised formations, thus preventing the complete destruction of the BEF and parts of the Belgian and French armies now being forced into a pocket around Dunkirk. Then, thankfully, the German High Command ordered a temporary halt to their headlong rush in order that their mechanised columns could rest, refit, and regroup, in preparation for an assault upon Paris and the rest of France, the Luftwaffe pressed their case for their Stukas be allowed to finish off the BEF in the Dunkirk pocket. The German pause was to prove a Godsend for the retreating, exhausted and demoralised Allied troops.

With the Belgian Army on the eastern flank of the BEF near to capitulation and the French Army to the south in considerable disarray, the War Cabinet, faced with the growing realisation that a general withdrawal from France was becoming likely, began to plan for the execution of Operation Dynamo: the evacuation of the BEF. Vice-Admiral Bertram Ramsay, Flag Officer Commanding Dover, was put in charge of the operation and Captain W.G. Tennant ordered to Dunkirk to take charge of the naval embarkation parties being sent over to control the evacuation process. Both were to prove crucial appointments.

On 22 May the Commanders-in-Chief of the Portsmouth and Nore commands were directed to take over and man nearly fifty 200-ton Dutch flat-bottomed motor barges called schuyts, which had come to Britain immediately prior to the Dutch capitulation, ready for use in any evacuation. The collection of many and varied other small vessels able to get close inshore – with many privately owned vessels among them – also began. Despite the many demands on the Royal Navy (from the still-on going struggle in Norway, the continuing need to protect the Atlantic convoys, and to provide a strong deterrent naval presence in the Mediterranean and Far East), the Admiralty was able to source a considerable armada of evacuating ships for Vice-Admiral Ramsay. He eventually had at his disposal the anti-aircraft cruiser *Calcutta*; 41 destroyers (albeit some of

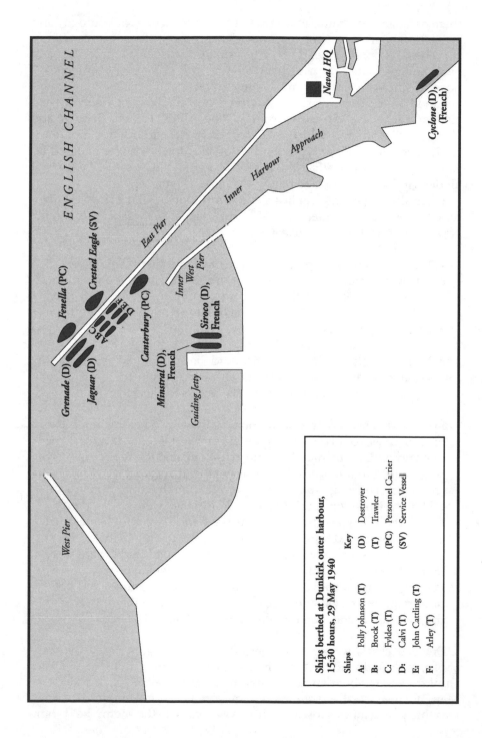

Ships berthed at Dunkirk outer harbour, 15:30 hours, 29 May 1940

Ships

A: Polly Johnson (T)
B: Brock (T)
C: Fyldea (T)
D: Calvi (T)
E: John Cattling (T)
F: Arley (T)

Key

(D) Destroyer
(T) Trawler
(PC) Personnel Carrier
(SV) Service Vessel

them damaged and battle-worn from their recent actions at Boulogne and Calais); 100 minesweepers and mine-clearing craft; 18 armed trawlers; 6 corvettes; 1 sloop and nearly 80 other small craft such as motor torpedo boats and gunboats. The Merchant Navy provided 36 passenger ferries; 7 hospital ships converted from passenger ferries; and over 260 tugs, trawlers and barges. There were in addition a miscellany of privately-owned civilian yachts and pleasure cruisers. The Allies, French, Belgian and Dutch, provided craft which included 19 French destroyers, 65 French civilian craft of various types, and 43 of the Dutch schuyts manned by Royal Navy crews. In all, as the evacuation unfolded, some 848 vessels of all descriptions were to take part in Operation Dynamo.

There also began, in great haste and unorthodoxy, all the detailed planning that was needed. Lieutenant G. Grandage, RNR, was working in the Naval Control Office at Ramsgate:

A London taxi drew up outside our office and three large boxes of charts were brought in. As I had not ordered them I telephoned the Hydrographic Office at the Admiralty, to be told "You will need them": 1,500 charts in all, 500 in each set, covering the route from Ramsgate to Dunkirk.[1]

The Ramsgate Naval Control Office had been allocated responsibility for despatching all the accumulating small craft from the ports around London, and the Essex and South coasts, across to Dunkirk:

I reported to my senior officer who was living in a nearby hotel. The only place we could discuss the situation was the gents' lavatory. The next morning I soon had the route made out, and the typist got busy producing four hundred copies; one copy and a set of three charts for each craft. Three light buoys had been laid on the route from northeast of the Goodwin Sands to Dunkirk. But they were not marked on the charts. The types of craft for which we were responsible included Dutch coasters and tugs, some of which were towing lifeboats. Most of these had some navigational equipment. In addition there were many river steamers, motor pleasure cruisers, fishing boats, etc. Few had any navigational gear. I decided to lay off the courses and positions required ourselves on the charts before issuing them. Two of us did this all day and well into the night on about 1000 charts.[1]

Detailed charts were needed because of the dangers posed by sandbanks, minefields and likely German air activity. Three routes to and from Dunkirk were to be used for the evacuation, designated X, Y and Z (see Map 3). The normal and shortest route from Dover to Dunkirk (Route Z) was thirty-nine miles. However, this passed close to the enemy-held shore to the east of Calais and was, for the last twenty miles of its passage , to prove very vulnerable to enemy attack and hence impractical for daylight use. The alternative northerly passage (Route Y) was therefore used in the early days of the evacuation, although the length of this passage (some eighty-seven miles) doubled the length of each ship's journey, and before it could be used it had to be swept free of mines. As the evacuation progressed, and speed of passage and hence time of evacuation became critical, a third central passage (Route X) of some fifty-five miles length was cleared for use.

By Sunday 26 May 1940, the position of the BEF had become desperate, and the War Cabinet decided that it had no option but to attempt a withdrawal from France. At 1030 Lord Gort, Commander-in-Chief of the BEF, received a signal from the Cabinet to evacuate.

This was apparently the first intimation that the C-in-C, who had been banking on a joint Allied counter-attack – The Weygand Plan – to break through the German stranglehold, had received that evacuation was now thought to be the only option. Lord Gort's reply concluded: "I must not conceal from you that a great part of the BEF and its equipment will inevitably be lost even in the best circumstances."[2]

During that fraught afternoon, the Admiralty was also busy putting into place its plans, and forewarned Vice-Admiral Ramsay: "it was imperative for Dynamo to be implemented with the greatest vigour."[2] At 1857 the Vice-Admiral was signalled to commence Operation Dynamo. The aim at that time was to evacuate 45,000 men in two days. It was considered unfeasible to expect to extract any more. The ships and men of the Royal Navy and the miscellaneous evacuation fleet were to prove both aims to be a gross underestimate. In the event seven times that many men were evacuated and the operation continued for nine days. The destroyers of the evacuating fleet were again to play the central key role, evacuating by far the greatest proportion of men, most of whom were evacuated from the moles of the outer harbour. Again the destroyers were to pay a heavy price: six British and three French destroyers were lost, and nineteen other British destroyers were badly damaged.

As it had been off the Low Countries, at Boulogne and again at Calais, so it was at Dunkirk; the destroyers led the operation with selfless gallantry and suffered most heavily. And these losses were to be felt grievously during the anxious months that followed…[3]

German bombing had devastated Dunkirk inner harbour and it was never used during the evacuation. However the outer harbour, protected by breakwaters or moles on both the east and west sides, could – although not designed for such use – accommodate the berthing of small cross channel passenger ships. *Mona Queen* was the first such ship to berth and bring back 1,200 troops, returning just after midnight on 27 May. She was followed at 0309 by *Canterbury* with 1,340 troops, the store-ship *Ngaroma* at 0500 with 100, and the *King Orry* at 1100 with 1,131. The use of hospital ships had to be discontinued when, despite their conspicuous white hulls and blazing lights and in disregard of the Geneva Convention, they were bombed and subjected to bombardment from shore batteries. Nevertheless, the hospital ships *Isle of Jersey* and *Worthing* each brought back three hundred stretcher cases.

Meanwhile, the three British Army corps making up the BEF were continuing their withdrawal into a defensive parameter around Dunkirk. The Luftwaffe continued its attacks on the town of Dunkirk, and more damage was inflicted on the harbour area such that it was decided that – at least for the time being – further evacuation from there was not possible. Troops were therefore directed to the beaches to await evacuation. Their hopes of a speedy return to England were to be quickly dashed. Jack Toomey, serving with the 42nd Postal Unit of the BEF, was later to write:

> …as dawn came up we found the main Dunkirk road and what a jam. After about ten hours of stopping and starting, diving into ditches and back into lorries, we got near Dunkirk…there were about seventy bombers…knocking hell out of the docks or what was left of them. From there to the beaches, they were black with troops waiting to go aboard, only there were no boats. They gave us a raid that afternoon and evening, and the following day they gave us a raid that lasted from dawn to dusk, about seventeen hours. The fellows laid down on open beaches with the bombs falling alongside us. Lucky it was sand it killed the effects of the bombs.[4]

The hopes of the troops on the beaches and in the sand dunes received a setback when German-manned shore batteries and artillery between Calais and Dunkirk started to fire on evacuating ships attempting to use Route Z, sinking and damaging them. The route had to be abandoned for use in daylight hours and the longer northerly Route Y had to be cleared for use.

Among the first ships to use Route Y on 27 May were the passenger vessels *St Helier* and *Royal Daffodil* which left Dover at 1054 under escort of the V and W class veteran of the Boulogne evacuations: the destroyer *Vimy*. Following the death of her Captain at Boulogne, Lieutenant-Commander R.G.K. Knowling assumed command of the *Vimy* on 23 May. Despite a German bombing attack, *Vimy* and her two ships arrived at Dunkirk safely, in company with the destroyer *Anthony* and the hospital carriers *St Andrew* and *St Julien*. When the convoy arrived at Dunkirk a heavy raid was in progress. *St Helier* and the two hospital ships could not enter; but *Vimy* and *Royal Daffodil* did, with the latter bringing off 840 troops. Then came a mystery – never explained – concerning *Vimy*: "Lieutenant Commander Knowling left the bridge at 2355 and was not seen again; he was officially reported as presumed lost overboard."[5] One of *Vimy*'s crew, Able Seaman Harris, expanded on the circumstances of the disappearance:

> The *Vimy* was engaged on this evacuation for a very arduous seven days. During which time we lost our replacement Captain. After the first day the First Lieutenant asked that he be awakened and called to the bridge during a German air raid. Despite numerous very thorough searches of the ship he could not be located. The Captain had been on board for such a short period of time that I had not even learned his name.[6]

After the ship search the First Lieutenant, Lieutenant A.P.W. Northey assumed command at 0300 on 28 May and escorted the *St Helier* and two hospital ships back to Dover. He remained in command for a further evacuation trip later that day, before handing over command to Lieutenant Commander M.W.E. Wentworth at 1545 on 29 May. *Vimy* thus had four commanding officers in six days. [5]

Throughout 27 May, Dunkirk was bombed and further damaged by the Luftwaffe, with at least twelve attacks being made upon the town and its sea approaches between 0825 and 2000. Captain Tennant, who had left Dover at 1315 in the destroyer *Wolfhound*, arrived at Dunkirk at 1655 in the middle of an air raid and took up his duties as Senior Naval Officer. He was accompanied by an initial staff of twelve officers and 160 naval ratings. They found a scene of devastation. Lieutenant S.A. Nettle, RNVR, was a member of Captain Tennant's embarkation control team:

> Coming in from seaward we could see the enormous pall of smoke from the oil storage tanks set on fire by bombing. An intense aerial bombardment was in progress when we arrived. This was the first time I had experienced that devastatingly frightening "screaming bomb". It seemed to screech into your brain, and you felt it was coming straight for you.[7]

Lieutenant Nettle was not the only person on *Wolfhound* to be terrified by their introduction to the Stuka dive-bomber as the destroyer approached Dunkirk; John Pearce, another member of the embarkation control party, wrote:

> Out of the blue there was a peculiar screaming noise. We all looked at each other for a second before we realised it was Stuka bombers overhead. They made a terrible noise – that was half the terror. The ship immediately heeled over to port and the next we heard was a

bomb screaming down. By that time you'd never seen such a panic in all your life. Rifles and kettles smashed against the walls, bodies were flying over and grabbing guard rails to stop them going over. Everybody was dashing to action stations with the alarm bell ringing simultaneously. It turned out three planes were attacking us and we eventually shot one down. This was our baptism of fire and a very frightening experience.[8]

By evening the situation in the town and harbour area had become so bad that Dunkirk was cleared of all troops, who were sent to the sand dunes behind the beaches to the east of the town to await embarkation. At 1958, Captain Tennant signalled Dover: "Please send every available craft to beaches east of Dunkirk immediately. Evacuation tomorrow night is problematical."[2] Barely half an hour later, another signal was sent to Vice-Admiral Ramsay:

> Port continuously bombed all day and on fire. Embarkation possible only from beaches east of harbour…Send all ships and passenger ships there to anchor. Am ordering *Wolfhound* to load there and sail.[2]

Unfortunately *Wolfhound*, which had been damaged by near-misses during a bombing attack *en route* for Dunkirk, was further damaged when a bomb struck the jetty some six feet away from the ship and when she later grounded in the shallow waters off the beaches. Nevertheless, she and *Wolsey* were among the first ships to take troops off the beaches. Up to midnight on 27 May, 7,669 troops had been evacuated.

Back in his Dover headquarters Vice-Admiral Ramsay, realising that the situation at Dunkirk had become critical – Belgium was going to capitulate at midnight – reacted immediately with great drive and energy, and overnight a period of intense organisational activity began. Any ships able to take troops off the beaches, mainly using their own boats to go inshore, were assembled: personnel ships, minesweepers and destroyers. Late that night a flurry of signals was sent out to ten destroyers and the anti-aircraft cruiser *Calcutta*. To the *Calcutta* and destroyers *Gallant*, *Vivacious*, *Windsor*, *Vimy*, *Anthony* and *Impulsive*: "Close beaches one to three miles east of Dunkirk with utmost dispatch and embark all possible British troops using your own boats. This is our last chance of saving them. Maid of Orleans, Lormont, seventeen drifters and other craft will be operating."[2] To the *Greyhound*, *Grafton*, *Sabre* and *Blyskawica*: Close the beach at La Panne at 0100 tomorrow, Tuesday, and embark all possible British troops using your boats. This is our last chance of saving them.[2]

Captain Tennant was signalled and ordered to report hourly on the situation on the beaches. This he did next morning at 0935:

Your 0758. There are at present 2,000 men on Dunkirk beach and 7,000 men on sand dunes for whom I have no ships. They are now in need of water which Army cannot supply. Unlimited numbers are falling back on this area and situation in present circumstances will shortly become desperate. I am doing my best to keep you informed but shall be unable to reply hourly.[2]

As a result of the overnight activity, early on 28 May there were assembling off the beaches some eight destroyers, the *Calcutta*, four paddle minesweepers, seventeen drifters, three Dutch schuyts and two transports. All these ships intended to use their own boats to get the men off the beaches. For Jack Toomey:

The following day dawn broke and we saw the most welcome sight of all – about a dozen destroyers off the beaches and more coming up – boats of all shapes and sizes…Fortunately the day was cloudy and misty, the bombers only came once and as they came low beneath the clouds the Navy let 'em have it. They slung everything up.[4]

28 May marked the beginning of the beach evacuations, but it was a slow beginning due to the chronic shortage of boats able to get close enough inshore to embark the exhausted and demoralised troops. The boat crews also quickly tired from rowing, and the exhausted and inexperienced troops were of little help. It was slow work.

From about 0300 onwards, destroyers making their first trip to the beaches had been arriving there; two (*Gallant* and *Wakeful*) braved going into Dunkirk. At 0320 *Vimy* returned and arrived off the beach at Zuydcoote, three miles east of Dunkirk and, using her boats, helped load the paddle minesweeper *Brighton Belle*. By 0400 the situation in Dunkirk harbour seemed to have eased, and Captain Tennant asked ships to start going alongside the east pier to try to speed up the evacuation by embarking troops from there. *Vimy* left her boats with *Brighton Belle* and entered the harbour at 0445 embarking 613 troops. Unfortunately *Brighton Belle*, returning with 350 troops to Ramsgate, struck a submerged wreck and sank, but not before her troops were rescued by nearby boats. At 0955 the destroyer *Mackay* reached Dunkirk, having travelled from her position in the Irish Sea, and within an hour had embarked 600 men, handing over her berth position to the waiting destroyer *Montrose*. A shuttle service was starting to develop. The destroyer *Sabre*, which had already returned to Dover with 158 troops picked off Malo beach, came back and berthed outside *Montrose*. An hour later the destroyers *Worcester* and *Anthony* arrived and berthed. With the two piers becoming crammed with troops, the Stukas returned, but were driven off by the combined gunfire of the destroyers.

At about lunchtime the destroyers *Codrington*, *Jaguar* and *Javelin*, diverted from patrol duties, arrived. *En route* they had picked up thirty-three survivors from the Belgian ship *Aboukir*, which had been torpedoed by an E-boat while carrying some 200 evacuees from Ostend to England. *Codrington* went to Dunkirk harbour, and the other two to the beaches to pick up troops using their own boats, while *Vivacious*, making her second trip, took back 359 troops. Operation Dynamo, despite the confusion and chaos, was gaining momentum; and during the day more destroyers were joining the evacuating force.

Other ships, naval and civilian, were playing an equally gallant role. Personnel carriers – civilian cross-channel ferries – had been pressed into service because of their large troop-carrying potential, but were incurring losses. *Queen of the Channel* was bombed and sunk, but the 904 troops she was carrying were safely transferred to *Dorrien Rose*, empty and *en route* for Dunkirk, before she sank. Some forty-five such civilian personnel carriers were to be used during Operation Dynamo, of which eight were sunk, and another eight so damaged by gunfire, bombing, or collision as to be rendered unserviceable.

The damage and losses that the unarmed and unprotected cross-channel ferries were suffering from coastal batteries and bombing, led to the decision that they could not be used in daylight hours. Such daylight evacuation had to be confined to warships and small vessels. These warships, particularly the larger destroyers which presented valuable strategic targets, were themselves coming under increasingly severe air attack, despite the best efforts of the RAF The whole of the Straits of Dover, not only the sea off Dunkirk, was subject to attacks from the Luftwaffe. Thus at 1145 the destroyer *Windsor*, on patrol off the South Goodwin Light Vessel, was attacked by fifteen dive bombers and ten fighters escorting them. *Windsor* survived, but was badly damaged by near misses and machine gun fire and suffered thirty casualties.

By now the stranded troops were suffering badly from hunger and thirst, and ships attempting to take off troops did their best to succour the exhausted troops from their own stocks. Jack Toomey was later to write:

> We got aboard and started, there were about 800 of us on one small destroyer. The Navy rallied round and dished out cocoa, tins of bully and loaves of new bread. This was the first grub some of us had for nearly four days and the first bread we had for a fortnight.[4]

As Operation Dynamo became more organised, ships were loaded with supplies of drinking water. The ferry *Maid of Orleans* took over 6,000 two-gallon cans of water to Dunkirk, and the lighter *Seine* took 5,000 cans to the beaches. Even so, no food or water reached Malo beach until 30 May.

During the afternoon of 28 May the troops on Bray beach were being heavily bombed. With little chance of early evacuation Captain Tennant ordered them to march into Dunkirk, despite the dangers of overcrowding there, and asked for ships to attempt to take them off from the eastern mole. The destroyers *Mackay, Montrose, Vimy, Worcester, Sabre* and *Anthony* all entered and embarked full loads of troops, while other destroyers continued to try to service evacuation from the beaches. At 1830 the destroyer *Grafton* reported that there were still several thousand troops on Bray beach, with still more arriving. Conditions on the exposed beaches were now becoming increasingly critical as more troops crowded into the defensive parameter. From H. Barwick in a letter to his father:

> When we arrived at Dunkirk there were lines and lines of men waiting for boats or anything afloat. Dave and I found our CQMS [Company Quarter-Master Sergeant] and Lieutenant Colonel Thomas with thirty one others and when we were going onto the mole to board a boat, a Captain of the Welsh Guards came along and said they were next in turn for evacuation, so we withdrew into the sand dunes to wait our turn.[9]

There was by now a desperate need for more boats to try to get home the growing numbers of the BEF withdrawing into the Dunkirk perimeter. In order to accelerate the evacuation, the Admiralty ordered a further seven destroyers to Dunkirk, where they arrived the next day 29 May: *Verity, Harvester, Esk, Malcolm, Express, Shikari* and *Scimitar*, as well as more minesweepers, some from as far away as Rosyth. At Dover, Vice-Admiral Ramsay signalled the Admiralty: "Request you send every available shallow draft power boat capable of ferrying from beaches to ships, direct to ships lying off beaches to eastwards of Dunkirk stocked with fuel and provisions for two days."[2]

Despite all the problems, by midnight on 28 May 17,804 troops had been evacuated back to England, of which 11,835 had gone in destroyers. 11,874 had left from Dunkirk east pier and 5,930 from the beaches.

The next day, 29 May, the Portsmouth and Nore Commands, the Thames estuary and the Port of London Authority were stripped of all available motor boats, lighters and barges, such that there was some difficulty in finding enough – even rudimentary – charts for the commandeered boats. The Master of the coaster *Hythe* claimed that he was given "an army road map" with which to navigate.[2]

At Dunkirk harbour, off the beaches and on the routes to and from Dover, Wednesday 29 May was to prove a testing day for the resources and resolve of the Royal Navy and the ships and boats of the mercantile fleets. As early as 0005 hours the first mishap occurred when the destroyer *Mackay, en route* to Bray beach with *Harvester*, ran aground and was unable to take any further part in the evacuation. *Harvester* meanwhile went on to Bray beach and found over 4000 troops awaiting embarkation. She was able to take off some 700 (including 100 wounded men) despite strong cross-seas and sand bars, which hindered the evacuation and led to the loss of boats, some through overcrowding.

One of the destroyers directed to the beaches was *Scimitar*; it was her first trip. Her Captain, Lieutenant Commander R.D. Franks, wrote:

> We joined up with *Malcolm* and followed her across the channel in the dark. My charts were not up to date with all the extra buoys etc, and I had little idea where we were when *Malcolm* stopped and told us to go a mile further on and embark troops. I went on gingerly, sounding all the way and then anchored and sent the motor boat in to where we thought the coast was.
>
> When the boat eventually came back I asked a military officer up to the bridge to tell me what was happening. He said he thought there were about 600 men to come off. He was wrong by about 316,000. I took rather a dim view of his alarmist report but as it got light we began to see the shore and curious dark patches which turned out to be soldiers waiting to come off. It was slow work with our two boats; the motor boat could only take six and the whaler about twelve. When we had about 70 soldiers embarked I thought we were pretty full and asked *Malcolm* if I should return to Dover. This provoked a dusty answer and we gradually filled to about 300 and this included filling up all our below deck spaces. Subsequently we found we could jam in about 500, standing room only, and this number made the ship feel dangerously unstable. Fairly early on the whaler was swamped by panicky soldiers rushing it. Morale at first was poor but improved all the time as we got to the fighting troops as opposed to the base and support men. [10]

The destroyer *Montrose* was also to have a very eventful time. One of her officers, Lieutenant E.A. Court-Hampton, was to record:

> While leaving Dunkirk on Wednesday 29 May 1940,* with 1200 soldiers on board, HMS *Montrose* was subjected to high level bombing. A stick of seven bombs fell across the ship. These fell approximately 20/30 yards on either side of the ship. Montrose was lifted about four feet out of the water while steaming at 18 knots, and suffered loss of half her lighting, damage to the steering and a small electrical fire. However the ship was worked to Dover and soldiers disembarked. The next day, patched up, while returning to Dunkirk to pick up more survivors the ship was in collision with a tug while steaming at 21 knots in a fog, suffering damage three feet above the waterline and flooding. She was towed, stern first, back to Dover harbour.[10]

---

* Thought in fact to be Tuesday 28 May.

The collision occurred in the very early hours of 29 May, at approximately 0013 hours, and resulted in severe damage to both the destroyer and the tug, *Sun V*, and the loss of the seven naval cutters being towed over to the beaches by the tug. Neither she nor the *Montrose* were able to take any further part in the evacuation.

These early incidents were to be a mere introduction to more severe and tragic setbacks as the night passed. At 0045 the destroyer *Wakeful*, returning from Bray beach with 650 troops on board, was torpedoed by the E-boat *S30*. A torpedo struck *Wakeful* in the forward boiler room. The destroyer broke in two and the two portions sank within about 15 seconds, each portion remaining upright with the bow and stern standing about 60 feet out of the water.[2] All 650 troops asleep below, except for one survivor, were lost, as were all *Wakeful*'s engine room crew except for two stokers.

Wakeful's Captain, Commander R.L. Fisher, was washed clear of the bridge to be picked up by the trawler *Comfort*, while the minesweepers *Lydd* and *Gossamer* searched for survivors. By the time *Lydd* had picked up ten survivors the destroyer *Grafton*, loaded with about 800 troops from Bray beach, had arrived on the scene, and ordered *Lydd* to circle around her. The *Gossamer* went on to Dover. *Comfort* had by now found that the stern portion of *Wakeful* had fallen over into the water, and went alongside *Grafton* to warn her of the danger of torpedoes, either from nearby enemy vessels or from any remaining on *Wakeful*. Then, at 0240, *Grafton* was indeed struck by a torpedo, later found to have been fired by the German submarine *U-62* which, together with E-boats, had been sent by the enemy to lie in wait across the routes being used by the evacuating ships.

The torpedo hit the *Grafton*'s port side to be followed almost immediately by a second explosion on the bridge, thought to be from a shell, which killed her Captain, Commander C.E.C. Robinson, and three of her crew. The torpedo blew off *Grafton*'s stern and broke her back. The torpedo explosion also almost swamped the alongside *Comfort*, and *Wakeful*'s survivor captain, Commander Fisher, was once more washed overboard. *Comfort* pulled away and came round in a wide circle to within about fifty yards of the stricken *Grafton* to render assistance. Tragically, in the darkness and confusion, *Comfort* was mistaken by the *Grafton* and the *Lydd* for a German E-boat and deluged with 4-inch and small-arms fire. Meanwhile Commander Fisher had reached the bow of *Comfort* and was about to clamber aboard when *Lydd*, coming in at full speed, rammed *Comfort* amidships, cutting her in half. Some of *Comfort*'s crew attempted to leap onto *Lydd* to save themselves but, mistaken for a German boarding attempt, were met with rifle fire. There were only five survivors from *Comfort*. Commander Fisher was picked up at 0515 by a boat lowered from the Norwegian SS *Hird*, bringing some 3,500 refugees and troops from Dunkirk back to England. The 800 troops from the *Grafton* were successfully transferred to the passenger ship *Malines*. The destroyer *Ivanhoe*, en route to Dunkirk in company with *Javelin, Icarus, Vanquisher* and *Intrepid*, went to the still-afloat *Grafton*'s aid at 0430 and took off the wounded, before sinking the by now heavily listing destroyer with gunfire. Following the loss of the valuable *Grafton*, the Admiralty sent out a signal a few hours later: "During present operations on Belgian coast where many small craft are present destroyers are not, repeat not, to stop to render assistance to ships in distress."[2]

Leaving *Ivanhoe* to help *Grafton, Vanquisher* went on to Malo beach while *Javelin* and *Icarus* entered Dunkirk harbour and *Intrepid* waited outside for a vacant berth, ahead of *Mona Queen* loaded with supplies of fresh water. Then at 0530 *Mona Queen* struck a magnetic mine and sank within two minutes. The Germans, it was subsequently found, had laid mines overnight in the approaches to Dunkirk: across Route X and at the entrances to Dover and Folkstone harbours. The anti-submarine trawlers *Thuringia, Westella_and_Blackburn Rovers* were thought to have been lost to some of these recently-laid mines.

During the rest of 29 May the ensuing heavy Allied shipping losses were caused by Luftwaffe air attack, despite frequent sweeps across the channel and over Dunkirk by RAF fighters. Destroyers were a sought-after target. At 1155 the destroyers *Jaguar, Gallant* and *Grenade*, on passage for Dunkirk by the central Route X, were attacked by seventeen Stuka dive-bombers. The destroyers, and the few RAF fighters striving to stem the dive-bomber onslaught, fought back as best they could. From a member of Jaguar's crew: "One dive-bomber was seen to be hit by pom-pom, and while losing height was dispatched by a fighter."[2]

This Stuka attack took place just when one of the RAF's main fighter patrols had turned for home with fuel running out. *Gallant* was badly damaged by a near miss and had to retire, to take no further part in Operation Dynamo. *Grenade* went on to berth at the east pier of Dunkirk at 1250 with *Jaguar* alongside. *Grenade* was ordered to remain as 'duty ship', at the disposal of Captain Tennant, the Senior Naval Officer, while *Jaguar* took off some 1,000 troops between 1400 and 1525.

By this time, fourteen ships were embarking troops, or awaiting to do so, at Dunkirk harbour. As the personnel carrier *Lochgarry* left with 1000 troops, she was replaced by six trawlers in two triple banks. Ahead were the double-banked *Grenade* and *Jaguar*, and astern the personnel carrier *Canterbury*. Astern of her again, in the inner harbour, was the French destroyer *Cyclone*. At the Guiding Jetty (see Map 4) were the two French destroyers *Mistral* and *Siroco*, and, outside the harbour, berthed on the seaward side of the east pier, were the service vessel *Crested Eagle* and the passenger vessel *Fenella*.

The crowded harbour was an ideal target for the Luftwaffe, and in the afternoon the bombing of the Dunkirk piers and beaches recommenced, in four separate attacks between 1530 and 2000. There was little apparent Allied fighter opposition. In the first raid, some twenty to thirty bombs were dropped by a force of twelve bombers. Most of the bombs fell wide of their targets, but the trawler *Polly Johnson* was severely damaged by a near miss, and at 1555 a bomb, striking the west Guiding Jetty, damaged the French *Mistral*, killing three of her crew and injuring four, including her Captain. While this raid was taking place the loaded destroyer *Jaguar* was ordered away from the harbour to accompany and escort home *Lochgarry* with her load of troops. At about 1630, as the destroyer was taking up station ahead of *Lochgarry*, the second air attack took place, with dive bombers each dropping a cluster of four bombs. Once again it was the valuable modern destroyer which was the prime target. Fourteen clusters were raining on *Jaguar*, and one on *Lochgarry*. A near-miss holed *Jaguar* near the waterline, putting her steering and engines out of action and causing a list to port. Drifting helplessly, *Jaguar* was quickly taken in tow by the destroyer *Express*, who came alongside and took off some of her troops. The small Dutch coaster *Riku*, on her way to La Panne beach, closed *Jaguar* and took off a further 295 troops. Despite further attacks at 2014 and 2026, *Jaguar* was towed to Dover and reached there at 2350, making the last part of the journey under her own power; but she was so damaged that she was unable to take any further part in Operation Dynamo.

Widespread bombing continued between 1530 and 1600, and the destroyer *Anthony*, with 550 troops lifted off La Panne beach on board, the destroyer *Greyhound*, the minesweepers *Sutton* and *Salamander*, and the paddle minesweeper *Sandown*, were attacked, but with little damage. However in a following dive-bomber attack, *Greyhound* was badly damaged and suffered twenty killed and a further seventy casualties. With 506 evacuated troops on board, *Greyhound* was taken in tow by the Polish destroyer *Blyskawica*, which had been on patrol with *Vega*. *Blyskawica* was one of those ships recalled from the Norwegian Campaign. One of the crewmen, Petty Officer B. Witkowski, remembers:

> Now we were on coastal patrol in the English Channel. We were one of eight destroyers [based] in Harwich. Soon the Dunkirk evacuation began, so we were guarding the small ships that were rescuing the soldiers from Dunkirk. One night one of the ships was sunk and we rescued several soldiers and landed them at Dover. Dunkirk Campaign was a frightening time.[12]

On this occasion, *Blyskawica* towed *Greyhound* as far as the North Goodwin lightship. Then, as the requested tugs had not materialised, took her on into Dover. *Greyhound* was too badly damaged to take any further part in the evacuation. [13]

At 1700 *Intrepid*, on her way back to Dunkirk having landed 661 troops at Dover, was severely damaged by a near miss when approaching La Panne beach. On fire, and with two killed and nineteen of her crew wounded, the destroyer was forced to return to Dover, and likewise had to be withdrawn from the evacuation. A little later, at 1730, the French destroyer *Siroco* together with the damaged *Mistral* left Dunkirk harbour for Dover with 500 troops. *Mistral* was also unable to take any further part in the operation.

The third air attack, at about 1750, saw waves of German bombers drop some 100 bombs on Dunkirk harbour area. Allied fighters were held off by strong formations of the escorting German fighters, and the bombing did much damage to Allied ships in the harbour. A near miss holed the destroyer *Grenade*, and the trawler *Calvi* was sunk by a direct hit. The personnel carrier *Fenella*, which had 650 troops, embarked and was hit on her promenade deck; a second bomb struck the pier and the concrete debris holed the thin-hulled passenger vessel below the waterline; a third bomb, exploding between the ship and the pier, wrecked the engine room. The surviving troops were disembarked and transferred to *Crested Eagle*, lying astern of *Fenella* (see Map 4.) which was towed away and left sinking. A few minutes later, *Grenade* received two direct hits, which destroyed her engine room and set her on fire. She was pulled clear of the pier at 1815 and, after narrowly missing the trawlers berthed nearby, was towed to the westward of the main harbour channel and allowed to burn herself out before finally exploding.

Stanley Allen was to write of his admiration for the trawler men:

> It really was incredible how they managed to clear the damaged ships and debris from their berths. This was fantastically brave work as they were sitting ducks to the aircraft. For the Luftwaffe pilots it must have been plain target practice because of the terrific sighting the line of the East Mole gave them.[8]

During this day of horrendous aerial onslaught of Dunkirk harbour – especially of the east pier – the nerve of some soldiers, overwrought by their ordeal which had by now lasted for several days, began to fail them. A number tried to escape the bombs by jumping into the sea or running back away from the pier. They were reportedly brought to order and a restored nerve by the intervention of Commander J. Clouston, pier master, brought over as a member of Captain Tennant's team. He is said to have intercepted them with drawn revolver, and firmly told them: "We have come to take you back to the UK. I have six bullets and I am not a bad shot. The Lieutenant behind me is an even better one. So that makes twelve of you. [Pause, and loudly bellowed] Now get on those bloody ships."[8] The men steadied.

The destroyer *Verity* left at 1755 followed by *Crested Eagle*. Clear of the harbour, the wooden-hulled *Crested Eagle* was struck by four bombs, caught fire and, out of control and blazing fiercely, ran aground west of Bray beach at 1830. Her 200 surviving crew and evacuated troops took to the shallow water, where they were machine-gunned by the Luftwaffe and the ships attempting rescue bombed. Some survivors, many badly burned, were picked up by the minesweepers *Hebe* and *Lydd*.

The fourth and final German air attack of 29 May took place between about 1830 and 2000. This attack was not concentrated upon the harbour but was more widespread. Bray beach was targeted as were the ships loaded with survivors returning to Dover. Off Bray beach, the destroyers *Sabre*, *Verity* and *Saladin* were heavily attacked. *Saladin* suffered ten attacks, during which her engine room was badly damaged by a near miss and she was forced to return to Dover at a best speed of 15 knots, to take no further part in the evacuation.

The destroyer *Icarus*, operating off Zuydcoote, had taken 470 troops off the coaster *Doggersbank* when she was attacked by ten dive-bombers at 1830. She survived this with only minor damage, but had one man killed and twenty-five wounded. The sloop *Bideford* arrived off Bray beach at 1730 and started to receive on board boatloads of mainly French troops some twenty minutes later. It was a difficult operation in the surf and swell, which typified many of the beach evacuations. Her Captain, Lieutenant Commander J.H. Lewes, described how:

> The boats were dangerously overcrowded and several swamped on the way off from the shore. On arrival alongside the men would all jump on board and let their boats drift off on the tide. Paddles were lost overboard, rendering the boats useless. *Bideford's* motor boat was lowered and ordered to collect and tow inshore any empty boats. The whaler was lowered and two officers and a signalman were sent in to endeavour to take charge on the beach…this was next to impossible. The men rushed the boats and capsized them I shallow water, and then left the boats without any attempt to right them and use them again.[2]

Bideford's journey home was an epic of tribulation and ultimate triumph. She was dive-bombed at 1915 and then machine-gunned by low-flying fighters. At 2007 four bombs were dropped on her. One missed by only thirty yards; one hit the quarter deck; one hit near the stern, detonating a depth charge which blew away forty feet of her stern. The main mast collapsed onto the searchlight and machine gun platforms wrecking both. Twenty-eight of her crew and evacuated troops were killed, and twenty-one wounded. A fire broke out and the magazine had to be flooded. After a further dive-bombing attack, she anchored in shallow water and transferred her troops to the minesweeper *Kellett*. During the night she took on another 400 troops. Then she was towed back to Dover at a speed of 2 to 3 knots by the gunboat *Locust*. *Bideford* finally reached Dover over forty hours away at 1130 on 31 May, and disembarked 436 men.

By midnight on 29 May, 47,310 men had been evacuated during the preceding twenty four hours, of which 13,752 had been lifted off the beaches. But the cost had been heavy: the destroyers *Wakeful*, *Grafton* and *Grenade* had been sunk; and seven more, *Saladin*, *Greyhound*, *Intrepid*, *Montrose*, *Mackay*, *Gallant* and *Jaguar* so badly damaged that they had to be withdrawn from the operation. Four personnel carriers had also been sunk together with nearly twenty other miscellaneous classes of vessel. So bad were the destroyer losses that the Admiralty feared that if the rate of attrition continued the Royal Navy would be crippled for future participation in the war, and an order was issued withdrawing the seven modern destroyers of the H, I and J classes - *Harvester*, *Havant*, *Icarus*, *Impulsive*, *Intrepid*, *Ivanhoe* and *Javelin* – from Operation Dynamo. This left only fifteen older destroyers to continue the evacuation – *Esk*, *Express*, *Anthony*, *Keith*, *Codrington*, *Malcolm*, *Whitehall*, *Winchester*, *Worcester*, *Windsor*, *Verity*, *Vanquisher*, *Sabre*, *Scimitar* and *Shikari*.

By the late evening of 29 May there was considerable confusion about whether or not Dunkirk harbour and piers were still operable, and little evacuation took place that night. Ashore, the defensive perimeter around Dunkirk was being gradually shrunk and thinned out. For the cause of Allied unity, the War Cabinet ordered that future evacuations should seek to lift off British and French troops in equal proportions, with the aim of final evacuation at midnight on 1–2 June. For the Royal Navy, 30 May was to be another difficult day. Because of the confused communications and conflicting reports from the ships returning from Dunkirk, it was not clear whether the harbour was still unusable because of the blockage of channels and piers by sunken ships. As a result, it was again only lightly used during the morning and early afternoon, with only one destroyer at a time entering and berthing alongside the east pier, and much more effort was concentrated that day upon beach evacuation.

Daylight found Rear Admiral Wake-Walker, freshly appointed Senior Naval Officer for the ships operating off the French coast, on board the destroyer *Esk* off Bray beach. He found "the ghastly sight of the shore, black with men standing in the water up to their waists... to watch the terribly slow progress of embarkation."[2] On the beaches themselves however, progress was being slowly made. Captain J.M. Howson, Naval Officer-in-Charge of the beaches, ashore at Bray recalled:

> ...in the lightening dawn, a number of destroyers, sloops and scoots (schuyts) were seen lying off, and embarkation was proceeding in such boats as were available. Several boats were aground, others were holed, and some had no oars...By about 0600, all destroyers, sloops, etc had cleared for England and there were no further ships available...[2]

Warrant Officer J.S. Walsham, serving with the Royal Artillery, was one of those awaiting rescue:

No ships arrived on the beaches that day so we had another night's sleep on the dunes. Awoke next morning and hove at anchor was a lovely sight to behold – a destroyer of the Royal Navy – HMS *Codrington*. I immediately reported to embarkation, 2nd Med. Regt. RA and [was] told "You have priority, get your men lined up at the water's edge in column." This was soon put into [action] and I reported ready to embark. Soon we were told to enter the water to waist deep. Small naval boats – 'whalers' I think they were called – pulled up to the head of the column. I sent the men three at a time. The strong arms of the sailors lugged each in turn into the boat, then the next three and so on until we were all safely on board. Another column of troops were already formed up behind to take their turn. When loaded to capacity we sailed away to Blighty and home.[14]

Despite the difficulties, 30 May was to be a peak for beach evacuations. 29,512 men were lifted off, compared with 24,311 from the harbour.

Because of the Dunkirk harbour restrictions only seven destroyers – *Vanquisher*, *Vimy*, *Malcolm*, *Wolsey*, *Sabre*, *Express* and *Scimitar* – went in during the morning and early afternoon of 30 May. By mid-afternoon a berth had been cleared for destroyer use some 400 yards down from the end of east pier, and *Vanquisher*, *Malcolm*, *Vimy* and *Wolsey* made their second trip of the day into the harbour. French ships also joined in the evacuation, including five destroyers and large torpedo boats. One of them was the *Bourrasque*. She had sailed from Dunkirk at 1530 loaded with over 600 mixed troops and base staff, including one woman. At about 1600 the *Bourrasque* came under heavy fire from shore batteries at Nieuport. To avoid the firing the ship moved further offshore, close to a French laid minefield. At 1625 a heavy explosion occurred aboard *Bourrasque*, which broke in two and rapidly sank with heavy loss of life. It was officially considered that she had probably struck a mine.

Up until the late afternoon, the disastrous losses of the previous day, caused by the Luftwaffe bombers against the massed shipping in the harbour, had been a major factor in forbidding entry into Dunkirk's choked harbour of more than one destroyer at a time. As the day wore on, and the build-up of troops awaiting evacuation continued to grow, it became a time for risk-taking. Commander G. O. Maund had temporarily taken over as SNO Dunkirk while Captain Tennant went off to confer with Lord Gort, the Military Commander of the BEF Commander Maund decided:

Towards the close of the day (30 May) a great number of ships had arrived, and I accordingly decided to accept the risk of further losses, and ordered the vessels waiting in the roads to proceed alongside and embark troops. Strong air attacks were launched by the enemy… I decided that the rate of embarkation must in some way be speeded up as the capacity of the ships now alongside was more than adequate for the rate of the flow of troops… I therefore went down to the Eastern Arm and rigged up a loudspeaker and addressed the troops in the following terms: "Remember your pals, boys. The quicker you get on board, the more of them will be saved." This worked like a miracle. The thousands of troops, tired, depressed and without food or water for days, broke into a double and kept it up for the whole of the length of the Eastern Arm for more than two hours. During that period I estimate that more than 15,000 troops were embarked. The Army certainly responded splendidly.[2]

On *Keith*, one of the eight destroyers to embark a total of 8,528 troops between 1802 and about 2100, Lieutenant G.J.A. Lumsden recalled:

Embarkation of tired troops, armed only with personal weapons, was extremely well controlled by a small naval party on the pier. In a few minutes we were fully loaded and sailed for Dover with 1500 men. A few enemy shells landed in the harbour while we were there.[15]

According to official figures,[2] *Keith* brought back 1,200 men, *Anthony* had 1,137, *Codrington* 1,100, *Esk* 1,041, *Vimy* 948, *Impulsive* 1,112, *Winchelsea* 925 and *Wolsey* 1,065. In addition, four personnel carriers brought out 5,694 troops, while other vessels – including the hospital carrier *Dinard* – brought out the remainder. On the journey home, *Anthony* was bombed, which put out all her lights, temporarily stopped her engines, and put out of action all her communications. After on-board repairs she was able to proceed, steering by her engines, escorted by *Keith* to Dover. By now all the ships' crews, especially those of the destroyers, were becoming exhausted, and it was thought that the evacuation would have to end by 0130 on 1 June.

Nevertheless, naval patrols and some embarkation still continued throughout the night hours. At approximately 0120 on 31 May the French destroyer *Cyclone*, on her way to Dunkirk was torpedoed and, badly damaged, forced to make a return to Dover at a laboured four knots, to take no further part in Operation Dynamo. Then at 0145 the French destroyer *Siroco*, on her way back to Dover with 700 troops on board, was struck by two torpedoes from a lurking E-boat and almost immediately capsized. 252 of her crew and the evacuated troops were picked up by nearby vessels, including fifteen by the Polish destroyer *Blyskawica*.

Back on the beaches in the early hours of Friday 31 May evacuation conditions were becoming critical. The destroyer *Icarus* off Bray beach felt it necessary to signal to Vice Admiral Ramsay at Dover:

0047/31. Situation at Bray impossible. No powerboats. Evacuation ten an hour. At least 2,000 men still ashore. Troops being bombed and shelled. Dunkirk being bombed continually. If no power boats become available propose withdraw at dawn. [2]

As the morning of 31 May broke, conditions for embarkation from the beaches worsened. At 0600 the RNLI Lifeboat *Lord Southborough* was ferrying troops out to *Icarus*, still waiting off Bray beach. Her coxswain reported:

There was a nasty surf. Troops were rushing out to us from all directions and were being drowned close to us and we could not get to them...it seemed to me we were doing more harm [than good] by drawing the men off the shore, as with their heavy clothing, the surf was knocking them over and they were unable to get up...The whaler from the destroyer was swamped, so was the motor pinnace that was working with the whaler, and so it was all along the sands as far as I could see, both sides of us, and there was not a boat left afloat.[2]

On the destroyer *Keith*:

On 31 May we cruised up and down the beach from Dunkirk to La Panne in the shallow and narrow stretch of water between the beach and shoals offshore, avoiding known mined areas and trying to marshal the various boats working there and persuade them to congested areas. The scene was amazing. Unbelievably long lines of soldiers, dark against the white sand, stretched patiently for miles from the area of La Panne to the harbour and queues down to places on the tide-line where rough, almost unusable, piers of abandoned vehicles had been built or where some boat was trying to embark men direct off the beach. Movement of these masses of men seemed very, very slow. A good number of small ships, destroyers, minesweepers and paddle ferries, were lying off the beach as close as they could in view of the very shallow water; and loaded boats, mostly clumsy ships' lifeboats towed over from London with one or two young naval ratings in charge, were pulling, oh so slowly, from the beach to the ships, where soldiers clambered aboard as best they could up the nets or ladders provided. But this operation was dreadfully frustrating and inefficient. As each heavy boat moved into the beach under the efforts of one of two men at the oars, and finally grounded a little way out from the water's edge it was rapidly filled with soldiers clambering over the side: the boat naturally sank a few inches and became immovable on the sand. A young sailor, or perhaps an army officer or NCO would instruct the last men to get out again to lighten the boat, but it will be realised that such an order in the dreadful circumstances, and when every man's thought was of reaching home, was very hard to accept. When boats did float off it was very difficult for soldiers, tired and untrained at sea, to find space to man the oars and row to any real effect to the waiting ships. Once there, many of the boats were abandoned to float aimlessly and uselessly offshore. With variations this was the real picture of the Dunkirk beaches and it accounts for the fact that the large majority of men who were evacuated successfully to England were properly marshalled from the beaches onto the pier in the harbour and thence into fast ships with trained and disciplined crews ready to receive them. This is not to belittle the bravery and determination of the volunteer crews of those yachts and other small craft who sailed straight into the maelstrom of war and did their uttermost to help their country in its hour of need; they lifted some10,000 men to England.[15]

Vice-Admiral Ramsay was doing his very best to meet the crisis. The order withdrawing the modern destroyers had to be rescinded, and every effort to send over more small boats to take the men off the beaches to the waiting destroyers and other larger ships was being made. The Admiralty's response showed how desperate was the situation on the beaches. At 1152 it signalled Vice Admiral Ramsay and the C-in-Cs of Portsmouth and Nore Commands: "War Office request maximum number of Carley floats and similar devices be left lying on beaches together with paddles after other craft have withdrawn."[2]

By 31 May, the remaining BEF troops were being withdrawn from the eastern end of the defensive pocket into the area of the French defences, and as such came under the orders of Admiral Abrial, the French Commander-in-Chief. The War Cabinet therefore decided that the BEF Commander-in-Chief, Lord Gort, and his senior staff should be brought home, to report and help in the regrouping and re-equipping of the rescued troops of the BEF together with the creation of the new formations in Britain, in preparation for the anticipated German follow-up invasion of the country. The remaining British troops in the pocket, estimated to be down to some 20,000, were put under the command of Major General H.R.L.G. Alexander – later to become Field Marshal Lord Alexander of Tunis – who took up his appointment at 1800 on 31 May as Lord Gort prepared for his return to England. *Keith* was off the beaches:

During the course of 31 May, still in glorious, calm weather, a few cars drove down onto the beach and signalled by lamp that they were the General Staff and needed a lift to England. We sent a motor boat and whaler to fetch them and circled off shore. More than a hundred enemy aircraft appeared and attacked everything in sight, including our boats; however they and we in the ships escaped damage. Lord Gort was transferred to a minesweeper for passage to England while most of his staff stayed in our Captain's cabin. Our ancient 3-inch high angle gun, so newly fitted, was without any effective fire control system and was firing virtually over open sights. By the evening of 31 May we had expended all our ammunition. I remarked to the Captain that unless we replaced this overnight I considered we would be sunk the next day; but the Admiral could not spare us.[15]

All this time Dunkirk harbour was being continuously bombarded, and the German artillery was gradually finding the exact range of the loading berths. Because of this, the use of the harbour by passenger transports and hospital carriers had to be suspended. Destroyers and other naval vessels however continued the evacuation. The Captain of *Scimitar* was to write:

Most of the time we embarked off Bray or La Panne using boats and soon there were large numbers of boats of all kinds, but one day (31 May) a bit of a sea got up and many boats were stranded or abandoned. We did one trip into Dunkirk itself, this was better and more exciting than the wearisome wait off the beaches. McBeath on *Venomous* was coming out of Dunkirk as we went in and gave us a great chuck up (cheer); we were good friends. We filled up in an hour, Guardsmen I think, and they were in splendid discipline. The well known naval embarkation officer, Commander Clouston* was an inspiring figure on the pier, and David Wellis of *Malcolm* was playing his pipes at intervals.[10]

Scimitar brought out 584 men from Dunkirk harbour.

The men embarking on *Malcolm* had other matters to contend with as well as the bagpipes of David Wellis. H. Barwick wrote:

When Jerry came across again dive-bombing and blasting the mole we had to move forward, putting duck boards over the craters and dropping the dead into the sea, leaving the wounded to be tended by some other persons, climbing, dropping down the rope scramble nets on the deck of the destroyer *Malcolm*. It was full steam ahead until we had a plane come over at about mast height and crash a few hundred yards away. It was one of ours, we heaved to, picking up two RAF men.[9]

---

* Commander J.C. Clouston did not survive the evacuation. He was drowned, returning to Dunkirk from discussions in Dover on 2 June, when his fast motor boat, Seaplane Tender 243, was sunk by enemy aircraft.

Captain A.M. Bell Macdonald, also of the BEF, remembered his rescue on the *Malcolm*:

> We left in the destroyer *Malcolm*, one thousand of us, but as we formed up to go the long expected air raid began and while the ship loaded men struggled down ladders from the jetty to the boat deck. While the harbour shook again to the thud of bombs, the *Malcolm* was missed. I shall never forget those fifteen minutes while we loaded, it was an eternity. At last we drew away…and tore out to sea at 30 knots…to Dover where we arrived at 7.30pm, safe and sound, thanks to the Navy.[16]

Other than the damaged minesweeper *Devonia*, which was beached to provide a beach jetty, no British warships were lost on 31 May. However, a number were damaged: among the destroyers, *Vivacious* was struck by a shell and had three killed and twelve wounded, *Wolsey* was in collision with the passenger vessel *Roebuck*, *Impulsive* struck an uncharted wreck, *Malcolm* collided with Dunkirk pier, and *Scimitar* was in collision with *Icarus*. The Captain of *Scimitar* was not best pleased:

> It was possibly fatigue that led to our collision with *Icarus* on the last day, although I have always maintained it was entirely his fault. *Icarus*, commanded by Colin Maude passed us at high speed in the Downs but came so close that our bow was drawn into his stern, making a hole in our bows. We completed the trip at slow speed with a collision mat out, and in fact we were saved a long trip because we went alongside the transport *Prague*, damaged and in danger of sinking, with a lot of troops on board some of whom transferred to us. Anyway on return to Dover they said we were too damaged to go on, so we had a rest then retired to London for repairs.[10]

Despite the slow and unpromising start, 64,429 troops were evacuated on 31 May. Back in London, hopes in the War Cabinet of averting a catastrophe were rising. In his diary entry for the day Private Secretary John Colville wrote of the Cabinet's mood:

> Everybody elated by the progress of the evacuation. One of the world's greatest defeats is being redeemed by an outstanding achievement of organisation and gallantry. The BEF rearguards, though decimated, are standing firm against fearful odds; the RAF activity over Dunkirk is ceaseless, the Navy has attempted and achieved the incredible. Two hundred and twenty two men of war have been used in the evacuation and 665 other vessels. The sailors are so tired that they are working automatically, but they are apparently quite undaunted.[17]

The evacuation began unpromisingly the following day, 1 June. There were increasing E-boat and U-boat attacks on returning ships in the channel, and heavy German artillery fire on the beaches east of Dunkirk, while the harbour area and the ships lying off shore were subjected to intense air attack. As on 29 May the destroyers and personnel carriers were the prime targets. Four destroyers, one of them French, and one personnel carrier were to be lost during the day.

Because of artillery fire, embarkation from La Panne and Bray beaches was becoming increasingly hazardous. At daybreak the minesweeper *Speedwell* was anchored to the west of La Panne, using her motor boat and two whalers to ferry troops aboard, when she grounded with the falling tide. She continued to embark troops, despite strafing machine gun fire from German aircraft, until towed off by the minesweeper *Albury*, and sailed towards Dunkirk harbour. On the way she met the destroyer *Ivanhoe* which had been damaged by a bomb. From the account of Lieutenant Jack Neale:

At 0900 we were ordered by W/T [radio] into Dunkirk harbour, so off we set at full speed to pick up troops from the jetty. The destroyer Ivanhoe came past us at 30 knots. Two hundred yards ahead of us a bomb scored a direct hit on her amidships, and she came to a stop belching clouds of steam. Speedwell went alongside her starboard side to take off her troops. A large diesel yacht went to the other side. I said to the Sub [sub-lieutenant] "Look, they got the paint locker" He replied, "That's not paint you fool."

I felt foolish at mistaking blood in the scuppers, from some forty sailors and soldiers dead on the deck, for red lead, but was otherwise unmoved by the sight. We had become so inured to death and destruction in the last five hours. We took off about 150 soldiers. Just as we were about to push off, one or two of Ivanhoe's ratings started climbing over too. Ivanhoe's Captain (Commander P.H. Hadow) looked down and said "Where do you think you are going?"

"I thought she might sink, Sir"

"Oh no she's not, you come back here"

From the tone of his voice, you would have thought he had just bumped the quay and scratched his paint."[18]

The yacht on the other side of *Ivanhoe* also pushed off, but was sunk as she left for home with her evacuated troops. *Speedwell* entered the harbour, securing alongside the East Jetty where she embarked more troops, and left for Dover at 0950, with a total of 972 troops on board. She arrived safely despite repeated air attack, and made two more evacuating trips to Dunkirk.

Ivanhoe was not the only destroyer to suffer at the hands of the Luftwaffe. On *Keith*, who had Rear Admiral W.F. Wake-Walker on board:

Early next day, 1 June, which again dawned calm and clear, a very large enemy aircraft formation appeared: I counted more than 200 as we began to circle. Once over the sea a number of Stukas peeled off and dived on us. The first three aircraft missed but jammed our steering gear and we were in hand steering from the tiller compartment when a further and heavier attack came in. A bomb from the second aircraft exploded on our starboard side and holed it between the engine room and the boiler room causing heavy casualties there and a total loss of power. The ship listed heavily and slowly came to a stop: we anchored her near a wreck for the tidal stream was quite strong. The Admiral and his staff boarded a fast launch to continue with their work as best they could from her. *Keith* was subjected to further Stuka attack: bomb splinters caused a fire aft and a number of men were wounded by machine-gun fire. Our pom-pom crews were again standing manfully to their guns, though some of their crew were wounded. The ship continued to list and settle and the Captain decided to abandon ship to save the lives of the crew, but asked for a few volunteers, including me, to stay on board with him in case a tow could be arranged to Dover. The crew left the ship over the stern, mostly onto rafts, in an orderly manner and were soon picked up by a Dutch coaster manned by a Royal Navy crew, which took them safely to Ramsgate. I bundled up all secret documents and charts in my charge and threw them over the side in a weighted bag. Soon afterwards *Keith* sank deeper. The Captain called an Admiralty tug alongside and she embarked our wounded and everyone else alive. A few minutes later as the tug pulled away, another onslaught by bombing aircraft on Keith blew her apart and sank her instantly, for we never saw her when the bomb splashes subsided.

Taking stock from the wheelhouse of the tug we were shocked to find that apart from *Basilisk*, a destroyer of our flotilla which was heavily on fire, we one our small tug were the largest vessel afloat off the miles of beach: all others had been sunk by that great air attack.[15]

The destroyer *Basilisk* was to suffer three separate air attacks. In the first, a bomb exploded in her engine rooms, cutting off all steam to her machinery, while six other bombs, exploding alongside, buckled the upper deck and ship's side. At 0945 *Basilisk*, still on an even keel, was taken in tow by the French trawler *La Jolie Mascotte*, which was forced to slip the tow when enemy aircraft again attacked, fortunately without securing any hits. Finally, at noon, the dive bombers returned for a third time, smothering *Basilisk* with bombs from a height of some 400 feet. The destroyer shuddered, heeled over, momentarily righted, and sank – all in three minutes, in shallow water. She was abandoned and, considered a danger to other evacuating ships, her destruction completed by gunfire and torpedoes from the *Whitehall*.

Meanwhile the destroyer *Havant*, having taken on board 500 men from *Ivanhoe*, was hit at 0906 by two bombs, which entered the engine room from the starboard side. Everyone in the engine room was killed. A third bomb, which dropped immediately ahead of the destroyer, exploded as she passed over it. Listing to port, out of control and on fire, *Havant* was taken on tow by the minesweeper *Saltash* who, with the yacht *Grive*, also took off her soldiers. Continuously bombed, further damaged, and with her list increasing until her decks were almost awash, *Havant* was finally abandoned by her crew. She rolled over and sank at 1015, with the loss of eight killed and twenty-five wounded.

A fourth destroyer, the French *Foudroyant*, was sunk before mid-day. She arrived at Dunkirk at 1030 during the third heavy air attack of the day, when she was hit by consecutive salvoes of bombs, blew up and sank in just over two minutes. The air attacks continued throughout 1 June. One heavy attack was directed at the personnel carrier *Scotia*, carrying 2,000 French troops from Dunkirk. At least four bombs in the massed attack hit *Scotia*, which heeled over until her forward funnel and mast were touching the water. She began to settle, while the enemy planes dropped more bombs and machine-gunned the men taking to the water. The destroyer *Esk* arrived and, placing herself alongside the sinking *Scotia*, started to take off her men while simultaneously fighting off the enemy planes. *Esk* took on board nearly one thousand of the French troops, and the destroyer *Worcester* also took on survivors. Even so, twenty eight of *Scotia*'s crew and an estimated 200 to 300 French troops were lost.

Not all the losses were confined to the bigger ships. Very many smaller vessels, some from the growing armada of small civilian boats now answering the rescue call and working valiantly off the beaches were lost. Some had never before sailed out of sight of land. Neither were the losses all due to bombing or shellfire. One such loss, to a German mine, was the cockle boat *Renown*, together with her crew of three, on the way back from Dunkirk after hours of ferrying out troops to the larger ships offshore.

Although the ship losses, big and small, sunk or damaged, had been high, the evacuated total of 64,429 for the day was the second highest of Operation Dynamo; 47,081 had been embarked from the harbour, and 17,348 from the beaches. However the losses, among destroyers in particular, were causing great concern. The C-in-C Nore Command proposed to the Admiralty that destroyers should only continue to be used in the Operation in positions where they could manoeuvre under heavy bombing attack. It was Norway all over again, with the inadequacy of the destroyers' anti-aircraft protection when operating in confined waters against concentrated dive bombing attack, being so clearly confirmed. The losses and damage were now rapidly outstripping the Navy's ability to meet all the demands being put upon the destroyers and their crews. They were at full stretch, simultaneously evacuating Allied troops from Norway as well as northern France. Indeed, on the Operation Dynamo days of 29, 30 and 31 May, when a large proportion of available destroyers were evacuating troops off Dunkirk, other destroyers, notably *Firedrake*, *Vanoc*, *Arrow*, *Havelock* and *Echo*, were evacuating troops from Bodo to Harstaad in Norway.*

During the afternoon of 1 June, Route X started to come under fire from German artillery ashore; and this, together with the accompanying loss of ships, often full of evacuating troops, was rapidly making impossible further evacuation during daylight hours. Vice-Admiral Ramsay therefore decided, despite the inherent difficulties, to attempt one last effort to complete the evacuation in a single operation on the following night between 2100 and 0330, by using both sides of Dunkirk pier and the remaining nearby beaches. As dusk fell on 1 June he sent across every ship which could be made ready. Minesweepers, schuyts and other small craft, including about one hundred French fishing boats and drifters, were directed to the beaches, while it was planned to send seven personnel ships and eight destroyers to the east pier of Dunkirk harbour. The destroyers, designated Force K, were ordered to proceed in pairs at hourly intervals to the east pier, and return to Dover when loaded. If there was a delay on the pier and no berth was readily available, then the destroyers were to go instead to the beaches to pick up troops. Four pairs were detailed off for the task: *Windsor* and *Icarus*, *Codrington* and *Sabre*, *Shikari* and *Esk*, *Winchelsea* and *Whitshed*. In the event *Esk*, her crew totally exhausted from running virtually continuously since 27 May, was unable to sail and was stood down for twenty four hours.

The loading off the beaches was still slow and inefficient, with the remaining trapped troops now desperate to get away before the ever-shrinking defensive perimeter finally collapsed under the renewed German onslaught.

Engaged in trying to control the loading of the boats ferrying the troops off the beach to the ships waiting offshore, Lieutenant S.A. Nettle watched as two boats were capsized by the rush of soldiers trying to climb aboard them:

> ...a third boat appeared, the troops again started wading out, so I went alongside them shouting to them to wait until it came into shallower water. They took no notice of a young RNVR Lieutenant. I drew my revolver and fired it into the water about three yards in front of the leading man. They all stopped. I waded across to them, waving my revolver indicating that they should return to the shore. Here I pay tribute to the British soldier and the natural discipline

---

* See Chapter Ten.

of the Services. They accepted the orders and moved slowly back. I detailed two men to go out and tow the boat into the shallow water so the others could embark. I asked two men to row it back, and I said I would ensure that they stayed in and went back to the rescue ship. But no one did, and we had to rely on boats drifting in on the tide. As for the troops, there was no depression or panic, just a quiet resignation to fate, and uplift of spirits when a boat floated in.[7]

In the harbour area there were still congregating BEF troops and an increasing number of French troops, now withdrawing into the area and assembling near to the west pier. Several thousand of those who wished to do so were evacuated back to Britain over the next two or three days. France was wavering and on the brink of capitulation. Winston Churchill was to make a number of visits to Paris during the days of early June, in an attempt to shore up French resolve and offer what little help Britain could in order to keep the Allies together. In a memo to the Chief of the Imperial General Staff on 29 May he had written regarding Operation Dynamo:

It is essential that the French should share in such evacuations from Dunkirk as may be possible. Nor must they be dependent only upon their own shipping resources. Arrangements must be concerted at once with the French Missions in this country, or, if necessary, with the French Government, so that no reproaches, or as few as possible, may arise.[19]

On 31 May a directive had been issued for a night-time operation which directed, *inter alia*, that "Tonight the special transport force designed for lifting last flight of 4000 is being concentrated on Eastern beaches. Tomorrow efforts are to be concentrated on the French evacuation."[2] The first pair of destroyers for the night evacuation of 1–2 June were the *Codrington* and *Sabre*. The former berthed at 2300, and the latter fifteen minutes later. Both only stayed for about 45 minutes. During that time *Codrington* embarked 878 troops and *Sabre* 756. They were followed by *Icarus*, who took off 677 troops, and *Windsor*. Unfortunately, on returning to Dover, *Icarus* was in collision with a trawler and had to be withdrawn from Dynamo. *Icarus* was having a bad time with collisions: only a day or so earlier she had collided with *Scimitar* and put the latter out of action.

Windsor had a fruitful but exhausting day. From her first trip, in the early hours of 2 June, she brought back to Dover 493 troops, sailed again for Dunkirk and brought back a further 624 soldiers. *Windsor* again left Dover at 1900 and embarked 1,022 men from Dunkirk East Pier, leaving there for her return to Dover at 0100 on 3 June. In total, in some twenty four hours, making three trips, she had safely brought home 2,139 men. With *Esk* unable to sail due to her crew's exhaustion, the *Skikari* made her night trip alone, berthing at 0125 and leaving Dunkirk harbour, again after a thirty-five minute stay, with 470 troops on board. The final night evacuation pair, the destroyers *Whitshed* and *Winchester*, scoured the harbour area for remaining troops and brought back between them some 1,600 men.

In the twenty-four hours of the operation, 1–2 June, by which time Operation Dynamo had been running for a full week, a total of 26,256 men were safely landed back in England; 19,561 from the Dunkirk harbour area and 6,695 from the beaches. Of these totals, French ships working from the harbour brought off 1,634, and Belgian trawlers 313. The total number of men evacuated to date under Operation Dynamo was 285,305.[2]

By now it was thought back in Britain that virtually all the British troops had been evacuated from their entrapment at Dunkirk:

> ...late on the evening of 2nd news reached Dover that, except for the wounded, whose evacuation had been prevented by continuous and callous German attacks on fully illuminated hospital ships, the whole of the British Expeditionary Force had reached England.[20]

Despite the Navy's best efforts it had not been possible to evacuate all the wounded. No hospital ships had sailed for Dunkirk in the previous twenty-four hours because of the bombing and the difficulties of evacuating badly wounded men from the chaotic congested harbour area. Priority had been given to getting off, in conditions of great haste, the men able to scramble aboard the rescue ships. Now it had been decided to try to evacuate, under daylight conditions, some of the wounded by using illuminated and clearly-marked hospital ships, which it was hoped the Germans would refrain from bombing. An "open and clear" radio message was sent out giving advance notice of the British intention.

Two unescorted, illuminated and clearly-marked hospital ships were despatched from Dover on 2 June; *Worthing* at 1255 and *Paris* at 1648. Neither reached Dunkirk. In clear visibility, twelve German aircraft bombed and machine-gunned *Worthing*, which was damaged by near-misses and returned to Dover. *Paris* was attacked at about 1900 by two aircraft, near misses putting out of action her engines and all lighting. One hour later she was attacked by three aircraft and further damaged. Three tugs attempted to take *Paris* in tow but, after further air attacks, she sank at 0400 on 3 June.

Although there was relief in London at the overall success of the evacuation, it became increasingly clear at Vice-Admiral Ramsay's headquarters at Dover during the day that there was some doubt as to whether, in the confusion, all the British Expeditionary Force had indeed been taken off. A British rearguard of 4,000 troops still remained within the perimeter, plus an estimated further 2,000 troops who were unaccounted for and thought to be still in the vicinity of Dunkirk. There were also an estimated 30,000 French troops who might or might not wish to be evacuated back to Britain, and by the evening of 2 June this estimate of still-encircled French troops had risen to between 50,000 and 60,000 men. There had to be another night time evacuation attempt.

At 1052 on 2 June, Vice-Admiral Ramsay signalled to his destroyer and minesweeper captains what amounted to a call for volunteers rather than an order: "The final evacuation is staged for tonight, and the Nation looks to the Navy to see this through. I want every ship to report as soon as possible whether she is fit to meet the call which has been made on our courage and endurance."[2] The captains and their crews responded magnificently; there was no shortage of volunteers. The Commanding Officer of the damaged destroyer *Scimitar*, refused permission to sail with her damaged bow, was to write:

> Afterwards I was sorry we did not stay for one more day to see the operation through: we could have continued at low speed, but I think I was too exhausted to carry that through and I suppose we should have been in a bad way to any further attack.[10]

Only the obsolete paddle minesweeper *Medway Queen* was unable to sail. She had returned to Dover from Dunkirk only three hours earlier, after five evacuation trips, and her crew were completely exhausted. She sailed later with a replacement crew lent from another incapacitated ship.

Despite the losses and damage to ships sustained during the week-long evacuation and the exhaustion of the sailors, Vice-Admiral Ramsay had been able to assemble a remarkably large armada for the night's operation. It included eleven destroyers, thirteen personnel carriers, two store carriers, fourteen minesweepers and over thirty tugs, drifters and yachts. The French Navy contributed three torpedo boats, two minesweepers, two patrol vessels and seventeen trawlers, and the Belgians one patrol vessel and some sixteen trawlers.

The first destroyers to reach Dunkirk were *Sabre* and *Shikari*, which had left Dover at 1845, and arrived undamaged despite having to run a gauntlet of fire from German shore batteries during their approach. Both destroyers left at 2200, with 500 and 700 troops respectively. *Venomous* was next in, and although she had difficulty in manoeuvring in the congested harbour to berth at a temporary makeshift pier head, she managed to take on 1,500 troops, including Major General Alexander, who had been in charge of the British rearguard, and successfully extricated herself. *Windsor* also had difficulty getting alongside, but managed to do so and take off 1,022 men. By now the flow of British troops appeared to be drying up, and *Winchelsea*, which arrived at 2300, found only 152 men awaiting evacuation. However, the gunboat *Locust*, arriving at the same time and tying up at a different berth, found 800 troops, including many French soldiers, awaiting embarkation. Only two of the personnel carriers lifted British troops from the East Pier that night: *King George V* embarked 1,460 men in twenty-seven minutes and left for England at 2225; and *St Helier* took on 2,000 troops and left at 2330, to complete the evacuation of the British rearguard troops.

The night evacuation had by now switched to the West Pier, now crowded with French troops, so that by the end of the night of 2–3 June a total of 26,700 allied troops had been evacuated.

Any hopes that the men of Operation Dynamo might have had of rest, time to recuperate, and time to repair their ships, were immediately dashed the next day. The operation was not yet over. The men and their ships were to be called upon to go back one more time to try to take off as many as possible of the many thousands of trapped French troops, still engaging the enemy, who had performed so gallantly in helping to hold the line of the defensive perimeter in order to allow the bulk of the British Expeditionary Force to escape. They were owed a debt of honour. Vice-Admiral Ramsay signalled his ships:

> I hoped and believed that last night would see us through but the French who were covering the retirement of the British rearguard had to repel a strong German attack and so were unable to send their troops to the pier in time to be embarked.
>
> We cannot leave our Allies in the lurch and I must call on all officers and men detailed for further evacuation tonight to let the world see that we never let down our ally.[2]

The Prime Minister, Winston Churchill, was to write:

> ...at dawn, great numbers of French troops, many still in contact with the enemy, remained ashore. One more effort had to be made. Despite the exhaustion of ships' companies after so many without respite, the call was answered...[19]

The sailors really were exhausted. On the minesweeper *Kellett*, one of her crew recounted:

> We had two stokers collapse in the stoke hold. They were severely burned having just collapsed absolutely exhausted...one telegraphist and one ordinary seaman were landed in straitjackets because they had gone absolutely mad through tension. The Chief ERA also went berserk – quite rightly too – because he was trying to get five minutes rest when a cannon shell came through the side and grazed his shoulder.[8]

The sailors' tenacity was beyond any reasonable expectations of human endurance. Not only had they had to cope for the last nine days with almost relentless bombing and shelling, travelling to and fro between Dover and Dunkirk through mine-infested waters while under constant threat from the torpedoes of U-boats and E-boats, but all were suffering from severe lack of sleep. They had not been able to rest properly due to the circumstances and conditions of the evacuation. With their mess decks, gangways and every available space both above and below decks packed with troops, the crews were unable to rest below, or even to prepare and consume their food.

Exhaustion was particularly marked in the destroyer force, the remnants of which had been executing a series of round trips without intermission for several days. Some of the ships had been working off the coasts of France and the Low Countries for two weeks preceding the beginning of Operation "Dynamo", engaged on various duties such as evacuating refugees and giving supportive fire to the army and evacuating Boulogne, work which had imposed an intense strain and resulted in heavy losses of ships and men."[2]

So concerned was Vice-Admiral Ramsay when he knew that further evacuation was required that he signalled the Admiralty in the early afternoon of 3 June:

After nine days of operations of a nature unprecedented in naval warfare, which followed on two weeks of intense strain, commanding officers, officers and ships companies are at the end of their tether.

I therefore view a continuance of the demands made by evacuation with the utmost concern as likely to strain to breaking point the endurance of officers and men.

I should fail in my duty did I not represent to Their Lordships the existence of this state of affairs in the ships under my command, and I consider it would be unfortunate, after the magnificent manner in which officers and men of the surviving ships have faced heavy loss and responded to every call made upon them, that they should be subjected to a test which I feel may be beyond the limit of human endurance.

If therefore evacuation has to be continued after tonight I would emphasise in the strongest possible manner that fresh forces should be used for these operations and any consequent delay in their execution should be accepted.[2]

The Admiralty accepted Vice-Admiral Ramsay's strongly worded report and the First Sea Lord, Admiral Pound, signalled his opposite number in France, Admiral Darlan:

I urge most strongly that evacuation be completed tonight, as after nine days of continuous work of this nature officers and men of both HM Ships and merchant ships are completely exhausted. Request early confirmation that evacuation will be completed tonight, and number to be evacuated.[2]

Just over two hours later came the French reply:

French Admiralty agree that evacuation should be terminated tonight, if possible, and estimate approximately 30,000 men remaining. In French opinion, only competent authorities are now Admiral Abrial and V.A. [Vice-Admiral Ramsay] Dover. Captain de Revoir and officer from V.A. Dover are *en route* Dunkirk to inform Admiral Abrial of plans for termination of evacuation. These officers should keep V.A. Dover informed of numbers involved as French Admiralty unable to communicate Dunkirk.[2]

The plan for the final night's evacuation envisaged an 'in and out' operation of short duration, with embarkation taking place between 2230 on 3 June and 0230 on 4 June from both East and West pier heads. Vice-Admiral Ramsay scraped together a flotilla of nine destroyers – all that now remained serviceable – nine personnel carriers, eleven minesweepers, two corvettes, four French torpedo boats and a large number of smaller vessels: drifters, motorboats including the Ramsgate and Dover lifeboats, French and Belgian fishing boats. The armada started to arrive at Dunkirk at 2200 to find an unexpectedly chaotic scene, with the harbour congested by French vessels – warships, fishing craft and small ships – all desperately trying, in a totally disorganised way, to embark the yelling troops crowding the pier heads. A Royal Navy lieutenant on one of the rescue vessels described the scene: "The congestion was chaotic, ships going astern into others coming ahead, French destroyers shrieking on their sirens, small craft nipping here and there, rendering the exit most dangerous."[2]

The Royal Navy ships trying to operate amid the chaos soon ran into difficulties. The corvette *Kingfisher*, with 200 evacuated French troops on board, was rammed when just clear of the harbour entrance by the French trawler *Edmond Rene*. The French vessel received only slight damage and was able to take off the French troops from *Kingfisher* who, with her port bow ripped open to the waterline, was able to struggle back to Dover, shipping water, in company with the minesweeper *Leda*, also damaged by collision in thick fog with the Belgian trawler *Marechal Foch*. These were but two of the many collisions and mishaps, caused by fog in the Channel and confusion and congestion in the harbour area.

The first Royal Navy destroyer to arrive was *Whitshed* at 2215. Due to the tide and wind conditions she could not get alongside her designated berth on the East Pier, but succeeded in putting her bows alongside the personnel ship *Autocarrier* and her stern against the destroyer *Sabre* to take on over four hundred men. *Sabre* had been operating since 30 May with a compass rendered unreliable by a German shell splinter, and had had to be led across to Dunkirk by *Venomous*. *Sabre* left Dunkirk at 0025, and was able to make her own way back to Dover with 592 men on board, by following other ships until she lost sight of them in fog, fortunately at a position where she was able to hear the horn of the North Goodwin Light Vessel. After locating the lightship by sound, *Sabre* was able to gingerly make her way from marker buoy to marker buoy until she reached Dover at 0500. Other destroyers came and went without mishap: *Vanquisher* at 0240 with 414 men, *Malcolm* at 0245 with 736, *Express* at 0300 with 611. *Venomous*, which had arrived to find the harbour too congested to enter, remained outside until she was able to do so, and took off an astonishing 1,200 men. In five trips, spread over four days, *Venomous* had evacuated 4,410 men. As a final act, three blockships (ancient vessels built between 1905 and 1911) escorted over to Dunkirk by the destroyer *Shikari*, were sunk in Dunkirk harbour entrance at about 0300 to deny access to the enemy. *Shikari* left at 0340, the last ship to do so, with 383 beach party and blockships' crews on board. At 1423 on 4 June the Admiralty finally signalled Operation Dynamo was concluded.

Operation Dynamo as originally envisaged was to last for two days with the hope of evacuating 45,000 men. It lasted for nine days and resulted in 338,226 men being rescued, of which 308,888 were brought back in British ships. Of the 338,226 total, British and French destroyers brought back to Britain the highest proportion, 102,843 men or 30%. The cost in destroyers was high: the Royal Navy used forty-one, of which six were lost and nineteen badly damaged. The French Navy used fourteen destroyers, of which three were lost.

Dunkirk was not a great victory. It was a miraculously-averted catastrophe and humiliation. The cost of rescuing the British Expeditionary Force had been high. The British Army was now in no position to repel an immediate follow-up German invasion. The BEF had suffered 68,111 men killed, wounded or taken prisoner. It had lost an immense amount of stores and equipment, destroyed or abandoned to the enemy: 2,472 guns, 90,000 rifles, 63,879 vehicles, 20,548 motor cycles, and over 500,000 tons of stores and ammunition. The Royal Air Force had lost 474 aircraft. The Royal and Merchant Navies had lost 243, or twenty-eight per cent, of the 860 vessels of all types used in the evacuation.

There was no time for the Royal Navy to regroup after Dunkirk: it was still heavily engaged in the evacuation of the Allied troops from Norway. Four days after the end of Operation Dynamo, on 8 June, the Navy was to lose the aircraft carrier *Glorious* and her escorting destroyers *Acasta* and *Ardent*, with over 1,500 men, off the Norwegian coast – and the battle for France was still being fought. To compound the Allies' problems, Italy entered the war on the German side on 10 June. The Germans continued to over-run France; Paris fell on the 14 June and on 22 June the French sought an armistice. France capitulated on 25 June, little more than six weeks after the German onslaught through the Low Countries had begun.

As the Germans over-ran France so the remaining troops of the British Expeditionary Force still there were forced westwards, with the Royal Navy again being called upon to evacuate the men, using many of the destroyers and troopships which had so recently been engaged in the same rescue operation in Norway. By the end of June 1940, Great Britain stood alone. It had lost the two Allies – Poland and France – with whom it had started the war ten months earlier, and had gained another enemy: Italy. Moreover, the country faced imminent invasion. Vice-Admiral Ramsay* was to write:

> The menace of invasion was very real. The collapse of France had come so suddenly that accurate information of German troop movements was difficult to obtain. But it was generally believed that Hitler would follow up his successful advance to the coast by invading England while the British Army was short of equipment. The German Army and Air Force were free of all major commitments and now, if ever, was the moment for them to launch the full weight of their might against England. The British naval losses had been heavy, and the Fleet was stretched to the limit in disputing Mussolini's bid for control of the Mediterranean while at the same time defending the vital supply lines in the North Atlantic. We did not know at the time how severely the German Navy had been hammered in the Norway campaign. Only two of their cruisers and about eight destroyers were fit for service.[20]

The invasion never came. If the Germans had tried they would have found the Royal Navy still implacably opposing them as it had done for the previous ten months; carrying the fight to the enemy and defending Great Britain to the last ship. And the destroyers would have been in the thick of it. In the first eight months of the war the Royal Navy lost twenty-three destroyers, with many more badly damaged; even more irreplaceable were the very many experienced men who had made up their crews. For

---

* Vice-Admiral Ramsey later became Allied Naval Commander for Operation Overlord, the D Day invasion of Europe on 6 June 1944. He was killed in an air crash in January 1945.

the destroyer crews of the Royal Navy the first nine months had been anything but a Phoney War.

NOTES TO SOURCES

1.   Grandage, Lieutenant G. Papers 87/16/1. Imperial War Museum. London.
2.   Gardner, W.J.R. (Ed.) *The Evacuation from Dunkirk: Operation Dynamo, 26 May–4 June 1940* (Frank Cass: London, 2000).
3.   Roskill, Captain S.W. *The War at Sea 1939–1945* (HMSO: London, 1945).
4.   Lewis, J.E. (Ed) *War Diaries and Letters: Life on the Battlefield in the Words of the Ordinary Soldier* (Robinson Publishing: London, 1998).
5.   de Clair, Commander H.G. *The Indiscretions of a Salthouse Commander* (Parapress: Tunbridge Wells, 1993).
6.   Harris, Able Seaman D.T.W. Papers 87/15/1. Imperial War Museum. London.
7.   Nettle, Lieutenant S.A. Papers 87/42/1. Imperial War Museum. London.
8.   Wilson, P. *Dunkirk–1940: From Disaster to Deliverance* (Pen and Sword Books: Barnsley, 2000).
9.   Barwick, H. Papers P474. Imperial War Museum. London.
10.   Franks, Captain R.D. Naval Diaries and correspondence with the author. October 2002.
11.   Court-Hampton, Lieutenant E.A. Papers 99/75/1. Imperial War Museum. London.
12.   Witkowski, B. Letter to the author, April 2001.
13.   Divine, A.D. *Navies in Exile* (John Murray: London, 1944).
14.   Walsham, Captain, Royal Artillery, J.S. Papers 80/18/1. Imperial War Museum. London.
15.   Lumsden, Captain G.J.A. Papers 66/24/1. Imperial War Museum, London.
16.   Bell Macdonald, Captain A.M. Con Shelf File. Imperial War Museum, London.
17.   Colville, Sir John. *The Fringes of Power: Downing Street Diaries 1939–1945* (Hodder and Stoughton: London, 1985).
18.   Neale, Lieutenant Commander J. Papers 92/50/1. Imperial War Mu seum, London.V
19.   Churchill, W.S. *The Second World War, Vol II: Their Finest Hour* (Cassell: London, 1949).
20.   Chalmers, Rear Admiral W.S. *The Biography of Admiral Sir Bertram Home Ramsay* (Hodder and Stoughton: London, 1959).

Appendix I

BRITISH AND DOMINION DESTROYERS IN COMMISSION, PREPARING TO COMMISSION
OR BUILDING AT THE OUTBREAK OF THE SECOND WORLD WAR*

Class		Quantity	Displacement (tons)	Armament (T.T. = torpedo tube)	Max Speed (knots)
L	LAFOREY (building)	1 Leader 7 Destroyers	1,935 1,920	6 x 4.7 inch 8 x T.T.	36
J	JAVELIN (1939)	2 Leaders 14 Destroyers	1.695 1,690	6 x 4.7 inch 10 x T.T.	36
K	KELLY (1939)	1 Leader 7 Destroyers	1,760	6 x 4.7 inch 1 x 4.0 inch A.A. 5 or 10 x T.T.	36
	AFRIDI ('TRIBAL') (1938-39)	2 Leaders 14 Destroyers	1,870	8 x 4.7 inch 4 x T.T.	36.5
I	INTREPID (1937-38)	1 Leader 8 Destroyers	1,530 1,370	4 x 4.7 inch 10 x T.T.	36.5
H	HERO (1936-37)	1 Leader 8 Destroyers	1,505 1,340	5 x 4.7 inch 8 x T.T. 4 x 4.7 inch 8 x T.T.	36.5
G	GREYHOUND (1936)	1 Leader 8 Destroyers	1,485 1,335	5 x 4.7 inch 8 x T.T. 4 x 4.7 inch 8 x T.T.	36.5

---

* From S.W. Roskill, *The War at Sea: 1939– 45* (HMSO: London, 1954).

Class		Quantity	Displacement (tons)	Armament (T.T. = Torpedo tube)	Max Speed
F	FEARLESS (1935)	1 Leader	1,460	5 x 4.7inch 8 x T.T.	36.5
		8 Destroyers	1,375	4 x 4.7inch 8 x T.T.	36
E	ECLIPSE (1934)	1 Leader	1,475	5 x 4.7 inch 8 x T.T.	36.5
		8 Destroyers	1,375	4 x 4.7inch 8 x T.T.	36
D	DEFENDER (1932-33)	1 Leader 8 Destroyers	1,400 1,375	4 x 4.7 inch 8 x T.T.	36
C	CRUSADER (1932)	1 Leader 4 Destroyers	1,390 1,375	4 x 4.7inch 8 x T.T.	36
B	BEAGLE (1931)	1 Leader 8 Destroyers	1,400 1,360	4 x 4.7inch 8 x T.T.	35
A	ACASTA (31-31)	1 Leader	1,540	5 x 4.7inch 8 x T.T.	
		8 Destroyers	1,350	4 x 4.7 inch 8 x T.T.	35
AMAZON (1927-31)		4 Destroyers	1,170 to 1,350	4 x 4.7inch 6-8 x T.T.	35-37
THORNEYCROFT DESIGN LEADERS (1919-1925)		3 Leaders	1,480	5 x 4.7 inch 6 x T.T.	36
ADMIRALTY DESIGN LEADERS (1918-19)		6 Leaders	1,530	5 x 4.7 inch 6 x T.T.	36.5
V and W Class Admiralty and Thorneycroft Designs (1917-24)		1 Leader 42 Destroyers	1,090 1,120	4 x 4.0 inch 5-6 x T.T.	34-35
R and S Classes (1917-1924)		11 Destroyers	905	3 x 4.0 inch 3 x T.T.	34.5-36

Appendix II

Number	Name	Displacement (tons)	Main Armament
Z1	*Leberecht Maass*	2,232	5 x 12.7cm (5.1 inch) 8 T.T.
Z2	*Georg Thiele*	2,232	
Z3	*Max Schultz*	2,232	
Z4	*Richard Beitzen*	2,232	
Z5	*Paul Jacobi*	2,171	
Z6	*Theodor Riedel*	2,171	
Z7	*Hermann Schoemann*	2,171	
Z8	*Bruno Heinemann*	2,171	
Z9	*Wolfgang Zenker*	2,270	
Z10	*Hans Lody*	2,270	
Z11	*Bernd von Arnim*	2,270	
Z12	*Erich Giese*	2,270	
Z13	*Erich Koellner*	2,270	
Z14	*Friedrich Ihn*	2,239	
Z15	*Erich Steinbrinck*	2,239	
Z16	*Friedrich Eckholdt*	2,239	
Z17	*Diether von Roeder*	2,411	
Z18	*Hans Ludemann*	2,411	
Z19	*Herman Kunne*	2,411	
Z20	*Karl Galster*	2,411	
Z21	*Wilkhelm Heidkamp*	2,411	
Z22	*Anton Schmitt*	2,411	

The first twenty-one of these destroyers were commissioned between January 14 1937 and the outbreak of war. Z22 was commissioned on September 24 1939. The destroyers had a designed top speed of 38 knots and a complement of 315. In addition, at the outbreak of war, the German navy had eleven torpedo boats of 925-935 tons displacement and armed with 3 x 10.5cm (4-inch) guns and up to 6 torpedo tubes. A further twelve torpedo boats had been launched up to the outbreak of the war.

---

* From J.C. Taylor, *German Warships of World War II* (Ian Allan Ltd: Shepperton).

Appendix III

GERMAN OPERATIONAL U-BOATS AT THE OUTBREAK OF THE SECOND WORLD WAR[*]

Type	Qty	Displacement (tons)	Radius of Operation (miles)	Armament	Crew
I.A.	2	862/983	6,700 miles at 12 knots	1 x 4.1inch (105mm) 1 x 20mm A.A. 6 x 21inch T.T. 14 torpedoes	43

These two boats were relegated to training submarine crew duties early in the war.

Type	Qty	Displacement (tons)	Radius of Operation (miles)	Armament	Crew
IIA	6	254/303	1,050 miles at 12 knots	1-4 x 20mm A.A. 3 x 21inch T.T. 6 torpedoes or 8 mines	25
IIB	18	279/329	1,800 miles at 12 knots	1-4 x 20mm A.A. 3 x 21inch T.T. 6 torpedoes or 8 mines	25
IIC	6	291/341	1,900 miles at 12 knots	1-4 x 20mm A.A. 3 x 21inch T.T. 6 torpedoes or 8 mines	25

Type II boats, because of their limited range, were largely used in coastal water operations. Later in the war, surviving Type II boats were relegated to training duties.

Type	Qty	Displacement (tons)	Radius of Operation (miles)	Armament	Crew
VIIA	10	626/745	4,300 miles at 12 knots	1 x 3.5inch (88mm) 1 x 20mm A.A. 5 x 21inch T.T. 11 torpedoes	44
VIIB	8	753/857	6,500 miles at 12 knots	1 x 3.5inch (88mm) 1 x 20mm A.A. 5 x 21inch T.T. 12 torpedoes or 14 mines	44

[*] From C. Bekker, *Hitler's Naval War* (Macdonald: London, 1974).

Type	Qty	Displacement (tons)	Radius of Operation (miles)	Armament	Crew
IXA	7	1,032/1,153	8,100 miles at 12 knots	1 x 4.1inch (105mm) 1 x 37mm A.A. 1 x 20mm A.A. 6 x 21inch T.T. 22 torpedoes or 6 torpedoes and 42 mines	48

Bibliography

Arthur, M., *Lost Voices of the Royal Navy* (Hodder and Stoughton: London, 2005).

Austin. J. and Leading Seaman Nick Carter, *The Man Who Hit the Scharnhorst* (Seeley Service: London, 1973).

Bekker, C., *Hitler's Naval War*, trans. F. Ziegler (Macdonald: London, 1974).

Brennecke, J., *The Hunters and the Hunted* (Burke Publishing, 1958).

Brice, M., *Axis Blockade Runners of World War II* (B.T. Batsford: London, 1981).

Broch, T., *The Mountains Wait* (Michael Joseph: London, 1943).

Brookes, E., *Prologue to War: The Navy's part in the Norwegian Campaign* (Jarrolds Publishers: London, 1966).

Brown, D. (ed), *Naval Operations of the Campaign in Norway: April–June 1940* (Frank Cass: London, 2000).

Brown, M. and P. Meehan, *Scapa Flow* (Penguin: London, 1968).

Carton de Wiart, Lieutenant General Sir Adrian, *Happy Odyssey* (Jonathan Cape: London, 1950).

Chalmers, Rear Admiral W.S., *Max Horton and the Western Approaches* (Hodder and Stoughton: London, 1954).

Chalmers, Rear Admiral W.S., *The Biography of Admiral Sir Bertram Home Ramsay* (Hodder and Stoughton: London, 1959).

Churchill, W.S., *The Second World War, Vol. 1: The Gathering Storm* (Cassell: London, 1948).

Churchill, W.S., *The Second World War, Vol II: Their Finest Hour* (Cassell: London, 1949).

Colville, J., *The Fringes of Power: Downing Street Diaries 1939-1945* (Hodder and Stoughton: London, 1985).

Connell, G.G., *Jack's War* (William Kimber: London, 1985).

Coulter, Surgeon Captain J.L.S., *The Royal Naval Medical Service: Vol VII* (HMSO: London, 1956).

Danchev, A. and D. Todman, (eds), *Field Marshal Lord Alanbrooke: War Diaries 1939–1945* (Wiedenfeld and Nicholson: London, 2001).

Dawson, Captain L., *Flotillas: A Hard Lying Story* (Rich and Cowan: London, 1933).

de Clair, Commander H.G., *The Indiscretions of a Salthouse Commander* (Parapress: Tunbridge Wells, 1993).

Derry, T.K., *The Campaign in Norway* (HMSO: London, 1952).

Divine, A.D., *Navies in Exile* (John Murray: London, 1944).

Doenitz, Grand Admiral J., *Memoirs: Ten Years and Twenty Days* (Lionel Leventhal: London, 1990).

Edwards, B., *The Merchant Navy Goes to War* (Hale: London, 1988).

Gardner, W.J.R. (ed), *The Evacuation from Dunkirk: Operation Dynamo, 26 May–4 June 1940* (Frank Cass: London, 2000).

Gilbert, M., *The Churchill War Papers: At the Admiraltym, Vol 1: Sept 1939 to May 1940* (Heinemann: London, 1993).

Gilbert, Sir Martin, *The Day the War Ended* (Harper-Collins: London, 1995).

Grimstone, A.V., Lyons, M.C., and Lyons, U., *Meredith Dewey: Diaries, Letters, Writings* (Pembroke College: Cambridge, 1992).

Haines, G., *Destroyer War* (Ian Allan: Shepperton, 1982).

Hardy, A.C., *Everyman's History of the Sea War* (Nicholson and Watson: London, 1948).

Hill, R., *Destroyer Captain: Memoirs of the War 1942–1945* (William Kimber: London, 1975).

James, Admiral Sir William, *The Portsmouth Letters* (Macmillan: London, 1946).

Jones, G.P. *Battleship Barham* (William Kimber: London, 1974).

Kennedy, Sir Ludovic, *On My Way to the Club* (Collins: London, 1989).

Lewis, J.E. (ed), *War Diaries and Letters: Life on the Battlefield in the Words of the Ordinary Soldier* (Robinson Publishing: London, 1998).

Macintyre, Captain D., *Narvik* (Evans Bros: London, 1959).

Maund, Rear Admiral L.E.H., *Assault from the Sea* (Methuen: London, 1949).

Mountbatten, Earl Louis, *Mountbatten: Eighty Years in Pictures* (Macmillan: London, 1979).

Mountevans, Admiral Lord, *Adventurous Life* (Hutchinson: London, 1946).

Peszke, M.A., *Poland's Navy 1918–1945* (Hippocrene Books: New York, 1999).

Plevy, T.A.H., *Battleship Sailors: The fighting career of HMS* Warspite *recalled by her men* (Chatham Publishing: London, 2001).

Poolman, K., *The Kelly* (William Kimber: London, 1954).

Pope, D., *The Battle of the River Plate* (William Kimber: London, 1974).

Rohwer, J., *War at Sea 1939–1945* (Chatham Publishing: London, 1996).

Rohwer, J. and G. Hummelchen, *Chronology of the War at Sea: 1939–1945: The Naval History of World War Two* (Lionel Leventhal: London, 1992).

Roskill, Captain S.W., *Churchill and the Admirals* (Collins: London, 1977).

Roskill, Captain S.W., *The Navy at War, 1939–1945* (Collins: London, 1960).

Roskill, Captain S.W., *The War at Sea: 1939–45* (HMSO: London, 1954).

Smith, P.C., *Hit Hard, Hit First: HMS* Renown *1916–1948* (William Kimber: London, 1979).

Vian, Admiral of the Fleet Sir Philip, *Action This Day* (Frederick Muller: London, 1960).

Warner, P., *Auckinleck: The Lonely Soldier* (Buchan and Enright: London, 1981).

Wells, Captain J., *The Royal Navy: An Illustrated Social History 1870–1982* (Alan Sutton Publishing: Stroud, 1994).

Whinney, Captain R., *The U-Boat Peril* (Blandford Press: London, 1986).

Whitley, M.J., *German Destroyers of World War Two* (Arms and Armour Press: London, 1991).

Wilson, P., *Dunkirk – 1940: From Disaster to Deliverance* (Pen and Sword Books: Barnsley, 2000).

Winton, J., *Carrier Glorious* (Leo Cooper: London, 1986).

Young, J., *A Dictionary of the Ships of the Royal Navy of the Second World War* (Patrick Stevens: Cambridge, 1975).

Ziegler, P., *Mountbatten: The Official Biography* (William Collins: London, 1985).

Index

INDEX